Lecture Notes in Computer Science 11479

Commenced Publication in 1973
Founding and Former Series Editors:
Gerhard Goos, Juris Hartmanis, and Jan van Leeuwen

Editorial Board Members

David Hutchison
Lancaster University, Lancaster, UK

Takeo Kanade
Carnegie Mellon University, Pittsburgh, PA, USA

Josef Kittler
University of Surrey, Guildford, UK

Jon M. Kleinberg
Cornell University, Ithaca, NY, USA

Friedemann Mattern
ETH Zurich, Zurich, Switzerland

John C. Mitchell
Stanford University, Stanford, CA, USA

Moni Naor
Weizmann Institute of Science, Rehovot, Israel

C. Pandu Rangan
Indian Institute of Technology Madras, Chennai, India

Bernhard Steffen
TU Dortmund University, Dortmund, Germany

Demetri Terzopoulos
University of California, Los Angeles, CA, USA

Doug Tygar
University of California, Berkeley, CA, USA

T0171821

More information about this series at http://www.springer.com/series/7407

Martin Schoeberl · Christian Hochberger ·
Sascha Uhrig · Jürgen Brehm ·
Thilo Pionteck (Eds.)

Architecture of Computing Systems – ARCS 2019

32nd International Conference
Copenhagen, Denmark, May 20–23, 2019
Proceedings

Springer

Editors
Martin Schoeberl
Technical University of Denmark
Lyngby, Denmark

Christian Hochberger
Technical University of Darmstadt
Darmstadt, Germany

Sascha Uhrig
Airbus Defence and Space GmbH
Taufkirchen, Germany

Jürgen Brehm
University of Hanover
Hanover, Germany

Thilo Pionteck
Otto-von-Guericke University
Magdeburg, Germany

ISSN 0302-9743   ISSN 1611-3349   (electronic)
Lecture Notes in Computer Science
ISBN 978-3-030-18655-5   ISBN 978-3-030-18656-2   (eBook)
https://doi.org/10.1007/978-3-030-18656-2

LNCS Sublibrary: SL1 – Theoretical Computer Science and General Issues

© Springer Nature Switzerland AG 2019
The chapter "MEMPower: Data-Aware GPU Memory Power Model" is Open Access This chapter is licensed under the terms of the Creative Commons Attribution 4.0 International License (http://creativecommons.org/licenses/by/4.0/). For further details see license information in the chapter.
This work is subject to copyright. All rights are reserved by the Publisher, whether the whole or part of the material is concerned, specifically the rights of translation, reprinting, reuse of illustrations, recitation, broadcasting, reproduction on microfilms or in any other physical way, and transmission or information storage and retrieval, electronic adaptation, computer software, or by similar or dissimilar methodology now known or hereafter developed.
The use of general descriptive names, registered names, trademarks, service marks, etc. in this publication does not imply, even in the absence of a specific statement, that such names are exempt from the relevant protective laws and regulations and therefore free for general use.
The publisher, the authors and the editors are safe to assume that the advice and information in this book are believed to be true and accurate at the date of publication. Neither the publisher nor the authors or the editors give a warranty, expressed or implied, with respect to the material contained herein or for any errors or omissions that may have been made. The publisher remains neutral with regard to jurisdictional claims in published maps and institutional affiliations.

This Springer imprint is published by the registered company Springer Nature Switzerland AG
The registered company address is: Gewerbestrasse 11, 6330 Cham, Switzerland

Preface

The 32nd International Conference on Computer Architecture (ARCS 2019) was hosted at the Technical University of Denmark (DTU) close to Copenhagen in Lyngby, Denmark, May 20–23, 2019. It was organized by the special interest group on "Architecture of Computing Systems" of the GI (Gesellschaft für Informatik e. V.) and ITG (Informationstechnische Gesellschaft im VDE).

The ARCS conferences series has over 30 years of tradition reporting leading-edge research in computer architecture, operating systems, and other related low-level system software, and a wide range of software techniques and tools required to exploit and build new hardware systems efficiently. ARCS addresses the complete spectrum from fully integrated, self-powered embedded systems up to plant-powered high-performance systems and provides a platform covering new emerging and cross-cutting topics, such as autonomous and ubiquitous systems, reconfigurable computing and acceleration, neural networks and artificial intelligence, as well as outlooks on future topics like post-Moore architectures and organic computing.

The focus of the 25th conference was set on architectures for complex real-time systems like autonomous control systems, as well as safety and security critical systems. This included upcoming architectures and technologies, exploitable architectural features, languages, and tooling.

ARCS 2019 attracted 40 submissions from authors in 19 countries world-wide, including Canada, New Zealand, Russia, Japan, and the USA. Each submission was reviewed by a diverse and dedicated Program Committee. Ten submissions received three qualified reviews and the remaining 30 submissions got the requested number of four reviews. There was a total of 150 reviews of which 99 were provided by the members of the Program Committee while 51 were from external reviewers.

The Program Committee selected 24 submissions to be presented at ARCS and published in the proceedings, which corresponds to a 60% paper acceptance rate. The accepted papers form eight entertaining sessions with 25-minute slots per presentation: Dependable Systems (2 papers), Real-Time Systems (3 papers), Special Applications (3 papers), Architecture (4 papers), Memory Hierarchy (3 papers), FPGA (3 papers), Energy Awareness (3 papers) as well as a session on NoC/SoC (3 papers).

Every conference day was opened by an interesting top-level keynote presentation from academia and industry, starting with "Static vs. Dynamic Hardware Security Protection Mechanisms" by Avi Mendelson from Technion, Israel. The second day was introduced by Benoît Dupond de Dinechin, CTO from Kalray (France) with "Kalray's MPPA® Manycore Processor: At the Heart of Intelligent Systems," followed by Wolfgang Schröder-Preikschat, University of Erlangen-Nürnberg (Germany), "Predictability Issues in Operating Systems" on the third day.

ARCS has a long tradition of hosting associated workshops. The following three workshops were held in conjunction with the main conference this year:

- VERFE 15th Workshop on Dependability and Fault Tolerance
- FORMUS^{3}IC 4th FORMUS^{3}IC Workshop
- SAOS 7th International Workshop on Self-Optimization in Autonomic and Organic Computing Systems

We thank the many individuals who contributed to the success of ARCS 2019, in particular the members of the Program Committee and all the additional external reviewers for their time and effort in carefully reviewing and judging the submissions. We further thank all authors for submitting their work to ARCS and presenting accepted papers. The workshops were organized and coordinated by Carsten Trinitis, the proceedings were compiled by Thilo Pionteck, and the website was maintained by Markus Hoffmann. Thanks to all these individuals and all the many other people who helped in the organization of ARCS 2019.

May 2019

Martin Schoeberl
Christian Hochberger
Sascha Uhrig
Jürgen Brehm

Organization

General Chairs

Martin Schoeberl   Technical University of Denmark, Denmark
Christian Hochberger   Technische Universität Darmstadt, Germany

Program Chairs

Sascha Uhrig   Airbus, Germany
Jürgen Brehm   University of Hannover, Germany

Workshop and Tutorial Chair

Carsten Trinitis   Technical University of Munich, Germany

Publication Chair

Thilo Pionteck   Otto von Guericke University Magdeburg, Germany

Web Chair

Markus Hoffmann   Karlsruhe Institute of Technology, Germany

Program Committee

Hamid Amiri	University of Tunis El Manar, Tunisia
Mladen Berekovic	Universität zu Lübeck, Germany
Jürgen Brehm	Leibnitz Universität Hannover, Germany
Uwe Brinkschulte	Goethe-Universität Frankfurt am Main, Germany
Rainer Buchty	Technische Universität Braunschweig, Germany
João M. P. Cardoso	Universidade do Porto, Portugal
Laura Carrington	San Diego Supercomputer Center/University of California, USA
Martin Daněk	daiteq s.r.o., Czech Republic
Nikitas Dimopoulos	University of Victoria, Canada
Ahmed El-Mahdy	Egypt-Japan University of Science and Technology, Egypt
Dietmar Fey	Friedrich-Alexander-Universität Erlangen-Nürnberg, Germany
William Fornaciari	Politecnico di Milano, Italy
Roberto Giorgi	University of Siena, Italy
Daniel Gracia Pérez	Thales Research and Technology, France

Jan Haase	Universität zu Lübeck, Germany
Jörg Hähner	University of Augsburg, Germany
Heiko Hamann	Universität zu Lübeck, Germany
Andreas Herkersdorf	Technical University of Munich, Germany
Christian Hochberger	Technische Universität Darmstadt, Germany
Gert Jervan	Tallinn University of Technology, Estonia
Ben Juurlink	Technische Universität Berlin, Germany
Wolfgang Karl	Karlsruhe Institute of Technology, Germany
Jörg Keller	Fernuniversität in Hagen, Germany
Andreas Koch	Technische Universität Darmstadt, Germany
Dirk Koch	University of Manchester, UK
Hana Kubátová	FIT CTU, Prague, Czech Republic
Erik Maehle	Universität zu Lübeck, Germany
Alex Orailoglu	University of California, San Diego, USA
Luis Miguel Pinho	CISTER, ISEP, Portugal
Thilo Pionteck	Otto von Guericke University Magdeburg, Germany
Pascal Sainrat	IRIT – Université de Toulouse, France
Luca Santinelli	ONERA, France
Toshinori Sato	Fukuoka University, Japan
Martin Schoeberl	University of Denmark, Denmark
Wolfgang Schröder-Preikschat	Friedrich-Alexander-Universität Erlangen-Nürnberg, Germany
Martin Schulz	Technical University of Munich, Germany
Muhammad Shafique	Vienna University of Technology, Austria
Leonel Sousa	Universidade de Lisboa, Portugal
Benno Stabernack	Fraunhofer Institute for Telecommunications, Heinrich Hertz Institute, Germany
Walter Stechele	Technical University of Munich, Germany
Jürgen Teich	Friedrich-Alexander-Universität Erlangen-Nürnberg, Germany
Sven Tomforde	University of Kassel, Germany
Eduardo Tovar	Polytechnic Institute of Porto, Portugal
Carsten Trinitis	Technical University of Munich, Germany
Nicolas Tsiftes	SICS Swedish ICT, Sweden
Sascha Uhrig	Airbus, Germany
Theo Ungerer	University of Augsburg, Germany
Hans Vandierendonck	Queen's University Belfast, UK
Stephane Vialle	CentraleSupelec and UMI GT-CNRS 2958, France
Lucian Vintan	Lucian Blaga University of Sibiu, Romania
Klaus Waldschmidt	Goethe-Universität Frankfurt am Main, Germany
Dominik Wist	BIOTRONIC Berlin, Germany
Stephan Wong	Delft University of Technology, The Netherlands
Sungjoo Yoo	Seoul National University, South Korea

Additional Reviewers

Abbas, Mostafa
Becker, Thomas
Blochwitz, Christopher
Brand, Marcel
Bromberger, Michael
Carle, Thomas
Doan, Nguyen Anh Vu
Eck, Darren
Eichler, Christian
Fezzardi, Pietro
Freitag, Johannes
Frieb, Martin
Ghasempouri, Tara
Gottschling, Philip
Guerreiro, Joao
Habermann, Philipp
Heinz, Carsten
Hofmann, Johannes
Iezzi, Domenico
Jana, Siddhartha
Khalili Maybodi, Farnam
Langer, Tobias
Mahmoody, Pouya

Mainardi, Nicholas
Mammeri, Nadjib
Niazmand, Behrad
Ozen, Elbruz
Passareti, Daniele
Pohl, Angela
Pratas, Frederico
Procaccini, Marco
Raoofy, Amir
Reif, Stefan
Sagi, Mark
Schmaus, Florian
Solis-Vasquez, Leonardo
Sommer, Lukas
Srinivas Prabakaran, Bharath
Stegmeier, Alexander
Ulbrich, Peter
Verchok, Nick
Vidya Achmad, Rachmad
Waldschmidt, Klaus
Wirsch, Ramon
Wolf, Dennis

Invited Talks

Static vs. Dynamic Hardware Security Protection Mechanisms

Avi Mendelson

Visiting Professor at the CS and EE Departments at the Technion and in the EEE Department, NTU Singapore

Abstract. As numbers of transistors on a single die increases in an exponential pace, the complexity of systems increases accordingly and so, it makes systems to be vulnerable to errors, incomplete specifications, and other cyber-related attacks. It seems that the overall complexity of modern systems reaches the point that it is near to impossible to truly test and verify the correctness of all the possible usage models and execution paths. Thus, this presentation will claim that static protection on the system is not feasible anymore and a new approach is needed.

In my talk, I will claim that more dynamic approach is needed in order to protect such complex systems and presents new ideas which are motivated by fault tolerance and systems' testing techniques.

Avi Mendelson is an IEEE Fellow and a second VP of the IEEE Computer Society. He is a visiting professor at the CS and EE departments at the Technion and in the EEE department, NTU Singapore. He has a blend of industrial and academic experience in several different areas such as Computer architecture, Power management, security and Real-Time systems.

Prof. Mendelson published more than 130 papers in refereed Journals conferences and workshops and holds more than 25 Patents. Among his industrial roles, he worked for National semiconductors, Intel and Microsoft.

Kalray's MPPA® Manycore Processor: At the Heart of Intelligent Systems

Benoît Dupont de Dinechin

CTO Kalray, France

Abstract. Intelligent systems can be defined as cyber-physical systems with integration of high-integrity functions, such as control-command, along with high-performance functions, in particular signal processing, image processing and machine learning. Such intelligent systems are required by defense and aerospace applications, and by automated vehicles.

The Kalray MPPA3 manycore processor is designed as a building block for such intelligent systems. Its architecture comprises multiple compute units connected by on-chip global fabrics to external memory systems and network interfaces. Selecting compute units assembled from fully programmable cores, a large local memory and an asynchronous data transfer engine enables to match the high performance and energy efficiency of GPGPU processors, while avoiding their limitations.

For the high-performance functions, we illustrate how the MPPA3 processor accelerates deep learning inference by distributing computations across compute units and cores, and by offloading tensor operations to the tightly coupled coprocessor connected to each core. For the high-integrity functions, we present a model-based systems engineering approach based on multicore code generation from the synchronous-reactive language SCADE Suite from Ansys.

Benoît Dupont de Dinechin is the Chief Technology Officer of Kalray. He is the Kalray VLIW core main architect, and the co-architect of the Multi-Purpose Processing Array (MPPA) processor. Benoît also defined the Kalray software roadmap and contributed to its implementation. Before joining Kalray, Benoît was in charge of Research and Development of the STMicroelectronics Software, Tools, Services division, and was promoted to STMicroelectronics Fellow in 2008. Prior to STMicroelectronics, Benoît worked at the Cray Research park (Minnesota, USA), where he developed the software pipeliner of the Cray T3E production compilers. Benoît earned an engineering degree in Radar and Telecommunications from the Ecole Nationale Supérieure de l'Aéronautique et de l'Espace (Toulouse, France), and a doctoral degree in computer systems from the University Pierre et Marie Curie (Paris) under the direction of Prof. P. Feautrier. He completed his post-doctoral studies at the McGill University (Montreal, Canada) at the ACAPS laboratory led by Prof. G. R. Gao.

Benoît authored 14 patents in the area of computer architecture, and published over 55 conference papers, journal articles and book chapters in the areas of parallel computing, compiler design and operations research.

Predictability Issues in Operating Systems

Wolfgang Schröder-Preikschat

Friedrich-Alexander-Universität Erlangen-Nürnberg, Germany

Abstract. Predictability is always subject to the underlying assumptions being made. For real-time systems, time response of processes in relation to the strictness of deadlines is of particular importance. With an additional focus on embedded systems, space and energy requirements become relevant as well and need to be considered in combination. As far as software is concerned, structure and organisation of the programs to be executed determines whether or not predictable processes will take place in a given computing system. Design for predictability is an overarching aspect that crosscuts the whole computing system and particularly addresses operating systems.

This talk is about structuring principles of non-sequential programs - in the shape of but not limited to operating systems - to abet predetermination of quality attributes of non-sequential (real-time) processes, it is not about analytical methods to effectively predetermine these attributes. Issues in operating systems as to space, timing, and energy requirement are touched. Emphasis thereby is on coordination of cooperation and competition between processes, namely synchronisation. It is shown how measures of process synchronisation against the background of many-core processors cater to these issues.

Dr. Wolfgang Schröder-Preikschat studied computer science at the Technical University of Berlin, Germany, where he also received his doctoral degree and venia legendi. After a decade of extra-university research at the German National Research Center of Computer Science (GMD), Research Institute for Computer Architecture and Software Technique (FIRST), Berlin, he became a full professor for computer science at the Universities of Potsdam, Magdeburg, and Erlangen-Nuremberg (FAU), Germany. He is elected member of the DFG (German Research Foundation) Review Board on subject area Operating, Communication, Database and Distributed Systems, his main research interests are in the domain of real-time embedded distributed/parallel operating systems. He is member of ACM, EuroSys, GI/ITG, IEEE, and USENIX.

Contents

Memory Hierarchy

FPGA

Energy Awareness

NoC/SoC

Dependable Systems

Hardware/Software Co-designed Security Extensions for Embedded Devices

Maja Malenko[(✉)] and Marcel Baunach

Institute of Technical Informatics, Graz University of Technology, Graz, Austria
{malenko,baunach}@tugraz.at

Abstract. The rise of the Internet of Things (IoT) has dramatically increased the number of low-cost embedded devices. Being introduced into today's connected cyber-physical world, these devices now become vulnerable, especially if they offer no protection mechanisms. In this work we present a hardware/software co-designed memory protection approach that provides efficient, cheap, and effective isolation of tasks. The security extensions are implemented into a RISC-V-based MCU and a microkernel-based operating system. Our FPGA prototype shows that the hardware extensions use less than 5.5% of its area in terms of LUTs, and 24.7% in terms of FFs. They impose an extra 28% of context switch time, while providing protection of shared on-chip peripherals and authenticated communication via shared memory.

Keywords: Memory protection · Resource protection ·
Inter-task communication · RISC-V · MPU

1 Introduction

The number and heterogeneity of embedded devices which are emerging with the rise of the IoT is increasing massively. Their span ranges from very small and lightweight devices up to very complex computer systems, many of which implement security and safety critical operations [7,11]. Therefore, they must offer some form of protection mechanism which will ensure isolated execution of applications. There is an extensive research in this area at the moment, focused on finding lightweight solutions and protection mechanisms. A lot of concepts have been developed, each with a different purpose, but so far, none of them has solved all the problems.

In this paper our focus are low-cost microcontrollers (MCUs) which operate in a single physical address space. Devices that are based on such MCUs are especially susceptible to attacks, intentional or not, and an efficient isolation mechanism is necessary to protect them. In order to reduce cost and energy usage, due to their lightweight nature, these devices often lack any form of protection. Thus, even though tasks might be designed to cooperate, not trying to intentionally harm each other, a small bug in one of them can potentially corrupt the whole system. The security solution must be implemented in a very

© Springer Nature Switzerland AG 2019
M. Schoeberl et al. (Eds.): ARCS 2019, LNCS 11479, pp. 3–14, 2019.
https://doi.org/10.1007/978-3-030-18656-2_1

efficient manner, regarding both memory and hardware consumption. If real-time constraints are present, the security implementation should not impose significant runtime overhead, but must still provide integrity and confidentiality guarantees. Many hardware and software-based security architectures have recently emerged, isolating the execution of sensitive operations on a wide range of devices. They all differ in the type of devices they are tackling and the amount of hardware and software in their Trusted Computing Base (TCB). In higher-end systems a very common approach is to have a trusted operating system which uses a Memory Management Unit (MMU) to isolate processes in their private virtual address space. This approach requires a lot of hardware and has big TCB. Researches recently have been working on developing Protected Module Architectures (PMAs) [15] as a more efficient and lightweight approach for memory isolation in a shared physical address space, using small-sized TCBs [5,6,8,12,14]. Some of them completely exclude the software from the TCB, while others implement just the most necessary software operations.

We propose a hardware/software co-designed embedded platform which provides dependability at low-cost. The architecture is based on a RISC-V *vscale*[1] implementation on which a minimal microkernel (*SmartOS*) [4] is running. All memory accesses are mediated by a tailored Memory Protection Unit (MPU) which provides three essential isolation concepts: isolation of private code and data regions of individual tasks, protecting the usage of shared on-chip memory-mapped peripheral devices from unauthorized access, and providing protected communication between tasks.

The paper is structured as follows. First we describe the protection concept and introduce the platform used for implementation and evaluation (Sect. 2). Then, a detailed description of each protection mechanism is given along with the hardware and software implementation (Sect. 3). Next, several test cases and measurement results are presented (Sect. 4). We relate our work to similar approaches (Sect. 5) and discuss the differences and benefits from our approach. Finally, we draw a conclusion (Sect. 6).

2   Concept and Platform Overview

The goal of most embedded computer systems is to run applications securely and efficiently. To achieve this goal both the hardware and the software should cooperate as effectively as possible. However, especially in today's security-related research the co-design aspect of hardware and software seems to be missing. In this work we explicitly target low-cost embedded devices and we try to close this gap by developing a hardware/software co-designed memory protection architecture.

In a multitasking environment where concurrent tasks reside in a single address space and extensively use shared resources, attacks from malicious or malfunctioning tasks are expected to happen. We propose an inexpensive and

---

[1] https://github.com/ucb-bar/vscale.

effective approach for isolated execution of preemptable tasks in an environment with frequent interactions. In order to have an isolated task execution, we must ensure several properties: protect the internal state of the running task (private code and data), ensure correct resource usage by enforcing access policies of the resources the task owns, and finally, authenticate communication between cooperating tasks using protected shared memory. The ultimate goal of our hardware/software co-designed architecture is to achieve efficient (in terms of hardware and software) task-based protection for low-cost MCUs, at the same time trying not to violate the real-time characteristics of the underlying OS by keeping the context switch time constant, and trying to avoid expensive system calls as much as possible. Thus, we implement kernel-based security mechanisms, which are then enforced by lightweight hardware extensions.

2.1 RISC-V

The MCU we are using is based on a *vscale* processor, which is a single-issue, three stage pipeline implementation of the RISC-V ISA [16,17]. We decided to use a RISC-V-based MCU mainly because of its simplicity, minimalism, openness, and room for extensions. The *vscale* implementation already comes with two privilege modes, which are the main prerequisite for implementing protection. Tasks can request services from the kernel only by system calls, which trap into machine mode. The MCU includes several on-chip peripherals, which, as in most embedded devices, are mapped into a single address space with the memories, and if no memory protection is available they are fully accessible to everyone. The architectural overview of the system is given in Fig. 1.

2.2 *SmartOS*

SmartOS is a small, modular, real-time operating system suitable for low-cost embedded devices [4]. It is ported to *vscale* and uses two operational modes: the kernel runs in privileged machine mode, while tasks as well as the libraries run in user mode. Tasks are preemptive, use individual stacks and execute all API functions in their context. The kernel uses its own stack and is responsible for priority-aware scheduling, system call execution, interrupt handling, dynamic resource management, and inter-task synchronization using events. The kernel code and data, including the control blocks for tasks, events, and resources, can only be accessed using system calls, which are atomic and executed in machine mode.

In order to properly design a secure system where tasks and OS coexist in a single address space, we must ensure that an incorrect (or malicious) task cannot interfere with the proper operation of the system and other tasks. That is why the linker is instructed to efficiently organize the memory map into regions, as shown in Fig. 1. Each task is associated with its individual code and data (stack) regions, as well as a shared region for API functions. On demand, the OS also grants access to additional regions for accessing peripherals and shared memory for inter-task communication.

Resource Management. In order to protect shared resources (i.e. peripherals) from unsynchronized access by several tasks and enable collaborative resource sharing, *Smart*OS uses a resource management concept, based on the Highest Locker Protocol (HLP) [18], which due to its simple implementation, is frequently used in RTOSs. It allows dynamic access coordination to temporarily shared, but exclusive resources and prevents a resource from being used by a task as long as it is allocated to another task. Each resource at compile time or system startup receives a ceiling priority, which is the highest priority of all registered tasks that announced the usage of that resource. As soon as a task successfully allocates a resource, its priority is raised to the resource's ceiling priority.

The resource concept in *Smart*OS enables, but does not enforce synchronization on physical resources without hardware support. The kernel can not prevent (neither detect, nor block) illegal access attempts to a peripheral by a task which does not hold it as a resource. To avoid this, instead of a very slow approach of allocating/deallocating the resource inside each driver function which has direct access to it, we are proposing a hardware-based enforcement of the HLP, which locks peripherals in order to protect them from unauthorized access. Without an additional hardware support there is a risk that even though one task has claimed the resource for itself, another task uses it in an unprotected way.

Inter-task Communication. Tasks in *Smart*OS are not self-contained, they frequently interact with each other and with the environment. For that reason, explicit synchronization between tasks is achieved through events, which can be invoked by tasks or interrupt service routines (ISRs). In this work we are extending the event synchronization concept of *Smart*OS and provide an effective solution for authenticated data exchange between tasks.

3   Implementation Details

In order to achieve flexible memory separation for variable-sized regions, each defined with its start and end address, we are using a segmentation-based memory protection approach. Our MPU is configured with four Control and Status Registers (CSRs), as specified in the RISC-V privilege architecture [17], which hold the address ranges of task's private code and data regions. Two more registers store the address range of the API functions, called libraries in Fig. 1, and are not reprogrammed on every context switch. By configuring few additional registers we also enable efficient and lightweight access protection to shared resources, including memory for communication (see Fig. 1).

3.1   Basic Memory Protection

When a programmer creates a task, she specifies the priority, the amount of stack to be used as well as the entry function of the task. When a task is loaded, the kernel assigns unique code and data (including stack) memory regions, which are stored in the Task Control Block. Since drivers in our system are executed in the

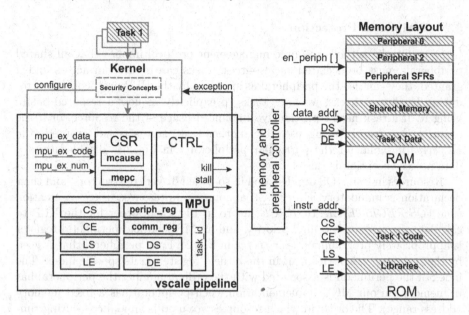

Fig. 1. Architectural overview of the system

context of the currently running task, by placing all API functions sequentially in memory, we reduce the number of MPU registers needed for protecting the shared code area accessible to all tasks.

In *vscale*, in order to achieve basic memory protection, we take advantage of its two privilege levels. The MPU configuration is allowed only in privileged machine mode and is done by the kernel on every dispatch of a newly scheduled task. While in user mode, the MPU monitors all bus activities and raises an exception in case of an access violation. We made several modifications to the *vscale* pipeline by introducing three new exception vectors: instruction access fault, load access fault, and store access fault vector. The MPU's data-access policy implies that memory locations accessed by store and load instructions can be performed only within the task's data regions (including the authorized peripheral and shared memory addresses) which are implicitly non-executable, while the control-flow policy implies that the control-transfer instructions must stay within the memory reserved for the task's code and library regions which are implicitly non-writable.

The MPU is attached to the *vscale* pipeline and the exception signal it produces is then handled by the controller module in the decode/execute stage. The processor invalidates the executing instruction by flushing the pipeline, saves the exception vector number in the *mcause* CSR, the faulty instruction in the *mepc* CSR, and immediately jumps to a predefined exception handler. From there, the kernel handles the exception appropriately.

3.2   Peripheral Protection

In *Smart*OS the kernel's resource management protocol implies that all shared peripherals must be declared as resources. Tasks can request an access and if granted, they can use the peripheral as specified by the HLP protocol. By introducing hardware checks, we force tasks to explicitly request a resource before using it. If a task hasn't previously announced usage of the resource, or if the resource is currently being used by another task, access is not granted (the *en_periph[i]* signal for the particular peripheral i in Fig. 2 is disabled) and a data access exception is raised.

Resources in *Smart*OS are declared in so-called driver constructors, and their declaration is mandatory. Every task announces its resource usage at creation time (*OS_REGISTER_RESOURCE* macro in Fig. 2), in order for the HLP to calculate the resource's ceiling priority, and an MPU bitfield peripheral register is appropriately programmed (*periph_reg* in Fig. 2). Each peripheral that is used by the task is encoded with a '1' in the bitfield register on its specific index. The index of the peripheral is associated with the ordinal number the peripheral has in memory (in our MCU implementation, each peripheral has a fixed memory address range). The order in which resources are used is announced during runtime by two system calls (*getResource()* and *releaseResource()*). Task-awareness is integrated into the hardware by storing the *id* of the currently executing task (*task_id* register in Fig. 2) as well as the *id* of the task which was granted access to a peripheral (*periph_owner* register in each peripheral in Fig. 2).

The MPU needs only one register for protecting up to 32-peripherals, which is sufficient for most small embedded systems. The peripheral access is checked by hardware on each peripheral register access (load or store), which is more efficient (both in terms of execution time and required software) than performing expensive software checks in device drivers.

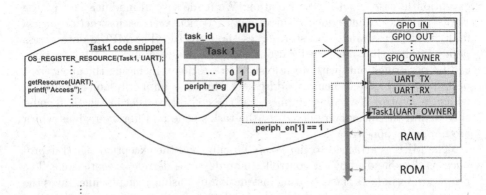

Fig. 2. Protected usage of shared peripherals

3.3   Protected Inter-Task Communication

We implement a shared memory approach for communication between tasks, since it has been proven to be a very versatile architectural choice, mainly because of the constant access time to variable-sized values. The shared memory region is divided into pages of configurable, but mutually equal sizes. Every page is easily indexed with the lower bits of the address (*page_index* in Fig. 3), which are used as the page's position in the MPU bitfield register (*comm_reg* in Fig. 3). For each task, this register has a '1' only if the communication is requested and acknowledged by both sending and receiving tasks. When the sender wants to communicate, it explicitly grants privileges for communication to the receiver task, by specifying the receiver task's id and the size of the message. But, only when the receiver task acknowledges the request, the shared memory region is open for both of them. The system calls (*registerSharedMem()* and *ackSharedMem()*) used for establishing the mutually authenticated communication are shown in Fig. 3, and are used to configure the values which will be placed inside the *comm_reg* register. After successful authentication, every communication between the two tasks is done in user mode, by calling the functions *sendData()* and *receiveData()*, thus preventing expensive system calls. When a task requests memory area for communication, the kernel inspects which pages are still free, and designates them to both communicating tasks. Tasks authenticate each other with their *id-s*, which are unique for each task and are maintained by the kernel. When running out of memory, the kernel rejects any request for new communication, until memory is freed. The nature of communication can be asynchronous in order to prevent blockage due to unresponsive tasks, or can be made synchronous by using the *SmartOS*'s event concept.

In hardware, every time a data memory operation is performed in the designated shared memory area for communication, the MPU calculates the page index, checks the *comm_reg* register, and raises a data memory access exception if the executing task has no privileges to use the indexed page. This approach is substantially faster then completely software-based implementation, because no system calls are involved for the communication itself. The more expensive authentication is only done once, before establishing the communication.

4   Test Cases and Performance Evaluation

We implemented the presented protection concept into our research platform consisting of a *vscale*-based MCU with several on-chip memory-mapped peripherals (e.g., UART, GPIO), on which *SmartOS* is running. For the MCU implementation we use the Basys3 Artix-7 FPGA board from Digilent[2].

First, we are going to present two test cases, along with the simulation results[3], which show an invalid way of accessing memory. On the left side of Fig. 4 the disassembly of *task1*'s entry function is shown. In this example *task1*

---

[2] https://reference.digilentinc.com/reference/programmable-logic/basys-3/start.
[3] Performed by Vivado Simulator 2017.3.

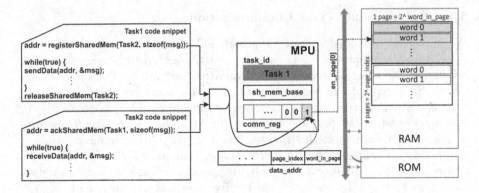

Fig. 3. Protected and authenticated communication between tasks

tries to change the control-flow by jumping into the address space of *task2*. As can be seen from the simulation output, at the time the jump instruction is executed with the address which does not belong to *task1*'s code region, an instruction access fault exception is raised. After the exception, the code continues from a predefined exception handling routine (0x100). The scenario in Fig. 5 shows a task trying to access the *GPIO_OUT* register, when it hasn't requested it before. A load access fault exception is raised, and as in the previous example, the processor jumps to the exception handling routine.

Hardware Footprint. To evaluate the used FPGA resources of our MPU implementation we measured the hardware footprint of the baseline system as well as the one just for the protection hardware components. The overall utilization of lookup tables for logic (LUTs) and flip-flops (FFs) as reported after synthesis by Xilinx Vivado 2017.3 is shown in Table 1.

Execution Time Overhead. Context switches are one of the most costly operating system operations in terms of CPU time. The context frame which is saved on the stack on each context switch when dispatching a newly scheduled task consists of a total of 36 load operations. Out of those, configuring the code and data regions takes only 4, while both peripheral and communication protection information counts for another 4 load operations, giving a total increase of 28%. However, except the initial peripheral allocation and communication authentication which happens at task's load time, during task execution the kernel does not perform any additional checks.

In order to compare the number of clock cycles needed for protected communication, besides the communication using shared memory, we implemented a simple message queue-based communication, as specified in [1]. As shown in Table 2 the number of clock cycles for creating a message queue and registering a shared memory address for same-sized messages are similar, since both are implemented as system calls. However, the number of clock cycles for actual communication is significantly lower when using shared memory, because *sendData()* unlike *xQueuePut()* is not a implemented as a syscall.

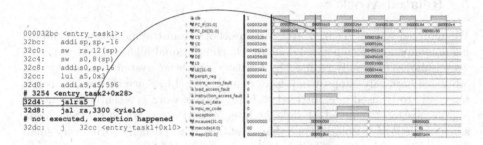

Fig. 4. Invalid control-flow memory access

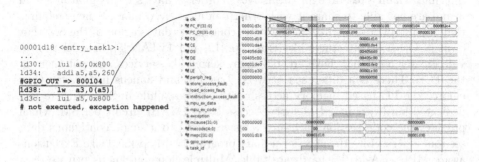

Fig. 5. Invalid GPIO peripheral access

Table 1. Synthesis results of our hardware extensions.

Category	Components	LUTs (Util%)	FFs (Util%)
Baseline system	vscale	2547 (4.02%)	1293 (1.02%)
Our hardware resources	Basic MPU	75 (0.36%)	192 (0.46%)
	Added resource protection	106 (0.51%)	256 (0.62%)
	Added communication protection	140 (0.67%)	320 (0.77%)
	Total % over Baseline system	5.5%	24.7%

Table 2. Clock cycles for protected communication.

Category	System call/Function	Clock cycles
Message queue	xQueueCreate (len, msgSize)	135
	XQueuePut (handle, msg)	115
Protected shared memory	registerSharedMem (taskId, msgSize)	150
	sendData (addr, msg)	30

5   Related Work

We analyzed several security architectures, both from the mainstream computing domain and the embedded domain. On conventional high-end systems, software isolation is usually realized by a trusted operating system, which relies on advanced hardware support in a form of an MMU [13]. Since this mechanism is too costly to be used in embedded systems, a lot of work is recently concentrating on creating Protected Module Architectures (PMAs) which provide cheap, small, and effective isolation in a shared address space, usually with a very small Trusted Computing Base (TCB). Architectures like SMART [9] and Sancus [14], with a zero-software TCB, have a static way of loading self-contained secure modules (SMs), which have very limited access to shared resources. This implies that SMs must claim a resource for themselves in order to have security guarantees on it and are not able to share it with other modules. Even more, Sancus requires that the peripheral is wired in the same contiguous data region of the SM that owns it. Other architectures like TrustLite [12] and TyTAN [5], in order to provide greater flexibility, have created many kernel-like services and put them in the TCB. There is a difference between Trustlite and Sancus in the way they enforce the PC-based memory access control rules. While in Sancus there is a dedicated hardware-based Memory Access Logic (MAL) circuit per SM, which provides the code section with an exclusive access to a single contiguous data section, in TrustLite the access rules are programmed in a fixed-size Execution-aware MPU (EA-MPU) hardware table. Multiple non-contiguous private data sections per trusted module, or protected shared memory between trusted modules can be configured, but such flexibility is limited by the number of entries in the hardware table. Regarding peripheral protection, TrustLite allows limited number of EA-MPU's data regions to be used for securing peripherals, which are allowed for access only to trusted modules. Our peripheral protection approach allows for configuration of up to 32 peripherals which do not have to be mapped in a contiguous memory addresses. ARM TrustZone [2] is another security architecture which separates a computer's resources into a secure and a non-secure world. While the secure world can access everything, the non-secure world is limited only to non-secure memory regions. Peripherals are also split between the two worlds. TrustZone requires a security kernel for managing the secure world, which increases the size of the TCB.

Since *Smart*OS has a very small kernel code base, which performs almost all the functions which in [5] are put in a TCB, we are considering it to be trusted and to be part of our system's TCB. In contrast to the above mentioned architectures, *Smart*OS does not distinguish between secure and non-secure worlds. It equally protects all tasks, not just their own code and data, but it allows for greater flexibility and more fine-grained protection regarding shared peripherals and shared memory for communication. The above mentioned architectures don't do much to improve the security of the software that runs in the secure world, except to prevent unwanted access by normal world software. Therefore, it is the developer who determines that software is trusted, typically through rigorous development processes, testing, and certification.

Regarding the communication between tasks, in many operating systems like L4 [10] and FreeRTOS [3] the communication for security reasons goes through the kernel, which is a very costly operation. In L4, each time a communication is performed, a task loads the receiver's id, the message, and executes a system call. Then, the kernel switches the address space to the receiver task's, loads the sender id, and returns to user mode. Only after that, the receiver task gets the message. On the other hand, in TrustLite, the ability to achieve fine-grained communication via shared memory is limited by the number of MPU regions the platform offers. In order to avoid expensive context switches every time tasks need to communicate, we are proposing hardware-checked authenticated communication, which the kernel establishes only once, and afterwards is performed in user mode. The communication memory that tasks use is configurable and fine-grained, in terms of consecutive memory locations.

6   Conclusion

In this paper we present a hardware/software co-designed architecture for isolated execution of tasks in low-cost embedded devices. Besides the basic isolation of private code and data regions, in an environment where tasks have frequent peripheral access and mutual communication, we allow for efficient protection of shared resources. By installing task-awareness into the MPU, kernel's operations are supported by inexpensive hardware-enforced security checks.

Acknowledgment. This work was conducted within the Lead-Project "Dependable Internet of Things in Adverse Environments", subproject "Dependable Computing" (funded by TU Graz).

References

1. embOS: Real-Time Operating System User Guide and Reference Manual. SEG-GER Microcontroller GmbH (2018)
2. ARM Limited. ARM Security Technology - Building a Secure System using Trust-Zone Technology (2009)
3. Barry, R.: FreeRTOS reference manual: API functions and configuration options. Real Time Engineers Limited (2009)
4. Baunach, M.: Towards collaborative resource sharing under real-time conditions in multitasking and multicore environments. In: ETFA, pp 1–9. IEEE (2012)
5. Brasser, F.F. Mahjoub, B.E., Sadeghi, A.R., Wachsmann, C., Koeberl, P.: Tytan: tiny trust anchor for tiny devices. In: DAC, pp. 34:1–34:6. ACM (2015)
6. Berkay Celik, Z., McDaniel, P., Tan, G.: Soteria: automated IoT safety and security analysis. In: 2018 USENIX Annual Technical Conference (USENIX ATC 2018), Boston, MA, pp. 147–158. USENIX Association (2018)
7. Checkoway, S. et al.: Comprehensive experimental analyses of automotive attack surfaces. In: Proceedings of the 20th USENIX Conference on Security, SEC 2011, Berkeley, CA, USA, p. 6. USENIX Association (2011)

8. Costan, V., Lebedev, I., Devadas, S.: Sanctum: minimal hardware extensions for strong software isolation. In: 25th USENIX Security Symposium (USENIX Security 2016), Austin, TX, pp. 857–874. USENIX Association (2016)

9. Defrawy, K.E., Perito, D., Tsudik, G., et al.: Smart: secure and minimal architecture for (establishing a dynamic) root of trust. In: Proceedings of the 19th Annual Network and Distributed System Security Symposium, pp. 5–8 (2012)

10. Heiser, G., Elphinstone, K.: L4 microkernels: the lessons from 20 years of research and deployment. ACM Trans. Comput. Syst. **34**(1), 1:1–1:29 (2016)

11. Humayed, A., Lin, J., Li, F., Luo, B.: Cyber-physical systems security-a survey. IEEE Internet Things J. **4**, 1802–1831 (2017)

12. Koeberl, P., Schulz, S., Sadeghi, A.-R., Varadharajan, V.: Trustlite: a security architecture for tiny embedded devices. In: Proceedings of the Ninth European Conference on Computer Systems, EuroSys 2014, New York, NY, USA, pp. 10:1–10:14. ACM (2014)

13. Maene, P., Götzfried, J., de Clercq, R., Müller, T., Freiling, F.C., Verbauwhede, I.: Hardware-based trusted computing architectures for isolation and attestation. IEEE Trans. Comput. **67**, 361–374 (2018)

14. Noorman, J. et al.: Sancus: low-cost trustworthy extensible networked devices with a zero-software trusted computing base. In: Presented as part of the 22nd USENIX Security Symposium (USENIX Security 13), Washington, D.C., pp. 479–498. USENIX (2013)

15. Patrignani, M., Agten, P., Strackx, R., Jacobs, B., Clarke, D., Piessens, F.: Secure compilation to protected module architectures. ACM Trans. Program. Lang. Syst. **37**(2), 6:1–6:50 (2015)

16. Waterman, A., Lee, Y., Asanović, K.: The RISC-V instruction set manual volume i: User-level ISA version 2.2. Technical report, EECS Department, University of California, Berkeley, May 2017

17. Waterman, A., Lee, Y., Asanović, K.: The RISC-V instruction set manual volume ii: Privileged architecture version 1.10. Technical report, EECS Department, University of California, Berkeley, May 2017

18. Zhang, T., Guan, N., Deng, Q., Yi, W.: Start time configuration for strictly periodic real-time task systems. J. Syst. Archit. **66**(C), 61–68 (2016)

S³DES - Scalable Software Support for Dependable Embedded Systems

Lukas Osinski[✉] and Jürgen Mottok

Laboratory for Safe and Secure Systems (LaS³),
Technical University of Applied Sciences Regensburg, Regensburg, Germany
{lukas.osinski,juergen.mottok}@oth-regensburg.de

Abstract. Scalable Software Support for Dependable Embedded Systems (S³DES) achieves fault tolerance by utilizing spatial software-based triple modular redundancy for computational and voter processes on application level. Due to the parallel execution of the replicas on distinct CPU cores it makes a step towards software-based fault tolerance against transient and permanent random hardware errors. Additionally, the compliance with real-time requirements in terms of response time is enhanced compared to similar approaches. The replicated voters, the introduced mutual voter monitoring and the optimized arithmetic encoding allow the detection and compensation of voter failures without the utilization of backward recovery. Fault injection experiments on real hardware reveal that S³DES can detect and mask all injected data and program flow errors under a single fault assumption, whereas an uncoded voting scheme yields approx. 12% silent data corruptions in a similar experiment.

Keywords: Fault tolerance · Multi-core · Arithmetic encoding ·
Triple modular redundancy · Replicated voting

1 Introduction

The availability of affordable, power efficient and high performance multi-core processors has impacted embedded system design considerably. An example among many includes the automotive industry where powerful systems—reasonably equipped for the radical changes in the industry by emerging topics such as autonomous driving, sensor fusion and new powertrain technologies—offer new possibilities in system design. In consequence of this development, the software code base, e.g., implementing automated driving functionality is growing in both complexity and size, which leads to a move to commercial off-the-shelf (COTS) hardware that provides high performance. Simultaneously, the semiconductor industry continues with structure and voltage down-scaling due to diminishing design margins and stringent power constraints. This trend leads to highly integrated hardware, on the one hand, whilst provoking an increase

© Springer Nature Switzerland AG 2019
M. Schoeberl et al. (Eds.): ARCS 2019, LNCS 11479, pp. 15–27, 2019.
https://doi.org/10.1007/978-3-030-18656-2_2

in sensitivity against random hardware faults. Recent studies provide supporting evidence of an increase in random hardware faults in CPUs and memories which, if not masked at hardware level or detected by fault detection mechanisms, can lead to Silent Data Corruptions (SDC), i.e., undetected incorrect results of computations [12]. These defects are reaching from transient faults, introduced by radiation effects or electromagnetic interference (e.g. bit flips or multi-bit flips [3,4,14,15,19]), to permanent faults arising from manufacturing process variations, aging and wear out effects [10,21] in memories and CPUs.

Established conservative fault tolerance solutions which ensure a safe execution of the software are based on hardware approaches which usually include triple/dual modular redundancy such as cycle-by-cycle synchronized lockstep processors, flip-flop hardening, watchdogs, etc. [2]. However, such hardware-based approaches imply higher hardware costs and commercially available processors that are especially designed and manufactured for safety-critical applications typically only offer limited computing power in comparison to modern COTS. Furthermore, the integrated hardware mechanisms commonly only support fail-safe operation since they are only able to detect errors. However, future safety-critical applications in domains such as autonomous driving will require a fail-operational execution on high-performance microcontrollers which are lacking specific fault detection and recovery mechanisms. Multi-core systems have strong potential to support cost-efficient fault tolerance due to their inherent spatial redundancy by the use of multiple cores. Suitable fault tolerance approaches could counteract the rising frequency of transient and permanent faults. To utilize this inherent redundancy, Software-Implemented Hardware Fault Tolerance (SIHFT) [8] approaches at different architecture levels such as instruction- [17], thread- [11], and process- [22,24] level redundancy are under active research. These methods could lower costs and increase flexibility by achieving fault tolerance via software-only methods whilst not requiring specialized hardware. However, in spite of experimental studies clearly indicating the occurrence of permanent and intermittent errors in CPUs and memories, most SIHFT techniques assume only transient errors. Furthermore, existing SIHFT techniques either yield low fault coverage [18], are impractical in terms of performance due to high execution time penalties [20] or utilize backwards recovery in presence of failures [24]. The latter could hamper compliance with real-time requirements in domains such as electrical powertrain system where the hardest real-time requirements for the application software are in the range of 200 microseconds deadline and the maximum allowed fault reaction time is in the area of a few milliseconds.

We propose a concept which utilizes software-based triple modular redundancy and arithmetic encoding on process-level (similar to [24]) while taking in the advantage of the inherent spatial redundancy of multi-core controller to enable software-based fault tolerance against permanent and transient single and multiple hardware errors within the CPU and memory. Scalable Software Support for Dependable Embedded Systems (S^3DES) achieves that by replicating computational and voter processes, enabling mutual voter monitoring and optimized arithmetic encoding to ensure fault detection and error handling on application level. Computational processes are replicated and executed in parallel on distinct cores, followed by replicated arithmetic encoded voting processes. The parallel executed replicated voters determines the majority among the encoded results to detect and compensate errors which occurred within the computation. The voters are arithmetic encoded to detect errors within each voter and are arranged in hierarchy which allows mutual monitoring and error compensation in case of a voter failure without the utilization of backwards recovery. Our contributions are: (1) Optimized arithmetic encoding which eliminates signature management and prevents fault propagation. (2) A voter replication concept with mutual voter monitoring, single voter output determination and failure compensation which is beneficial for real-time requirements. (3) An evaluation of the concept with fault injection by injecting transient faults in the underlying hardware which trigger data and program flow errors on application level.

2 Background and Related Work

2.1 Arithmetic Encoding

Arithmetic Encoding, commonly referred to as coded processing, is a non systematic encoding scheme based on the theory of arithmetic codes which allows error detection and recovery of random hardware errors in CPUs and memory. Arithmetic codes were already successfully applied by several error detection techniques [5,17,25,26]. There exist different strategies and coding rules for the implementation of arithmetic encoding which differ mainly in their supported arithmetic operations and their coverage with regard to the fault model. The simplest representative of arithmetic codes is called AN-encoding. With AN-encoding, an integer n is encoded by multiplying it with a constant A. The resulting integer $\hat{n} = A * n$ is called a code-word and the number of bits for the word representation is doubled. Due to the multiplication with the constant, the distance between two valid code-words is increased. The original domain of 2^n words is extended by k check bits which results in 2^{n+k} possible code-words. As a consequence, if a random hardware error alters the code-word $\hat{n}$, it results in an invalid word with high probability. If $\hat{n}$ still represents a code word, $\hat{n} \bmod A$ equals 0; if the result of the modulo operation is unequal to 0, a random hardware error is detected. To decode the code word, a division $n = \hat{n}/A$ is performed. The number of tolerable faults depends on the value of the encoding constant A. Several publications identified suitable values for A in a 32-bit AN-encoding scheme such as 58659, 59665, 63157, 63877 by Ulbrich [24] which is compliant with the results of Braun et al. [6]. These values are characterized by their hamming distance of six and therefore allow the detection of up to five faults in a code word. AN-encoding supports all relevant operations including the division of the encoded values. However, some operations (e.g. bit-wise operations) require more sophisticated implementations which can hamper performance and/or require intermediate decoding of operands. Furthermore, AN-encoding allows the detection of data errors but is not able to detect control flow errors and erroneous or lost data access. To detect these types of errors, variants of AN-encoding were developed, namely ANB- and ANBD-encoding. ANB-encoding introduces the static signature B which allows the determination of the identity of the data [26]: $\hat{n} = A * n + B$. B represents a unique signature for each operation (e.g constant value) [25]. As a result, swapped data/operations and control flow errors can be detected during the decoding phase. To allow the detection of a lost update, i.e., in case a store operation was omitted, the additional dynamic signature D is introduced: $\hat{n} = A * n + B + D$ where D is represented by a timestamp [5]. ANBD-encoding provides very high fault coverage, but if applied on source-level, i.e., encoding every operation (e.g. by code-transformation tools), it incurs very high penalties regarding execution time since more computational effort is required for executing the encoded operations and performing complex signature calculations during run-time. Execution time penalties range form 3x (AN-encoding) [18] up to 250x (ANBD-encoding) [20] compared to uncoded execution. This fact makes encoding on source-level—in combination with further drawbacks—impractical for most use cases.

2.2   Redundancy and Replication

A key mechanism to achieve fault tolerance is the replication of components in e.g. hardware (processors, memory) or software (entire programs or parts of it) [7]. A widely used replication paradigm is represented by the N-modular redundancy (NMR) pattern, where N characterizes the number of replicated components which process the same data. A well-known representative is triple modular redundancy (TMR) which uses three elements and a majority voter. After completing the operation, the voting element compares the three results and selects the correct one by majority [7]. TMR is—besides the higher cost in terms of resources—a powerful approach since the system can continue the execution by masking the faulty element. This contributes to a higher system availability and depending on the type of realization the number of replicas can be increased as long as the necessary resources are available [7]. TMR can be implemented as a temporal or spatial design. While spatial redundancy performs the same operation on distinct hardware components, temporal redundancy indicates that the same operation is independently performed sequentially on the same hardware.

The weak spot of TMR, if implemented purely in software, is the majority voter. It depicts a single point of failure (SPOF) and therefore has to meet high reliability requirements [7]. To eliminate this SPOF in software, a concept called Combined Redundancy (CoRed) was proposed [24]. CoRed protects an application by temporal (sequential) software-based triple modular redundancy on process-level, applying ANBD-encoding to increase the reliability of the software voter and utilizing rollback recovery in case of a voter failure. Experimental evaluation of the voter by fault injection experiments depicts full single and dual bit-flip data error fault coverage [24]. Drawbacks of this approach are e.g. increased response time due to temporal redundancy as well as re-execution of the voting process in case of a failure (rollback recovery). Furthermore, the concept does not consider permanent faults, does not take into account floating-point values as input for the computational or voting process and requires additional external logic for the management of the arithmetic encoding signatures so that subsequent processes following the voter are able to decode the voting result.

3   S³DES

Scalable Software Support for Dependable Embedded Systems (S³DES) utilizes process-level redundancy for computational (P) and voter (V) processes, mutual voter monitoring and optimized arithmetic encoding to ensure fault detection and error handling on application level. S³DES exploits the inherent spatial redundancy of multi-core systems and reduces the response time by executing the replicated processes in parallel (on different cores) and utilizing compensation in case of process (computation and voting) failures.

3.1   Fault Assumption

Figure 1 establishes two different fault assumptions: (1) For the replicated computational processes (P) only a single fault assumption is considered. (2) Whereas the replicated voting processes can tolerate up to two voter failures. This was deliberately chosen and only serves as a reference example for the concepts described in the following sections. In this paper and the subsequent evaluation we consider—as most of the public available concepts—a single fault assumption where exactly one transient fault occurs during the replica execution within the CPU and memory. Nevertheless, we argue that the transient single fault assumption is not sufficient as studies [10,21] showed that memories are not only affected by transient bit flips, but also permanent faults. Although the permanent fault rate is lower than the fault rate of transient faults, we will consider this extended assumption in our future work and discuss the aspects which are

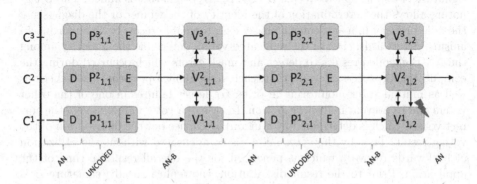

Fig. 1. Replicated computational $(P_{i,j}^r)$ and voting $(V_{i,j}^r)$ processes on each core (C^n) and the applied arithmetic encoding scheme (application i, job j, replica r, core number n)

already covered by S^{3}DES. Furthermore, we assume that the occurring fault in the CPU and memory leads to data and program flow errors on application level and do not consider timing and byzantine errors. Additionally, since multi-core processors represent a single-chip solution, purely software-implemented fault-tolerance approaches cannot prevent common mode failures by nature. Faults affecting shared chip logic, e.g., the power supply, require further measures such as redundant hardware designs, but these concerns are out of scope.

3.2   Concept

Figure 1 depicts a model example of the concept. For the sake of simplicity we assume the input values for the computational processes (P) are already AN-encoded, replicated correctly and are provided to the process in a deterministic way. The considered multi-core platform provides three processing elements respectively cores (C), which execute the replicated processes (P and V) in parallel. The parallel execution has two advantages over a sequential execution on one core (temporal redundancy): (1) it makes a step towards fault tolerance against permanent random hardware errors, since a repeated execution of a replica on a faulty core would probably lead to the same faulty result and therefore would stay undetected and (2) it enhances the compliance with real-time requirements in terms of response time of the application compared to a sequential execution on one core. In contrast to other approaches such as Safely Embedded Software (SES) [5], arithmetic encoding is not applied to the entire calculation process to minimize the run-time execution overhead which would be otherwise introduced by complex signature calculation [24]. During the process prologue (D), each replicated computational process decodes the received AN-encoded values and executes the computation (P). During the time-span where values are processed uncoded, the execution is protected by the replicated execution. After the computation is finished, the computation results are AN-B-encoded during the process epilogue (E), i.e., the replica result is multiplied with the constant signature A and a replica specific B (B_x, B_y, B_z) signature is added. The B signature allows the determination of the identity of the winner or the diagnosis of the failed replica in a subsequent phase, e.g., to enable recovery or repair mechanisms. Afterwards, each of the replicated voters determine the majority among the AN-B-encoded results to detect and mask errors which occurred during the computational process. Beyond that, each voter replica performs a self-check as well as mutual voter monitoring in order to detect failures in one of the other voters and to prevent fault propagation. In case of a voter failure, one of the correct voters which is determined by a hierarchy carries out the distribution of the voting result. Thereby the voter failure is compensated without the utilization of backwards recovery which is beneficial for the overall response time of the application. Prior to the result distribution, the replica specific signature B is substracted and an AN-encoded value is forwarded to the subsequent (replicated or non-replicated) process.

Require: B_x, B_y, B_z

```
1: function PRECALCULATE_STATIC(x_c, y_c, z_c)
2:     if (x_c - y_c) = (B_x - B_y) then
3:         if (x_c - z_c) = (B_x - B_z) then
4:             return (B_x - B_y) + (B_x - B_z)
5:         else
6:             return (B_x - B_y)
7:         end if
8:     else if (y_c - z_c) = (B_y - B_z) then
9:         return (B_y - B_z)
10:    else if (x_c - z_c) = (B_x - B_z) then
11:        return (B_x - B_z)
12:    else
13:        SIGNAL_ERROR()
14:    end if
15: end function
```

(a)

Require: A

```
1: function SELFCHECK(B_precalc, result_c)
2:     if (result_c mod A) = B_precalc then
3:         return result_c - B_precalc
4:     else
5:         SIGNAL_ERROR()
6:     end if
7: end function
```

(b)

```
1: function APPLY(v_c, B_dyn)
2:     if B_dyn > B_max then
3:         SIGNAL_ERROR()
4:     else
5:         return v_c + B_dyn
6:     end if
7: end function
```

(c)

Require: B_x, B_y, B_z

```
1: function VOTE(x_c, y_c, z_c)
2:     if (x_c - y_c) = (B_x - B_y) then
3:         if (x_c - z_c) = (B_x - B_z) then
4:             result_c ← APPLY(x_c - B_x, (x_c - y_c) + (x_c - z_c))
5:             return result_c
6:         else
7:             result_c ← APPLY(x_c - B_x, (x_c - y_c))
8:             return result_c
9:         end if
10:    else if (y_c - z_c) = (B_y - B_z) then
11:        result_c ← APPLY(y_c - B_y, (y_c - z_c))
12:        return result_c
13:    else if (x_c - z_c) = (B_x - B_z) then
14:        result_c ← APPLY(x_c - B_x, (x_c - z_c))
15:        return result_c
16:    else
17:        result_c ← V_invalid
18:        SIGNAL_ERROR()
19:    end if
20: end function
```

(d)

Fig. 2. (a) Calculation of the static control flow signature; (b) Self-check for control flow and data errors; (c) Determination and application of dynamic control flow signature; (d) Encoded voting procedure.

3.3 Optimization of Encoding Signatures

Beside the parallel execution of the replicas and the replication of the voter, the initially proposed encoding (AN-BD) of the voting procedure [24] allows several optimizations while maintaining the established fault assumption: (1) Elimination of B signature management required for subsequent decoding within the computational processes. (2) Reduction of potential fault propagation between voter and computational processes. In the original approach, the voting procedure returns a result value which was encoded as follows: $v_c = A * n + B_{dyn} + B_{replica}$ and a constant jump signature B_e which are both provided to the subsequent process replicas. B_{dyn} represents the dynamic jump signature which is calculated during the voting based on the AN-B-encoded input values, $B_{replica}$ describes the replica-specific B signature of the voting winner and B_e the constant jump signature which is uniquely defined for each control flow branch and is calculated from the replica-specific B signatures during the voting. B_e is persisted together with the voting result or managed by an external data structure to allow the subsequent processes to lookup the value in order to evaluate if the control flow of the voting was correct and to decode the voting result. We assume the control flow check is performed in the following way: $(v_c - B_e mod A) = B_{\text{replica}}$. For a correct control flow of the voter, the remainder of the check has to correspond to one of the replica-specific B signatures which are stored in a lookup table, otherwise an error is detected. This causes two issues: (1) The B_e signatures have to be managed by an external data structure for each result of the voting process and the replica-specific B signature must be stored in lookup tables. This increases the complexity and the susceptibility to errors as well as the memory consumption and (2) because the control flow is only checked during the decoding phase of the consuming process, errors could propagate beyond the borders of the voter. In the event of a control flow error during the voting, the subsequent process could detect the deviation, but none of the replicas could determine the correct value which would lead to a detected but unrecoverable error.

For our optimization we aim to eliminate the static signature B_e and to reallocate the checks for voting errors to the voter itself. We first calculate the expected static value for the correct control flow B_{precalc} based on the voters input values (see Fig. 2(a)). During the voting the replica specific B signature is subtracted from the input value (see Fig. 2(d) - lines 7, 11, 14) and replaced by a control flow dependent signature B_{dyn} (see Fig. 2(b)) which results in an $A * n + B_{\text{dyn}}$ encoded value. After the winner of the voting is identified, a self-check is performed in which the precalculated control flow signature B_{precalc} is compared with the remainder of $A * n + B_{\text{dyn}} mod A$. An equal remainder and precalculated signature implies that the control flow was correct and no data error occurred. Subsequently, the control flow dependent signature B_{dyn} is substracted from the result which leaves an AN-encoded winner. An AN-encoded result is sufficient for the protection against data errors during the transaction to the subsequent processes. Due to this optimization only AN-encoded values are stored or transmitted and as a consequence the external management logic for the B signature and the resulting additional complexity are eliminated as any subsequent process can decode the value by the division with the constant signature A. Furthermore, the error detection is moved to the voter instead of the subsequent processes, and thus error propagation can be prevented as voter errors are detected and compensated by one of the replicated voters during the mutual voting monitoring. This optimization still holds with the transient single fault assumption and the results of the evaluation by fault injection will be provided in a latter section.

3.4   Mutual Voter Monitoring

The parallel executed replicated voters determine the majority among the encoded results to detect and compensate errors which occur during the computation. The voters are arithmetic encoded as described earlier and perform mutual monitoring. In case of a voter failure errors are compensated by an available correct voter (see Fig. 3). After the self-check of the voting result for control

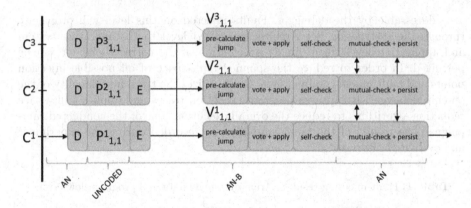

Fig. 3. Mutual voter monitoring for error detection

flow and data errors of each voter was executed, each voter checks the other voters for errors prior to the output of the result. The control flow of each voter is represented by a voter-specific flag (B signatures) which is calculated during the voter execution and contains the information, if every critical function (e.g. pre_calculate jump, vote, apply, self-check) was executed. Depending on the flag value (1) each voter knows if the other voters were executed correctly and (2) the output hierarchy between the voter is determined. In the case that the control flow flag of a voter is incorrect, one of the correct voter persists the result. In case an erroneous voter transmits its result without performing, e.g., a self-check or the voting itself, the other voters detect the error due to an erroneous flag and overwrite the already persisted value. The current design is able to compensate up to two voter failures. Due to this design change the compliance to real-time requirements can be eased and—depending on the system configuration—permanent or multiple fault coverage can be introduced to a certain degree. The singular output of the replicated voters prevents—in comparison to a common TMR system with replicated voters – error propagation to the subsequent computational processes and allows the output of a single result without having to repeat or perform a final voting on the voting result.

4   Evaluation

The evaluation of the dependability properties of an application can be accomplished by applying Software-Implemented Fault Injection (SWiFI) techniques which emulate random hardware faults at software level [13,23]. SWiFI techniques are widely adopted [1,9,27] and typically operate at the assembly level of the application to emulate hardware faults at the low level which propagate up to the application level. For our fault injection campaigns we used our self-implemented framework called PyFI (Python-backend for Fault Injection) [16]. PyFI utilizes an iSystem iC5000 on-chip analyzer to inject faults in the elements of the microarchitectural level (e.g. register and memory locations) which are addressable by the debugger. Faults injected on this level will propagate through the Instruction Set Architecture (ISA) level to the operating system and application level where finally a deviation of the correct behavior can be perceived. In order to reduce the spanned fault-space of all possible injection points and fault model combinations, PyFI utilizes the trace functionality of the on-chip debugger. It captures program execution traces and applies fault-space reduction algorithms to reduce the overall execution time of the conducted campaigns. The results of the fault campaign are recorded during the experiment and evaluated afterwards.

Table 1. Fault injection results - Transient single data and program flow errors

	Data error		Program flow error	
	Uncoded	Encoded	Uncoded	Encoded
Benign fault	1956	16234	490	997
Detected - S³DES	-	5440	-	2942
Detected - Trap	52	936	20	0
SDC	**264**	**0**	**73**	**0**
Sum	2272	22640	583	3939

For the assessment of the fault tolerance properties of our concept was implemented on an Infineon AURIX TriBoard TC277 [1] (three cores) with Erika Enterprise 2.7.0 and fault injection campaigns were performed with PyFI. To simplify our fault injection analysis, the implemented application consists only of three parallel executed voting processes which receive their AN-encoded input data from our fault injection framework. The processes are scheduled by a fixed priority non-preemptive scheduling policy and the code is executed from RAM. For our experiments we implemented an encoded voter (146 instructions) which consists of the functions shown in Fig. 3 and an uncoded voter (17 instructions). The uncoded voting experiment is not fully suited for a comparison but acts as a baseline for the evaluation of silent data corruptions. Each voting experiment is conducted with four different input value sets for the voter which represent the four possible branch decisions of the voter. We do not evaluate the voter under three different input values which would lead to detected unrecoverable errors and leave this evaluation for future work. Our goal was to trigger two types of errors on application level: (1) Data errors and (2) program flow errors. Data

---

[1] We selected the Aurix TriBoard platform to allow comparability with other approaches which used similar hardware. In the future S³DES will be evaluated on a more suitable and representative ARM system such as the Renesas R-Car series which executes a POSIX compliant operating system and lacks already integrated hardware safety mechanisms. The R-Car platform provides two Quad-Core CPUs and consequently states reduced requirements regarding resource consumption in terms of core usage.

errors are represented by single transient bit-flips which were injected prior to the read and write access of every used data and address register during the voting. Furthermore, faults were also injected into registers containing condition variables (e.g. PSW register). Program flow errors are injected by manipulating the program counter. The target addresses for the program counter which represent the erroneous jumps were determined automatically by PyFI through extracting the basic blocks of the program and generating all possible jump or sequence faults for the voting process. The results of the fault injection experiments are sorted into 4 categories: benign faults (do not affect execution), S³DES detected (detected and masked by S³DES voting scheme), trap detected (a fault triggered a hardware exception), SDC (undetected silent corruption of data). Further categories which are not listed because none of the injected faults triggered them in the current setup are OS detected (detected by OS) and hang (program hanged because of the fault).

The results of our fault injection experiments are shown in Table 1. An total of 2855 faults were injected into the uncoded voter. 2446 of the injected faults were masked on hardware level and had no effect on the application while a significant number of 337 SDCs were observed which corresponds to approx. 12% of all injected data and program flow errors. On the other side, the S³DES variant which utilizes the optimized arithmetic encoding, replicated voters in combination with mutual monitoring experiences no SDCs during the injection of a total of 26579 faults. The higher number of injected faults compared to the uncoded variant can be explained by the higher number of instructions of the coded voter.

5   Conclusion

Many concepts consider only transient errors. Although the error rate for permanent errors is significantly lower, we include this assumption in our considerations. Due to the execution of the replicated processes on different cores, a step towards the detection and compensation of permanent errors on homogeneous systems can be made, which could be reinforced by applying the concept on heterogeneous platforms. In addition, the parallel execution of the process replicas (computation and voters) reduces the response time of the system and thus the real-time capability is promoted. Due to the replication of the majority voter, mutual monitoring and the established voter hierarchy, the previously required backward recovery can be eliminated. In case of a voter failure, one of the correct voter detects the failure and persists the correct results depending on the output hierarchy. We showed by fault injection that the mutual voting monitoring in combination with the arithmetic encoding optimizations is able to detect all injected faults which lead to program and data flow errors.

Depending on future system requirements (e.g. fail-safe, fail-operational), system design (e.g. static, dynamic) and optimization goals (e.g. memory consumption, number of available cores) different variants of the concept regarding the system configuration will be evaluated. In case a system design only requires a fail-safe operation and no hardware mechanisms such lockstep cores are available, the concept could be scaled to dual modular redundancy with an encoded comparison instead of voting. This would decrease the maximum overall CPU load while allowing the detection of CPU and memory faults.

References

1. Arlat, J., et al.: Fault injection for dependability validation: a methodology and some applications. IEEE Trans. Softw. Eng. **16**(2), 166–182 (1990)
2. Bartlett, W., Spainhower, L.: Commercial fault tolerance: a tale of two systems. IEEE Trans. Dependable Secure Comput. **1**(1), 87–96 (2004). https://doi.org/10.1109/TDSC.2004.4
3. Baumann, R.: Soft errors in advanced computer systems. IEEE Des. Test Comput. **22**(3), 258–266 (2005). https://doi.org/10.1109/MDT.2005.69
4. Borkar, S.: Designing reliable systems from unreliable components: the challenges of transistor variability and degradation. IEEE Micro **25**(6), 10–16 (2005). https://doi.org/10.1109/MM.2005.110
5. Braun, J., Mottok, J.: Fail-safe and fail-operational systems safeguarded with coded processing. In: Eurocon 2013, pp. 1878–1885, July 2013. https://doi.org/10.1109/EUROCON.2013.6625234
6. Braun, J., Mottok, J.: The myths of coded processing. In: 2015 IEEE 17th International Conference on High Performance Computing and Communications, 2015 IEEE 7th International Symposium on Cyberspace Safety and Security, and 2015 IEEE 12th International Conference on Embedded Software and Systems, pp. 1637–1644, August 2015. https://doi.org/10.1109/HPCC-CSS-ICESS.2015.24
7. Echtle, K.: Fehlertoleranzverfahren (1990)
8. Goloubeva, O., Rebaudengo, M., Reorda, M.S., Violante, M.: Software Implemented Hardware Fault Tolerance, vol. 2005. Springer, New York (2006)
9. Hsueh, M.C., Tsai, T.K., Iyer, R.K.: Fault injection techniques and tools. Computer **30**(4), 75–82 (1997). https://doi.org/10.1109/2.585157
10. Kim, Y., et al.: Flipping bits in memory without accessing them: an experimental study of DRAM disturbance errors. In: 2014 ACM/IEEE 41st International Symposium on Computer Architecture (ISCA), pp. 361–372, June 2014. https://doi.org/10.1109/ISCA.2014.6853210
11. Koser, E., Berthold, K., Pujari, R.K., Stechele, W.: A chip-level redundant threading (CRT) scheme for shared-memory protection. In: 2016 International Conference on High Performance Computing Simulation (HPCS), pp. 116–124, July 2016. https://doi.org/10.1109/HPCSim.2016.7568324
12. Li, M.L., Ramachandran, P., Sahoo, S.K., Adve, S.V., Adve, V.S., Zhou, Y.: Understanding the propagation of hard errors to software and implications for resilient system design. In: Proceedings of the 13th International Conference on Architectural Support for Programming Languages and Operating Systems. ASPLOS XIII, pp. 265–276. ACM, New York (2008). https://doi.org/10.1145/1346281.1346315
13. Maia, R., Henriques, L., Costa, D., Madeira, H.: XceptionTM - enhanced automated fault-injection environment. In: Proceedings International Conference on Dependable Systems and Networks, p. 547 (2002). https://doi.org/10.1109/DSN.2002.1028978
14. Narayanan, V., Xie, Y.: Reliability concerns in embedded system designs. Computer **39**(1), 118–120 (2006). https://doi.org/10.1109/MC.2006.31

15. Nightingale, E.B., Douceur, J.R., Orgovan, V.: Cycles, cells and platters: an empirical analysis of hardware failures on a million consumer PCs. In: Proceedings of the Sixth Conference on Computer Systems, EuroSys 2011, pp. 343–356. ACM, New York (2011). https://doi.org/10.1145/1966445.1966477

16. Osinski, L., Langer, T., Schmid, M., Mottok, J.: PyFI-fault injection platform for real hardware. In: ARCS Workshop 2018; 31st International Conference on Architecture of Computing Systems, pp. 1–7. VDE (2018)

17. Reis, G.A., Chang, J., August, D.I.: Automatic Instruction-Level Software-Only Recovery, pp. 36–47 (2007)

18. Reis, G.A., Chang, J., Vachharajani, N., Rangan, R., August, D.I.: SWIFT: software implemented fault tolerance. In: Proceedings of the International Symposium on Code Generation and Optimization, CGO 2005, pp. 243–254. IEEE Computer Society, Washington, DC (2005). https://doi.org/10.1109/CGO.2005.34

19. Saggese, G.P., Wang, N.J., Kalbarczyk, Z.T., Patel, S.J., Iyer, R.K.: An experimental study of soft errors in microprocessors. IEEE Micro **25**(6), 30–39 (2005). https://doi.org/10.1109/MM.2005.104

20. Schiffel, U.: Hardware error detection using AN-codes (2010)

21. Schroeder, B., Pinheiro, E., Weber, W.D.: DRAM errors in the wild: a large-scale field study. In: ACM SIGMETRICS Performance Evaluation Review, vol. 37, pp. 193–204. ACM (2009)

22. Shye, A., Moseley, T., Reddi, V.J., Blomstedt, J., Connors, D.A.: Using process-level redundancy to exploit multiple cores for transient fault tolerance. In: 2007 37th Annual IEEE/IFIP International Conference on Dependable Systems and Networks, DSN 2007, pp. 297–306. IEEE (2007)

23. Stott, D.T., Floering, B., Burke, D., Kalbarczpk, Z., Iyer, R.K.: NFTAPE: a framework for assessing dependability in distributed systems with lightweight fault injectors. In: Proceedings IEEE International Computer Performance and Dependability Symposium, IPDS 2000. pp. 91–100 (2000). https://doi.org/10.1109/IPDS.2000.839467

24. Ulbrich, P.: Ganzheitliche Fehlertoleranz in Eingebetteten Softwaresystemen. Ph.D. thesis (2014)

25. Wappler, U., Fetzer, C.: Hardware failure virtualization via software encoded processing. In: 2007 5th IEEE International Conference on Industrial Informatics, vol. 2, pp. 977–982, June 2007. https://doi.org/10.1109/INDIN.2007.4384907

26. Wappler, U., Muller, M.: Software protection mechanisms for dependable systems. In: 2008 Design, Automation and Test in Europe, pp. 947–952, March 2008. https://doi.org/10.1109/DATE.2008.4484802

27. Ziade, H., Ayoubi, R., Velazco, R.: A survey on fault injection techniques. Int. Arab J. Inf. Technol. **1**(2), 171–186 (2004). https://doi.org/10.1.1.167.966

Real-Time Systems

A Hybrid NoC Enabling Fail-Operational and Hard Real-Time Communication in MPSoC

Max Koenen$^{(\boxtimes)}$ ⬥, Nguyen Anh Vu Doan ⬥, Thomas Wild,
and Andreas Herkersdorf

Chair of Integrated Systems, Technical University of Munich, Munich, Germany
{max.koenen,anhvu.doan,thomas.wild,herkersdorf}@tum.de

Abstract. Multi-core processors, despite their technical and economic advantages, are yet hesitantly adopted in safety-critical embedded application domains such as automotive and avionics. A key issue is the potential interference on shared resources, such as interconnect and memory, between applications of different criticality which are running on a Multi-Processor System-on-Chip (MPSoC) with tens of individual cores. In this paper we propose the introduction of established protection switching, known from synchronous data networks, to a hybrid Network-on-Chip (NoC) in order to provide fault-tolerance for critical connections. Our hybrid NoC combines configurable Time-Division-Multiplexing (TDM) for critical task traffic with conventional packet switching for Best-Effort (BE) traffic. We analyze three different protection switching schemes for their worst case latencies in case of faulty NoC links and their resource overheads. Simulations with random traffic and 10% reserved resources for TDM connections reveal that the degradation of BE traffic performance due to the proposed TDM protection switching for critical traffic remains limited to about a 5% lower injection rate even in case of 1+1 protection, which can hence be considered affordable. We conclude that the proposed hybrid NoC is a suitable way to provide both hard real-time guarantees and fault-tolerance for critical connections in advanced MPSoCs.

Keywords: NoC · TDM · Hybrid · Fail-operational ·
Hard real-time · Fault-tolerance · Protection switching

1 Introduction

Modern Multi-Processor System-on-Chips (MPSoC) can embed tens to, in the near future, hundreds or even thousands of processing elements [5]. All these processing elements must be connected to each other and, due to scalability issues, bus-based solutions are no longer feasible and are dropped in favor of Network-on-Chips (NoC) [4].

When integrating multiple applications on such an MPSoC it is vital to ensure strict isolation between applications of different criticality and to provide

© Springer Nature Switzerland AG 2019
M. Schoeberl et al. (Eds.): ARCS 2019, LNCS 11479, pp. 31–44, 2019.
https://doi.org/10.1007/978-3-030-18656-2_3

Guaranteed Service (GS) to critical applications so that all safety critical hard real-time applications run unobstructed by any low- or non-critical application and always meet their deadline. Moreover, in order to enable fail-operational applications the communication of a critical application must not be affected by a fault in the NoC. All this must be considered when implementing a NoC for an MPSoC that is to be used in a safety-critical environment.

There are two common types of NoCs: packet-switched and circuit switched. Today, most research seems to concentrate on packet-switched NoCs [15]. They offer a good flexibility and different approaches to implement fault-tolerance exist. However, it has proven rather difficult to implement hard-real-time guarantees and most implementations give only statistical latency guarantees [11]. Circuit-switched NoCs on the other hand are well suited for providing guarantees since resources are reserved for every connection [9,15]. However, this typically leads to a lower utilization and less flexibility than in packet-switched NoCs. Furthermore, to the best of our knowledge, no work exists considering fault-tolerance in circuit switched NoCs.

Hybrid NoCs were proposed to combine the strengths of both NoC types but the proposed approaches are mostly targeted towards maximizing the utilization of the NoC rather than guaranteeing hard real-time communication [6,16,20]. Other works use circuit switching to provide GS but typically set up the connections at runtime by using packet switched best-effort (BE) traffic. This means that guarantees can be given once a connection is established, but not about the time it takes to set the connection up or whether it can be established at all.

In our work we propose a hybrid NoC combining Time-Division-Multiplexing (TDM) and packet-switching that can not only provide GS but also fault-tolerance to safety critical applications, while still providing BE traffic for non-critical applications. We do that by applying a protection switching scheme to the NoC, as known from SONET/SDH [2]. We define two paths for the critical applications at compile time which are then set up at the startup time of the system. In case of a fault along the main path, the system can immediately (and transparently to the application) switch to the predefined backup path.

The remainder of the paper is structured as follows. In Sect. 2 we discuss related work. We describe the basic concept of our approach in Sect. 3 before providing a formal analysis of the achievable guarantees in Sect. 4. In Sect. 5 we describe our experimental setup and evaluate our proposed design. Section 6 concludes our results and gives an outlook to future work.

2   Related Work

Several NoC designs that provide GS have been proposed in prior research. To the best of our knowledge, Goossens et al. have been the first to propose a hybrid NoC design in their Æthereal NoC [8], composed of a TDM part for GS and packet switching for BE traffic. The TDM schedules in the Æthereal NoC are defined at design time. Other works based on the Æthereal NoC are aelite [10] and dAElite [19] which both only implement GS traffic.

The Argo NoC [12] uses TDM to provide GS and describes how a TDM scheme can be applied to asynchronous and mesochronous environments. It uses a completely static scheduling. Sørensen et al. have proposed an extension of the Argo NoC in order to support reconfiguration at run-time in [18].

XNoC [17] also uses TDM to provide GS and provides a non-intrusive way to reconfigure connections at runtime within a predictable latency. This is done by using a distributed control plane.

A combination of Space-Division-Multiplexing (SDM) and TDM based circuit-switching together with packet-switching has been proposed by Lusala and Legat [16]. They effectively use two separate networks. One implementing several links between neighboring routers (SDM), each with their own TDM schedule, for GS traffic, the other implementing a standard packet-switched NoC for BE traffic.

Yin et al. have proposed a hybrid NoC composed of a packet-switched NoC with virtual channels and a TDM part [20]. Packet-switched messages are used to set up TDM channels for bandwidth-heavy applications. Slot table sizes can be adjusted at runtime (causing a reset of all TDM connections). Their main concern has been energy-efficiency and network utilization.

Another TDM/packet-switched hybrid NoC has been proposed by Chen et al. [6,7]. Their network applies the TDM schedule either by using slot tables in each router and Network Interface (NI) or by using source routing and slot tables only in the NIs. A central NoCManager is responsible for scheduling connections per request. Dedicated wires or TDM channels are used for the connection requests. Their main concerns have been power-efficiency, higher utilization, and channel set up time.

Kostrzewa et al. have proposed an approach to provide GS in a packet-switched NoC by introducing a Resource Manager (RM) [13,14]. Each NI implements a client that requests a channel from the RM. The path of each channel is pre-calculated at design time so the RM only has to arbitrate overlapping paths.

An extension layer for the NI of an existing NoC has been proposed by Ahmadian et al. in [3]. They differentiate between time-triggered and event-triggered messages and ensure that time-triggered messages can traverse the NoC unobstructed by other messages by restricting traffic injection.

To provide GS the approaches mentioned above use either completely static scheduling that cannot be changed at runtime or dynamic scheduling that tries to set up communication channels on demand and tears them down afterwards. The latter makes it impossible to give hard real-time guarantees, which always require that at least the critical connections are reserved and mapped at compile time [11]. None of these works consider fault-tolerance. To the best of our knowledge our proposed approach is the first one to provide not only hard real-time guarantees but also fault-tolerance for the critical communication, while at the same time providing the flexibility of run-time reconfigurations and BE traffic.

3   Hybrid TDM NoC Architecture with Protection Switching

This section describes the concept for the hybrid NoC and the implementation of fault-tolerance. First, the definition of the applied TDM scheme will be covered, as different approaches are taken in related work and there does not seem to be a single state of the art solution. Furthermore, the composition of the hybrid NoC as well as the protection switching scheme and its adoption for NoC are described.

3.1   The Hybrid NoC Architecture

In our work we use the "contention-free routing" scheme for TDM NoCs described in [8] as a basis. Each network node (i.e. router and NI) has a slot table T with S slots that stores the routing information for each output and each time slot. All nodes cycle through their slot tables synchronously. In each time slot t, the output ports of the routers forward a flit from a defined input port according to their slot table entry. A path for a connection is set up by configuring consecutive slot tables along the path to forward flits in subsequent time slots $t + 1$. The NIs write/read flits to/from the network according to their slot tables.

This form of routing is advantageous for GS traffic since the pipelined forwarding guarantees a deterministic latency. A formal analysis of the achievable worst case latencies (of both, a single TDM connection as well as the protection switching schemes proposed in Sect. 3.2) is given in Sect. 4. Contentions cannot occur per design, since the time slots for each connection are reserved beforehand. The disadvantage, however, is that reserved resources cannot be used by other connections, even if they are not used at a time. This typically leads to a low resource utilization.

To mitigate the downsides of pure TDM routing and to support applications with different and more flexible communication requirements, we use a hybrid NoC, similar to the one proposed in [20]. The idea is to use the described TDM schedule for the critical connections and use the remaining time slots for packet-switched BE traffic. This requires buffers at each router input in order to store incoming BE flits in case of contention between BE and TDM traffic, or between two BE flits that request the same output port of a router. It is important to note that the TDM routing is still contention-free since a scheduled TDM flit will always have precedence over BE traffic and two TDM flits can never collide. The described router architecture is shown on the right side of Fig. 1.

The use of a hybrid NoC increases the overall network utilization compared to a pure TDM NoC since the BE flits fill otherwise unused time slots. The BE traffic can even use reserved but unoccupied TDM slots, a technique known as slot-stealing [20]. Furthermore, the BE part of the NoC is more flexible which can be useful in case non-critical applications are started and dynamically mapped at runtime. On the downside, the implementation of BE traffic adds complexity to the routers which now not just require buffers but also routing and arbitration logic. However, the implementation does not need to be as complex as a pure packet-switched NoC that wants to implement Quality of Service (QoS) since packet-switching is not used for any critical communication. A system developer has a degree of freedom regarding the complexity of the packet-switched part of the NoC (e.g. number of virtual channels, traffic classes, etc.).

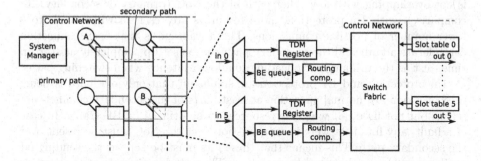

Fig. 1. Proposed architecture with system manager and control network

3.2   Protection Switching in NoC

In this section we describe the implementation of fault-tolerance for the critical connections by applying protection switching. The basic idea behind protection switching is to define alternative paths that can instantly be switched to in case a fault occurs on the active path. The principle is known from SONET/SDH [2] and requires some adjustments of the NoC in order to be applicable. It is important to note that we give the fault-tolerance and hard real-time guarantees of the critical traffic the highest priority which is why these connections are determined at compile time, set up at startup time, and only reconfigured in case of a fault.

To implement protection switching in our NoC two (or more) disjunct paths are reserved for each connection at compile time. For the remainder of this paper we will always consider two paths, and we will call the path that is actively being used for communication the *primary* path, and the backup path the *secondary* path. The first necessary adjustment to the NoC is to provide a second link between each NI and the router it is connected to. Otherwise, no two paths could ever be completely disjunct (i.e. have no common links). Both paths can traverse the same router as long as they use different input and output ports (we assume that each output port has its own slot table and no single fault can affect the whole router). We examine three protection switching variants in our research: 1:n, 1:1, and 1+1 protection.

In SONET/SDH 1:n protection means that several connections share the same backup path. In a TDM NoC it means that the alternative paths of 2 or more connections overlap in at least one time slot of at least one router port. This has three consequences. Firstly, n connections can tolerate one fault on any of their paths at most. Secondly, more connections can be scheduled in a NoC, since fewer time slots need to be reserved for secondary paths. Lastly, at least parts of each secondary path, specifically the overlapping time slots, cannot be configured at startup time, which leads to a longer delay when a fault occurs. This is because only when a fault occurs it is known which secondary path must actually be activated.

When using 1:1 protection, each connection has its own secondary path that is not overlapping with any other path in the NoC (primary or secondary). In comparison with 1:n protection, more resources are reserved which leads to a lower number of possible connections. The advantage is that each connection can tolerate a fault and the secondary path can be set up completely at startup time, just as the primary path, leading to a lower latency when switching paths.

1:n protection and 1:1 protection are similar in that only one path is being used at a time. In normal operation at least parts of the secondary channels are set up but not used, allowing the resources to be utilized by BE traffic. In case of a fault, any flits that were in transmission over the NoC must be resent over the secondary path. This means that these flits must be kept at the sending NI until it can be sure that they have arrived. The switching is done at the sending NI, which requires another adjustment to the NoC: a feedback channel from the routers to all NIs to inform the NIs about the occurrence of a fault. For our proof-of-concept described in Sect. 5 we use a low-throughput overlay network as control network. This network is used for two things. At startup time a central system manager uses this network to configure the slot tables of the NIs and routers before the normal operation of the system starts. During operation this network is used to broadcast the occurrence of any fault in the NoC to all NIs, which then decide whether or not they need to switch paths. It is important to note that the described central system manager is not required for the protection switching, which is done in a distributed manner by the sending NIs. However, in case of a fault the system manager can try to find and set up a new secondary path for any broken connection to return the system into a fault-tolerant state. Figure 1 shows the proposed architecture with system manager, control network, and a primary and secondary path from node A to node B.

A different approach is taken with 1+1 protection, which sends each flit over both paths. This again has several consequences. Firstly, there is hardly any flit delay in case of a fault, since no retransmission is necessary. Secondly, the sending NI does not need to store any flits, since in case of a fault on one channel all flits will still arrive on the other channel. The consequence is that the sending NI does not need to know about the fault, which means solutions without the previously mentioned control network as feedback channel are possible. The fault can simply be detected at the receiving NI, which can then inform a higher software layer about the lost fault-tolerance. However, the downside is that more resources are used, leading to fewer time slots available for BE traffic.

To guarantee that all sent data is received and nothing is delivered twice to the receiving task some kind of data synchronization is necessary. For instance, if a fault occurs on the primary path while multiple flits are being transmitted it is possible that the first few flits still arrive. When the sending NI sends the same flits again over the secondary path the receiving NI needs to know which flits are duplicates that must be discarded. To solve this issue, we periodically insert checkpoints into the data stream. If some data is retransmitted over the secondary path the last checkpoint number is retransmitted as well. The receiving NI can thereby detect any duplicate flits in the received data.

The proposed protection switching scheme does not differ between permanent and transient faults. The highest priority is given to the fault-tolerance which is why in case of any fault the connection will switch to the secondary path. However, it would be possible to send test vectors over the primary path after a switch to check whether the path is still faulty and, if not, use it as new backup path.

4   Formal Analysis

In this section we present a formal analysis of the three different protection switching schemes regarding their worst case latency. There are several parameters that have an impact on the worst case latency of a TDM connection: the latency per hop, the number N of hops, the size S of the slot tables, and the number of slots s assigned to a connection.

The latency per hop in a TDM NoC is typically 1 cycle and is therefore not further considered here. The hop-count N in our proposed architecture will typically be relatively low since the critical applications are mapped at compile time which allows to optimize the mapping for short paths. The size S of the slot tables is a major design parameter and must be decided at system design time. This parameter limits the number of connections that can share a single link. It also defines the minimal bandwidth BW_{min} that can be assigned to any TDM connection, which at the same time denotes the quantization of the available bandwidth BW ($BW_{min} = BW/S$). The number of slots s assigned to a connection defines the maximum bandwidth BW_{max} the connection can use ($BW_{max} = s \cdot BW_{min}$) but also has an influence on the worst case latency of a single flit or a packet composed of multiple flits.

From the cycle that a TDM flit is injected into the NoC its latency is: $N + 1$ (one cycle per hop plus one cycle until it reaches the NI). However, a flit might have to wait for up to $S - s$ cycles at the sending NI until it can get injected into the NoC. Hence, the worst case latency C_1 in cycles for a single flit is:

$$C_1 = (S - s) + (N + 1) \tag{1}$$

When sending multiple flits between two checkpoints the total latency heavily depends on the slot table size S, the number of assigned slots s, and the number of flits f, and only to a minor degree on the hop count N. The reason is that only s flits can be sent every S cycles. After the initial worst case delay, flits can be sent in the following $s - 1$ cycles before the next flit must wait for another $S - s$ cycles. In the simplest case ($s = 1$) the flits following the first flit have an additional delay of $S \cdot (f - 1)$ cycles, causing a total worst case latency C_2 of:

$$C_2 = (S - s) + (N + 1) + (S \cdot (f - 1)) = S \cdot f - s + N + 1 \qquad (2)$$

This equation can be further generalized to also include cases where more than one slot is reserved for a connection. Equation 3 describes the worst case latency C for any TDM path. It can easily be seen that the hop count only has a minor influence on the worst case latency when sending multiple flits.

$$C = (S - s) + (N + 1) + (S \cdot \left\lfloor \frac{f - 1}{s} \right\rfloor + (f - 1) \bmod s) \qquad (3)$$

For 1+1 protection C also denotes the worst case latency in case of a fault during the transmission, since it can be applied to both the primary and the secondary path. In case of 1:n or 1:1 protection two other parameters must be considered: the latency F caused by the feedback via the overlay network described in Sect. 3.2, and, in case of 1:n protection, the latency P to set up the secondary path. In both cases all flits since the last safe checkpoint must be retransmitted over the secondary path, which also has the worst case latency C (assuming the two paths are equidistant, otherwise N is different for the two paths). A checkpoint can be considered *safe* as soon as the next checkpoint has been inserted and $C + F$ cycles have passed. Assuming a fault occurs on the last hop for the last flit before a new checkpoint, the total worst case latency of transmission and retransmission is: $2C - 1$. In combination with the parameters F and P ($P = 0$ for 1:1 protection) we get the worst case latency for 1:n and 1:1 protection.

$$C_3 = (2C - 1) + F + P \qquad (4)$$

Both F and P are implementation dependent parameters, and can only be approximated here. It can be assumed, though, that both parameters will, in the worst case, grow linearly with the number of hops, making short paths more desirable. Furthermore, since for 1:n and 1:1 protection all flits since the last safe checkpoint must be retransmitted and C heavily depends on the number of flits f between two checkpoints, it makes sense to keep f low by inserting more checkpoints. For an actual application the tolerable worst case latency must be considered when deciding which protection switching to use and how to dimension S, s, f, and N.

5   Experimental Setup and Evaluation

The following subsections describe the experimental setup and the simulation that has been done to evaluate the proposed architecture. No simulation would be required for the critical communication and the fault-tolerance since they are deterministic by design. Instead, the simulation is intended to evaluate the impact the TDM traffic has on the BE traffic and the overall network utilization.

5.1   Experimental Setup

To get adequate results concerning the interference of TDM and BE traffic we made cycle-accurate simulations. We implemented a hybrid router in SystemVerilog HDL and created an 8×8 NoC mesh. The implemented packet switched part of the router uses static X-Y-routing and does not employ virtual channels. Synopsys VCS is used to simulate the implemented NoC. The remaining parts of the system (i.e. the NIs, the overlay network, the system manager, the computing nodes, and the processes running on them) are currently abstracted in a testbench created with cocotb [1] and Python.

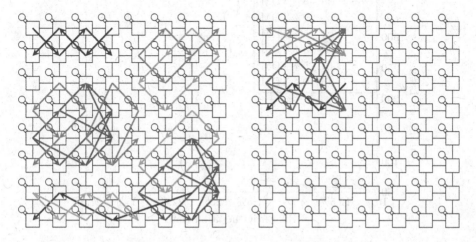

Fig. 2. Scenario 1 - 11 task graphs   **Fig. 3.** Scenario 2 - 3 task graphs

We used 4 randomly-generated task graphs to represent a set of critical applications for our simulations. All graphs have one source and one sink vertex, are directed, acyclic, and have vertices with a degree of up to 3. We simulated two scenarios with different sets of task graph mappings, different TDM injection rates, and different protection switching schemes.

For the first scenario we spread 11 task graphs taken from the set of randomly-generated task graphs across the entire 8×8 system. We simulated both a 5% and 10% flit injection rate for the TDM traffic. These injection rates describe the net traffic meaning they are effectively twice as high for 1+1 protection. Furthermore, the injection rates define the average across all nodes, meaning that the injection rate of a single node can be significantly higher as not all nodes inject TDM traffic into the NoC. Figure 2 shows the logical connections that are configured for the critical communication (each connection has a disjunct primary and a secondary path, not shown in the figure). All nodes send and receive uniform random BE traffic to measure the effect the TDM traffic has on the packet-switched traffic.

For the second scenario we mapped 3 task graphs to just 16 nodes clustered in one quarter of the system, shown in Fig. 3. In this scenario, due to the dense mapping only an overall TDM flit injection rate of 5% could be achieved (which means the 16 participating nodes have an average per node injection rate of 20%, or 40% for 1+1 protection, since only a quarter of the NoC is used). Random BE traffic is sent and received by the remaining 48 nodes meaning the critical and BE applications are separate.

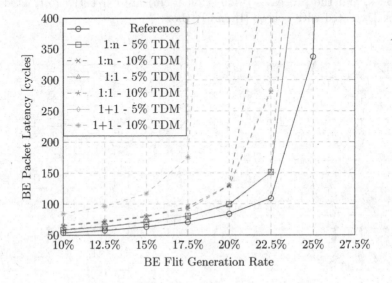

Fig. 4. Average BE latency - Scenario 1

The BE packets have an average size of 30 flits and each router has an input buffer that can hold 16 flits. We simulated a per node BE flit generation rate of 10% to 30% in 2.5% steps to measure at which point the network would saturate. After a warmup period of 10 000 cycles, after which the link load has stabilized, we simulated 100 000 cycles. Longer simulation runs did not change the results significantly.

5.2   Results and Evaluation

The Figs. 4 and 5 show the average BE packet latencies for the two simulated scenarios. Both figures include a reference simulation without any TDM traffic in the NoC. The measured packet latencies are from the applications point of view, i.e. from the generation of a packet (and queuing at the NI) until its delivery (not from injection into the NoC until delivery). For the results this means that at a certain threshold the flit generation rate exceeds the achievable injection rate and the BE buffer queues at the sending NIs would grow infinitely.

The results for scenario 1, depicted in Fig. 4, show that the TDM traffic negatively affects the BE traffic, which causes the earlier saturation points for BE traffic. However, this degradation of the BE traffic was expected and is still acceptable considering the trade-off for real-time guarantees and fault-tolerance for the critical communication. The results also show that the combined flit injection rate of BE and TDM traffic (obtained by adding the 5% or 10% TDM injection rate to the respective curve in the diagram) can even be higher than the one of the reference simulation with only BE traffic. The simulations for 1:n and 1:1 protection show very similar results which is caused by the fact that they both only use one path at a time. Furthermore, the results for 1+1 protection with a 5% injection rate and the ones for 1:n and 1:1 protection with a 10% injection rate are also similar, which reflects the fact that 1+1 protection uses twice the amount of resources.

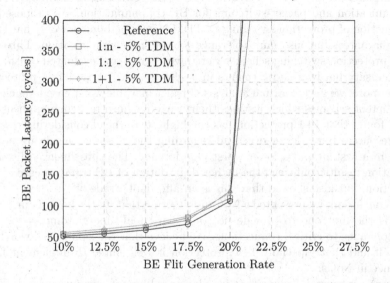

Fig. 5. Average BE latency - Scenario 2

The results of scenario 2, depicted in Fig. 5, show a different outcome. Here, the TDM traffic has almost no effect on the BE traffic. Furthermore, the saturation point for the reference simulation is considerably lower than in scenario 1. The results can be explained by two effects. First, the nodes creating and consuming BE traffic are no longer evenly distributed throughout the NoC. This causes an uneven utilization of the available links in the NoC (caused by the static X-Y-routing) which creates bottlenecks on some links and thereby leads to an earlier saturation point. Second, only a small amount of the BE traffic traverses the area with the TDM traffic, which is also caused by the X-Y-routing. Therefore, only a small amount of the BE traffic is affected by the TDM traffic.

The results indicate that it is beneficial to spread out the critical applications rather than clustering them. This would also increase the overall resilience since a single fault in the NoC would affect fewer critical paths. However, more simulations with different mappings are needed to verify this assumption, which will be done in future work. Furthermore, different BE routing schemes and network topologies should be investigated as the results of scenario 2 indicate a strong influence on the BE traffic performance of both. Overall, we believe that the results justify the use of 1+1 protection rather then 1:n or 1:1 protection. In our opinion the additional resource utilization of 1+1 protection is tolerable, especially when considering the lower worst case latency and the fact that 1+1 protection would allow for an architecture without additional control network.

6   Conclusion and Future Work

In this paper we described a hybrid NoC architecture using TDM for critical communication and packet-switching for BE communication. We proposed the introduction of protection switching to TDM NoCs, enabling not only hard real-time guarantees but also fault-tolerance for critical communication. Three different protection switching schemes were investigated and evaluated considering the necessary hardware adjustments in a system: 1:n, 1:1, and 1+1 protection. Furthermore, we gave a formal analysis of the achievable worst case latencies for the different schemes which justifies their usage for hard real-time applications. It was found that 1+1 protection has the highest overhead considering reserved NoC resources but a lower overhead regarding the necessary hardware adjustments in a system and a lower worst case latency. The subsequently discussed simulation results confirmed the higher degradation of BE traffic in case of 1+1 protection, but also showed that this is an affordable trade-off.

In conclusion, we presented a NoC architecture that, to the best of our knowledge, is the first one to provide not only hard real-time guarantees but also fault-tolerance to critical connections. We believe that the gain is well worth the trade-off and that especially 1+1 protection is well suited to implement fault-tolerance in NoCs.

There are several aspects that we plan to address in our future work. First, we want to investigate tools that automatically find possible mappings and the required slot table size for a given set of critical applications with provided constraints, since mapping is currently done manually. This will allow us to simulate a larger number of mapping scenarios to validate our current results as well as examine different network topologies and their effect on the overall achievable NoC utilization. We also plan to research ways to deal with accesses to heavily shared resources (such as I/Os and memories), possibly by using different slot table sizes throughout the NoC, or multiple interfaces. Lastly, we want to examine the protection switching schemes in combination with the migration of a critical task and in combination with multicasts.

Acknowledgement. The work presented in this paper is supported by the German BMBF project ARAMiS II with funding ID 01 IS 16025.

References

1. Cocotb manual. https://cocotb.readthedocs.io/en/latest/. Accessed 22 Nov 2018
2. ITU-T G.841: Types and characteristics of SDH network protection architectures. Technical report. International Telecommunication Union, October (1998)
3. Ahmadian, H., Obermaisser, R., Abuteir, M.: Time-triggered and rate-constrained on-chip communication in mixed-criticality systems. In: 2016 IEEE 10th International Symposium on Embedded Multicore/Many-core Systems-on-Chip, MCSOC, pp. 117–124, September 2016
4. Benini, L., Micheli, G.D.: Networks on chips: a new SoC paradigm. Computer **35**(1), 70–78 (2002)
5. Borkar, S.: Thousand core chips: a technology perspective. In: Proceedings of the 44th Annual Design Automation Conference, DAC 2007, pp. 746–749. ACM, New York (2007)
6. Chen, Y., Matus, E., Fettweis, G.P.: Combined packet and TDM circuit switching NoCs with novel connection configuration mechanism. In: 2017 IEEE International Symposium on Circuits and Systems, ISCAS, pp. 1–4, May 2017
7. Chen, Y., Matus, E., Fettweis, G.P.: Register-exchange based connection allocator for circuit switching NoCs. In: 2017 25th Euromicro International Conference on Parallel, Distributed and Network-based Processing, PDP, pp. 559–566, March 2017
8. Goossens, K., Dielissen, J., Radulescu, A.: Æthereal Network on Chip: concepts, architectures, and implementations. IEEE Des. Test Comput. **22**(5), 414–421 (2005)
9. Goossens, K., Hansson, A.: The Æthereal network on chip after ten years: goals, evolution, lessons, and future. In: Design Automation Conference, pp. 306–311, June 2010
10. Hansson, A., Subburaman, M., Goossens, K.: Aelite: a flit-synchronous Network on Chip with composable and predictable services. In: 2009 Design, Automation Test in Europe Conference Exhibition, pp. 250–255, April 2009
11. Hesham, S., Rettkowski, J., Goehringer, D., Ghany, M.A.A.E.: Survey on real-time Networks-on-Chip. IEEE Trans. Parallel Distrib. Syst. **28**(5), 1500–1517 (2017)
12. Kasapaki, E., Sparsø J.: The Argo NOC: combining TDM and GALS. In: 2015 European Conference on Circuit Theory and Design, ECCTD, pp. 1–4, August 2015
13. Kostrzewa, A., Saidi, S., Ernst, R.: Dynamic control for mixed-critical Networks-on-Chip. In: 2015 IEEE Real-Time Systems Symposium, pp. 317–326, December 2015
14. Kostrzewa, A., Saidi, S., Ecco, L., Ernst, R.: Ensuring safety and efficiency in Networks-on-Chip. Integr. VLSI J. **58**(Suppl. C), 571–582 (2017)
15. Liu, S., Jantsch, A., Lu, Z.: Analysis and evaluation of circuit switched NoC and packet switched NoC. In: 2013 Euromicro Conference on Digital System Design, pp. 21–28, September 2013
16. Lusala, A.K., Legat, J.D.: A hybrid NoC combining SDM-TDM based circuit-switching with packet-switching for real-time applications. In: 10th IEEE International NEWCAS Conference, pp. 17–20, June 2012
17. Nguyen, T.D.A., Kumar, A.: XNoC: A non-intrusive TDM circuit-switched Network-on-Chip. In: 2016 26th International Conference on Field Programmable Logic and Applications, FPL, pp. 1–11, August 2016

18. Sorensen, R.B., Pezzarossa, L., Sparso, J.: An area-efficient TDM NoC support-ing reconfiguration for mode changes. In: 2016 Tenth IEEE/ACM International Symposium on Networks-on-Chip, NOCS, pp. 1–4, August 2016
19. Stefan, R.A., Molnos, A., Goossens, K.: dAElite: a TDM NoC supporting QoS, multicast, and fast connection set-up. IEEE Trans. Comput. **63**(3), 583–594 (2014)
20. Yin, J., Zhou, P., Sapatnekar, S.S., Zhai, A.: Energy-efficient time-division multi-plexed hybrid-switched NoC for heterogeneous multicore systems. In: 2014 IEEE 28th International Parallel and Distributed Processing Symposium, pp. 293–303, May 2014

Resource-Aware Parameter Tuning
for Real-Time Applications

Dirk Gabriel[1](✉), Walter Stechele[1], and Stefan Wildermann[2]

[1] Chair of Integrated Systems, Technical University of Munich,
Munich, Germany
{dirk.gabriel,walter.stechele}@tum.de
[2] Chair of Computer Science 12,
Friedrich–Alexander University Erlangen–Nürnberg, Erlangen, Germany
stefan.wildermann@fau.de

Abstract. Executing multiple applications on a multi-core system while the workload of all applications varies brings the challenge of dynamically adapting resource allocations and parametrizing with respect to constraints e.g. timing limits of real-time applications. We present a hybrid approach which extracts a set of Pareto-optimal operating points during design time which are used to dynamically parameterize the periodic application during run-time. The setup is done at the beginning of each iteration of the execution and exclusively allocates processing elements from the system depending on the current workload. The parametrization is performed with the observed information about workload complexity and allocated resources. Therefore guarantees on time limits can be granted for all iterations including situations when the number of available processing elements has been decreased sharply.

Keywords: Self-aware application · Resource-aware application ·
Reliability · Parameter tuning · Resource reservation

1 Introduction and Related Work

Multi-core systems are commonly used in data-centers and consumer electronics like mobile devices and desktop workstations. Multiple applications running on such systems share the available hardware resources and can adapt their distribution dynamically during run-time. This allows an adjustment according to the current workload and optimizes the resource utilization.

But still the majority of automotive and aviation systems is built up by hundreds of single core control units. This results in a more inefficient design as more hardware components are required while their utilization remains low. Nevertheless, single core architectures are preferred in real-time systems as they simplify the granting of guarantees for the maximum execution time of a single application. Calculating worst-case execution times (WCETs) on multi-core platforms is in some cases achievable [6,11] but requires a known and therefore static task assignment.

© Springer Nature Switzerland AG 2019
M. Schoeberl et al. (Eds.): ARCS 2019, LNCS 11479, pp. 45–55, 2019.
https://doi.org/10.1007/978-3-030-18656-2_4

Furthermore, applications in embedded system usually follow a periodic pattern. They repeat a basic processing task which handles a single input data set, e.g. a network packet or camera image. We use this behavior to adapt the resource allocation and configuration of run-time parameters between two iterations. For being able to give guarantees on the WCET of the task for processing one input data, no changes are allowed during the execution of one iteration. This way workload changes can be compensated while still giving processing time guarantees.

1.1 Feedback Control System

Hoffmann et al. [5] introduced the PowerDial Control System which enables applications to adapt their dynamic parameters in order to achieve constant latency while the available power capacity changes. The user defines a set of parameters and their corresponding ranges. The influence of the parameters on the execution time and quality of service (QoS) is analyzed. All points which lead to an optimal combination of speedup versus QoS are collected and build a Pareto-optimal front.

During run-time the application can switch between different operating points of the precalculated Pareto-front. Therefore, the inserted Dynamic Knobs are controlled by a feedback loop based on the Heartbeats Framework presented in [4]. The system measures the error of the current execution time and calculates the required speedup to compensate the error. The speedup value is used to select a new optimal operating point and setup the Dynamic Knobs and respective all application parameters for the next iteration. This way the QoS is maximized with respect to the timing constraint.

As long as only slight changes occur on the workload and set of available hardware resources, the PowerDial Control System achieves very good results. Since the system relies on a feedback mechanism based on a measured error, sudden changes in the amount of available resources or the input complexity lead to an high error before the system adapts to the new situation. This control delay affects real-time applications which have to rely on a guaranteed WCET.

1.2 Explicit Resource Allocation

Even without variations of the workload other applications might influence the timing behavior by sharing the same resources. To overcome this impact Teich [9] introduced a method of explicit resource allocation. The applications perform the allocation in a cyclic pattern consisting of three stages. First they request processing elements like general purpose cores and accelerators from the system using an *invade* call. Then the jobs are distributed on the granted resources by calling *infect*. After the execution has been completed the resources are given back to the system by triggering *retreat*.

Weichslgartner et al. [10] extended this approach with a graph structure representing the required resources and a methodology how to map them onto the hardware. This graph representation and mapping algorithm is used in the run-time system of this work.

2   Resource-Aware Parameter Tuning

To overcome the delay of feedback mechanisms (like [5]) we propose a direct control flow for real-time applications as depicted in Fig. 1. It relies on a known set of operating points provided by a design space exploration (DSE). During run-time, the selection of the optimal operating point is based on the information available within one single iteration and does not depend on an error calculated by previous runs. In order to achieve reliable decisions it is mandatory to predict the current workload. This information is presented by a complexity class which is directly calculated or estimated based on the input data. It is not necessary for the complexity class to have a mathematical relation to the execution time. It is only required that different inputs with the same complexity class show the same timing behavior.

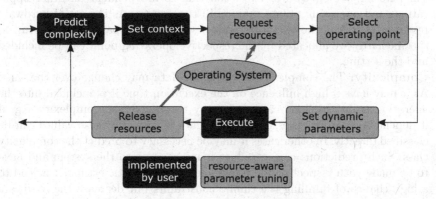

Fig. 1. Run-time workflow of resource-aware parameter tuning.

Based on the complexity class, a set of operating points that match this class is selected and the corresponding hardware resources are requested from the system. The point with the highest quality of service level whose resource request can be fulfilled by the system is finally selected. The dynamic parameters are now used to configure the application and execute the job within the granted resource set. After the execution has been completed the resources are given back to the system or a new iteration starts immediately.

2.1   Operating Points

One operating point is characterized by the setting of the Dynamic Knobs (or run-time parameters) together with the achievable quality of service. This is similar to Hoffmann et al. [5]. However, in addition, we associate each operating point with hardware resource requirements (given by a constraint graph according to Weichslgartner et al. [10]). Furthermore, each operating point is provided with the set of complexity classes for the processing of which it is suitable. This combination leads to following entries building a single operating point:

- **Hardware Resources:** The parameter tuning system allocates the resources at the beginning of each iteration which are used exclusively by the application. The resource graph contains the number and type of the used processing elements like cores and accelerators, the minimal required operating frequency and bandwidth of communication channels between the different elements. Following this (spatial) isolation scheme, we obtain *composability* (see Akesson et al. [1]). This allows independent analysis of multiple applications which are combined on the heterogeneous multi-core system.
- **Run-time Parameters:** The setting of all configuration parameters is provided by the selected operating point. Each point contains only one valid set of dynamic parameters. Their values remain constant during the execution of a single iteration. Due to the composability property of our approach, we can determine and evaluate the parameter setting per operating point at design time: Its impact on QoS or execution time is independent on other applications and operating points running in the system. As the set of hardware resources is part of the operating points even run-time parameters relying on specific hardware allocated by the respective operating point can be included into the setting.
- **Complexity:** The complexity of the input data may change over the time. As it may have a high influence on the execution time it is included into the operating point. In some cases it is easy to observe the complexity, e.g. if it depends on the compression ratio or data packet size these values can be classified directly. In other cases it may be necessary to predict the complexity class. Such predictions can introduce inaccuracies into the system and have to be made with respect to the requirements. Pessimistic estimations lead to a high chance of fulfilling the timing constraints but decrease the hardware utilization and QoS. Therefore the user selects a suitable trade-off respective to the application and usecase.
- **Quality of Service:** Modifications of the run-time parameters usually influence the quality of service. As this metric needs to be maximized, their calculation is be provided by the user. This value is only used during design time, hence the calculation can be based on information which is not available during run-time but the design process.
- **Execution Time:** The execution time is the major constraint of real-time applications and depends on the other values of the operating point. Whenever a static WCET analysis is applicable, it can be used to determine the execution time. In soft-real-time systems an observation based measurement can be used instead.
- **Non-functional Requirements:** Further goals can be included into the optimization process. Thus it is possible to optimize non-functional requirements e.g. minimizing the energy consumption.

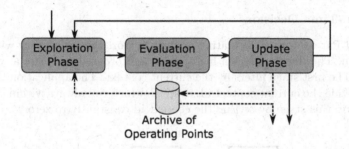

Fig. 2. Evolutionary workflow of design space exploration [10].

2.2 Design Space Exploration

During design time, a list of possible operating points is extracted from the application and optimized to form a Pareto-front. For this purpose an evolutionary algorithm is used. Weichslgartner et al. [10] presented the workflow consisting of three stages as shown in Fig. 2. The stages are iteratively executed to achieve an optimal result over time. In the exploration phase, new hardware constraints and dynamic parameters are derived from previous operating points. For the first iteration, random operating points are generated. During the evaluation phase, the quality of service levels and execution times are determined. Therefore, either a static WCET analysis or a hardware profiling approach is used. After gathering all values, the archive of operating points is updated in order to contain dominating points building the Pareto-front. This workflow is carried out for each relevant complexity class. Corner cases which might happen on the complexity class are included into the DSE to ensure proper behavior in all cases.

2.3 Context Conditions

Depending on the current situation, the user might change application constraints. In some cases, it is for example necessary to achieve the best result whereas a long execution time can be tolerated. In other cases, a low time limit must not be exceeded. Each situation is described by a set of constraints for resource and time limits. This set is called context within the following descriptions. During run-time, the current context of different applications is usually selected by a global control unit.

The design space exploration is performed for each context defined by the user. Each evaluated operating point is stored in a global storage. Thus different executions of the DSE need not to rerun the evaluation step but can use the stored values directly if one operating point is generated for different contexts. This is possible as the context only influences the update stage which decides whether a point is accepted and included into the Pareto-front. The other stages are independent of the context.

2.4   Run-Time Decision

The found Pareto-optimal operating points are stored in a directory within the application. The directory has a hierarchical and ordered structure as depicted in Fig. 3. The first stage filters by the current context. The application therefore has to provide the current context id. Systems which run always within the same context skip this stage by setting the context id constantly to zero.

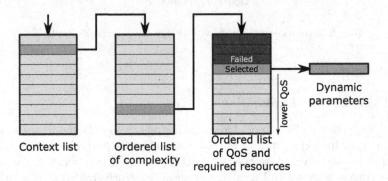

Fig. 3. Hierarchical structure of operating point directory stored in run-time system.

The second stage selects a list of possible resource graphs based on the current complexity. The complexity is provided by a function added by the user. It estimates the class based on the observed data input. The resource set returned by the directory is requested from the system using the *invade* call. As multiple applications are executed on the system, resources may be granted to other applications. Thus the first *invade* call can fail. Then the next setting with a lower known QoS is tried to be allocated until the request can be fulfilled. The resource sets are stored in decreasing order of QoS levels which results in the selection of the highest QoS value currently achievable by the system.

The last stage of the directory contains the dynamic parameters which are used to setup the application for the current iteration. After the resources are allocated and the allocation is configured the application is executed. At the end of the iteration immediately a new iteration is configured and executed or the resources are returned to the system.

3   Experimental Setup and Results

The full resources-aware parameter tuning workflow is shown with an application developed by Azad et al. [2]. The application takes a camera image as input and searches for textured objects within the frame. Therefore multiple steps are executed after each other.

The Harris Corner algorithm [3] is used to find pixel regions with high entropy. If the corner score of a pixel is higher than the defined threshold a scale invariant feature transform (SIFT) is calculated to describe the region [7]. The calculated SIFT-features are compared with pretrained features of a known object. If enough features match the known object it is considered to be found within the image and a affine transformation is calculated using the RANSAC algorithm in order to determine the position. This application supports high parallelization and parametrization with values like the Harris Corner threshold and number of RANSAC iterations. Paul et al. [8] has shown that the threshold can be used to trade of between execution time and the number of considered feature points which is used as a quality of service metric.

The complexity value is derived from the previous frame. Therefore the number of pixels in the Harris Corner image above a specific threshold value are counted. The weight of the pixels is increasing in steps from 1 for pixels above a threshold of 100 up to 5 if the value is higher than 1900.

The application is executed on a multi-core platform consisting of 4 Intel® Xeon® E7-4830 CPUs with each 12 physical cores. The cores support Hyper-threading hence the overall systems contains 96 virtual cores. The application has to process images with a size of 2048 × 1536 pixels within 500 or 800 milliseconds, depending on the selected context. This setup has been optimized using the design space exploration with application profiling method.

Simultaneously two further applications following the same approach are executed on the system. Thus some resources are occupied by them and are not available to the object detection application. The workload of all applications varies over the time which influence the set of available resources.

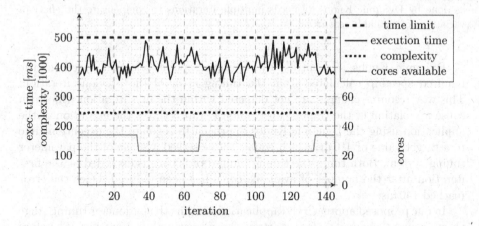

Fig. 4. Compensated effect of reduced amount of processing elements on the execution time with the proposed approach.

Figure 4 shows the execution time of the object detection application using the resource-aware parameter tuning while the number of available cores changes but complexity and context remain the same. Even directly after a reduction of the number of available cores the execution time stays reliably below the time limit of 500 ms. The increasing threshold reduces the computational amount so the result can be produced with fewer processing elements. Although the number of extracted SIFT-features and likewise the quality of service is decreased the trained object is detected always during the test. Increasing amounts of available resources can be used immediately. Thus iterations with underutilization are prevented the quality is increased as soon as possible.

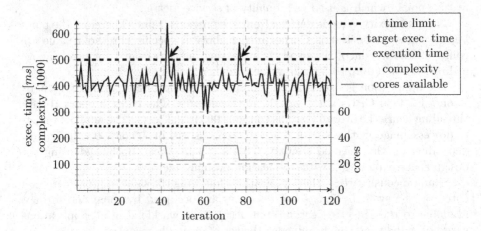

Fig. 5. Calculating the required speedup based on the timing error of the last iteration as done by Dynamic Knobs [5] needs multiple iterations to compensate the effect of variations of available resources.

Dynamic Knobs [5] controls the operating point selection based an the required speedup calculated from the timing error of the previous iteration. This way resource changes are not detected within the first iteration which can cause a violation of the timing constraints. Figure 5 shows the execution of the application using the Dynamic Knobs approach to regulate the execution time to a target value of 410 ms which equals the observed average of the parameter tuning system. Both times the timing limited of 500 ms is exceeded at the first iteration after the number of available cores has been reduced. Once the error reached 140 ms.

In our proposed approach the application informs the parameter tuning stage about context changes before starting the corresponding iteration. Therefore the selection of a suitable operating point happens immediately. Figure 6 shows the adaption to context changes. The execution time directly jumps to the new range. The higher execution time limit in the middle of the test causes a reduced resource requirement while the threshold and thus the quality of service remains at an optimal value.

The workload complexity of this application depends to a large extent on the features contained in the input image. As it is not possible to determine this

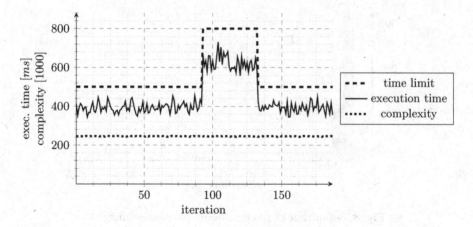

Fig. 6. Immediate adaption to context changes with the proposed approach.

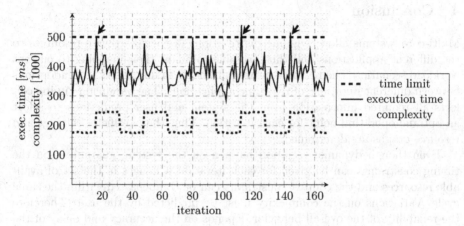

Fig. 7. Violation of timing constraint at first iteration of increased complexity due to wrong user based prediction.

number without intensive calculations, our estimation of the complexity is based on previous frames. This approach can lead to wrong predictions of the complexity class. Figure 7 shows the execution time raising above the timing constraint. This happens at a single iteration when the complexity has increased suddenly. Further iterations are not affected because then the complexity prediction is based on the high value of the previous frame.

The overhead of all functions added by the resource-aware parameter tuning is depicted in Fig. 8. The configuration time depends on the number of failed *invade* calls but stayed below 25 µs for all 512 iterations executed during the tests. Compared to the execution time of the algorithm the setup makes up less than 0.1% and is negligible.

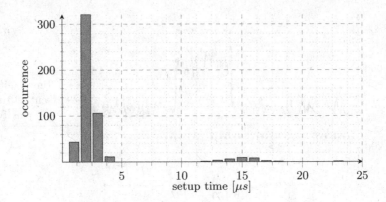

Fig. 8. Setup time of resource-aware parameter tuning.

4 Conclusion

Multi-core systems allow dynamic distributions of their hardware resources to the different applications and thus are able to adapt their mapping to current workload scenarios. The resource-aware parameter tuning allows such adoptions between different iterations of real-time applications. The parameter tuning collects all required information from the system and user predictions to select an optimal operating point for each iteration. Thus the parameter settings and resource graphs are determined.

Even though dynamic variation happen on the system, guarantees on the timing constraints can be given for each iteration. Changes in the set of available resources and the context constraints can be compensated within the same cycle. Variations on the complexity must be predicted by the user. Therefore the reliability of the overall behavior depends on the accuracy and delay of the complexity estimation.

Additionally it was shown that the added overhead is negligible which allows the usage of the proposed approach in embedded systems.

Acknowledgement. This work was partly supported by the German Research Foundation (DFG), Projectnumber 146371743, TRR 89 Invasive Computing.

References

1. Akesson, B., Molnos, A., Hansson, A., Angelo, J.A., Goossens, K.: Composability and predictability for independent application development, verification, and execution. In: Hübner, M., Becker, J. (eds.) Multiprocessor System-on-Chip, pp. 25–56. Springer, New York (2011). https://doi.org/10.1007/978-1-4419-6460-1_2
2. Azad, P., Asfour, T., Dillmann, R.: Combining Harris interest points and the sift descriptor for fast scale-invariant object recognition. In: 2009 IEEE/RSJ International Conference on Intelligent Robots and Systems, pp. 4275–4280, October 2009. https://doi.org/10.1109/IROS.2009.5354611

3. Harris, C., Stephens, M.: A combined corner and edge detector. In: Proceedings of Fourth Alvey Vision Conference, pp. 147–151 (1988)
4. Hoffmann, H., Eastep, J., Santambrogio, M.D., Miller, J.E., Agarwal, A.: Application heartbeats: a generic interface for specifying program performance and goals in autonomous computing environments. In: Proceedings of the 7th International Conference on Autonomic Computing, ICAC 2010, pp. 79–88. ACM, New York (2010). https://doi.org/10.1145/1809049.1809065
5. Hoffmann, H., Sidiroglou, S., Carbin, M., Misailovic, S., Agarwal, A., Rinard, M.: Dynamic knobs for responsive power-aware computing. In: Proceedings of the Sixteenth International Conference on Architectural Support for Programming Languages and Operating Systems, ASPLOS XVI, pp. 199–212. ACM, New York (2011). https://doi.org/10.1145/1950365.1950390
6. Kelter, T., Falk, H., Marwedel, P., Chattopadhyay, S., Roychoudhury, A.: Bus-aware multicore WCET analysis through TDMA offset bounds. In: Proceedings of the 2011 23rd Euromicro Conference on Real-Time Systems, ECRTS 2011, pp. 3–12. IEEE Computer Society, Washington, DC (2011). https://doi.org/10.1109/ECRTS.2011.9
7. Lowe, D.G.: Object recognition from local scale-invariant features. In: Proceedings of the Seventh IEEE International Conference on Computer Vision, vol. 2, pp. 1150–1157, September 1999. https://doi.org/10.1109/ICCV.1999.790410
8. Paul, J., et al.: Resource-aware Harris corner detection based on adaptive pruning. In: Maehle, E., Römer, K., Karl, W., Tovar, E. (eds.) ARCS 2014. LNCS, vol. 8350, pp. 1–12. Springer, Cham (2014). https://doi.org/10.1007/978-3-319-04891-8_1
9. Teich, J.: Invasive algorithms and architectures. IT - Inf. Technol. **50**(5), 300–310 (2009). https://doi.org/10.1524/itit.2008.0499
10. Weichslgartner, A., Wildermann, S., Gangadharan, D., Glaß, M., Teich, J.: A design-time/run-time application mapping methodology for predictable execution time in MPSoCs (2017). https://doi.org/10.1145/3274665
11. Yan, J., Zhang, W.: WCET analysis for multi-core processors with shared L2 instruction caches. In: Proceedings of the 2008 IEEE Real-Time and Embedded Technology and Applications Symposium, RTAS 2008, pp. 80–89, IEEE Computer Society, Washington, DC (2008). https://doi.org/10.1109/RTAS.2008.6

Asynchronous Critical Sections
in Real-Time Multiprocessor Systems

Michael Schmid[✉] and Jürgen Mottok

Laboratory for Safe and Secure Systems - LaS³,
University of Applied Sciences Regensburg, Regensburg, Germany
{michael3.schmid,juergen.mottok}@oth-regensburg.de

Abstract. Sharing data across multiple tasks in multiprocessor systems has intensively been studied in the past decades. Various synchronization protocols, the most well-known being the Priority Inheritance Protocol or the Priority Ceiling Protocol, have been established and analyzed so that blocking times of tasks waiting to access a shared resource can be upper bounded. To the best of our knowledge, all of these protocols share one commonality: Tasks that want to enter a critical section, that is already being executed by another task, immediately get blocked. In this paper, we introduce the Asynchronous Priority Ceiling Protocol (A-PCP), which makes use of aperiodic servers to execute the critical sections asynchronously, while the calling task can continue its work on non-critical section code. For this protocol, we provide a worst-case response time analysis of the asynchronous computations, as well as necessary and sufficient conditions for a feasibility analysis of a set of periodic tasks using the proposed synchronization model on a system that preemptively schedules the tasks under the rate-monotonic priority assignment.

1 Introduction

Sharing data between various tasks plays a very important role in real-time systems. Therefore, over the last few decades, synchronization protocols have intensively been established and studied in order to provide bounded blocking times for tasks. The best known of such protocols are the Priority Inheritance Protocol (PIP) and the Priority Ceiling Protocol (PCP), both covered by Sha et al. in [8]. However, all of the real-time synchronization protocols we found in the state of the art are based on mutual exclusion and thus, immediately block tasks that want to enter the critical section which is already being executed by another task. In this paper, we consider asynchronous critical sections, i.e. the execution of the critical section is relocated to an aperiodic server associated with the shared resource while the tasks waiting on the result of the asynchronous computations can continue their execution in order to carry out other work that does not access shared resources. The proposed model introduces a few benefits:

(1) The data locality is improved as the computations always take place on the same processor and thus, reduces the amount of data moved around in distributed systems and non-uniform memory access (NUMA) architectures.

© Springer Nature Switzerland AG 2019
M. Schoeberl et al. (Eds.): ARCS 2019, LNCS 11479, pp. 56–67, 2019.
https://doi.org/10.1007/978-3-030-18656-2_5

(2) Tasks that make use of asynchronous critical sections continue their execution with their normal priority and thus, priority inversions can only occur on processors running aperiodic servers.
(3) Blocking times and the amount of context switches are reduced as the tasks only block and yield when the results of the asynchronous computations are not available at the time instant when they are needed.

The last item is only beneficial when the work that the task performs after raising a request for the asynchronous critical section is larger than the execution time of the critical section. As an example, we assume that the shared resource is not being accessed and a task raises a request for an asynchronous critical section. The execution of the critical section will immediately start while the task runs non-critical code in the meantime. Both threads are considered to execute without preemption. As soon as the task finishes running the non-critical code, it self-suspends to wait for the result of the asynchronous computations. This does not happen when the task tries to acquire the result of the asynchronous computations after the execution of the critical section has finished or in the case where the critical section is executed directly by the task as it is done in common synchronization protocols. However, as critical sections tend to be short compared to non-critical sections [1], tasks should rarely be blocked by asynchronous critical sections.

1.1 Contribution and Structure

Following contributions are added to the state of the art:

(1) A real-time multiprocessor synchronization protocol that allows the asynchronous execution of critical sections through the use of aperiodic servers.
(2) A model for the proposed protocol that upper bounds the worst-case response times of the asynchronous critical sections under rate-monotonic preemptive scheduling.
(3) Necessary and sufficient conditions for a feasibility analysis of a task set using the Asynchronous Priority Ceiling Protocol.

The rest of this paper is organized as follows: Sect. 1.2 presents related work on real-time synchronization. The notations used throughout this paper are presented in Sect. 2 together with the model of the A-PCP. Subsequently, in Sect. 3, the response time analysis of asynchronous critical sections on systems using rate-monotonic preemptive scheduling is conducted and followed by the feasibility analysis in Sect. 4. At last, the outcome of this paper is summarized in Sect. 5.

1.2 Related Work

Many different real-time synchronization protocols can be found in the state of the art. The two best-known are described by Sha et al. in [8], namely the Priority Inheritance Protocol and the Priority Ceiling Protocol. They derive a set of sufficient conditions under which a set of periodic tasks can be scheduled by rate-monotonic preemptive scheduling on a single processor. Both protocols deal with uncontrolled priority inversion problems by temporarily raising the priority of the task holding the critical section. An important advantage of the PCP over PIP is that the former protocol prevents transitive blocking and deadlocks. In [5,6], Rajkumar et al. made necessary adaptions to the Priority Ceiling Protocol that allow a schedulability analysis for tasks executing in parallel on distributed (Distributed PCP, D-PCP) and shared (Multiprocessor PCP, M-PCP) memory multiprocessor systems, respectively. Both previously mentioned papers provide a pessimistic analysis of worst-case blocking times of tasks. A more detailed analysis of the Multiprocessor PCP is covered in various papers, e.g. by Lakshmanan et al. [2] and Yang et al. [10]. For a more detailed survey of real-time synchronization protocols the reader is referred to [4].

As mentioned before, all real-time resource sharing protocols known to us share the commonality that a task that wants to enter a critical section is blocked when the shared resource is already being accessed by another task. In the sector of distributed computing, the Active Object pattern [7] describes a way of providing synchronized access to a shared resource by relocating the computations to a thread of execution residing in the control of the shared resource. Thereby, the execution of the critical sections is done asynchronously, allowing the task to continue its computation on non-critical section code. To the best of our knowledge, no real-time analysis of this pattern has been conducted in order to prevent unbounded blocking times and priority inversions of tasks using this pattern. As a result, our work is the combination of the Active Object pattern and the D-PCP.

2   Notations and Model

We now present the notations used for the task model and the asynchronous critical sections, as well as the assumptions that are necessary for the response time and feasibility analysis of the A-PCP.

2.1   Asumptions and Notations

In this paper, we consider a task set Γ of n periodic tasks scheduled on a shared-memory multiprocessor with m identical processing cores $p_1, p_2, ..., p_m$. Note that we will use the words processor and cores interchangeably. Each task τ_i (with $1 \leq i \leq n$) is represented by a 2-tuple $\tau_i = (T_i, C_i)$, where T_i is the period of the task and C_i denotes the worst-case execution time (WCET). The task periodically releases a job, at multiples of T_i, which executes for C_i units of time. The l-th job of task τ_i is denoted as $J_{i,l}$ and is released at time instant $r_{i,l}$. An arbitrary job of τ_i is denoted as $J_{i,*}$ with its release time being $r_{i,*}$. Furthermore, we consider implicit deadlines, i.e. the deadline of $J_{i,l}$ is equal to the release time $r_{i,l+1}$ of the subsequent job. Each job may be preempted by higher priority jobs and resume its execution later on. The time instant at which job

$J_{i,l}$ finishes its execution is denoted as the completion time $f_{i,l}$. The worst-case response time (WCRT) of a task τ_i is defined as $R_i = \max_{\forall l}(f_{i,l} - r_{i,l})$. As in [6], we assume that tasks are statically allocated to processors and assigned a fixed priority based on the rate-monotonic algorithm. The priority P_i is shared by all jobs of task τ_i. We assume that lower indices represent a higher priority, i.e. task τ_i has a higher priority than τ_j if $i < j$. The sets of tasks with a higher and lower priority than τ_i are denoted as $hp_i(\Gamma)$ and $lp_i(\Gamma)$, respectively.

Throughout this paper, the accesses to shared resources $\varrho_1, \varrho_2, ..., \varrho_x$ are protected by aperiodic servers $\alpha_1, \alpha_2, ..., \alpha_x$ following the rules of A-PCP. Whenever a job of τ_i wants to access a shared resource, it raises a request to the corresponding aperiodic server of the shared resource. This server is responsible for executing the critical section. Each request $\mu_{i,l}$ is characterized by a 3-tuple $\mu_{i,l} = (\rho_{i,l}, \zeta_{i,l}, \gamma_{i,l})$, where l denotes the l-th request raised by an arbitrary job of task τ_i, $\rho_{i,l}$ indicates the time instant when $J_{i,*}$ raises the request, $\zeta_{i,l}$ represents the worst-case execution time of $\mu_{i,l}$ and $\gamma_{i,l}$ is the time instant when the result is needed by $J_{i,*}$ in order to continue its execution. It must be noted that the execution requirements $\zeta_{i,*}$ do not contribute to the execution time C_i of task τ_i. The completion time $\phi_{i,l}$ denotes the time instant when the aperiodic server has finished the computation of $\mu_{i,l}$ and has provided a result to the respective job. If $\phi_{i,l} > \gamma_{i,l}$, i.e. the task needs the result of an asynchronous critical section that has not yet finished its execution, the task is suspended until $\phi_{i,l}$. The worst-case response time $\sigma_{i,l}$ is defined as the maximum difference $\phi_{i,l} - \rho_{i,l}$ among all jobs of τ_i. Arbitrary requests and their properties are denoted as $\mu_{i,*}$, $\rho_{i,*}$, ..., $\sigma_{i,*}$. The set of requests raised by τ_i to an aperiodic server α_n is represented by M_i^n, in addition $M_i = \cup_{\forall n} M_i^n$ is the set of all requests raised by task τ_i. The priority of all requests in M_i is equal to the priority of τ_i. Finally, we do not allow nested asynchronous critical sections, i.e. aperiodic server α_x is not allowed to raise a request to α_y when $x \neq y$ and each task may only have one pending request, i.e. $\gamma_{i,l} < \rho_{i,l+1}$.

To clarify the notations, an example is shown in Fig. 1. Two tasks τ_x, τ_y and the aperiodic server run on three distinct processors p_1, p_2 and p_3. In the interval $[0, 3)$, the aperiodic server is executing a critical section with a computation time $\zeta_{...}$ from a request which was raised before $t = 0$. During the same interval the queue of the aperiodic server is considered empty. When task τ_y raises an arbitrary request $\mu_{y,*}$ at $t = \rho_{y,*} = 1$, the request is stored in the queue of the server for later execution. At $t = \rho_{x,*} = 3$, task τ_x also raises a request $\mu_{x,*}$ which is stored in the queue and the aperiodic server finishes the computations of $\zeta_{...}$. The server then decides which request to run next. In this case, we consider the priority of task τ_y greater than the priority of τ_x and thus, request $\mu_{y,*}$ is executed next for $\zeta_{y,*}$ units of time. At time $t = \gamma_{y,*} = 5$, task τ_y needs the results of the computations $\zeta_{y,*}$ in order to continue its execution. As the results are not available yet, the task suspends itself. At time instant $t = \phi_{y,*} = 8$, the aperiodic server finishes the execution of $\zeta_{y,*}$ and returns the result to τ_y which allows the task to continue its execution. Again, the aperiodic server picks the next request from the queue, which is request $\mu_{x,*}$, and executes it. At $t = \phi_{x,*} = 10$, the

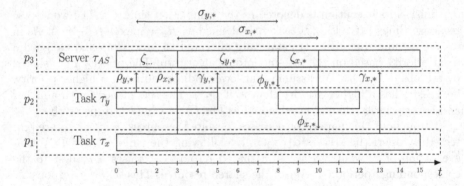

Fig. 1. Example of an asynchronous critical section

server finishes $\zeta_{x,*}$ and returns the result to τ_x. As $\gamma_{x,*} > \phi_{x,*}$, task τ_x does not need to self-suspend.

In concurrent programming languages, a way of returning the results of asynchronous computations is through the use of future-objects: On the function call which raises a request, tasks receive a future-object from the aperiodic server. When the task needs to retrieve the result, it calls the respective method of the future (in C++ and Java, this method is called get), which blocks the task in case the server has not yet stored the result in the future. An example is shown in the C++ code of Listing 1: In line 2, the task raises a request to the aperiodic server and receives a future in return. The server is responsible for executing the function int modify_resource(int arg) which modifies a shared resource. In the meantime, the task is able to perform some different non-critical section code. As soon as the task needs the result of the asynchronous computations, i.e. the return value of modify_resource, it calls the method get of the future, which either blocks when the result is not ready or returns the result otherwise.

```
1  // raise request to the aperiodic server task
2  future<int> future_obj = T_as.raise(modify_resource, 5);
3
4  // perform other work here, while the aperiodic server
       calls modify_resource with the argument '5'
5
6  int r = future_obj.get() //this line blocks if the
       result was not stored in the future yet
```

Listing 1. Programming example of a task raising a request

2.2   Asynchronous Priority Ceiling Protocol

Due to its simplicity and its ability to suspend itself when the job queue is empty and restart once a new job is enqueued, we decided to use a deferrable server for the execution of the asynchronous critical sections. Typically, a deferrable server is used to provide high responsiveness to aperiodic tasks. In our case, we will use the server to serialize the execution of the critical sections and thus, introduce synchronized access to a shared resource. We therefor briefly revisit the deferrable server model introduced by Strosnider et al. [9]: Each deferrable server is represented by a periodic task τ_{DS} with period T_{DS} and a capacity C_{DS}. The server is ready to execute at the beginning of its period and services aperiodic tasks until it exhausts its execution budget C_{DS}. The capacity is fully replenished at the end of each period.

Before deriving the worst-case response time and feasibility analysis, we define the properties of the A-PCP. In the A-PCP, each shared resource ρ_n is assigned a deferrable server α_n with period T_{DS}^n and execution budget C_{DS}^n. Tasks that want to access a shared resource, raise a request to the corresponding deferrable server. The request is stored in a priority ordered queue, while the server repeatedly pops the highest prioritized request from the queue and executes the respective critical section. As a shared resource is only accessed by one deferrable server and the critical sections are run to completion by the server, accesses to shared resources take place in a synchronized fashion.

Notation. We use Γ_n to denote the set of tasks that access the resource ρ_n at any given time.

Notation. We denote the set of tasks, both periodic and aperiodic server tasks, running on the same processor as the aperiodic server α_n as $sp(\alpha_n)$.

Definition. Let P_H be the priority of the highest priority task in the system. The priority ceiling Ω_n of a shared resource ρ_n is defined to be the sum of P_H and the highest priority of the tasks accessing ρ_n:

$$\Omega_n = P_H + \max_{\tau_i \in \Gamma_n} \{P_i\}$$

Every aperiodic server must run with the priority given by the priority ceiling of the corresponding shared resource. As a result of the rate-monotonic priority assignment, we need to determine a suitable period and a capacity which is large enough to handle the critical sections of all tasks accessing the shared resource. The period T_{DS}^n can be defined such that it is slightly smaller than the period of the next lesser prioritized task running on the same processor. Having the value of T_{DS}^n, the execution budget can be calculated by summing up the execution times ζ of all requests by all jobs running in the given period:

$$T_{DS}^n = \min_{\forall i} \{T_i | (\tau_i \in sp(\alpha_n)) \wedge (P_i < \Omega_n)\} - 1$$

$$C_{DS}^n = \sum_{\tau_i \in \Gamma_n} \left\lceil \frac{T_i}{T_{DS}^n} \right\rceil \sum_{\mu_{i,j} \in M_i^n} \zeta_{i,j}$$

Note that the aperiodic server tasks with smaller priority ceilings also have to be considered for the determination of T_{DS}^n.

3 Response Time Analysis

In this section, we derive upper bounds for worst-case response times of asynchronous critical sections. We start by showing that the execution of the asynchronous critical sections only depends on other asynchronous critical sections:

Lemma 1. *The response times of asynchronous critical sections is a function of other asynchronous critical sections only.*

Proof. As the deferrable server tasks are given the highest priorities on the processor, they are not subject to preemption by periodic tasks and also do not depend on the execution of tasks in other circumstances. Therefore, a deferrable server can only be preempted by a higher priority aperiodic server running on the same processor. As a result, the response times of asynchronous critical sections is only dependent on the execution of other asynchronous critical sections.

Following Lemma 1, we now consider job $J_{i,*}$ to raise an arbitrary request $\mu_{i,*}$ and derive the maximum amount of computations done by the deferrable server before it is able to execute $\mu_{i,*}$.

Lemma 2. *Each time a job $J_{i,*}$ raises a request $\mu_{i,*}$ for an asynchronous critical section to a deferrable server α_n, the execution of the critical section is delayed by lower priority critical sections running on α_n for at most*

$$d_i^l = \max\{\zeta_{j,k}|\mu_{j,k} \in \{M_j^n|\tau_j \in lp_i(\Gamma_n)\}\} - 1. \tag{1}$$

Proof. The proof follows from the fact that the execution of asynchronous critical sections on the deferrable server α_n can not be preempted by other requests to the same server. As lower priority requests will not be scheduled prior to $\mu_{i,*}$, only a request which is already being executed by the deferrable server delays the execution of $\mu_{i,*}$. The maximum delay d_i^l occurs when the longest request by lower priority tasks starts execution exactly one time instant before $\mu_{i,*}$ is raised.

Lemma 3. *Each time a job $J_{i,*}$ raises a request $\mu_{i,*}$ to a deferrable server α_n, the execution of the critical section is delayed by higher priority critical sections running on α_n for at most*

$$d_i^h(\Delta t) = \sum_{\tau_j \in hp_i(\Gamma_n)} \left\lceil \frac{\Delta t}{T_j} \right\rceil \sum_{\mu_{j,k} \in M_j^n} \zeta_{j,k} \tag{2}$$

during the interval Δt.

Proof. During the interval Δt, a higher priority task τ_j can release at most $\left\lceil \frac{\Delta t}{T_j} \right\rceil$ jobs. Every time a job $J_{j,*}$ runs, it can request $\sum_{\mu_{j,k} \in M_j^n} \zeta_{j,k}$ time units of computation from the deferrable server α_n. Summing up the amount of work imposed on the deferrable server by all higher priority jobs results in $d_i^h(\Delta t)$.

As aperiodic servers can be subject to preemption by higher prioritized servers, the execution time of the critical sections run by those servers has to be taken into account as well. The delay is accounted for in the equation shown in Lemma 4. It must be noted that servers always run with the priority ceiling of the shared resource. Due to this constraint, also a lower prioritized task τ_L can increase the response time of a request raised by a high priority task τ_H, if the aperiodic server of the request $\mu_{L,*}$ has a higher priority than the server of request $\mu_{H,*}$.

Notation. We denote the set of aperiodic server tasks that run on the same processor and have a higher priority than α_n as $hp_n(\alpha)$.

Lemma 4. *Each time a job $J_{i,*}$ raises a request $\mu_{i,*}$ to a deferrable server α_n, the execution of the critical section is delayed by higher prioritized aperiodic servers for at most*

$$d_i^\alpha(\Delta t) = \sum_{\alpha_m \in hp_n(\alpha)} \sum_{\substack{\tau_j \in \Gamma_m, \\ \tau_j \neq \tau_i}} \left\lceil \frac{\Delta t}{T_j} \right\rceil \sum_{\mu_{j,k} \in M_j^m} \zeta_{j,k} \tag{3}$$

during the interval Δt.

Proof. All higher prioritized servers can preempt α_n. During the time interval Δt, jobs of a task other than τ_i raising requests to higher prioritized servers can execute for at most $\lceil \frac{\Delta t}{T_j} \rceil$ times. Every time such a job $J_{j,*}$ executes, it will impose $\sum_{\mu_{j,k} \in M_j^m} \zeta_{j,k}$ time units of work to the higher prioritized server α_m. Summing up the work of all tasks imposed to higher priority aperiodic servers running on the same processor as α_n results in Eq. 3.

Notation. We use $d_i(\Delta t)$ to denote the sum of the previously derived delays of Lemmas 2, 3 and 4 and denote $e_{i,*}(\Delta t)$ as the sum of $d_i^\alpha(\Delta t)$ and the execution time $\zeta_{i,*}$:

$$d_i(\Delta t) = d_i^l + d_i^h(\Delta t) + d_i^\alpha(\Delta t) \tag{4}$$

$$e_{i,*}(\Delta t) = \zeta_{i,*} + d_i^\alpha(\Delta t) \tag{5}$$

Equation 4 characterizes the delay imposed on the execution of $\mu_{i,*}$ by requests that run before $\mu_{i,*}$ is scheduled on α_n, as well as higher prioritized servers. Once $\mu_{i,*}$ starts executing, only requests to higher prioritized servers can delay the response time $\sigma_{i,*}$. This is represented by Eq. 5 which accounts for the execution time of $\mu_{i,*}$ and the amount of time higher priority servers execute prior to the aperiodic server α_n. The maximum delay can be determined by finding the solutions d_i^{max} and $e_{i,*}^{max}$ of the recursive functions $d_i^{z+1}(d_i^z)$ and $e_{i,*}^{z+1}(e_{i,*}^z)$, respectively. The iteration starts with $d_i^0 = d_i^l$ and ends when $d_i^{z+1} = d_i^z$. Equivalently, $e_{i,*}^{z+1}(e_{i,*}^z)$ starts and ends with $e_{i,*}^0 = \zeta_{i,*}$ and $e_{i,*}^{z+1} = e_{i,*}^z$, respectively. Note that the above computations of d_i^{max} and $e_{i,*}^{max}$ yield a pessimistic estimation and can be reduced by considering the exact amount of asynchronous critical sections requested to the deferrable servers in the two intervals.

Combining our previous results we can derive an upper bound for the worst-case response time $\sigma_{i,*}$ of a request $\mu_{i,*}$.

Theorem 1. *Each time a job $J_{i,*}$ raises a request $\mu_{i,*}$ the worst-case response time $\sigma_{i,*}$ of $\mu_{i,*}$ can be upper bounded by:*

$$\sigma_{i,*} = d_i^{max} + e_{i,*}^{max} \tag{6}$$

Proof. This theorem follows directly from the previous lemmas: Lemma 1 states that the computations of the deferrable server are only a function of other asynchronous critical sections, while Lemmas 2, 3 and 4 consider the amount of computations imposed by critical sections of other tasks. Finally, according to the model, $J_{i,*}$ may only have one pending request at a time and thus, only the computations $\zeta_{i,*}$ are imposed on the deferrable server by $J_{i,*}$. Before $\mu_{i,*}$ is scheduled by the server the requests considered in Lemmas 2, 3 and 4 contribute to $\sigma_{i,*}$. The maximum amount of time those requests execute prior to $\mu_{i,*}$ is accounted for in d_i^{max}. As soon as $\mu_{i,*}$ is running on the aperiodic server α_n, only higher priority servers can delay the response time $\sigma_{i,*}$ by preempting α_n. This is considered by $e_{i,*}^{max}$. Therefore, the sum of d_i^{max} and $e_{i,*}^{max}$ results in the worst-case response time.

4 Feasibility Analysis

Following the results of the previous section, we now provide sufficient conditions for a schedulability analysis. In our model, tasks can be considered to self-suspend themselves if the result of an asynchronous critical section is not available in time. We utilize this behavior to conduct the schedulability analysis conformable to [3,6], where the total amount of time a task remains suspended is added to the computation of the schedulability test. We rephrase Theorem 10 of [6] to match the wording of [3]:

Theorem 2. *A set of n periodic self-suspending tasks can be scheduled by the rate-monotonic algorithm if the following conditions are satisfied:*

$$\forall i, 1 \le i \le n, \frac{C_1}{T_1} + \frac{C_2}{T_2} + \ldots + \frac{C_i + B_i}{T_i} \le i(2^{1/i} - 1), \tag{7}$$

where B_i is the worst-case suspension time of task τ_i and n is the number of tasks bound to the processor under test.

Notation. We denote M_i^b as the set of requests to aperiodic servers that lead to a self-suspension of job $J_{i,*}$:

$$M_i^b = \{\mu_{i,j} | \phi_{i,j} > \gamma_{i,j}\}$$

Every processor has to be tested separately with the conditions of Eq. 7. If the processor under test does not run a deferrable server, the following portions contribute to B_i (adapted from [3]):

(1) The blocking time $b_i(np)$ of non-preemptive regions (e.g. local critical sections) of lower priority tasks on the processor that runs τ_i: Each time a job $J_{i,*}$ suspends itself it can be blocked for $b_i(np) = \max_{i+1 \leq k \leq n} \theta_k$ units of time, where θ_k denotes the worst-case execution time of non-preemptive regions on the processor. In this paper, we do not consider local critical sections, however, it is possible to run the common Priority Ceiling Protocol on local shared resources. If $|M_i^b|$ requests lead to a self-suspension of job $J_{i,*}$, then $(|M_i^b| + 1) * b_i(np)$ is added to B_i.

(2) The duration $b_i(ss^1)$ due to self-suspension of τ_i: The upper bound of the duration that a job of τ_i remains self-suspended due to $\mu_{i,j}$ can be determined by subtracting the instant when $J_{i,*}$ self-suspends from the worst-case completion time ($\phi_{i,j} = \rho_{i,j} + \sigma_{i,j}$) of the asynchronous critical section. Summing up the durations a job remains self-suspended due to all of its requests yields in $b_i(ss^1)$:

$$b_i(ss^1) = \sum_{\mu_{i,j} \in M_i^b} (\phi_{i,j} - \gamma_{i,j})$$

(3) The duration that accounts for deferred execution of higher priority self-suspending tasks on the same processor as τ_i:

$$b_i(ss^2) = \sum_{\tau_k \in hp_i(\Gamma)} \min(C_k, b_k(ss^1))$$

Notation. We use $sp_i(M_j)$ to denote the set of requests a task τ_j raises to aperiodic servers running on the same processor as task τ_i.

Since tasks allocated to a processor that runs at least one deferrable server can be blocked by every asynchronous critical section (even by their own requests and requests of lower priority tasks), B_i has to be computed differently:

$$B_i = \sum_{\tau_j \in \Gamma} \sum_{\mu_{j,k} \in sp_i(M_j)} \zeta_{j,k}$$

Theorem 2 provides sufficient conditions for a feasibility analysis. In [3], Liu derives a set of necessary and sufficient conditions based on the time-demand analysis. We can use the previously calculated values of B_i in order to determine the worst-case response time R_i of the tasks and identify the feasibility of the system:

Theorem 3. *A set of n periodic self-suspending tasks can be scheduled by the rate-monotonic algorithm if the following conditions are satisfied:*

$$\forall i, 1 \leq i \leq n, R_i^{l+1} = C_i + B_i + \sum_{k=1}^{i-1} \left\lceil \frac{R_i^l}{T_k} \right\rceil C_k \leq T_i, \tag{8}$$

where B_i is the worst-case suspension time of task τ_i and n is the number of tasks bound to the processor under test.

The worst-case response time of task τ_i can be determined by finding the solution to the recursive function in Eq. 8. The iteration starts with $R_i^0 = C_i + B_i$ and ends either when $R_i^{z+1} = R_i^z \leq T_i$, indicating that the task τ_i is schedulable or when $R_i^{z+1} > T_i$, which means that the task set is not feasible.

5   Conclusion and Future Work

In this paper, we introduced the asynchronous execution of critical sections through our proposed synchronization protocol named Asynchronous Priority Ceiling Protocol, which is a combination of the Distributed Priority Ceiling Protocol [6] and the Active Object pattern [7]. In the Asynchronous Priority Ceiling Protocol, each shared resource is assigned to a distinct aperiodic server that is responsible for executing the critical sections in a sequential manner. We therefor established a model and subsequently derived a worst-case response time analysis of the asynchronous computations for task sets using the proposed protocol and scheduled under rate-monotonic preemptive scheduling. The worst-case response times of the asynchronous critical sections allowed us to derive the worst-case suspension times of tasks and by making adaptions to the schedulability analysis of Rajkumar et al. [6] and Liu [3], we provided necessary and sufficient conditions that allow to determine the feasibility of a task set using the proposed synchronization protocol.

Our computation of the worst-case response times of the asynchronous critical sections yields a pessimistic bound and can be improved by considering the exact amount of requests a task raises to aperiodic servers. As a result, schedulability tests would benefit greatly from more accurate computations. Another important item of future work are evaluations and comparisons to common mutual exclusion based synchronization protocols. This can be done in terms of schedulability tests, simulations or on an actual system.

References

1. Brandenburg, B.B., Anderson, J.H.: A comparison of the M-PCP, D-PCP, and FMLP on LITMUS[RT]. In: Baker, T.P., Bui, A., Tixeuil, S. (eds.) OPODIS 2008. LNCS, vol. 5401, pp. 105–124. Springer, Heidelberg (2008). https://doi.org/10.1007/978-3-540-92221-6_9
2. Lakshmanan, K., de Niz, D., Rajkumar, R.: Coordinated task scheduling, allocation and synchronization on multiprocessors. In: 2009 30th IEEE Real-Time Systems Symposium, pp. 469–478, December 2009
3. Liu, J.W.S.: Real-Time Systems. Prentice Hall, Upper Saddle River (2000)
4. Midonnet, S., Fauberteau, F.: Synchronizations: Shared Resource Access Protocols, pp. 149–191. Wiley, Hoboken (2014)
5. Rajkumar, R.: Real-time synchronization protocols for shared memory multiprocessors. In: Proceedings, 10th International Conference on Distributed Computing Systems, pp. 116–123, May 1990

6. Rajkumar, R., Sha, L., Lehoczky, J.P.: Real-time synchronization protocols for multiprocessors. In: Proceedings Real-Time Systems Symposium, pp. 259–269, December 1988
7. Schmidt, D.C., Stal, M., Rohnert, H., Buschmann, F.: Pattern-Oriented Software Architecture, Patterns for Concurrent and Networked Objects, vol. 2. Wiley, Hoboken (2000)
8. Sha, L., Rajkumar, R., Lehoczky, J.P.: Priority inheritance protocols: an approach to real-time synchronization. IEEE Trans. Comput. **39**(9), 1175–1185 (1990)
9. Strosnider, J.K., Lehoczky, J.P., Sha, L.: The deferrable server algorithm for enhanced aperiodic responsiveness in hard real-time environments. IEEE Trans. Comput. **44**(1), 73–91 (1995)
10. Yang, M.L., Lei, H., Liao, Y., Rabee, F.: Improved blocking time analysis and evaluation for the multiprocessor priority ceiling protocol. J. Comput. Sci. Technol. **29**(6), 1003–1013 (2014)

Special Applications

DSL-Based Acceleration of Automotive Environment Perception and Mapping Algorithms for Embedded CPUs, GPUs, and FPGAs

Jörg Fickenscher$^{(\boxtimes)}$ ⓘ, Frank Hannig ⓘ, and Jürgen Teich ⓘ

Hardware/Software Co-Design, Department of Computer Science,
Friedrich-Alexander University Erlangen-Nürnberg (FAU), Erlangen, Germany
`joerg.fickenscher@fau.de`

Abstract. The availability and sophistication of Advanced Driver Assistance System (ADASs) are becoming increasingly important for customers when making purchasing decisions and thus also for the manufacturers of such systems. The increased demands on functionality have also increased the demands in computing power and today's standard processors in automotive Electronic Control Unit (ECUs) struggle to provide enough computing power for those tasks. Here, heterogeneous systems, for example consisting of Central Processing Unit (CPUs), embedded Graphics Processing Unit (GPUs), and Field-Programmable Gate Array (FPGAs) provide a remedy. These heterogeneous systems, however, increase the development effort and the development costs enormously.

In this paper, we analyze the extent to which it is possible to automatically generate code with the help of a Domain-Specific Language (DSL) for typical algorithms in the field of environment perception and environment mapping. We show that with the Heterogeneous Image Processing Acceleration (Hipacc) framework it is possible to generate program code for CPUs, GPUs, and FPGAs. After that, we compare for selected algorithms the execution times of the automatically generated code with hand-written variants from the literature.

Keywords: Advanced Driver Assistance Systems ·
Domain-specific languages · Code generation

1 Introduction and Related Work

The sector for ADAS and autonomous driving has experienced enormous growth in recent years, but the most significant growth is yet to come. However, this enormous increase is accompanied by increasing demands on sensors, algorithms, and hardware. Sensors must have higher resolutions in order to perceive the environment more accurately, e.g., cameras with a higher resolution have to be used to detect the facial expressions of humans. More complex algorithms must be

© Springer Nature Switzerland AG 2019
M. Schoeberl et al. (Eds.): ARCS 2019, LNCS 11479, pp. 71–86, 2019.
https://doi.org/10.1007/978-3-030-18656-2_6

used to evaluate the sensor data more precisely. In the end, this leads to enormously increasing computing power requirements that can no longer be met with conventional single-core processors, which are in today's standard ECUs. Here, heterogeneous systems that include besides a CPU an accelerator such as a GPU, an FPGA, or both can show their advantages. Even embedded GPUs have hundreds of Arithmetic Logic Unit (ALUs) at a similar power envelope as a standard CPU despite significantly higher computing power. To use these architectures efficiently, the programming model has to be switched from the predominant single-threaded programming model to a multi-threaded one or to specific hardware development paradigms, which increase the development effort for such systems enormously. The manual implementation of the algorithms for the different architectures would, on the one hand, cost a lot of time and money, and on the other hand, would require software specialists for the respective hardware architectures. Here, DSLs, like Hipacc, can exploit their benefits. With Hipacc it is possible to write the desired algorithm in a language close to C++ and automatically generate code for CPUs, GPUs, or FPGAs. The Hipacc framework has knowledge about the respective target architecture, e.g., cache/memory hierarchy, which can be used directly for optimization. Initially, this framework was developed for image processing, but also other algorithms can be implemented in Hipacc. In this work, we examine to what extent algorithms from the automotive sector can be realized in this framework. Furthermore, we analyze for each architecture, how the different algorithms scale with different sensor resolutions. On the one hand, we picked computer vision algorithms that are used to extract information from camera images for ADAS. These include the Sobel filter and the Harris corner detector [12]. On the other hand, we analyze algorithms for creating environment maps [6,7], at the example of the occupancy grid map. Finally, we compare our results with results known from the literature for these algorithms.

The remainder of the paper is structured as follows: Next, we discuss the differences of our approach compared to related work. In Sect. 2, we describe the framework Hipacc, the basics of the analyzed algorithms and also the implementation of the algorithms in the framework. In Sect. 3, experimental results are presented and discussed. Finally, we conclude the paper in Sect. 4 and give an outlook on future work.

1.1   Related Work

DSLs are used in many different fields, such as financial services [1], machine learning [22], virtual reality [10], operating systems [18], or image processing [17]. Some of these DSLs also focus on specific computer architectures or programming dogmas, e.g., ExaSlang, which is used for the specification of numerical solvers based on the multigrid method targeting distributed memory systems [20]. Some works focus only on domain-specific optimization, like [9], which adopts its algorithm to the hardware to generate highly optimized code. Another approach in the image processing domain is PARO [11], but it generates only dedicated hardware accelerators and does not support multi- and many-core architectures. A DSL-based approach similar to ours is Darkroom [13], but it does not support advanced language constructs such as border treatment. In the automotive area, many works combine DSLs with Controlled Natural Language (CNLs). CNLs are a subset of natural languages, which reduce language proficiency to decrease complexity and eliminate ambiguity. Bock et al. used such a language in [2] to describe the requirements of an automotive system, to improve the transitions between the different development stages. In [23], Volker et al. introduced a framework, based on a DSL to support the development process and the safeguarding of algorithms in C in the automotive domain, e.g., it is possible to annotate mathematical expressions with which the tool verifies the correctness of the code. The two DSLs above are used for specification and validation, but none of them deals with parallelization and code generation for heterogeneous architectures. In this paper, we focus on the code generation for image processing and environment maps in the automotive area. We evaluate, how and which of those algorithms can be implemented in Hipacc [17] and appraise the performance of the generated code across multiple platforms. To the best of our knowledge, it is the first time that code for algorithms for creating environment maps is generated by a DSL-based approach automatically.

2   DSL-Based Approach and Algorithmic ADAS Building Blocks

2.1   Hipacc

Hipacc [17,19] is a DSL embedded in C++ and a compiler framework for the domain of image processing. It captures domain knowledge in a compact and intuitive language and employs source-to-source translation combined with various optimizations to achieve excellent productivity paired with performance portability. The Hipacc approach has been applied and evaluated for a broad variety of parallel accelerator architectures, including many-core processors such as Nvidia and AMD GPUs and Intel Xeon Phi, embedded CPUs and GPUs, Xilinx and Intel/Altera FPGAs, and vector units. The structure and the different target platforms of Hipacc are illustrated in Fig. 1.

2.2   ADAS Building Blocks

In the following, we select and briefly introduce characteristic algorithmic building blocks, which are widely used in ADAS applications. Here, we further distinguish between two main algorithm categories: (a) computer vision and (b) environment maps.

Computer Vision: A critical basis for many ADAS applications is the apparent motion of surfaces and other objects, the so-called *optical flow*. Optical flow algorithms serve as a basis for object detection and tracking, and they are in turn often based on feature extraction (e.g., edges or corners of an image).

The Sobel operator, named after Irwin Sobel and Gary Feldman, is used in image processing for detection of edges. An example application for the Sobel

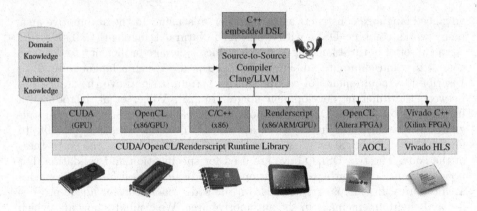

Fig. 1. Overview of the structure of Hipacc [19].

operator is the extraction of vehicles from camera images, where the operator is part of the processing cascade [16]. The goal of this work is to track objects, and the Sobel filter is used in a preprocessing step to find out right-angled objects. To detect edges, changes in intensity to adjacent pixels are considered. The Sobel operator is a convolution operator, which calculates the first derivative of the pixel brightness values, where at the same time the orthogonal to the direction of derivation is being smoothed.

The Harris operator [12] detects corners in images. Corners are points where two edges intersect or pixels where the neighbors are brighter or darker. These areas are called points of interest. With the help of that points, for example, the same objects in different images can be recognized. For ADAS it can be used, e.g., for estimating the motion vector of a pedestrian [15].

Environment Maps: Environment maps are essential for ADASs and autonomous driving. Such maps store all information from the vehicle environment that is important for ADASs. That information can be other vehicles, obstacles, lane markings, or other objects of interest. One of the best known environmental maps is the occupancy grid map.

The idea of an occupancy grid map [5] is to represent the environment through a fine-grained grid. It was originally designed to map the environment of a robot but is now also used in ADAS. As illustrated in Fig. 2, the environment is rasterized in equally sized rectangles, so-called cells. For every cell, a probability $p \in [0,1]$ is calculated, whether the cell is occupied ($p = 1$) or free ($p = 0$), based on sensor measurements. Typically, the posterior probability is used in the occupancy grid map algorithm [21]:

$$p(m|z_{1:t}, x_{1:t}) \tag{1}$$

where m is the map, $z_1, ..., z_t$ are the measurements from the first to the measurement at time t, and x denotes the corresponding known poses of the vehicle also from the first to the measurement at time t. Due to the high-dimensional space, the posterior cannot be determined readily. So the problem is reduced to calculate the posterior of each cell separately:

$$p(m_i|z_{1:t}, x_{1:t}) \tag{2}$$

To take into account all previous measurements without explicit storage, the Bayes rule is applied to $p(m_i|z_{1:t})$, and we get:

$$p(m_i|z_{1:t}) = \frac{p(m_i|z_t) \cdot p(z_t) \cdot p(m_i|z_{1:t-1})}{p(m_i) \cdot p(z_t|z_{1:t-1})} \tag{3}$$

To eliminate some hard computable terms and to avoid numerical instabilities for probabilities near zero or one, the so-called *log-odds* form is used:

$$\log \frac{p(m_i|z_{1:t})}{1 - p(m_i|z_{1:t})} = \log \frac{p(m_i|z_t)}{1 - p(m_i|z_t)} + \log \frac{1 - p(m_i)}{p(m_i)} + \log \frac{p(m_i|z_{1:t-1})}{1 - p(m_i|z_{1:t-1})} \tag{4}$$

To recover the probabilities, as later shown in Listing 1.2, the following equation is used:

$$p(m_i|z_{1:t}) = 1 - \frac{1}{1 + \exp^{\log(\frac{p(m_i|z_t)}{1 - p(m_i|z_t)}) + \log(\frac{p(m_i|z_{1:t-1})}{1 - p(m_i|z_{1:t-1})})}} \tag{5}$$

It is assumed that the Markov property holds. Typically the real world 3D environment is broken down to a 2D occupancy grid map. With the aid of this assumption and the fact that the probability for each cell is computed separately, without dependencies to any other cells, the problem is ideal to be calculated on a GPU.

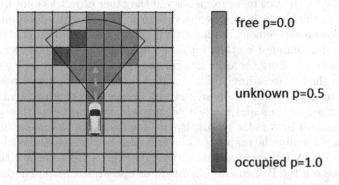

Fig. 2. Illustration of an occupancy grid map. The direction of travel is indicated with the orange arrow and the measurement range of the laser sensor by the black line. (Color figure online)

The creation of environment maps often requires the basic algorithms as identified in [6] and illustrated in Fig. 3. At this point, only a brief description of the individual basic algorithms will be given, and for a detailed description,

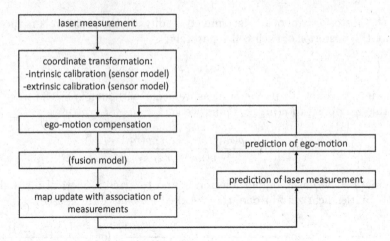

Fig. 3. Overview of the sub-algorithms which are necessary to create an environment map.

we refer to the corresponding literature. A laser sensor is often used to create an occupancy grid map. However, this sensor provides the measurements in polar coordinates, whereas the occupancy grid map is in Cartesian coordinates. Therefore, in a first step, a coordinate transformation from polar to Cartesian coordinate space has to be performed. After that, the ego-motion of the vehicle has to be compensated. The compensation of the vehicle's own motion is necessary so that the measurements made at time $t - 1$ can be correctly associated with the measurements from time t. For example, if the vehicle has moved ten meters forward between the two measurements and the other object has not moved, the laser beam to the object is ten meters shorter in the current measurement than in the previous measurement. Various methods exist for the compensation of the ego-motion. The simplest method for an occupancy grid map, however, is to use a 2d ring buffer to store the cells [3]. For the ego-motion in x- and y-direction, a pointer is shifted accordingly. The rotation of the vehicle is compensated by rotating it on the map. If there are several sensors, the measurements have to be synchronized in time and merged accordingly together, e.g., the speed of a vehicle, measured by a radar sensor, is combined with the detected vehicle by a laser scanner. Finally, the map has to be updated. Several methods exist for this purpose, such as the Bresenham algorithm [4] or the cell-based algorithm [8]. In our work, we use the Bresenham algorithm to update the map. The laser beam is entered in the map from the origin of the measurement, the laser sensor, to the measured object. This method is like the standard Bresenham line drawing algorithm, where a line on a rasterized grid is drawn between two points. The probability of occupancy of the affected cells is calculated with Eq. (4). Since the measurements often contain noise, a Kalman filter is used to reduce it [14]. In this work, due to space constraints, we will focus on coordinate transformation, ego-motion compensation, and map update.

Listing 1.1: Hipacc kernel code for the coordinate transformation from polar (angle, distance) to Cartesian (x, y) coordinate space.

```
1  void kernel() {
2    float x_coord = 0;
3    float y_coord = 0;
4
5    if(valid()!=-1.){ //ray is valid!
6      x_coord = distance() * cosf((angle()*PI)/180.f);
7      y_coord = distance() * sinf((angle()*PI)/180.f);
8      if(y_coord <0){
9        y_coord *=-1;
10     }
11     x_coord = x_coord + carth_width/2;
12     int x_final = (int) x_coord;
13     int y_final = (int) y_coord;
14     output() = (x_final |(y_final<<16));
15   }
16 }
```

Since the Hipacc framework was originally developed for image processing, there are some peculiarities in the implementation of the basic algorithms for the environment maps, which will be discussed in more detail below. The underlying algorithms must always be adapted in such a way that they resemble the processing of images, e.g., a pixel in an image is representing a cell of an occupancy grid map. The Hipacc kernel code for the coordinate transformation from polar to Cartesian coordinate space is shown in Listing 1.1. A kernel in Hipacc is similar to a kernel in CUDA. The kernel is executed in parallel for each element (Hipacc: over the complete *IterationSpace*). Accessors are in Hipacc objects that access the input data or a certain region of interest. Furthermore, interpolation is supported, such as *nearest neighbor*, *bilinear filtering*, *bicubic filtering*, and *Lanczos resampling*. The *angle* and the *distance* of a laser beam should be passed to the kernel, which are then converted to x and y coordinates. As accessors, we have for the kernel *distance*, *angle*, and *valid*. All structures, including the output structure, have the same size, which corresponds to the number of laser beams. Since Hipacc does not support complex data structures, such as *structs*, some workaround has to be implemented. After the coordinate transformation has been applied, the x and y coordinate has to be placed in an *integer* using a bitshift operator. This is necessary to place the two coordinates in one element (a.k.a. pixel). It would also be possible for storing the x and y coordinate in two different elements. However, this is not necessary and would only increase the memory transfer.

In the next step, the occupancy grid map from time $t - 1$ is updated with the measurement from time t with the Bresenham algorithm [4]. The algorithm gets as input data the list with the x and y coordinates. The data structure for the input is an image that consists of one line. Each entry (pixel) in this line consists of an x and y coordinate, which was obtained using the algorithm in Listing 1.1. The output of the algorithm is an image that has the same size as the occupancy grid map. One pixel of the image corresponds to one cell of the occupancy grid map.

Listing 1.2: Hipacc kernel code for the ego-motion compensation and the map update with the Bresenham algorithm.

```
1  void kernel() {
2      int x0 = input() & 0xFFFF; //undo bitshifting
3      int y0 = (input() >> 16) & 0xFFFF; //undo bitshifting
4      int dx = abs(x1 - x0), sx = x0 < x1 ? 1 : -1;
5      int dy = abs(y1 - y0), sy = y0 < y1 ? 1 : -1;
6      int err = (dx > dy ? dx : -dy) / 2, e2;
7      for (;;) {
8          if (((x0) + out_width_bres * (out_height - y0 - 1)) < 0) {
           break; }
9          float map_value = input_map.pixel_at(x0+vel_x,out_height-y0
           -1+vel_y);
10         float meas_value = 0.1f;
11         float new_probability = 1.0f / ((1.0f + expf(logf((1.0f -
           meas_value) / meas_value) + logf((1.0f - map_value) /
           map_value))));
12         output_at(x0,out_height - y0 - 1) = new_probability;
13         if (x0 == x1 && y0 == y1) {
14             meas_value = 0.9f;
15             new_probability = 1.0f / ((1.0f + expf(logf((1.0f -
           meas_value) / meas_value) + logf((1.0f - map_value) /
           map_value))));
16             output_at((int)x_coord,(out_height - (int) y_coord - 1) )
           = new_probability;
17             break;
18         }
19         e2 = err;
20         if (e2 > -dx) { err -= dy; x0 += sx; }
21         if (e2 < dy) { err += dx; y0 += sy; }
22     }
23 }
```

Here, the problem is that the input image has not the same size as the output image. Therefore, to update the map with the Bresenham algorithm, global indexing is necessary. This is possible in Hipacc for output data with the function *output_at()*. Listing 1.2 shows the Hipacc code for the map update with ego-motion compensation. In line 15, the calculation of the new occupancy probability of a cell takes place. In this case, the ego-motion of the vehicle is directly compensated by calculating the new probability of a cell, taking the momentary measured value and accessing the relevant old position of the cell, i.e., the cell's old position, which has been cleared for the velocity vector of the vehicle. If the coordinates of a measured obstacle coincide with the coordinates of the measurement, this cell is assumed to be occupied. Due to the uncertainty of measurement, the probability of occupancy is given with $p = 0.9$ (line 13–15). Otherwise, if no object was detected at the cell's location, the probability of occupancy is assumed to be $p = 0.1$ (lines 10–11).

3   Evaluation

3.1   Evaluation Platform

For the evaluation of the algorithms, we used on the one hand, the Nvidia Jetson board. The board embodies an embedded GPU, the Nvidia Tegra K1 with 192 CUDA Cores clocked at 850 MHz. The CPU is a quad-core ARM Cortex-A15 with 2.3 GHz. On the other hand, the execution time of the code generated for the FPGA is only determined by a post-place and route simulation on an xc7z045ffg900-2 FPGA from Xilinx. This FPGA is among others on the Xilinx Zynq-7000 SoC ZC706 board. Generally, in our experiments and the experiments in the literature, the block size was set to 128 threads arranged in 32×4 threads. Furthermore, the CPU versions of the algorithms are a single-threaded ones.

3.2   Evaluation of Computer Vision Algorithms

In the first experiment on the computer vision algorithms, we evaluated the execution time of the Sobel filter on the three different platforms (ARM CPU, GPU, and FPGA). In order to keep the measurement noise as low as possible, the respective filter is used 100 times, and the results are illustrated in box plots. The box plots contain the median, the quartiles, as well as the 5th and 95th percentile. In order to ensure that the execution times of the computer vision algorithms have a high independence from a specific image, ten different ones were used for the experiments. Each of these images is available in six different resolutions (128×128, 256×256, 515×152, 1024×1024, 2048×2048, 4096×4096). In Fig. 4, the execution times for the Sobel filter are shown. The reason for the high standard deviation in the execution time on the CPU and the FPGA is that one of the ten images contains relatively many black pixels. For these pixels, the algorithm does not has to be executed on the CPU and the FPGA. However, this has hardly any influence on the execution times on the GPU. Once a pixel in a warp (consisting of 32 threads) has to be computed, the other 31 threads must wait until that calculation is completed. As can be seen in Fig. 4, the filter on the CPU needs the longest execution time. Both the FPGA and the GPU have a significantly shorter execution time for the algorithm, with the GPU beating the FPGA. The reason that the GPU is faster than the FPGA is that the Sobel filter has only little mathematical complexity. For the FPGA, the execution time depends mainly on the amount of data to be processed. For an FPGA, only the processing of one new pixel can be started per cycle. A cycle is also called Iteration Interval (II). In this case, the II is 1 and 93 cycles are required to process one pixel. The smallest resolution of the input images is 128×128 pixels. So already $128 \times 128 = 16384$ cycles are necessary to start the calculation of all pixels. Therefore, the calculation time for the FPGA depends hardly on the complexity of the calculation, which does not apply to the GPU. Here, the mathematical complexity has a much stronger influence, because the calculation of a pixel on a CUDA core lasts much longer and therefore, the whole execution time increases. Furthermore, Hipacc also optimizes the GPU code, for example by using *shared memory*.

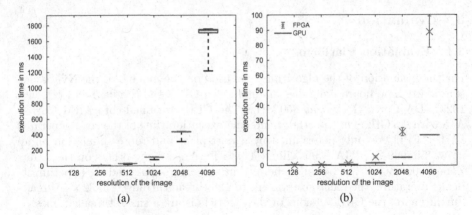

Fig. 4. In (a), the execution times of the Sobel filter on the CPU are shown. In (b), the execution times of the Sobel filter on the GPU and FPGA are shown.

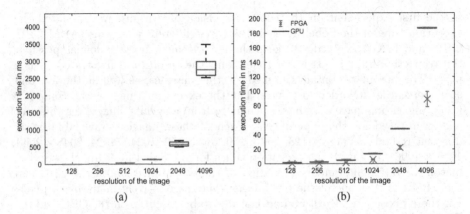

Fig. 5. In (a), the execution times of the Harris corner filter on the CPU are shown. In (b), the execution times of the Harris corner filter on the GPU and FPGA are shown.

The Harris corner filter runs with the same settings and on the same three hardware architectures as the Sobel filter. The results of the Harris corner filter are given in Fig. 5. It can be seen again that the CPU needs the longest execution time for the Harris corner filter. Comparing the execution time with the Sobel filter, it can be realized, that the Harris corner filter takes much longer on the CPU and GPU. However, on the FPGA, the absolute execution time does not increase very much, compared to the Sobel filter. As a result, the execution time for this filter on the FPGA is lower than on the GPU. The rationale is that the Harris filter has a higher mathematical complexity. This has a much greater impact on the execution time of the CPU and GPU, as described above for the Sobel filter, than on the execution time of the FPGA.

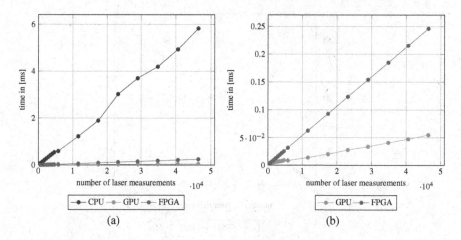

Fig. 6. In this experiment, the coordinate transformation from polar to Cartesian coordinate space was evaluated on an embedded CPU, GPU, and FPGA. The program code for the different platforms was generated with Hipacc. In (a), the results for the CPU, GPU, and FPGA are shown and in (b) only the results for the GPU and FPGA are shown for a better overview.

3.3 Evaluation of Environment Mapping Algorithms

In the following experiments for the basic algorithms of the environment map, an occupancy grid map of size 2048×2048 is used. At first, we evaluated the coordinate transformation from polar to Cartesian coordinate space. For this algorithm, it was possible to generate automatically code for all three platforms. The results are shown in Fig. 6. As can be seen from Fig. 6, the algorithm has on the CPU the longest execution time. The execution time on the CPU and FPGA increases linearly with the increase of the laser measurements. For a small number of laser measurements, the algorithm has on the FPGA a smaller execution time as on the GPU. This can be explained on the one hand, for a small number of laser measurements, the GPU is not fully exploited because there are not enough threads to use every CUDA core since each thread enters a laser beam into the occupancy grid map. On the other hand, the threads on the GPU are always grouped into blocks of 128 threads. Since the number of measurement data is often not a multiple of 128, not all threads may be fully utilized. This is particularly important for a small number of measurements. Compared to the work in [6], the execution time of our automatic generated code is ten times faster on the GPU and five times slower on the CPU. The reason for this is that although the coordinate transformation can be described as a Hipacc kernel, Hipacc does not provide any abstraction for this algorithm. Yet, GPU results were better than the handwritten code.

In the next experiment, we evaluated the map update with the Bresenham algorithm, including the ego-motion compensation. The results are shown in Fig. 7. It is again clearly visible that the execution time on the CPU is much longer compared to the GPU. That the execution time on the GPU, in relation

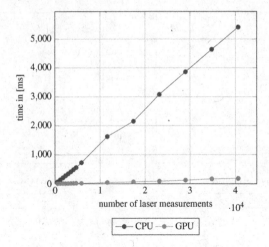

Fig. 7. Execution times of the occupancy grid map update with the Bresenham algorithm, including the ego-motion compensation in *ms*.

to the CPU, is quite short has two main reasons. The first reason is the high parallelizability of the algorithm. The second reason is that the cache that is available to the individual blocks can be used very well for this algorithm. If the same cells are being updated by threads that are in the same block, then the corresponding data can to be cached. Threads are grouped on GPUs into blocks, which often consist of 128 threads. If a cell of the environment map is then updated by several threads, which are within a block, they can immediately access the data in the cache. This is especially relevant for cells near to the laser sensor, as multiple beams often cover these cells. Unfortunately, it was not possible to synthesize the Bresenham algorithm for Vivado with Hipacc. The reason is that Hipacc does not support global indexing of output images for FPGAs. One possible solution to synthesize a larger part of the algorithm for an FPGA would be to perform only the Bresenham algorithm on a CPU or GPU without the map update and ego-motion compensation. After that, with this method, code for all three hardware platforms could then be automatically generated for the ego-motion compensation and for the map update, i.e., merging the previous map with the current map. Compared to the work in [6], the generated code for the CPU and GPU is slower. The main reason for this is that in the referenced work the used algorithm filters out a lot of data in advance and therefore the data does not enter the map anymore. If we compare our work with the work in [7], then our execution times on the CPU are about 30% longer, but our code for the GPU is seven times faster.

To further analyze the performance of the algorithms (coordinate transformation and the Bresenham algorithm with motion compensation), a roofline model [24] was created for both the CPU and GPU. Figure 8 shows the roofline model for the CPU and Fig. 9 shows the roofline model for the GPU. The compute intensity (number of operations per fetched/stored byte) remains constant for the respective algorithm since we only changed the number of measurements

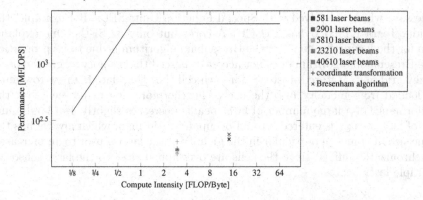

Fig. 8. Classification of the coordinate transformation and the Bresenham algorithm with ego-motion compensation within the roofline model for different numbers of laser measurements on the CPU. Please note especially the y-axis scaling.

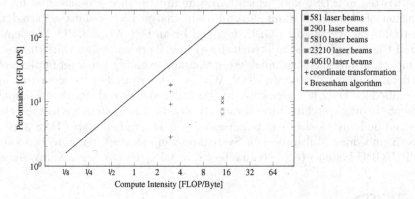

Fig. 9. Classification of the coordinate transformation and the Bresenham algorithm with ego-motion compensation within the roofline model for different numbers of laser measurements on the GPU.

without modifying any code. Both algorithms are compute-bound on the CPU. On the contrary, on the GPU, only the map update is compute-bound, and the coordinate transformation is memory-bound. This is due to the significantly lower processing power of the CPU in relation to the GPU. When comparing the coordinate transformation with the Bresenham algorithm, one recognizes that the former has a much lower computation intensity than the latter. This can be explained by the fact that relatively few computations are required for the coordinate transformation (see Listing 1.1) in contrast to the map update (see Listing 1.2). With increasing measurement data for the coordinate transformation, the utilization of the hardware also increases, especially on the GPU. The reason is that for a small number of measurement data the GPU cannot be fully utilized. For both algorithms, there is a clear distance to the roofline. For the coordinate transformation, the reason is that trigonometric functions are necessary which are solved with Special Function Units SFUs. For example, the Nvidia Tegra K1 GPU has 192 CUDA cores but only 32 SFUs. One explanation for the low performance of the Bresenham algorithm is due to its properties. The Bresenham algorithm does not access coalesced the memory where the occupancy grid map is stored. Instead, for each cell that is updated, a new row must be loaded from memory into the cache. Furthermore, it can be seen that the performance of a large number of laser beams decreases slightly. If a large number of laser beams is entered into an occupancy grid map, which always has the same size, it comes in particular in the vicinity of the laser sensor to an increased synchronization effort, since the cells are overlapped close to the laser sensor of multiple laser beams.

4   Conclusion and Future Work

In this paper, we have examined typical ADAS algorithms for their suitability to be written in a DSL and, which hardware architecture is best suited for the execution of these algorithms. Overall, our analyzed algorithms achieved the best results on average on a GPU, followed by an FPGA and CPU. We demonstrated that a DSL-based approach drastically shortens design time thanks to a compact, intuitive algorithmic description and avoiding low-level implementation details and parallelization effort. With one description of the algorithm in a C++-embedded DSL, it was possible to generate program code for three complete different hardware architectures automatically. In a next step, we use the characterized building blocks to systematically co-partition and map ADAS applications to embedded Multiprocessor System-on-Chip (MPSoC) architectures such as CPU/GPU systems (e.g., Nvidia Tegra) or CPU/FPGA (e.g., Xilinx Zynq).

References

1. Arnold, B., Deursen, A.V., Res, M.: An algebraic specification of a language for describing financial products. In: ICSE-17 Workshop on Formal Methods Application in Software Engineering, pp. 6–13. IEEE (1995)
2. Bock, F., German, R., Siegl, S.: Domain-specific languages for the definition of automotive system requirements. In: Workshop CARS 2016 - Critical Automotive Applications: Robustness & Safety, September 2016. https://hal.archives-ouvertes.fr/hal-01375453
3. Bouzouraa, M.E.: Belegungskartenbasierte Umfeldwahrnehmung in Kombination mit objektbasierten Ansätzen für Fahrerassistenzsysteme. Dissertation, Technische Universität München, München (2012)
4. Bresenham, J.E.: Algorithm for computer control of a digital plotter. IBM Syst. J. 4(1), 25–30 (1965). https://doi.org/10.1147/sj.41.0025
5. Elfes, A.: Using occupancy grids for mobile robot perception and navigation. Computer 22(6), 46–57 (1989). https://doi.org/10.1109/2.30720
6. Fickenscher, J., Hannig, F., Teich, J., Bouzouraa, M.: Base algorithms of environment maps and efficient occupancy grid mapping on embedded GPUs. In: Proceedings of the 4th International Conference on Vehicle Technology and Intelligent Transport Systems (VEHITS), pp. 298–306. SciTePress, March 2018. https://doi.org/10.5220/0006677302980306

7. Fickenscher, J., Reiche, O., Schlumberger, J., Hannig, F., Teich, J.: Modeling, programming and performance analysis of automotive environment map representations on embedded GPUs. In: Proceedings of the 18th IEEE International High-Level Design Validation and Test Workshop (HLDVT), pp. 70–77. IEEE, October 2016. https://doi.org/10.1109/HLDVT.2016.7748257

8. Fickenscher, J., Schlumberger, J., Hannig, F., Teich, J., Bouzouraa, M.: Cell-based update algorithm for occupancy grid maps and hybrid map for ADAS on embedded GPUs. In: Proceedings of the Conference on Design, Automation and Test in Europe (DATE), pp. 443–448. EDAA, March 2018. https://doi.org/10.23919/DATE.2018.8342050

9. Frigo, M., Johnson, S.G.: The design and implementation of FFTW3. Proc. IEEE 93(2), 216–231 (2005). https://doi.org/10.1109/JPROC.2004.840301

10. Gill, A.: AFrame: a domain specific language for virtual reality. In: Proceedings of the 2nd International Workshop on Real World Domain Specific Languages (RWDSL), p. 4:1. ACM (2017). https://doi.org/10.1145/3039895.3039899

11. Hannig, F., Ruckdeschel, H., Dutta, H., Teich, J.: PARO: synthesis of hardware accelerators for multi-dimensional dataflow-intensive applications. In: Woods, R., Compton, K., Bouganis, C., Diniz, P.C. (eds.) ARC 2008. LNCS, vol. 4943, pp. 287–293. Springer, Heidelberg (2008). https://doi.org/10.1007/978-3-540-78610-8_30

12. Harris, C., Stephens, M.: A combined corner and edge detector. In: Proceedings of Fourth Alvey Vision Conference, pp. 147–151 (1988)

13. Hegarty, J., et al.: Darkroom: compiling high-level image processing code into hardware pipelines. ACM Trans. Graph. 33(4), 144:1–144:11 (2014). https://doi.org/10.1145/2601097.2601174

14. Kalman, R.E.: A new approach to linear filtering and prediction problems. Trans. ASME J. Basic Eng. 82(Series D), 35–45 (1960)

15. Kuo, Y.C., Fu, C.M., Tsai, C.T., Lin, C.C., Chang, G.H.: Pedestrian collision warning of advanced driver assistance systems. In: International Symposium on Computer, Consumer and Control (IS3C), pp. 740–743, July 2016. https://doi.org/10.1109/IS3C.2016.189

16. Kuo, Y.C., Pai, N.S., Li, Y.F.: Vision-based vehicle detection for a driver assistance system. Comput. Math. Appl. 61(8), 2096–2100 (2011). https://doi.org/10.1016/j.camwa.2010.08.081

17. Membarth, R., Reiche, O., Hannig, F., Teich, J., Körner, M., Eckert, W.: HIPAcc: a domain-specific language and compiler for image processing. IEEE Trans. Parallel Distrib. Syst. 27(1), 210–224 (2016). https://doi.org/10.1109/TPDS.2015.2394802

18. Pu, C., Black, A., Cowan, C., Walpole, J.: Microlanguages for operating system specialization. In: Proceedings of the SIGPLAN Workshop on Domain-Specific Languages. ACM, January 1997

19. Reiche, O., Özkan, M., Membarth, R., Teich, J., Hannig, F.: Generating FPGA-based image processing accelerators with Hipacc. In: Proceedings of the International Conference on Computer Aided Design (ICCAD), pp. 1026–1033. IEEE, November 2017. https://doi.org/10.1109/ICCAD.2017.8203894

20. Schmitt, C., Kuckuk, S., Hannig, F., Köstler, H., Teich, J.: ExaSlang: a domain-specific language for highly scalable multigrid solvers. In: Proceedings of the 4th International Workshop on Domain-Specific Languages and High-Level Frameworks for High Performance Computing (WOLFHPC), pp. 42–51. IEEE Computer Society, November 2014. https://doi.org/10.1109/WOLFHPC.2014.11

21. Thrun, S., Burgard, W., Fox, D.: Probabilistic Robotics. The MIT Press, Cambridge and London (2005)

22. Sujeeth, A.K., et al.: OptiML: an implicitly parallel domain-specific language for machine learning. In: Proceedings of the 28th International Conference on International Conference on Machine Learning (ICML), pp. 609–616. Omnipress (2011)

23. Voelter, M., Ratiu, D., Kolb, B., Schaetz, B.: mbeddr: instantiating a language workbench in the embedded software domain. Autom. Softw. Eng. **20**(3), 339–390 (2013). https://doi.org/10.1007/s10515-013-0120-4

24. Williams, S., Waterman, A., Patterson, D.: Roofline: an insightful visual performance model for multicore architectures. Commun. ACM **52**(4), 65–76 (2009). https://doi.org/10.1145/1498765.1498785

Applying the Concept of Artificial DNA and Hormone System to a Low-Performance Automotive Environment

Uwe Brinkschulte[1]([✉]) and Felix Fastnacht[2]

[1] Institut für Informatik, Goethe Universität Frankfurt am Main,
Frankfurt, Germany
`brinks@es.cs.uni-frankfurt.de`
[2] Intedis GmbH & Co. KG, Würzburg, Germany
`Felix.Fastnacht@intedis.com`

Abstract. Embedded systems are growing very complex because of the increasing chip integration density, larger number of chips in distributed applications and demanding application fields e.g. in autonomous cars. Bio-inspired techniques like self-organization are a key feature to handle the increasing complexity of embedded systems. In biology the structure and organization of a system is coded in its DNA, while dynamic control flows are regulated by the hormone system. We adapted these concepts to embedded systems using an artificial DNA (ADNA) and an artificial hormone system (AHS). Based on these concepts, highly reliable, robust and flexible systems can be created. These properties predestine the ADNA and AHS for the use in future automotive applications.

However, computational resources and communication bandwidth are often limited in automotive environments. Nevertheless, in this paper we show that the concept of ADNA and AHS can be successfully applied to an environment consisting of low-performance automotive microcontrollers interconnected by a classical CAN bus.

Keywords: Artificial DNA · Artificial hormone system ·
Self-organization · Automotive environment · CAN bus

1 Introduction

Embedded systems are growing very complex because of the increasing chip integration density, larger number of chips in distributed applications and demanding application fields e.g. in autonomous cars. Bio-inspired techniques like self-organization are a key feature to handle the increasing complexity of embedded systems. In biology the structure and organization of a system is coded in its DNA, while dynamic control flows are regulated by the hormone system. We adapted these concepts and developed the Artificial DNA (ADNA) by which

© Springer Nature Switzerland AG 2019
M. Schoeberl et al. (Eds.): ARCS 2019, LNCS 11479, pp. 87–99, 2019.
https://doi.org/10.1007/978-3-030-18656-2_7

the blueprint of the structure and organization of an embedded systems can be described. The ADNA can be stored in every processor of the system (like the biological DNA is stored in every cell of an organism). The tasks described by the ADNA are distributed to the processors in a self-organizing way by an artificial hormone system (AHS). The combination of ADNA and AHS allows to create very robust and flexible systems providing so-called self-X features like self-configuration, self-optimization and self-healing. We have already demonstrated these features in previous publications [8] using an autonomous self-balancing robot vehicle (see e.g. a video in [5]).

In this publication we investigate the applicability of the ADNA and AHS concept to automotive environments. Today's cars are equipped with several processors (electronic control units, ECUs) which perform the tasks necessary to operate the cars' powertrain, safety systems, driving assistants and board entertainment. These systems have to operate at a very high level of robustness and fault-tolerance. So the self-X capabilities of the ADNA and AHS would offer a great potential in this area. However, computational resources and communication bandwidth are often limited in automotive environments. To save costs, ECUs frequently use low-performance microcontrollers with limited computational and memory resources. Furthermore, common automotive bus systems like the CAN bus strictly limit the bandwidth and message sizes.

In the following we show that these limitations can be overcome and the concept of ADNA and AHS can be successfully applied to an environment consisting of low-performance automotive microcontrollers interconnected by a classical CAN bus. Our contribution in this paper is four-fold:

1. We demonstrate the applicability of ADNA and AHS for automotive ECU systems.
2. We compute the memory needs of the ADNA and AHS.
3. We propose an efficient communication scheme for the ADNA and AHS on CAN bus.
4. We evaluate performance measures and the resulting communication and processor load in these systems.

The paper is structured as follows: Related work is presented in Sect. 2. Section 3 describes both the ADNA and the AHS and its application to automotive systems. The adaptation to the target platform of automotive ECUs is presented in Sect. 4. Section 5 shows the evaluation results while Sect. 6 concludes this paper.

2   Related Work

Our approach relies on self-organization in automotive applications. IBM's and DARPAS's Autonomic Computing project [13, 15] deals with self-organization of IT servers in networks. Several so-called self-X properties like self-optimization, self-configuration, self-protection and self-healing have been postulated.

The German *Organic Computing* Initiative was founded in 2003. Its basic aim is to improve the controllability of complex embedded systems by using principles found in organic entities [26,27]. Organization principles which are successful in biology are adapted to embedded computing systems.

Self-organization for embedded systems has been addressed especially at the ESOS workshop [4]. Furthermore, there are several projects related to this topic like ASOC [1,21], CARSoC [16,17] or DoDOrg [14]. In the frame of the DoDOrg project, the Artifical Hormone System AHS was introduced [9,14]. [28] describes self-organization in automotive embedded systems. None of these approaches deal with self-organization using DNA-like structures.

DNA Computing [10] uses molecular biology instead of silicon based chips for computation purposes. In [20], e.g. the traveling salesman problem is solved by DNA molecules. In contrast, our approach uses classical computing hardware.

Several authors in [22] emphasize the necessity of redundant processors and sensors in future autonomous cars, however, they do not propose such a fine-grained approach as possible by the ADNA.

In [11] a redundancy scheme for processors in automotive applications is proposed where a voting algorithm is used to determine the validity of results of redundant processors. This is different from our approach which improves the exploit of redundancy using the ADNA.

Our approach relies on classical computing hardware using DNA-like structures for the description and building of the system. This enhances the self-organization and self-healing features of embedded systems, especially when these systems are getting more and more complex and difficult to handle using conventional techniques. Our approach is also different from generative descriptions [12], where production rules are used to produce different arbitrary entities (e.g. robots) while we are using DNA as a building plan for a dedicated embedded system.

To realize DNA-like structures, we have to describe the building plan of an embedded system in a compact way so it can be stored in each processor core. Therefore, we have adapted well known techniques like netlists and data flow models (e.g. the actor model [19]) to achieve this description. However, in contrast to such classical techniques our approach uses this description to build the embedded system dynamically at run-time in a self-organizing way. The description acts like a DNA in biological systems. It shapes the system autonomously to the available distributed multi/many-core hardware platform and re-shapes it in case of platform and environment changes (e.g. core failures, temperature hotspots, reconfigurations like adding new cores, removing cores, changing core connections. etc.). This is also a major difference to model-based [23] or platform-based design [25], where the mapping of the desired system to the hardware platform is done by tools at design time (e.g. a Matlab model). Our approach allows very high flexibility and robustness due to self-organization and self-configuration at run-time while still providing real-time capabilities.

3 Conception of the Artificial Hormone System and DNA

This section briefly describes the concept of the artificial DNA and the underlying artificial hormone system (AHS). For detailed information see [6,7,9].

3.1 Artificial DNA

The approach presented here is based on the observation that in many cases embedded systems are composed of a limited number of basic elements, e.g. controllers, filters, arithmetic/logic units, etc. This is a well known concept in embedded systems design. If a sufficient set of these basic elements is provided, many embedded real-time systems could be completely built by simply combining and parameterizing these elements. Figure 1 shows the general structure of such an element. It has two possible types of links to other elements. The *Sourcelink* is a reactive link, where the element reacts to incoming requests. The *Destinationlink* is an active link, where it sends requests to other elements.

Each basic element is identified by a unique Id and a set of parameters. The sourcelink and the destinationlink of a basic element are compatible to all other basic elements and may have multiple channels.

The Id numbers can be arbitrarily chosen, it is important only that they are unique. Figure 2 gives an example for a PID controller which is often used in closed control loops. This element has the unique Id = 10 and the parameter values for P, I, D and the control period. Furthermore, it has a single sourcelink and destinationlink channel.

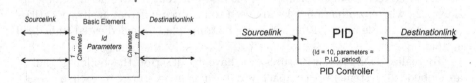

Fig. 1. Structure of a basic element (task)   **Fig. 2.** Sample basic element

Embedded systems can be composed by using these basic elements as building blocks. Figure 3 shows a very simple example of a closed control loop based on

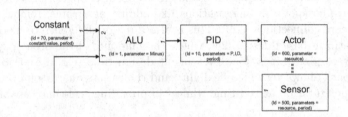

Fig. 3. A closed control loop consisting of basic elements

basic elements. An actor (defined by its resource id, e.g. a motor) is controlled by a sensor (also defined by its resource id, e.g. a speed sensor) applying a constant setpoint value. If we consider the closed control loop to be the *function* of the embedded system, it is divided by the ADNA into *tasks*: the basic elements.

If a sufficient set of standardized basic elements with unique Ids is available, an embedded system will no longer be programmed, but composed by connecting and parametrizing these elements. The building plan of the system can be described by a compact netlist containing the basic elements, its parameters and interconnections. This netlist can be stored in each processor of the system. It therefore represents a digitial artificial DNA (ADNA) which allows to partition and build the system at run-time. Detailed examples and a very memory efficient format to store an ADNA are presented in [6] and [7].

3.2 Building the System from Its ADNA by the AHS

Using the ADNA the system is divided into functions (e.g. control functions, closed control loops, data processing, filtering, etc.) and tasks (the basic elements of a function). Each processor has a local copy of the ADNA and therefore knows all these functions, tasks and their interconnections. It passes this information to the local instance of its artificial hormone system (AHS). The AHS is a completely decentralized mechanism to assign tasks to distributed computing nodes, see [9]. It uses artificial hormones (emulated by short messages) to find the most suitable computing node for each task based on node capability, load and tasks interconnection. It can also detect failing nodes and tasks by missing hormone values. So all basic elements of the ADNA are assigned as tasks at run-time by the AHS to the available processors. These elements are then interconnected according to the ADNA. This means the functions build themselves at runtime in the best possible way on the available processor resources. In case of a processor failure the basic elements are autonomously reassigned and reconnected to other processors as long as there is enough computing power left. Assignment and reassignment of tasks is done in real-time (with a time complexity of $\mathcal{O}(n)$, where n is the number tasks) as proven in [9] and demonstrated by a self-balancing robot vehicle in [7]. The ADNA therefore enables an extremely robust and fine-grain distribution of functions to processors. A function is not bound to a single processor but can be split among several processors on the task (basic element) level. In case of processor failures only the affected basic elements are automatically moved to other processors. Also the importance of basic elements can be derived from the ADNA and used to operate the most important parts if not enough computation power is left to assign all tasks. A detailed description of building a system from the ADNA and complex examples can be found in [7].

3.3 Application of the ADNA and AHS Concept to Automotive Systems

In automotive applications the system functions (anti-locking brake, traction control, stability control, engine control, driving assistants, infotainment, etc.)

are executed by the car's processors, the ECUs. Many of these systems require fail-operational behavior. So a highly robust design is necessary. In classical approaches a function is usually mapped to an ECU (e.g. anti-locking brake to the anti-locking brake ECU). To provide fail-operational behavior, critical ECUs have a backup ECU (1:1 redundancy). In more advanced approaches like e.g. the AutoKonf project [2], several ECUs share a single backup ECU (n:1 redundancy) to reduce the overhead. These approaches apply redundancy on the *function level*. In contrast, the self-healing process of the ADNA and AHS concept provides redundancy on the *task (basic element) level*. This enables the best possible use of the available ECU resources.

If we have e.g. f critical functions, the classical 1:1 redundancy approach requires $2f$ ECUs. Fail-operational behavior can no longer be guarantied if 2 or more ECUs fail (the failure of 2 ECUs can disable a function, if the original and the backup ECU are affected). So the fail-operational limit is $\frac{2}{2f} = \frac{1}{f}$. In a 2:1 redundancy approach, $\lceil 3f/2 \rceil$ ECUs are required. Like for the 1:1 approach, fail-operational behavior can no longer be guarantied if 2 or more ECUs fail. However, due to the lower number of ECUs used, the fail-operational ECU limit is better: $\frac{2}{\lceil 3f/2 \rceil}$. In general, the classical n:1 redundancy results in a fail-operational ECU limit of $\frac{2}{\lceil (1+1/n)f \rceil}$.

Using the ADNA/AHS approach, the self-healing mechanism reassigns the tasks of the functions to the remaining ECUs in case of an ECU failure. As long as enough ECUs are available, all functions will stay operational. If we use the same number of $2f$ ECUs for f critical functions like in the classical 1:1 redundancy approach, f ECUs might fail without the loss of a function (since f ECUs are sufficient to execute f functions). So the fail-operation ECU limit is $\frac{f+1}{2f}$. If we use $\lceil 3f/2 \rceil$ ECUs like in the 2:1 approach, this limit calculates to $\frac{\lceil 3f/2 \rceil - f + 1}{\lceil 3f/2 \rceil}$. In general, if we use $e \geq f$ ECUs, the fail-operational limit calculates to $\frac{e-f+1}{e}$. Figure 4 compares the fail-operational limits for different approaches and different number of functions. It can be seen that from this theoretical point of view the ADNA/AHS approach clearly outperforms the classical solutions. Furthermore, in current safety-critical automotive applications usually a fail-safe state is entered if one more failure would lead to a critical event. For the classical redundancy approaches shown above this happens after 1 ECU failure. For the ADNA/AHS approach this happens not before $e - f$ failures. Therefore, it seems reasonable to apply the ADNA/AHS concept to the automotive area. The major question is if the available computational, memory and bandwidth resources are sufficient there to operate this concept. This will be investigated in the next sections.

4   Adaptation to the Target Platform

As target platform we have chosen the Renesas μPD70F35XX microcontroller family [24]. This family contains a dual lockstep V850E2 32 bit processor core and is a common controller for safety-critical ECUs. It is e.g. also used for the

AutoKonf project [2] mentioned above. The controller offers a classical CAN bus interface [3], which is a frequently used communication bus in automotive systems. Table 1 shows key features of the family. The main bottleneck is the low amount of data memory, together with the limited bandwidth and message size of the CAN bus. Clock frequency and program memory are less critical since the ADNA/AHS requires low computational resources and has a small program memory footprint [8].

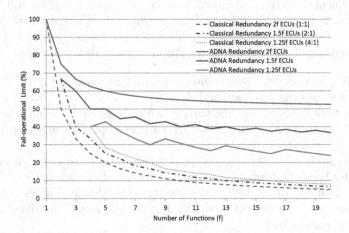

Fig. 4. Fail-operational limits of different redundancy configurations

Table 1. μPD70F35XX microcontroller family key features

Controller:	μPD70F3504	μPD70F3506	μPD70F3508
Data memory:	24 kBytes	40 kBytes	80 kBytes
Program memory:	384 kBytes	512 kBytes	1024 kBytes
Data flash:	32 kBytes	32 kBytes	32 kBytes
Max. clock frequency:	80 MHz	80 MHz	160 MHz

The ADNA/AHS system is completely written in Ansi C 99 and therefore could be easily compiled for the target platform using a GreenHill C compiler for this microcontroller family. Mainly, two modules had to be adapted:

- *AHSBasicOSSupport*, which implements the basic multithreading and synchronization mechanisms for the AHS and ADNA.
- *AHSBasicCommunication*, which implements all basic communication functions for the AHS and ADNA.

In the following sections, we describe these adaptions as well as the resulting data and program memory footprint.

4.1 Basic Operating System Support

This module usually connects the ADNA/AHS system to the operating system. Implementations for Windows and Linux already exist. On this automotive microcontroller target platform, no Windows or Linux support exists. Therefore we have chosen AtomThreads [18] as a basis to implement the AHSBasicOSSupport module. AtomThreads is a lightweight open source multithreaded library, which can be easily adapted to a dedicated microcontroller. AHSBasicOSSupport implements functions to create, terminate, suspend, resume and schedule threads preemptively with different fixed priorities. Furthermore it realizes synchronization functions like mutexes, semaphores, events and timers. To build this efficiently on top of AtomThreads, the AtomThreads library has been extended:

- Functions to suspend, resume and terminate threads have been added.
- Event management has been added.
- To save data memory, the idle thread (which is active when no other thread is ready to run) has been replace by an idle loop. This idle loop does not require its own stack.
- To save more data memory, the initial thread activating the AtomThread scheduler has been turned into a regular thread of the scheduler so it can be further used. In the original implementation this thread is never used again.
- Idle time measurement has been added to the idle loop. This allows to determine the system load.

Overall, using the modified AthomThreads library a very lightweight and efficient basic operating system support module could be built.

4.2 Basic Communication with CAN Bus

The ADNA/AHS system sends messages and hormones via the AHSBasicCommunication module. Hormones are bundled up to a telegram length of 256 Bytes. The maximum length of message telegrams is also 256 Bytes. So the AHSBasiCommunication module has to offer functionality to send and receive telegrams up to that size. The user accessible fields of a classical CAN bus telegram consist of an identifier section of 11 Bits (standard CAN format), a length section of 4 bits and a data section of up to 64 bits (8 bytes). The identifier section also serves for bus-arbitration using a CSMA/CR policy. A logical 0 dominates a logical 1 so as more 0 are in the identifier as higher is the priority of the telegram. To transfer telegrams of up to 256 Bytes via the classical CAN bus, they have to be divided in chunks. We have chosen a division scheme shown in Fig. 5, which is optimized for the format of the hormone and message telegrams. The first byte of these telegrams distinguishes between hormones and messages. Hormone telegrams are broadcasted to all ECUs, while the receiver ECU id of a message telegram is given in the second byte. So we use the 11 bit identifier field to contain the 8 bit sender ECU id, a hormone/message distinction bit (to allow different priorities for hormones and messages) and a 2 bit chunk id to determine the first chunk of a telegram (10), an even chunk (00), an odd chunk (01) and a last chunk[1] (11). So we can fully use the CAN bus data payload to send and receive hormones and messages, a n byte telegram is divided into $\lceil n/8 \rceil$ chunks. As mentioned above, in case of a message the second byte of the payload of the first chunk indicates the receiver ECU id. Since a sender ECU never sends a new message or hormone telegram before the previous one is completely transmitted, the receiver ECU id of the first chunk can be applied to all following chunks from the same sender ECU id. The distinction of even and odd chunks additionally allows to detect an odd number of lost chunks.

8 Bit	1 Bit	2 Bit	4 Bit	up to 64 Bits
Sender ECU Id	Hormone/Message	Chunk Id	Len	Payload
Identifier			Length	Data

Fig. 5. CAN Bus telegram organization

4.3 Memory Footprint

One of the most critical issues is the low amount of data memory on the target platform. The data memory needs of the ADNA/AHS system can be divided into static and dynamic memory needs. Both could be optimized during the adaption process by e.g. reducing list management overhead, using bit based structures and shrinking oversized buffers. As a result, the dynamic memory needs of the ADNA/AHS could be reduced to:

$$dynMem = 221 + (gt \cdot 32) + (at \cdot 80) + (lt \cdot (96 + mb)) + (rt \cdot 15) + cb + ab \text{ Bytes}$$

with: gt: global number of tasks (basic elements) in the system, at: number of tasks the ECU applies for, lt: number of tasks running on the ECU, rt: number of related tasks, mb: task communication message buffer size, cb: CAN bus communication buffer size, ab: ECU communication message buffer size.

Additionally, AtomThreads need 900 Bytes stack per thread, which is also allocated dynamically. Since we have 2 system threads, the stack memory needs related to the number of running tasks on an ECU calculates to:

$$dynMem_{stack} = 900 \cdot (lt + 2) \text{ Bytes}$$

Finally, when a DNA is read from the data flash memory, administrative memory to operate this DNA is allocated dynamically:

$$dynMem_{DNA} = (dl \cdot 14) + (ln \cdot 4) + ps \text{ Bytes}$$

with: dl: number of DNA lines, ln: number of destination links, ps: parameter size

---

[1] Only needed if the payload data of a chunk is completely filled, otherwise a length less than 8 bytes indicates the last chunk.

The static data memory needs of the ADNA/AHS system are constant at

$$statMem = 11960 \text{ Bytes}$$

To give a real-number example, an ADNA to realize an anti-locking brake and traction control system[2] requires 16 DNA lines (dl) with 23 destination links (ln) and 210 Bytes parameter space (ps). The resulting number of tasks[3] is 9 (gt). If each ECU in the system applies for all tasks ($at = 9$) and in worst case a single ECU runs all of them ($lt = 9$), each task is related to another task ($rt = 9$) and we have a message buffer size for each task of 128 Bytes (mb), the CAN bus buffer size is 3000 Bytes (cb) and the ECU communication message buffer size is 128 Bytes (ab), the overall data memory needs for this application are:

$$data \; memory = dynMem + dynMem_{stack} + dynMem_{DNA} + statMem$$
$$= 6508 + 9900 + 582 + 11960 = 28950 \text{ Bytes}$$

This easily fits the two bigger controllers of the family (μPD70F3506 and μPD70F3508), see Table 1. For the smallest controller (μPD70F3504) it is a bit too much. However, a major part of the data memory is consumed by the thread stack. So the smallest controller could run 4 tasks at maximum. Due to the dynamic nature of the AHS (a memory overflow automatically produces a suppressor hormone which reduces the number of running tasks on an ECU) the system would autonomously adapt to this situation. This enables the use of the smallest controller if enough are present.

The program memory footprint of the entire ADNA/AHS system is 138 kBytes. So this easily fits all three controllers. Please note that this includes all basic elements, the application itself does not require any additional program and data memory. The running application is stored via the DNA in the data memory using $dynMem_{DNA}$ bytes as calculated above. Also the data flash memory (32 kBytes) used to persistently store different DNAs is by far large enough for a big number of DNAs.

5   Evaluation Results

For the evaluation we have chosen the mid-size controller μPD70F3506. We have used several DNAs from our self-balancing robot vehicle (Balance, BalanceAGV, BalanceFollow, BalanceTurn) as well as two experimental automotive DNAs realizing an anti-locking brake plus traction control (AntiLockTraction) and an anti-locking brake plus traction and cruise control (AntiLockTrCruise). Three different configurations were used: (1) A single ECU was interconnected with the environment via CAN bus. (2) Two ECUs were interconnected to each other and the environment via CAN bus. (3) Two ECUs were interconnected via CAN bus, two more virtual ECUs (on a Windows PC) were interconnected via UDP

---

[2] Experimental AntiLockTraction DNA from Sect. 5.
[3] Not necessarily all DNA lines require a task, e.g. actor lines.

and UDP/CAN was interconnected by a hub. The results are given in Table 2. The table shows the resulting CAN bus load (at 1 MHz CAN bus frequency) and the computational load of the most occupied real (not virtual) ECU. The hormone cycle time used was 50 ms and the fastest message cycle time was 15 ms. It can be seen that neither the CAN bus load nor the ECU load exceeds critical bounds.

Table 2. Evaluation results

DNA	1 × CAN (1)		2 × CAN (2)		2 × (CAN + UDP) (3)	
	CAN load	ECU load	CAN load	ECU load	CAN load	ECU load
Balance	21%	9%	21%	6%	10%	3%
BalanceAGV	26%	12%	26%	10%	15%	5%
BalanceFollow	28%	13%	28%	10%	23%	8%
BalanceTurn	28%	12%	28%	10%	23%	7%
AntiLockTraction	40%	14%	40%	12%	37%	9%
AntiLockTrCruise	45%	18%	46%	15%	31%	10%

6 Conclusion

In this paper we have shown that it is possible to apply the self-organizing ADNA/AHS concept to an automotive environment with low performance microcontrollers and a classical CAN bus. Due to its self-healing capabilities, this approach can contribute to improve the fail-operational behavior and flexibility of automotive systems. Its failure robustness exceeds traditional approaches. In future, more powerful controllers and busses (like e.g. CAN-FD) will even increase the potential of the ADNA/AHS concept.

In the work presented we have used a modified AtomThreads OS and a proprietary CAN bus protocol. As next step we are investigating the possibility to adapt this concept also to a pure automotive OS like classical AUTOSAR and an AUTOSAR compliant use of the CAN bus. This is challenging due to the static nature of classical AUTOSAR. However, first experiments made using e.g. thread pools show these limitations can be overcome. This would add a completely new quality to AUTOSAR.

References

1. Bernauer, A., Bringmann, O., Rosenstiel, W.: Generic self-adaptation to reduce design effort for system-on-chip. In: IEEE International Conference on Self-Adaptive and Self-Organizing Systems (SASO), San Francisco, USA, pp. 126–135 (2009)
2. BMBF: Autokonf projekt. http://autokonf.de/
3. Bosch: CAN Specifications Version 2.0. http://esd.cs.ucr.edu/webres/can20.pdf

4. Brinkschulte, U., Müller-Schloer, C., Pacher, P. (eds.): Proceedings of the Work-shop on Embedded Self-Organizing Systems, San Jose, USA (2013)
5. Brinkschulte, U.: Video of the KDNA controlled robot vehicle. http://www.es.cs.uni-frankfurt.de/index.php?id=252
6. Brinkschulte, U.: An artificial DNA for self-descripting and self-building embedded real-time systems. Pract. Exp. Concurr. Comput. **28**, 3711–3729 (2015)
7. Brinkschulte, U.: Prototypic implementation and evaluation of an artificial DNA for self-describing and self-building embedded systems. In: 19th IEEE International Symposium on Real-time Computing (ISORC 2016), York, UK, 17–20 May 2016
8. Brinkschulte, U.: Prototypic implementation and evaluation of an artificial DNA for self-descripting and self-building embedded systems. EURASIP J. Embed. Syst. (2017). https://doi.org/10.1186/s13639-016-0066-2
9. Brinkschulte, U., Pacher, M., von Renteln, A.: An artificial hormone system for self-organizing real-time task allocation in organic middleware. In: Brinkschulte, U., Pacher, M., von Renteln, A. (eds.) Organic Computing. UCS, pp. 261–283. Springer, Heidelberg (2009). https://doi.org/10.1007/978-3-540-77657-4_12
10. Garzon, M.H., Yan, H. (eds.): DNA 2007. LNCS, vol. 4848. Springer, Heidelberg (2008). https://doi.org/10.1007/978-3-540-77962-9
11. Yi, C.H., Kwon, K., Jeon, J.W.: Method of improved hardware redundancy for automotive system, pp. 204–207 (2015)
12. Hornby, G., Lipson, H., Pollack, J.: Evolution of generative design systems for modular physical robots. In: Proceedings of the IEEE International Conference on Robotics and Automation, ICRA 2001, vol. 4, pp. 4146–4151 (2001)
13. IBM: Autonomic Computing (2003). http://www.research.ibm.com/autonomic/
14. Becker, J., et al.: Digital on-demand computing organism for real-time systems. In: Workshop on Parallel Systems and Algorithms (PASA), ARCS 2006, Frankfurt, Germany, March 2006
15. Kephart, J.O., Chess, D.M.: The vision of autonomic computing. IEEE Comput. **1**, 41–50 (2003)
16. Kluge, F., Mische, J., Uhrig, S., Ungerer, T.: CAR-SoC - towards and autonomic SoC node. In: Second International Summer School on Advanced Computer Architecture and Compilation for Embedded Systems (ACACES 2006), L'Aquila, Italy, July 2006
17. Kluge, F., Uhrig, S., Mische, J., Ungerer, T.: A two-layered management architecture for building adaptive real-time systems. In: Brinkschulte, U., Givargis, T., Russo, S. (eds.) SEUS 2008. LNCS, vol. 5287, pp. 126–137. Springer, Heidelberg (2008). https://doi.org/10.1007/978-3-540-87785-1_12
18. Lawson, K.: Atomthreads: open source RTOS, free lightweight portable scheduler. https://atomthreads.com/
19. Lee, E., Neuendorffer, S., Wirthlin, M.: Actor-oriented design of embedded hardware and software systems. J. Circ. Syst. Comput. **12**, 231–260 (2003)
20. Lee, J.Y., Shin, S.Y., Park, T.H., Zhang, B.T.: Solving traveling salesman problems with dna molecules encoding numerical values. Biosystems **78**(1–3), 39–47 (2004)
21. Lipsa, G., Herkersdorf, A., Rosenstiel, W., Bringmann, O., Stechele, W.: Towards a framework and a design methodology for autonomic SoC. In: 2nd IEEE International Conference on Autonomic Computing, Seattle, USA (2005)
22. Maurer, M., Gerdes, J.C., Winner, B.L.H.: Autonomous Driving - Technical, Legal and Social Aspects. Springer, Heidelberg (2016). https://doi.org/10.1007/978-3-662-48847-8
23. Nicolescu, G., Mosterman, P.J.: Model-Based Design for Embedded Systems. CRC Press, Boca Raton, London, New York (2010)

24. Renesas: V850E2/Px4 user manual. http://renesas.com/
25. Sangiovanni-Vincentelli, A., Martin, G.: Platform-based design and software design methodology for embedded systems. IEEE Des. Test **18**(6), 23–33 (2001)
26. Schmeck, H.: Organic computing - a new vision for distributed embedded systems. In: 8th IEEE International Symposium on Object-Oriented Real-Time Distributed Computing (ISORC 2005), pp. 201–203. Seattle, USA, May 2005
27. VDE/ITG (Hrsg.): VDE/ITG/GI-Positionspapier Organic Computing: Computer und Systemarchitektur im Jahr 2010. GI, ITG, VDE (2003)
28. Weiss, G., Zeller, M., Eilers, D., Knorr, R.: Towards self-organization in automotive embedded systems. In: González Nieto, J., Reif, W., Wang, G., Indulska, J. (eds.) ATC 2009. LNCS, vol. 5586, pp. 32–46. Springer, Heidelberg (2009). https://doi.org/10.1007/978-3-642-02704-8_4

A Parallel Adaptive Swarm Search Framework for Solving Black-Box Optimization Problems

Romeo Shuka[✉] and Jürgen Brehm

Institute of Systems Engineering, Leibniz Universität Hannover,
Hannover, Germany
{shuka,brehm}@sra.uni-hannover.de

Abstract. This paper presents a framework to support parallel swarm search algorithms for solving black-box optimization problems. Looking at swarm based optimization, it is important to find a well fitted set of parameters to increase the convergence rate for finding the optimum. This fitting is problem dependent and time-consuming. The presented framework automates this fitting. After finding parameters for the best algorithm, a good mapping of algorithmic properties onto a parallel hardware is crucial for the overall efficiency of a parallel implementation. Swarm based algorithms are population based, the best number of individuals per swarm and, in the parallel case, the best number of swarms in terms of efficiency and/or performance has to be found. Data dependencies result in communication patterns that have to be cheaper in terms of execution times than the computing in between communications. Taking all this into account, the presented framework enables the programmer to implement efficient and adaptive parallel swarm search algorithms. The approach is evaluated through benchmarks and real world problems.

Keywords: Particle Swarm Optimization · Parallelization ·
Adaptive algorithm · Optimization problems ·
Interplanetary space trajectory

1 Introduction

Numerical optimization presents a comprehensive and contemporary description of the most effective methods in continuous optimization and it has been widely used in engineering to solve a variety of complex problems in different areas such as finance [7], medicine [21], electrical engineering [15], and aerospace [13] to name but a few. It responds to the growing interest in optimization in these fields by focusing on methods that are best suited to practical real-world problems. Due to the lack of information about the internal working of these systems and their complexity, they can be classified as black-box problems.

Stochastic iterative global search methods such as Evolutionary Algorithms (EAs) and swarm algorithms have been shown to solve many real-world complex problems. The Particle Swarm Optimization (PSO) [17] algorithm is one

© Springer Nature Switzerland AG 2019
M. Schoeberl et al. (Eds.): ARCS 2019, LNCS 11479, pp. 100–111, 2019.
https://doi.org/10.1007/978-3-030-18656-2_8

of the most important representative of the swarm algorithms paradigm. The advantage of using PSO is that it does not use the gradient of the problem to be optimized, thus, it can be successfully applied to both, large scale and complex optimization problems. This versatility comes at a price, as three major restrictions limit the solution efficiency. Firstly, real-world problems are getting larger and complicated, which requires significant resources in time and hardware. Secondly, optimization problems are characterized by multiple local optima, requiring a method to avoid early stagnation. Thirdly, PSO may need some problem dependent tuning of its behavioral parameters.

The first problem can be solved by taking advantage of the computer architecture. Most of the publications concentrate on implementing the PSO on Graphics Processing Units (GPUs) [14,18,22]. Furthermore, there are a few shared memory, usually via Open Multi-Processing (OpenMP)[1], implementations [8,20]. All the referred approaches focus either on the algorithm or on how to implement it on a cluster or GPUs processor. None of the implementations investigates how the algorithm can preferably be mapped on a parallel architecture.

The second problem is treated in several ways: on one hand, once a stagnation is detected it can be remedied by restarting the algorithm [5,28]; on the other hand, early stagnation can be averted by using a decentralized approach [1].

The third problem, as well as the second one, is treated in several ways too. The spectrum goes from a brute-force search [24] to meta-heuristic approaches for finding the best parameters [6]. While a brute-force search is associated with a lot of time, the meta-heuristic approach just shifts the dilemma of the best parameters one level above.

Eventually, almost all the presented approaches focus either on solving one of the mentioned problems, or changing the PSO to fit a specific problem domain. This leads to a better performance for the investigated domain, but a deterioration in other domains.

In this study, we present a Parallel Adaptive Swarm Search (PASS) framework for solving a wide range of different optimization problems. Our goal is to smooth out simultaneously all the major PSO obstacles and to increase the effectiveness of the algorithm. Considering the 'No Free Lunch Theorems for Optimization' [26], we tend to achieve good performance over diverse classes of problems, without focusing on a specific one. As it will be shown, this approach can lead to improved overall optimization performance.

2   Background

The PSO is a population-based, non-deterministic optimization algorithm, proposed by Kennedy and Eberhard in 1995 [17]. In the original definition of PSO, the main idea is to model all solution candidates as a moving swarm of particles, which is attracted in the direction of the swarm-wide best position found so far, as well as each particle's individual best position from previous measurements.

---

[1] https://www.openmp.org/. Accessed 2 Dec 2018.

Given the position $x_i^t = (x_{i,1}^t, x_{i,2}^t, \ldots, x_{i,D}^t) \in S$, where S is the search space, and velocity $v_i^t = (v_{i,1}^t, v_{i,2}^t, \ldots, v_{i,D}^t) \in \mathbb{R}^D$ of the ith particle at the tth iteration, as well as the swarm-wide best position $g^t = (g_1^t, g_2^t, \ldots, g_D^t) \in S$ and the ith particle's best position $l_i^t = (l_{i,1}^t, l_{i,2}^t, \ldots, l_{i,D}^t) \in S$, the next position x_i^{t+1} can be calculated by the following equations,

$$v_{i,d}^{t+1} = wv_{i,d}^t + c_1 u_1^t(g_d^t - x_{i,d}^t) + c_2 u_2^t(l_i^t - x_i^t) \tag{1}$$

$$x_{i,d}^{t+1} = x_{i,d}^t + v_{i,d}^{t+1} \tag{2}$$

$$g^{t+1} = \begin{cases} x_i^t & f(x_i^t) < f(g^t) \\ g^t & \text{otherwise} \end{cases} \tag{3}$$

$$l_i^{t+1} = \begin{cases} x_i^t & f(x_i^t) < f(l_i^t) \\ l_i^t & \text{otherwise} \end{cases} \tag{4}$$

where $i \in \{1, 2, \ldots, P\}$ and $d \in \{1, 2, \ldots, D\}$, with P denoting the number of particles and D denoting the dimensionality at S. The so called inertia weight w, the maximal global attraction c_1 and maximal local attraction c_2 are user defined values, used to parameterize the algorithm. u_1 and u_2 are independent and uniformly distributed random values within $[0, 1]$.

Several modifications have been applied to the original algorithm to improve its performance [10, 23], which led to the current Standard Particle Swarm Optimization 2011 (SPSO2011) [27], a baseline for future PSO improvements and performances. The SPSO2011 algorithm is the basis of our approach.

3   Parallel Adaptive Swam Search Framework

Figure 1 illustrates the proposed approach. PASS consists of three main parts:

(a) Hardware Analysis: the goal is to find out if it is worth using shared memory for parallelization. For further details, refer to Sect. 3.1.
(b) Parameter Selection: the goal is to find the best parameters for the considered black-box problem. For further details, refer to Sect. 3.2.
(c) Parallel Swarm Search: is an extended PSO algorithm implementation explained in Sects. 3.1 and 3.3.

Both, *Hardware Analysis* and *Problem Specific Best Parameters* generate a result which can be used in the future. The first result is an *Architecture Cost Model* and the second one is a result with the best parameters for the actual problem. The first two steps above are only done once for a target machine, till the computer architecture changes or we have to optimize a new black-box problem.

3.1   Parallelization

One strategy to parallelize the PSO algorithm is to use shared memory. The parallelization process through OpenMP always comes together with overhead like

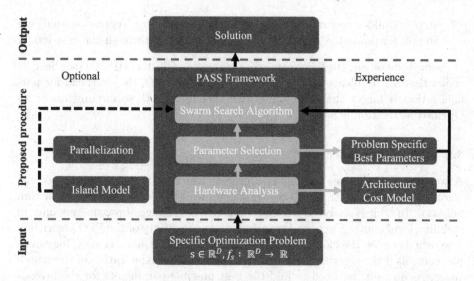

Fig. 1. PASS approach.

thread start-up time, synchronization, thread termination time etc. The implementations in [8,20] deliver a parallel version of PSO without considering the costs of overhead. Consequently, we have to identify the process with the largest computational time. Accordingly, the evaluation step is a candidate than will be parallelized. Through this change in the algorithm, we go from an asynchronous (Algorithm 1) version of PSO to a synchronous one (Algorithm 2). According to [11] the sequential method seems to be slightly more efficient, experimentally. On the other hand, for big problems with a large evaluation time, it should be necessary to run the algorithm in parallel.

Algorithm 1. Asynchronous	**Algorithm 2.** Synchronous

while *not stopping condition* **do**
  for all *Particles p in Swarm* **do**
    p.evaluate();
    p.update();
  end for
end while
	while *not stopping condition* **do**
	  for all *Particles p in Swarm* **do**
	    p.evaluate();
	  end for
	  for all *Particle p in Swarm* **do**
	    p.update();
	  end for
	end while

The *Hardware Analysis* procedure of PASS identifies through Machine Learning if the problem is big enough to activate parallelization. This is done in four steps:

Step 1: Generate training data (i.e. problems with different evaluation time)
Step 2: Evaluate the problems and calculate the speedup[2]

---

[2] The ratio of the sequential execution time to the parallel execution time.

Step 3: Build a cost model with the gathered data (e.g. regression analysis)

Step 4: Estimate the speedup of the given problem through the cost model

Some tests on our High Performance Computing Cluster (HPCC) (see Sect. 4) shows that for problems with very small evaluation time, the overhead for parallelization is larger than the achievable speedup. In these circumstances no OpenMP activation is needed.

3.2   Parameter Selection

A well fitted parameter setting is a crucial factor in the performance of the algorithms. Changing the PSO constants can lead to a change of the algorithm behavior. In [9] it is analyzed what an influence the change of parameters have in stability, local convergence, and transformation sensitivity of the PSO algorithm. The ratio between the global attraction c_1 and the social attraction c_2, for example, controls if the algorithm aims to an exploration or exploitation of the search space. As a result, we need to find the best possible parameters for the investigated problem. The difficulty in this process lies on the wide configuration range of the parameters. Through the literature (e.g. [9]), we can reduce the configuration range to a minimum possible. That enables us to develop a method which is noticeably faster than brute force or meta-heuristic search. Global attraction c_1 and social attraction c_2 have values within $[0, 2.5]$. The number of particles P are in the range $[10, 100]$ and the inertia weight w in $[-1, 1]$. The main idea of the parameter selection is to use a binary search[3] finding the best parameter setting. At the first step of the binary search, a random element from every side is picked. Then, we run the PSO algorithm with this parameter setting and compare the two parts with each other. Equation 5 is used to determine the *winner*. The side with the higher score is selected. This process continues iteratively up to a defined granularity. The finer the granularity, the longer the search process will be.

$$Score_{left} = \frac{|\#Eval._{left} - \#Eval._{right}|}{\#Eval._{left}} + \frac{Success_{left}}{|Success_{left} - Success_{right}|}$$

(5)

$$Score_{right} = \frac{|\#Eval._{right} - \#Eval._{left}|}{\#Eval._{right}} + \frac{Success_{right}}{|Success_{right} - Success_{left}|}$$

3.3   Island Model

The island model has been proposed in [19] and it has evolved through the last years. With the dawn of parallel computing machines, this model gained significant importance. Its intention is to improve the diversity of solutions and thus delaying stagnation. In a parallel implementation of an island model, each

---

[3] https://xlinux.nist.gov/dads/HTML/binarySearch.html. Accessed 2 Dec 2018.

machine executes a PSO algorithm and periodically exchanges a piece of their population. A multi-swarm can be defined as a triple $\langle \mathcal{MP}, \mathcal{T}, \mathcal{C} \rangle$, where $\mathcal{MP} = \{MP_1, ..., MP_n\}$ is the number of swarms, $\mathcal{T}$ is the topology of the swarm, and $\mathcal{C}$ is the migration-selection strategy.

$\mathcal{C}$ is defined as a four-tuple $\langle \alpha, \beta, \gamma, \delta \rangle$, where α is the frequency of the exchange, β indicates the number of particles that will migrate from one swarm to another, γ shows which particles have to be migrated and δ indicates how the replacement is done.

A wide variety of tests to find out the best parameters for the island model led us to the following configuration: $\mathcal{MP} = 14$, for $\mathcal{T}$ we use a maximum communication (i.e. every swarm communicates with the rest). After every swarm iteration (α), we change the worst particle of each swarm (δ) with the best global particle (γ).

4 Experimental Setup

All tests have been conducted on a HPCC with 17 compute nodes. Each node consists of 12 cores, each with an Intel(R) Xeon(R) CPU with 2.67 GHz clock rate. All source codes were written in C++ and compiled with gcc (version 8.2.0) using openMP (see Sect. 3.1) when needed. The implementation of the island model (see Sect. 3.3) is done through the Message Passing Interface (MPI)[4]. Each node serves as a unique swarm. Figure 2 gives an overview of the HPCC parallel implementation. On the basis that we use the same algorithm for every population $\mathcal{MP}$ (i.e. the execution time is almost the same), the communication is done synchronously. Further implementation details can be gathered from the website[5].

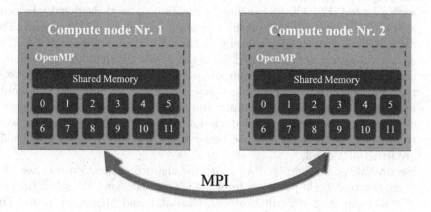

Fig. 2. Parallel implementation of PASS in HPCC.

---

[4] https://www.mcs.anl.gov/research/projects/mpi/. Accessed 2 Dec 2018.
[5] https://github.com/rshuka/PASS. Accessed 2 Dec 2018.

To evaluate our approach, we consider some non-linear benchmark functions with diverse properties (e.g. separability, uni- and multimodal). They are reported in Table 1. Next, we select some cases from the Global Trajectory Optimization (GTOP) database (see Sect. 4.1).

Within this paper, the problems used for evaluation are real-parameter, real-valued, bound-constraint black-box optimization problems (BBOPs). By convention, the optimization problem is viewed as a minimization problem (6).

$$\text{Minimize} \qquad f(x) \qquad (x \in \mathbb{R}^n)$$
$$\text{subject to:} \qquad x_1 \leq x \leq x_2 \qquad (x_1, x_2 \in \mathbb{R}^n) \qquad (6)$$

Table 1. Benchmark problems from [12].

Name	Benchmark functions	Domain $[X_{min}, X_{max}]^D$	Error goal	Dim. D
De Jong	$f1 = \sum_{i=1}^{n} x_i^2$	$[-5.12, 5.12]^D$	10^{-6}	40
Rastrigin	$f2 = 10n + \sum_{i=1}^{n}(x_i^2 - 10cos(2\pi x_i))$	$[-5.12, 5.12]^D$	10^{-4}	5
Rosenbrock	$f3 = \sum_{i=1}^{n-1}(100(x_i^2 - x_{i+1})^2 + (1 - x_i)^2)$	$[-2.048, 2.048]^D$	10^{-1}	10
Griewank	$f4 = 1 + \frac{1}{4000}\sum_{i=1}^{n} x_i^2 - \prod_{i=1}^{n} cos(\frac{x_i}{\sqrt{i}})$	$[-600, 600]^D$	10^{-6}	40
Schwefel	$f5 = \sum_{i=1}^{n}(-x_i sin(\sqrt{|x_i|})) + 418.982887 \cdot n$	$[-500, 500]^D$	10^{1}	5

The evaluation process is divided into two steps:

- **First step:** as mentioned in Sect. 2, the SPSO2011 algorithm is the baseline for the PASS algorithm. In order to demonstrate the performance increase of the proposed approach, five well-known benchmark functions from literature were adopted [12]. All the benchmark functions have their global minimum at 0.0. Table 1 reports the formula, domain, error goal and dimension. The SPSO2011 algorithm is initialized with the default values (see Sect. 4.2). The optimization process terminated when the global minimum was found or a maximum of 10,000 function evaluations was reached. Every experiment was repeated 50 times. If the problem was solved, the success rate, maximum number of evaluations, minimum number of evaluations, average number of iterations and the standard deviation of the benchmark functions were recorded. In order to display the best results, we bolded them. The results are listed in Table 3.
- **Second step:** we compare PASS with the algorithms mentioned in Sect. 4.2 using two real-world problems from the GTOP database. We select the easiest and the most difficult problem: Cassini 1 and Messenger (full). The optimization process terminated when a maximum of 500,000 function evaluation was reached. Every experiment was repeated **1000** times. For each set of data, the best objective function, the worst objective function, average of objective functions and the standard deviation were recorded.

4.1   Global Trajectory Optimization

Since 2005, the Advanced Concept Team (ACT) of the European Space Agency (ESA) publishes a database of GTOP problems [3] which can be used as benchmark of interplanetary space mission problems. A set of eight different real-world benchmark problems like Cassini, Sagas, and Messenger are included in this database.

Table 2. GTOP database benchmark problems.

Problem name	Variables	Number of submissions	Time between first and last submission
Messenger (reduced)	18	3	11 months
Messenger (full)	26	10	63 months
Cassini2	22	7	14 months
Rosetta	22	7	6 months
Sagas	12	1	-
GTOC1	8	2	24 months
Cassini1	6	3	6 months
Tandem*	18	-	-

*Tandem has 50 different instances and each instance has its own submissions

The GTOP benchmark problems are all highly non-linear and non-convex and they are known to be very difficult to solve. This difficulty can be seen at the time span between the first and last solution submission as reported in Table 2. It took more than 5 years for the community to achieve the current best found solution for the hardest problem (Messenger full). The complexity of this problem is represented with a state from the ESA website [4]:

> ...it was hardly believable that a computer, given the fly-by sequence and an ample launch window, could design a good trajectory in complete autonomy without making use of additional problem knowledge.

All the problems in the GTOP database are represented as optimization problems [2].

4.2   Algorithms

We selected some of the most popular algorithms that have proved their effectiveness in the past years.

1. SPSO2011: Standard Particle Swarm Optimization 2011 - We use the default recommended parameters in [11].
2. DE: Differential Evolution - This algorithm was introduced by Storn and Price [25] in 1997. The algorithm parameters are set to be $CR = 0.9$ and $F = 0.8$.

3. ABC: Artificial Bee Colony - This algorithm was introduced by Karaboga [16] in 2007. We use the default recommended parameters.

5   Numerical Results

5.1   Experiment #1: PASS vs. SPSO2011

The accumulated results presented in Table 3 show that the proposed approach out-performs the SPSO2011 algorithm. Using the parameter setting, we adapt the algorithm better to the problem characteristics and using the island model we can avoid early stagnation. Although having to compute more function evaluations we observe a better overall performance for our approach. We can even solve problems that are not solved through the SPSO2011. Taking a look at the *De Jong* benchmark function, we notice that both algorithms achieve a 100% success, but PASS converges faster than SPSO2011.

Table 3. Comparison between PASS and SPSO2011.

Benchmark	Algorithm	Suc. (%)	Min.	Max.	Mean	St.D
De Jong	PASS	100	200	310	**252.4**	25.3
	SPSO2011	100	455	589	532.46	28.1
Rastrigin	PASS	**100**	17391	25619	21456.38	2038.3
	SPSO2011	48	195	1209	510.95	309.8
Rosenbrock	PASS	**96**	20440	24640	22904	1613.5
	SPSO2011	78	1693	2492	2233.66	181.9
Griewank	PASS	**76**	1904	2082	1092.81	403.2
	SPSO2011	54	1007	1196	1080	45.7
Schwefel	PASS	**92**	1840	29400	11821.33	6840
	SPSO2011	10	346	1087	682.6	353.9

5.2   Experiment #2: PASS vs. DE vs. ABC vs. SPSO2011

Figure 3 presents a histogram of values in data using the number of bins equal to the square root of the number of elements. The X-axis represents the objective function value and the Y-axis represents the frequency of such values among all 1000 solutions. The red curve represents the normal distribution fit. Table 4 presents detailed information of the algorithms.

Comparing the results from all test runs, it can be seen that on average PASS had a better performance than the other algorithms on both problems. The overall best solutions are achieved by PASS. For Cassini 1, it corresponds to an objective value of $f(x) = $ **4.9486** and for Messenger full, it corresponds to an objective value of $f(x) = $ **8.6049**.

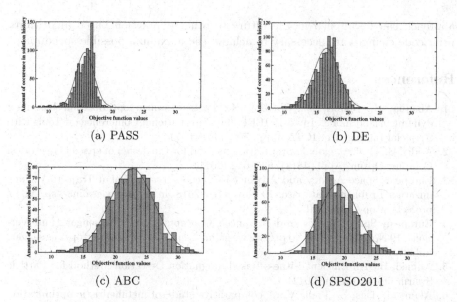

Fig. 3. Histogram of the algorithms for the messenger full problem.

Table 4. Results from 1000 runs.

Benchmark	Algorithm	Min.	Max.	Mean	St.D
Cassini 1	PASS	4.9486	5.357	**5.258**	0.086
	SPSO2011	5.3309	19.915	12.188	3.571
	DE	4.9507	16.715	8.789	3.359
	ABC	5.4286	11.390	6.745	0.801
Messenger full	PASS	8.6049	19.154	**15.693**	1.409
	SPSO2011	11.8651	30.770	19.025	2.974
	DE	9.6816	22.873	16.566	1.987
	ABC	10.8451	33.132	22.629	3.523

6   Conclusions

In this paper, we present a framework for solving black-box optimization problems. We introduce an effective selection strategy for finding the best parameters for the PSO algorithm. Furthermore, mapping the algorithm to the hardware and using the benefits of parallel computing can lead to a noticeable speedup. The island model is used to avoid early stagnation and to increase the PSO algorithm convergence. Through these steps, we can solve the major problems that face stochastic iterative global search methods like the PSO. It is important to say that no code changes are needed and everything is automated.

We do not restrict ourselves only to one specific problem class (e.g. GTOP). We can deliver good results for all kind of black-box problems. The presented approach can be applied in the future to other population based algorithms, prior code changes are necessary to achieve the maximum possible speedup.

References

1. Abadlia, H., Smairi, N., Ghedira, K.: Particle swarm optimization based on dynamic island model. In: 2017 IEEE 29th International Conference on Tools with Artificial Intelligence (ICTAI), pp. 709–716 (2017)
2. Addis, B., et al.: A global optimization method for the design of space trajectories. Comput. Optim. Appl. **48**(3), 635–652 (2011)
3. European Space Agency and Advanced Concepts Team: Global Trajectory Optimization Problems Database, 19 November 2018. http://www.esa.int/gsp/ACT/projects/gtop/gtop.html
4. European Space Agency and Advanced Concepts Team: Messenger (Full Version), 19 November 2018. http://www.esa.int/gsp/ACT/projects/gtop/messenger_full.html
5. Ahmed, H.: An Efficient Fitness-Based Stagnation Detection Method for Particle Swarm Optimization (2014)
6. Alam, M., Das, B., Pant, V.: A comparative study of metaheuristic optimization approaches for directional overcurrent relays coordination. Electr. Power Syst. Res. **128**, 39–52 (2015)
7. Allugundu, I., et al.: Acceleration of distance-to-default with hardware-software co-design, August 2012, pp. 338–344 (2012)
8. Altinoz, O.T., Yılmaz, A.E.: Comparison of Parallel CUDA and OpenMP Implementations of Particle Swarm Optimization
9. Bonyadi, M.R., Michalewicz, Z.: Analysis of stability, local convergence, and transformation sensitivity of a variant of the particle swarm optimization algorithm. IEEE Trans. Evol. Comput. **20**, 370–385 (2016). ISSN 1089–778X
10. Chen, T.-Y., Chi, T.-M.: On the improvements of the particle swarm optimization algorithm. Adv. Eng. Soft. **41**(2), 229–239 (2010)
11. Clerc, M.: Standard Particle Swarm Optimization, 19 November 2018. http://clerc.maurice.free.fr/pso/SPSO_descriptions.pdf
12. Molga, M., Smutnicki, C.: Test functions for optimization needs, 19 November 2018. http://new.zsd.iiar.pwr.wroc.pl/files/docs/functions.pdf
13. Isikveren, A., et al.: Optimization of commercial aircraft utilizing battery-based voltaic-joule/Brayton propulsion. J. Airc. **54**, 246–261 (2016)
14. Jong-Yul, K., et al.: PC cluster based parallel PSO algorithm for optimal power flow. In: Proceedings of the International Conference on Intelligent Systems Applications to Power Systems (2007)
15. Kahar, N.H.B.A., Zobaa, A.F.: Optimal single tuned damped filter for mitigating harmonics using MIDACO. In: 2017 IEEE International Conference on Environment and Electrical Engineering (2017)
16. Karaboga, D., Basturk, B.: A powerful and efficient algorithm for numerical function optimization: artificial bee colony (ABC) algorithm. J. Glob. Optim. **39**(3), 459–471 (2007)
17. Kennedy, J., Eberhart, R.: Particle swarm optimization. In: Proceedings of ICNN 1995 - International Conference on Neural Networks (1995)
18. Laguna-Sánchez, G.A., et al.: Comparative study of parallel variants for a particle swarm optimization algorithm implemented on a multithreading GPU. J. Appl. Res. Technol. **7**, 292–307 (2009)

19. Latter, B.D.H.: The island model of population differentiations: a general solution. Genetics **73**(1), 147–157 (1973)
20. Liu, Z., et al.: OpenMP-based multi-core parallel cooperative PSO with ICS using machine learning for global optimization problem. In: 2015 IEEE International Conference on Systems, Man, and Cybernetics (2015)
21. Mahajan, N.R., Mysore, S.P.: Combinatorial neural inhibition for stimulus selection across space. bioRxiv (2018)
22. Roberge, V., Tarbouchi, M.: Comparison of parallel particle swarm optimizers for graphical processing units and multicore processors. J. Comput. Intell. Appl. **12**, 1350006 (2013)
23. Shi, Y., Eberhart, R.: A modified particle swarm optimizer. In: Proceedings of the IEEE International Conference on Evolutionary Computation (1998)
24. Shi, Y., Eberhart, R.C.: Parameter selection in particle swarm optimization. In: Porto, V.W., Saravanan, N., Waagen, D., Eiben, A.E. (eds.) EP 1998. LNCS, vol. 1447, pp. 591–600. Springer, Heidelberg (1998). https://doi.org/10.1007/BFb0040810
25. Storn, R., Price, K.: Differential evolution - a simple and efficient heuristic for global optimization over continuous spaces. J. Glob. Optim. **11**, 341–359 (1997). ISSN 1573–2916
26. Wolpert, D.H., Macready, W.G.: No free lunch theorems for optimization. IEEE Trans. Evol. Comput. **1**, 67–82 (1997)
27. Zambrano-Bigiarini, M., Clerc, M., Rojas, R.: Standard particle swarm optimisation 2011 at CEC-2013: a baseline for future PSO improvements. In: Proceedings of the Congress on Evolutionary Computation (2013)
28. Zhang, J., et al.: A fast restarting particle swarm optimizer. In: 2014 IEEE Congress on Evolutionary Computation (CEC) (2014)

Architecture

Leros: The Return of the Accumulator Machine

Martin Schoeberl[✉] and Morten Borup Petersen

Department of Applied Mathematics and Computer Science,
Technical University of Denmark, Kongens Lyngby, Denmark
masca@dtu.dk, s152999@student.dtu.dk

Abstract. An accumulator instruction set architecture is simpler than an instruction set of a (reduced instruction set computer) RISC architecture. Therefore, an accumulator instruction set that does within one instruction less than a typical RISC instruction is probably more "reduced" than a standard load/store register based RISC architecture.

This paper presents Leros, an accumulator machine and its supporting C compiler. The hypothesis of the Leros instruction set architecture is that it can deliver the same performance as a RISC pipeline, but consumes less hardware and therefore also less power.

Keywords: Embedded systems · Minimal processor

1 Introduction

The invention of the reduced instruction set computer (RISC) [9,12,13] in the early 80's was a sort of a revolution. Since then most embedded processors have been designed as RISC processors, and from the Pentium Pro, the x86, a typical complex instruction set computer (CISC), uses RISC style instructions internally. Recently the free RISC-V instruction set [19], also developed at the University of California, Berkeley is gaining momentum. First silicon implementations are available. Even a many-core architecture with more than 4096 RISC-V processors on a single die is under development by Esperanto [7] and expected to ship mid-2019.

The RISC architecture promises to provide a simpler instruction set that is cheaper to implement and more natural to pipeline to achieve high performance by a higher clock frequency and fewer clocks per instructions. A typical RISC architecture has: 32-bit instructions, 32 registers, operation with two source and one destination register, and load and store instructions with displacement addressing.

This paper takes the RISC approach one step further and provides an even more *RISCy* instruction set: Leros, an accumulator machine. An accumulator instruction set is even simpler than a RISC instruction set. This processor is

© Springer Nature Switzerland AG 2019
M. Schoeberl et al. (Eds.): ARCS 2019, LNCS 11479, pp. 115–127, 2019.
https://doi.org/10.1007/978-3-030-18656-2_9

named Leros, after the Greek island Leros.[1] Leros is an accumulator machine with direct addressing of 256 memory words. Those 256 words are considered a large register file. Leros implements basic logic and arithmetic operations with an accumulator and one of the registers or a constant. Memory is accessed indirectly via an address register. All instructions are 16-bit wide. Leros can be configured to be a 16, 32, or 64-bit architecture. We optimize Leros for an FPGA, by using an on-chip memory for the large registers file.

The Leros architecture hypothesizes that it will deliver the same performance as a RISC pipeline, but consumes fewer hardware resources and therefore also less power. The Leros accumulator architecture will execute more instructions than a RISC architecture. However, the accumulator architecture compensates this by two facts: (1) The simple architecture shall allow clocking the pipeline with a higher clock frequency. (2) The shorter instructions (16 instead of 32 bits) need less instruction memory and instruction cache.

A further goal of Leros is to be a good target for a C compiler. Therefore, the data width shall be 32 bits. We present a port of the LLVM [10] C compiler for Leros.

The contributions of this paper are: (1) a definition of a minimal accumulator based instruction set architecture (ISA), (2) an implementation of that ISA in two simulators and in an FPGA, and (3) a C compiler ported to target the Leros ISA.

This paper is organized in 7 sections: The following section presents related work. Section 3 describes the Leros instruction set architecture. Section 4 describes one possible implementation of the Leros processor. Section 5 introduces the C compiler for Leros. Section 6 evaluates the architecture, the compiler, and an FPGA implementation of Leros. Section 7 concludes.

2   Related Work

Many small processor cores for FPGAs have been developed or are developed as assignments for courses in computer architecture. With Leros, we also aim to be an instruction set definition that can be used in teaching. In this section, we restrict the discussion to a few successful cores and point out the differences from our Leros design.

PicoBlaze is an 8-bit processor for Xilinx FPGAs [21]. PicoBlaze is optimized for resource usage and therefore restricts the maximum program size to 1024 instructions and data to 64 bytes. PicoBlaze can be implemented with one on-chip memory and 96 logic slices in a Spartan-3 FPGA. PicoBlaze provides 16 8-bit registers and executes one instruction in two clock cycles.

The central theme behind Leros is similar to PicoBlaze. However, we target a processor that is useful with a C compiler. Thus, the resource consumption of Leros is slightly higher as PicoBlaze. The PicoBlaze code is at a low level of abstraction composed out of Xilinx primitive components. Therefore, the design

---

[1] The initial version of the processor has been designed on the island Leros: https://www.leros.gr/en/.

is optimized for Xilinx FPGAs and practically not portable. Leros is written in vendor agnostic Chisel [2] and compiles unmodified for Altera and Xilinx devices.

The SpartanMC is a small microcontroller with an instruction and data width of 18 bits [8]. The authors optimized this width for FPGAs that contain on-chip memories that can be 18-bit wide (the additional bits are initially for parity protection). The processor has two operand instructions with 16 registers and is implemented in a three-stage pipeline. The register file uses on-chip memory and a sliding register window is used to speed up function calls (similar to the SPARC architecture). SpartanMC performs comparably to the 32-bit RISC processors LEON-II [6] and MicroBlaze [22] on the Dhrystone benchmark.

Compared to the SpartanMC, we further optimized Leros for FPGAs using fewer resources. Leros simplifies the access to registers in on-chip memory by implementing an accumulator architecture instead of a register architecture. Although an accumulator architecture is, in theory, less efficient, the resulting maximum achievable clock frequency may offset the higher instruction count.

Intel (former Altera) provides the Nios II [1] processor, which is optimized for Intel FPGAs. Nios is a 32-bit RISC architecture with an instruction set similar to MIPS [9] with three register operations. The sizes of its instruction and data caches are configurable.

Although Nios II represents a different design from Leros, it is a clear competitor, as one can configure Nios for different resource consumption and performance targets. Three different models are available: the *Fast* core is optimized for high performance, the *Standard* core is intended to balance performance and size, and the *Economy* core is optimized for smallest size. The smallest core needs less than 700 logic elements (LEs). It is a sequential implementation, and each instruction takes at least six clock cycles. Leros is a smaller, accumulator-based architecture, and with a pipelined implementation of Leros, most instructions can execute in a single clock cycle.

The *Supersmall* processor [15] is optimized for low resource consumption (half of the Nios economy version). This is achieved by serializing ALU operations to single bit operations. The LE consumption is comparable to Leros.

The Ultrasmall MIPS project [11] extends the Supersmall architecture. The main difference is the change of the ALU serialization to perform two-bit operations each cycle instead of single bits. Therefore, a 32-bit operation needs 16 clock cycles to complete. The Ultrasmall processor consumes 137 slices in a Xilinx Spartan-3E, which is 84% of the resource consumption of Supersmall. The serialization of the ALU operations results in an average of 22 clock cycles per instructions. According to the authors, "Ultrasmall is the smallest 32-bit ISA soft processor in the world". We appreciate this effort of building the smallest 32-bit processor. With Leros, we aim similar for a small 32-bit processor.

Wolfgang Puffitsch developed the ∅ processor.[2] It is an accumulator machine aiming at low resource usage. The bit width of the accumulator (and register width) is configurable. An instance of an 8-bit ∅ processor executing a blinking function consumes 176 LEs and 32 memory bits.

---

[2] https://github.com/jeuneS2/oe.

An early processor targeting FPGAs is the DOP processor [3]. DOP is a 16-bit stack oriented processor with additional registers, such as address registers and a work register. As the work register is directly connected to the ALU, DOP is similar to Leros an accumulator oriented architecture. The authors do not provide resource consumptions for the DOP design.

Lipsi is a processor that aims to be one of the smallest processors available for an FPGA [18]. Lipsi is small as it can use just a single block RAM for instructions and data. Therefore, each instruction executes in at least two clock cycles. The datapath of Lipsi is 8-bit. The aims of Lipsi and Leros are similar to build small embedded processors. However, with Leros, we target a processor that is well suited for a modern C compiler. Therefore, the default datapath width is 32-bit but is configurable to be 16, 32, or 64 bits.

The first version of Leros [16] was a hardcoded 16-bit accumulator machine. It consisted of a two-stage pipeline, where the pipeline delays are visible in the instruction definition. Compared to this initial version of Leros, we make a clear definition of the instruction set architecture, independent from any implementation in this paper. Furthermore, we allow that the bit width is configurable. And we provide a port of the LLVM C compiler for Leros. The porting of the C compiler also provided feedback on the instruction set that we changed accordingly. Therefore, the presented version of Leros is not binary compatible with the early version of Leros.

3   The Leros Instruction Set Architecture

The instruction set architecture, or short ISA, is the most important interface of a processor. It defines the language that the processor understands. It is the interface between the hardware and the compiler. IBM first introduced an ISA with the 360 series of computers. IBM introduced several implementations of the 360 series, with different price tags, that all implemented the same ISA. Therefore, it was possible to reuse software and compilers on different computers.

The ISA defines the programmer visible state, e.g., registers and memory, and instructions that operate on this state. The processor state that is not visible to the programmer, e.g., caches, are not part of the ISA. Some parts of a processor, e.g., address translation and memory protection, are not visible in the user ISA, but only available in a supervisor mode (usually used by an operating system kernel).

Leros is an accumulator machine. Therefore, the dominant register is the accumulator A. Furthermore, Leros defines a small memory area that can be directly addressed. We call those 256 memory words registers. Leros performs operations with the accumulator and those registers. E.g., Adding a register to the accumulator, storing the accumulator into a register. Basic operations are also available with immediate values, e.g., adding a constant to A.

Memory operations use an address register, called AR, plus an 8-bit displacement. All memory accesses use this address register. The load destination is the accumulator, and the store source is also the accumulator.

Table 1. The Leros instruction set.

Opcode	Function	Description
add	$A = A + Rn$	Add register Rn to A
addi	$A = A + i$	Add immediate value i to A (sign extend i)
sub	$A = A - Rn$	Subtract register Rn from A
subi	$A = A - i$	Subtract immediate value i from A (sign extend i)
shr	$A = A \ggg 1$	Shift A logically right
and	$A = A$ and Rn	And register Rn with A
andi	$A = A$ and i	And immediate value i with A
or	$A = A$ or Rn	Or register Rn with A
ori	$A = A$ or i	Or immediate value i with A
xor	$A = A$ xor Rn	Xor register Rn with A
xori	$A = A$ xor i	Xor immediate value i with A
load	$A = Rn$	Load register Rn into A
loadi	$A = i$	Load immediate value i into A (sign extend i)
loadhi	$A_{31-8} = i$	Load immediate into second byte (sign extend i)
loadh2i	$A_{31-16} = i$	Load immediate into third byte (sign extend i)
loadh3i	$A_{31-24} = i$	Load immediate into fourth byte (sign extend i)
store	$Rn = A$	Store A into register Rn
jal	$PC = A, Rn = PC + 2$	Jump to A and store return address in Rn
ldaddr	$AR = A$	Load address register AR with A
loadind	$A = \text{mem}[AR + (i \ll 2)]$	Load a word from memory into A
loadindbu	$A = \text{mem}[AR + i]_{7-0}$	Load a byte unsigned from memory into A
storeind	$\text{mem}[AR + (i \ll 2)] = A$	Store A into memory
storeindb	$\text{mem}[AR + i]_{7-0} = A$	Store a byte into memory
br	$PC = PC + o$	Branch
brz	if $A == 0$ $PC = PC + o$	Branch if A is zero
brnz	if $A\ != 0$ $PC = PC + o$	Branch if A is not zero
brp	if $A >= 0$ $PC = PC + o$	Branch if A is positive
brn	if $A < 0$ $PC = PC + o$	Branch if A is negative
scall	scall A	System call (simulation hook)

All instructions are 16-bit. The data width of Leros is configurable to be: 16, 32, or 64 bits. The default implementation of Leros is 32-bit.

A set of branch instructions perform unconditional and conditional branches depending on A (zero, non-zero, positive, or negative). For larger branch targets, indirect jumps, and calls, Leros has a jump and link instruction that jumps to the address in A and stores the address of the next instruction in a register. Furthermore, we define a system call instruction for operating system calls.

Leros is designed to be simple, but still a good target for a C compiler. The description of the instruction set fits in less than one page, see Table 1. In that table A represents the accumulator, PC is the program counter, i is an immediate value (0 to 255), Rn a register n (0 to 255), o a branch offset relative to PC, and AR an address register for memory access.

4   A Leros Implementation

With the Leros ISA, we do not define any specific implementation. Sequential, single cycle, or pipelined implementations are all proper implementations of the Leros ISA. The initial Leros 16-bit processor [16] used the pipeline implementation as part of the ISA definition, which limits the usefulness of an ISA definition. Therefore, we remove this restriction with the current definition. Instruction dependencies within a pipeline need to be resolved in hardware (by forwarding or stalling). No pipeline effects shall be visible in the ISA (except in the execution time of an instruction).

As a golden reference, we have implemented a Leros ISA simulator in Scala. The simulator is a large match/case statement and is implemented in around 100 lines of code. The simulator also reflects the simplicity of the Leros ISA.

Writing an assembler with an expressive language like Scala is not a big project. Therefore, we wrote a simple assembler for Leros, which is possible within about 100 lines of code. We define a function getProgram that calls the assembler. For branch destinations, we need a symbol table, which we collect in a Map. A classic assembler runs in two passes: (1) collect the values for the symbol table and (2) assemble the program with the symbols obtained in the first pass. Therefore, we call the assembler twice with a parameter to indicate which pass it is.

The ISA simulator and the hardware implementation of Leros call the function getProgram to assemble a program at simulation or hardware generation time.

We have chosen Scala for the simulator and the assembler as we use Chisel, which is a Scala library, to describe the hardware implementation. We can share constants that define the instruction encoding between the simulator, the assembler, and the hardware implementation.

The 256 registers of Leros are similar to the work registers of the TMS9900 CPU, the processor that was used in the first 16-bit personal computer TI-99/4A.[3] The TMS9900 had 16 registers, which are kept in RAM.

---
[3] https://en.wikipedia.org/wiki/Texas_Instruments_TI-99/4A.

An implementation of Leros may map those registers into the main memory and cache it in a data cache. Or it can implement the registers in on-chip memory, also called scratchpad memory. The Leros ISA does not define this implementation details. The ISA specification does not assume that the registers can be read or written with memory load and store instructions.

For testing, we wrote a few test programs in assembler with the convention that at the end of the test the accumulator shall be 0. Those tests are executed in the software simulator of Leros and in the hardware simulation in Chisel.

Furthermore, as we implemented the hardware description and the software simulator in the same language, we can do co-simulation. With co-simulation, we compare after each instruction the content of A between the software simulation and the hardware. Any (relevant) difference/error will eventually show up in A as all data flows through A.

5   The Leros C Compiler

We implemented a C compiler and accompanying toolchain for the Leros instruction set with the LLVM compiler infrastructure. A detailed description of the compiler and tools for Leros can be found in [14].

The LLVM compiler infrastructure is a collection of toolchain applications built around the LLVM core libraries. The LLVM core is a modular compiler infrastructure, allowing for separate implementation of front-, optimizer, and backends. We implemented an LLVM backend that targets the Leros instruction set.

5.1   Using LLVM for Accumulator Machines

A difficulty in using LLVM for Leros arises when we directly use the intermediate representation (IR) of LLVM. LLVM follows the common notion of compiler IR wherein the IR should resemble the target instruction set format, to facilitate various steps such as optimizations and instruction selection. An example LLVM IR sequence may be the addition of two variables:

```
%c = add i32 %a, %b
```

The format of the LLVM IR resembles 3-operand RISC instruction sets, which facilitates instruction selection and emission for instruction sets such as ARM and RISC-V. For Leros, virtually no LLVM IR instructions can be directly matched to Leros instructions.

The method for matching the LLVM IR during instruction selection has been to implement a 3-operand version of the Leros instruction set, denoted as the Leros pseudo instruction set. An example expansion of a Leros pseudo instruction is as follows:

```
%c = add %a %b        load    %a
                      add     %b
                      store   %c
```

Having mappings such as shown above allows for instruction selection with the ease enjoyed by the 3-operand upstream backends of LLVM. After scheduling, SSA optimizations and register allocation the Leros pseudo instructions are expanded to their corresponding sequence of Leros machine instructions. Whilst incurring a code-size overhead, the method does not require any modifications to the DAG which is provided as the input for the backend as well as the built-in scheduler, SSA optimization- and register allocation passes, which are desired to be left as default to minimize implementation time as well as the possibility for compiler issues.

5.2   Accumulator Optimizations

A consequence of the pseudo instruction set is an overhead in the size of the compiled programs, mainly due to redundant instructions which are a side-effect of the pseudo instruction set. Therefore, we implemented various optimizations to detect and modify code sequences where a program may reuse the accumulator content. An example is the removal of redundant load and stores. Figure 1 shows an example of Leros machine code after pseudo instruction expansion. We can see that the intermittent load- and store to %tmp is redundant, and the compiler may remove it if the register %tmp is dead after the load %tmp instruction.

	load	%a	load	%a
	add	%b	add	%b
%tmp = add i32 %a %b	store	%tmp	add	%a
%d = add i32 %a %tmp	load	%tmp	store	%d
	add	%a		
	store	%d		

Fig. 1. Left: the LLVM IR sequence, center: expanded pseudo instructions, and right: an optimal sequence.

As of this writing, we have implemented three optimization passes in the backend:

Redundant loads: Identifies code sequences as shown in Fig. 1 where a register is loaded wherein the value of the register is already present in the accumulator.

Redundant stores: Identifies code sequences as shown in Fig. 1 where a register is used to store an intermediate result. Redundant store instructions are identified and removed by reverse traversal of a basic-block, checking register liveness and usage.

Redundant ldaddr: All ldind and stind instructions emit a ldaddr instruction, resulting in code sequences where multiple ldaddr instructions will load an unmodified value into the address register. This pass mimics the redundant store pass, tracking the usage of the register which is currently loaded into the address register and removes ldaddr instructions if deemed redundant.

5.3 Further Optimizations

Some pseudo instruction expansions require the use of bit masks. An example is the expansion of arithmetic right shift instructions. In this, the bitmask **0X80000000** is required for sign-extending a (logically right shifted) value. The compiler generates immediate values through subsequent **loadi#** instructions.

Given that the compiler knows the required set of constants for instruction expansion at compile time, these constant can be stored in registers. The abundance of registers in Leros allows for using some of the registers for constants. With this, we define some constant registers for Leros, which the **_start** function initializes. These constant registers are furthermore able to be referenced during instruction selection.

For custom inserters in which more instructions are required to express the action than what the compiler emits as function call overhead, we should move these to a runtime library. Using library functions addresses the current issue of identical pseudo instruction expansions being repeated multiple times throughout code. Furthermore, given that these runtime functions will be often called the addresses of these functions may be kept in registers. The expected effect of this is a slight performance decrease given the call overhead but a significant reduction in code size.

5.4 Toolchain

By leveraging the LLVM compiler infrastructure, a number of different tools have been integrated with support for the Leros instruction set. Clang is used as the C frontend of choice, as well as being a compiler driver for the remainder of the toolchain. LLVMs **lld** linker has been modified with support for the Leros relocation symbols, and shall be used in place of system linkers like **gold**. Furthermore, LLVM provides a slew of binary utilities akin to the GNU Binutils collection of applications such as **llvm-dis**, the LLVM disassembler, **llvm-readelf**, the LLVM ELF reader with support for Leros relocation flags, **llvm-objcopy**, **llvm-objdump** and others.

For simpler simulators as well as executing Leros code on hardware the **llvm-objdump** tool may be used to extract the **.text** and **.data** segment of the

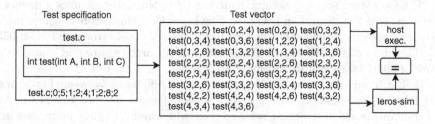

Fig. 2. The test suit compiles and executes the test specification (source file and input ranges) for all combinations of the input ranges on the host- and target systems, with host results serving as golden references.

compiled program, yielding a flat binary which may be executed from address 0X0, removing the need for a simulater reading ELF files or some hardware to interpret ELF files.

6   Evaluation

6.1   Automated Test Suite

While LLVM contains many fuzzing tools used for verifying that a backend can select all instructions of the LLVM IR, it cannot check the semantics of the produced code. We developed an automated test suite to check the semantics of the generated code. The test suite compiles the programs with a host compiler and with our compiler for Leros and executes them on the host and in the Leros simulator. The test compares then the outputs of the two runs.

The test suite is a Python script which given a test specification file may control the host and Leros compilers as seen in Fig. 2. Each line in the test specification file contains a reference to a test file as well as a range and step for all input arguments. The test source file is compiled for the host system as well as using the Leros compiler, whereafter the program is executed using the set of all combinations of arguments. All test programs return a value. The test suit compares the test return value of the host and simulator execution. The test suite has proved a valuable asset in identifying issues and verifying the correctness of instruction expansion and optimization passes. Furthermore, it functions as a regression test suite allowing for fewer errors to propagate to the source repositories.

6.2   Leros ISA Performance

To validate the compiler as well as generate indicators of the efficacy of the ISA, we use the CoreMark benchmark [4]. CoreMark is a synthetic benchmark designed for embedded systems which aims to be an industry standard benchmark for embedded systems, replacing the older DhryStone benchmark [20].

Figure 3 shows the Leros CoreMark score and ELF .text section size for various optimization levels.

The CoreMark scores generated from the Leros simulator assumes a memory access time of 1 cycle and an IPC of 1. The Leros CoreMark score is comparable to other low-end embedded devices, such as the STMicroelectronics STM32L053 [5]. This device is based on the Arm Cortex-M0+ architecture and manages a score of 39.91 at a clock frequency of 16 MHz.

In Fig. 3 we can see a significant code size difference between Leros and the RISC-V compilation. We can find several factors for this overhead. An accumulator-based instruction set as Leros will usually require more instructions to execute an action than a 3-operand instruction set (such as RISC-V). A single RISC instruction may need up to three instructions (load, op, store) in an accumulator machine.

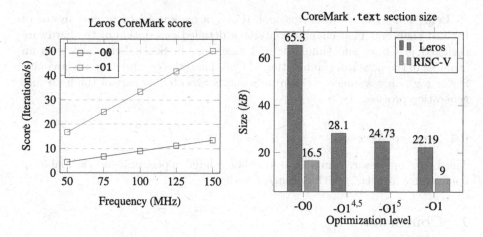

Fig. 3. Leros CoreMark results

The custom inserters used by Leros incurs an overhead through the requirement to emit many instructions, in place of what a single instruction in RISC-V can express, e.g., arbitrary shifts and sign-extended loads.

In general, code size will correlate to the efficacy of the instruction set. For CISC instruction sets code size will be smaller compared to the semantically equivalent code produced for a RISC instruction set. The same pattern shows for Leros in comparison to RISC-V, wherein Leros is arguably more RISC than RISC-V.

Comparing $-O1^{4,5}$ to $-O1^5$, the accumulator optimization passes manage a code size reduction of 12.75%. Comparing $-O1^5$ to $-O1$, the introduction of constant registers shows a further decrease of 10.82%. These are significant reductions in code size. We expect to decrease further when we implement more accumulator optimizations and build a runtime library for the custom inserters.

The successful compilation and execution of the CoreMark benchmark show that the Leros ISA is a valid C target.

6.3 Leros in Teaching

The simplicity of Leros makes it a good candidate for teaching an introductory class in computer architecture. The description of the Leros ISA fits in less than one page in this paper format, see Table 1. Therefore, one can quickly memorize the ISA. A simple exercise for a lab would be the implementation of a Leros software simulator and then explore the usage of the instructions from compiled C programs. In a larger project, for students with hardware design knowledge, implementing Leros in an FPGA would be a good project, as the infrastructure (C compiler, assembler, and simulator) are available.

---

[4] No accumulator optimizations
[5] No constant registers

Leros is used in a Chisel textbook [17] as a medium sized project in one of the last chapters. That chapter contains a detailed description of the hardware designed in Chisel and simulator and assembler in Scala. Leros serves as an example of the powerful combination of Chisel and the general purpose language Scala. E.g., an assembler, written in Scala, is executed as part of the hardware generation process.

6.4   Source Access

The Leros processor, compiler, and other related repositories are available in open source at https://github.com/leros-dev.

7   Conclusion

In this paper, we present a minimal instruction set architecture (ISA): the Leros accumulator machine. The idea behind this ISA is the same as the one for a RISC instruction set: provide just basic instructions and let the more complex functions be done by the compiler. Leros takes that step further and defines an even simpler ISA than a RISC processor, which shall still be a useful target for C.

That simple ISA leads to the simple implementation of simulators and hardware in an FPGA. We have ported the LLVM compiler to support Leros. Besides serving as a small embedded processor, the simplicity of Leros makes it also a good example for an introductory course in computer architecture. Leros also serves as a running example in a final chapter of a digital design textbook in Chisel.

References

1. Altera Corporation: Nios II processor reference handbook, version NII5V1-11.0, May 2011. http://www.altera.com/literature/lit-nio2.jsp
2. Bachrach, J., et al.: Chisel: constructing hardware in a scala embedded language. In: The 49th Annual Design Automation Conference (DAC 2012), pp. 1216–1225. ACM, San Francisco, June 2012
3. Danecek, J., Drapal, F., Pluhacek, A., Salcic, Z., Servit, M.: DOP-a simple processor for custom computing machines. J. Microcomput. Appl. 17(3), 239–253 (1994). https://doi.org/10.1006/jmca.1994.1015
4. EEMBC: Coremark - an EEMBC benchmark (2018). https://www.eembc.org/coremark/. Accessed 12 Dec 2018
5. EEMBC: Coremark benchmark score - stmicroelectronics stm32l053 (2018). https://www.eembc.org/benchmark/reports/benchreport.php?suite=CORE&bench_scores=1689. Accessed 12 Dec 2018
6. Gaisler, J.: A portable and fault-tolerant microprocessor based on the SPARC v8 architecture. In: DSN 2002, Proceedings of the 2002 International Conference on Dependable Systems and Networks, p. 409. IEEE Computer Society, Washington, DC, USA (2002). http://doi.ieeecomputersociety.org/10.1109/DSN.2002.1028926

7. Gwennap, L.: Esperanto makes out RISC-V. Technical report, The Linley Group, Microprocessor Report, December (2018)
8. Hempel, G., Hochberger, C.: A resource optimized processor core for FPGA based SoCs. In: Kubatova, H. (ed.) Proceedings of the 10th Euromicro Conference on Digital System Design (DSD 2007), pp. 51–58. IEEE (2007)
9. Hennessy, J.L.: VLSI processor architecture. IEEE Trans. Comput. **C−33**(12), 1221–1246 (1984). https://doi.org/10.1109/TC.1984.1676395
10. Lattner, C., Adve, V.S.: LLVM: a compilation framework for lifelong program analysis & transformation. In: International Symposium on Code Generation and Optimization (CGO 2004), pp. 75–88. IEEE Computer Society (2004)
11. Nakatsuka, H., Tanaka, Y., Chu, T.V., Takamaeda-Yamazaki, S., Kise, K.: Ultrasmall: the smallest MIPS soft processor. In: 2014 24th International Conference on Field Programmable Logic and Applications (FPL), pp. 1–4, September 2014. https://doi.org/10.1109/FPL.2014.6927387
12. Patterson, D.A.: Reduced instruction set computers. Commun. ACM **28**(1), 8–21 (1985). https://doi.org/10.1145/2465.214917
13. Patterson, D.A., Sequin, C.H.: RISC I: a reduced instruction set VLSI computer. In: Proceedings of the 8th Annual Symposium on Computer Architecture, ISCA 1981, pp. 443–457. IEEE Computer Society Press, Los Alamitos (1981)
14. Petersen, M.B.: A compiler backend and toolchain for the leros architecture. B.Sc. Engineering thesis, Technical University of Denmark (2019)
15. Robinson, J., Vafaee, S., Scobbie, J., Ritche, M., Rose, J.: The supersmall soft processor. In: 2010 VI Southern Programmable Logic Conference (SPL), pp. 3–8, March 2010. https://doi.org/10.1109/SPL.2010.5483016
16. Schoeberl, M.: Leros: a tiny microcontroller for FPGAs. In: Proceedings of the 21st International Conference on Field Programmable Logic and Applications (FPL 2011), pp. 10–14. IEEE Computer Society, Chania, September 2011
17. Schoeberl, M.: Digital Design with Chisel. TBD V 0.1 (2018). https://github.com/schoeberl/chisel-book
18. Schoeberl, M.: Lipsi: probably the smallest processor in the world. In: Berekovic, M., Buchty, R., Hamann, H., Koch, D., Pionteck, T. (eds.) ARCS 2018. LNCS, vol. 10793, pp. 18–30. Springer, Cham (2018). https://doi.org/10.1007/978-3-319-77610-1_2
19. Waterman, A.: Design of the RISC-V instruction set architecture. Ph.D. thesis, EECS Department, University of California, Berkeley, January 2016
20. Weicker, R.P.: Dhrystone: a synthetic systems programming benchmark. Commun. ACM (1984). https://doi.org/10.1145/358274.358283
21. Xilinx: PicoBlaze 8-bit embedded microcontroller user guide (2010)
22. Xilinx Inc.: MicroBlaze processor reference guide, version 9.0 (2008)

A Generic Functional Simulation
of Heterogeneous Systems

Sebastian Rachuj$^{(\boxtimes)}$, Marc Reichenbach, and Dietmar Fey

Friedrich-Alexander University Erlangen-Nürnberg (FAU), Erlangen, Germany
{sebastian.rachuj,marc.reichenbach,dietmar.fey}@fau.de

Abstract. Virtual Prototypes are often used for software development
before the actual hardware configuration of the finished product is available. Today's platforms often provide different kinds of processors forming a heterogeneous system. For example, ADAS applications require
dedicated realtime processors, parallel accelerators like graphics cards
and general purpose CPUs. This paper presents an approach for creating a simulation system for a heterogeneous system by using already
available processor models. The approach is intended to be flexible and to
support different kinds of models to fulfill the requirements of a heterogeneous system. Simulators should easily be exchangeable by simulators
with the same architecture support. It was possible to identify the SystemC connection of the considered general purpose CPU models as a
bottleneck for the simulation speed. The connection to the realtime core
suffers from a necessary connection via the network which is evaluated
in more detail. Combining the GPU emulator with the rest of the system reduces the simulation speed of the CUDA kernels in a negligible
manner.

1 Introduction

The degree of automation in vehicles rises every year. There are already many
different Advanced Driver Assistance Systems (ADAS) that help the driver and
are even capable of taking full control of the car [7,8]. Providing the necessary
performance and still allowing the safety-critical parts to get certified requires
heterogeneous systems. These kinds of systems are already established in the
realm of ADAS. They include general purpose processors, many core accelerators, and real-time processors. The Nvidia *Drive PX 2* is an example for a
development board of a system that contains AArch64 compatible ARM cores,
Nvidia Pascal GPUs, and an Infineon *AURIX* [16]. Audi proposes another platform called *zFAS* containing multi-core processors, reconfigurable hardware and
specialized DSPs [2].

During the software development of new ADAS systems, the final hardware
setup is usually not yet determined. Depending on the real-time requirements,
kind of algorithm and necessary computing power, different characteristics of the
final processing system have to be satisfied. For that reason, choosing the correct
components and writing the software should be done cooperatively. This can be

© Springer Nature Switzerland AG 2019
M. Schoeberl et al. (Eds.): ARCS 2019, LNCS 11479, pp. 128–141, 2019.
https://doi.org/10.1007/978-3-030-18656-2_10

achieved by using virtual prototypes of the hardware that offer different levels of abstraction [11]. While very abstract emulation reaches high execution speeds, it suffers in accuracy of predicting the nonfunctional properties like required energy and runtime behavior. On the other hand, a very detailed simulation of the heterogeneous system might reach nearly real world values for the predicted values but is too slow for greater workloads as they might occur in ADAS algorithms.

Since a heterogeneous system contains multiple different kinds of processors (e.g. CPUs, GPUs, specialized ASICs, etc.), a virtual platform is required that also provides models for all of these components including their interconnections. A lot of processor simulators are available separately but can be connected to a SystemC runtime, a framework for implementing discrete simulations [10]. This allows the usage of already available models within virtual prototypes of heterogeneous systems.

The goal of this paper is to show how to combine multiple unrelated simulation models with the help of their SystemC bindings to create a mere functional simulation of a heterogeneous system as it might be used in current or future vehicles. Especially models that can be extended by means of determining nonfunctional properties are taken into account. However, their ability is not used yet. Another aim is to stay generic in a way that allows the inclusion and interchangeability of arbitrary SystemC compatible simulation models into the heterogeneous virtual platform and to avoid changes within the taken models. Hence, the approach was implemented with gem5 [3], OVP from Imperas, and the ARM Fast Models to simulate general purpose CPUs, GPU Ocelot [6] and GPGPU-Sim [1] to provide support for a CUDA-compatible accelerator core, and the AURIX model from Infineon to offer a realtime processor. After presenting the connection approaches, the simulation runtime performance impacts are identified and evaluated.

2   Related Work

Heterogeneous simulators are no new invention. Coupling virtual prototypes of general purpose processors with GPU emulation tools has been done before. A prominent example is *gem5-gpu* which also uses GPGPU-Sim and connects it to gem5 [13]. Power et al. created patches that modify the source code of the two simulators to allow the integration. They also took care about modeling the memory system including cache coherency protocols. Software can be run on the simulated GPU by using a wrapper for the CUDA runtime library. This enables the usage of available CUDA code but requires the binary to be linked to the wrapper before it can be deployed on gem5-gpu. In this paper a similar approach is presented that implements the coupling in a more generic way by offering memory mapped input and output registers. This allows not only gem5 to be used as a simulator for the general purpose CPU but also OVP and the ARM Fast Models. Still, a small software wrapper for the applications is required to exploit the simulated GPU.

A direct integration of a GPU simulation into gem5 was done by AMD. They added an accelerator model that is compatible to the GCN version 3 instruction set architecture and achieved an average absolute error of 42% [9]. Major difference to *gem5-gpu* and this paper is the supported runtime environment. AMD's approach is available to all languages supported by their HCC compiler including OpenCL, C++AMP, etc. while only CUDA and OpenCL is supported by GPGPU-Sim.

Further works include FusionSim (formerly on www.fusionsim.ca but not available anymore) and Multi2Sim [17] which both don't support SystemC coupling out of the box. Thus, they were not in line for connecting the real-time processor since that would have meant changes within the provided models. To the authors' knowledge, there is no generic coupling of processor models and many core accelerator models to realtime processor simulators available yet.

3   Virtual Prototype for Heterogeneous Systems

The proposed virtual prototype for heterogeneous systems uses the TLM library of SystemC for loosely timed simulations as its core because most available simulation models allow coupling with it. Figure 1 shows an overview of the system that was created for this paper. An arrow denotes a possible connection between an initiator socket (beginning of the arrow) and a target socket (end of the arrow). The prototype includes components often found on today's embedded ADAS platforms like general purpose CPUs, parallel accelerators and a dependable realtime CPU which is certified according to ISO 26262. There are already simulator models for these processors available. However, the connection to the realtime CPU and the linkage to the CUDA accelerators was newly created for this paper. Additionally, the central router which is the only strictly required part of the prototype and the peripherals had to be supplied. Excluding the bus, all models can freely be replaced or omitted allowing a generic adaption to the needs of the developed application. However, connecting the native simulators comes with an impact that is analyzed in Sect. 4.

3.1   General Purpose CPU

Most heterogeneous systems still contain a powerful general purpose CPU. Since the target application is an embedded system as it might be deployed in an ADAS application, the choice was to use the AArch64 instruction set architecture as a reference. Hence, it is sensible to consider the ARM Fast Models as an ARM instruction set simulator which allow a high simulation speed. Like the other processor models, it offers SystemC bindings and can easily be connected to the bus system. For this paper it was used in combination with the support libraries provided by Synopsys. Open Virtual Platforms (OVP) which is offered by Imperas is similar to the ARM Fast Models but also support many different instruction set architectures. It has already been used in research and was extended by runtime and power estimation functionality [5,15].

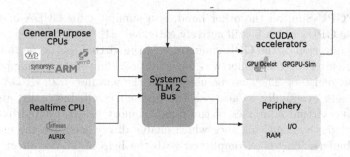

Fig. 1. The heterogeneous virtual prototype. General purpose CPUs can be provided by OVP, gem5 and the ARM Fast Models, the CUDA accelerator is implemented by GPU Ocelot or GPGPU-Sim. The real-time CPU is supplied by the Infineon AURIX model. Only the central bus is required.

Another simulation framework that was investigated for this paper is gem5 which supports different instruction set architectures and also offers multiple architecture backends. Available backends are the TimingSimple model implementing a single cycle CPU with the possibility to add a fine grained memory hierarchy. Additionally, the O3 model offers an out-of-order processor pipeline simulation which requires simulated caches to work correctly. In comparison to the previous two simulators, gem5 is much slower since it does not provide just-in-time compilation of the guest code. However, due to the detailed architecture description, a better runtime prediction can be achieved when using the detailed backends. The SystemC connection was established by Menard et al. who added a new slave type to gem5 allowing to interface with custom TLM targets [12]. Since the goal of this paper is to provide a heterogeneous virtual platform for functional emulation, the TimingSimple backend of gem5 was used. It allows adding a custom memory hierarchy but avoids an in-depth simulation of the microarchitecture. The generic approach presented in this paper allows all of these three general purpose CPU simulators to be chosen and integrated into the prototype. They can act as initiators of a TLM connection which makes it possible to directly connect them to the central bus system without further modifications.

3.2 GPU

Alongside the general purpose CPUs, an approach for emulating CUDA compatible accelerator cores was also accomplished. Parallel processors of this kind are very important for supporting computer vision applications like required for pedestrian or traffic sign recognition. There are two GPU simulators available that provide a CUDA runtime library to intercept the API calls and forward it to the backend. One of them is GPU Ocelot which implements a dynamic translation framework for translating PTX code into native machine code of the host CPU using LLVM [6]. To the authors' knowledge, it is not developed any more. GPGPU-Sim, on the other hand, is a simulator for CUDA or OpenCL compatible GPUs which is still actively extended[1] [1].

The connection of the GPU simulators to the virtual prototype that had to be implemented for this paper was done by providing memory mapped input and output registers. They can be used to set the parameters of CUDA runtime functions and eventually to also call the function itself. Internally, arguments representing virtual addresses of the main memory are translated into global pointers of the SystemC instance which enable direct access to the underlying memory buffers. This is accomplished with the help of TLM's direct memory interface (DMI) that is used to request pointers from the central bus (compare the arrow from the CUDA accelerator back into the bus in Fig. 1). Delivering a pointer also requires the RAM implementation to support the DMI. Finally, the processed parameters are forwarded to the global CUDA runtime function available in the simulator. Depending on the library, the simulation binary is linked to, the functions of GPU Ocelot or GPGPU-Sim are used. It is even possible to use the real graphics card of a system by taking the standard CUDA runtime library deployed by Nvidia. This allows a Hardware-In-The-Loop approach which might be helpful for evaluation tasks with a fixed GPU architecture.

Another approach to integrate a GPU simulator implementing a runtime API into processor simulators is realized by *gem5-gpu* and the GCN3 implementation of AMD which use the Syscall Emulation (SE) facilities of gem5 [9,13]. However, this requires strongly simulator dependent code which should be avoided for the generic virtual prototype. OVP also supports adding additional syscalls by using the intercept library that allows the definition of callbacks when the requested syscalls are executed. But this method is not portable between different simulators and contradicts to the stated aim of this paper to offer a generic virtual prototype with exchangeable processor cores. Hence, this mode was not considered for the proposed platform.

3.3   Realtime Processor

The automotive industry always had a requirement for reliable and deterministic processor cores. As a result, specialized CPUs were created that offer distinct features like lockstep execution and the possibility to get accurate runtime predictions. Examples include the ARM Cortex-R and the Infineon TriCore families offering ISO 26262 compliance. Latter can be simulated by a so-called c-model that offers simulation models of an AURIX System-On-Chip. It contains multiple TriCores, common accelerators and bus transceivers for protocols often found in vehicles like CAN and FlexRay.

Due to platform restrictions of the involved models and their supported operating systems, it was not possible to run the whole heterogeneous system on the same machine within the same SystemC runtime environment. For this reason, a method for distributed SystemC simulation had to be implemented for this paper to enable a combined simulation of the realtime processor with the rest of

---

[1] As of February 2019.

the proposed prototype. It is loosely based on SystemC-Link [18] in the way that it uses latencies within the modelled design to reduce the experienced latency of the host network. To realize this connection, two major challenges had to be managed. First, a synchronization mechanism of simulation time was required to avoid one simulation instance to run ahead of the other one. Second, a possibility for data exchange had to established.

Synchronization can be done by periodically sending messages containing the current simulation time stamp of one SystemC instance to the other one. At the beginning of the simulation or after the last received foreign time stamp message, a time equal to the predefined latency can be simulated. If during this time another time stamp message is received, the simulation will execute with its maximal speed and no waiting times have to be introduced. This corresponds to the best case part of Fig. 2 where both simulators run their full speed. However, if one SystemC instance is faster than the other one, it will find out that the received time stamps lack far behind. When the difference between the local and the remote time gets greater than a predetermined threshold, the faster simulation will be paused until the difference got smaller again. This allows the both parts to be run with a resulting simulation speed, in terms of simulated seconds, of the slower participating simulation. If no further foreign time stamp message was received during the latency time, the simulation also has to be paused until new information about the other part arrived. This can be seen as the worst case part of Fig. 2 where the execution of both SystemC instances cannot resume until the new message is received.

Data exchange is accomplished by directly sending messages containing a write or a read request. While the initiating process is waiting for a response, the simulation time can proceed until the simulated round-trip time is reached. If there is still enough local work available, the speed of the virtual prototype will not be diminished. In case, the read data is mandatory for continuing the local simulation, the SystemC instance has to be paused until the response was received. This is depicted in Fig. 2 at the right-hand side.

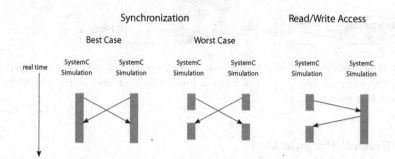

Fig. 2. Best and worst case of the presented approach for time synchronization and a data exchange example between two SystemC instances. Gray boxes are show when the simulation on the machine progresses. The arrows depict messages.

3.4   Peripherals

Components like memory are often provided by frameworks like OVP and gem5. However, accessing the data is only possible from within these simulators which makes usage from the outside difficult. As a consequence, the necessary memory and the input and output devices had to be implemented as reusable SystemC modules. This allows access of the GPU and realtime CPU models with their specific requirements like the need to directly access the data using pointers. After the creation of the virtual prototype, an evaluation of possible bottlenecks was done. The following Section gives an insight into the hindrances of the given approach.

4   Evaluation

All of the presented simulation models are already available as standalone versions. However, connecting them to a SystemC runtime causes speed impacts by making certain optimization methods like just-in-time compilation difficult or even impossible. Figure 3 shows the data paths that are analyzed in this Section. Section 4.1 covers the overhead introduced by using the SystemC connectors of the mentioned general purpose CPU simulators. This corresponds to data path (1) within the Figure. (2) belongs to the overhead of the newly written CUDA connector module and the data exchange between the CUDA runtime library and a test memory which is measured in Sect. 4.2. Data path (3) of the module created for the distributed SystemC simulation is evaluated in Sect. 4.3. Its messages are exchanged with another SystemC instance which can be located on the same computer or on another computer.

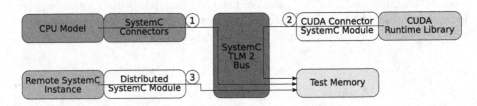

Fig. 3. The analyzed impacts. Each arrow represents one of the three analyzed data paths. The white, purple, and gray boxes are modules that were implemented for this paper. (Color figure online)

4.1   General Purpose CPU

To evaluate the impact of modeling the bus and memory system with the means of SystemC instead of the native possibilities of gem5 and OVP, two virtual prototype designs were created for each model. For gem5, the first design includes the *SimpleMemory* module as main memory. The second one uses the presented bus and memory system for heterogeneous simulation. Similar to this, the first design of OVP uses its native main memory while the second variant uses the presented memory layout. The ARM Fast Models use the SystemC Modeling Library, which is developed by Synopsys and compatible to TLM 2, to connect to the memory. Since there is no native way to provide a memory implementation, the SystemC overhead could not be analyzed in an isolated way.

As reference benchmarks CoreMark[2], an implementation of the Ackermann function, a Monte Carlo algorithm for calculating Pi, and the Sieve of Eratosthenes were used. These programs are expected to represent different kinds of real world problems that could be run on a general purpose processor. Table 1 shows the slowdown experienced for each benchmark from the native use of peripherals in comparison to the SystemC versions.

Table 1. The overhead introduced by coupling the simulators with SystemC. A value of one means no overhead while a value of two means that twice the time is required.

	CoreMark	Ackermann	Monte Carlo	Sieve
gem5	2.7	3.0	3.1	3.1
OVP	798	377	284	1291

Gem5's slowdown ranges from 2.7 to 3.1 which means that the time required to run one of the programs with SystemC is approximately three times as long as the native implementation. An investigation about the cause of this slowdown using the SystemC version showed that around 43.8% of the simulation time was spent in the runtime and peripheral code. Additionally, marshalling and unmarshalling packages from gem5 to and from TLM takes some time. This in combination with memory allocations and memory copy operations is accountable for another 19.3% of the time. Only 32.7% of the time is actually used for simulating the processor. The remaining 4.2% are spent in various C or C++ runtime functions.

OVP suffers a much larger slowdown due to lost optimization potentials when using the SystemC coupling for the main memory. The code morphing (OVP's name for Just-In-Time compilation) cannot deliver enough speedup any more because OVP cannot assume that the instructions stay the same. Thus, it has to fetch them every time anew always suffering a round-trip time to the SystemC memory implementation and back. In total, 85% of the simulation time is spent in the SystemC part of the virtual platform.

As shown in this Section, the simulation performance of the general purpose simulators is tremendously diminished when the SystemC binding is used. This is caused by the overhead introduced by converting the data requests from the internal representation to a TLM compatible one. Additionally, no features of TLM are used which would allow a speedup again. For example, the DMI can be

---

[2] https://www.eembc.org/coremark (accessed on 2018-12-04).

used to obtain a pointer into the memory which avoids a lot of overhead which was measured in this Section. Hence, some optimizations should be implemented to increase simulation speed.

4.2   GPU

The SystemC module for linking against GPU Ocelot and GPGPU-Sim does not introduce relevant overhead. This was evaluated by measuring the time of the CUDA simulations once without the SystemC connection as the libraries are intended to be used and once with a CPU model and the SystemC connection in place. To get only the impact on the accelerator code without interference from the required host code, the CUDA runtime library source code was modified to cumulate the time used within the CUDA runtime functions. Multiple different algorithms were run to even out software specific anomalies. The benchmarking applications include a vector addition (vecAdd) which was done for a vector containing one million elements, ten matrix multiplications (matrixMult) of 320 × 320 and 320 × 640 matrices, 128 iterations of the Black Scholes algorithm [4] with a problem size of 5000, and a sobel algorithm which is sometimes used as a component of an ADAS application, e.g. in lane detection algorithms [14]. From a set of at least ten measurements always the fastest results were used and the overhead determined. It is shown in Table 2 for all four algorithms. The Host Runtime corresponds to the time measured without any SystemC involvement while the simulation runtime (Sim. Runtime) corresponds to the time measured with the CUDA library connected to the virtual prototype.

Table 2. Overhead introduced by the SystemC connection module in comparison to native usage of the CUDA simulation libraries for different benchmark algorithms.

	vecAdd	matrixMult	Black Scholes	Sobel
Overhead	3.7%	0.5%	1.3%	2.0%
Host Runtime	6.6 s	587.6 s	13.3 s	23.4 s
Sim. Runtime	6.8 s	590.7 s	13.5 s	23.9 s

As can be seen from Table 2 the overhead is relatively small and stays below 4% for all investigated benchmarks. Especially long running algorithms like the matrix multiplication are hardly affected by the SystemC module. Short running ones like the vector addition display a bigger overhead which is still small in comparison to the overhead introduced to the general purpose CPU models for example. The source of the overhead lies within the SystemC connector that has to copy the operands from the virtual prototype to the CUDA runtime library and is responsible for performing the address translations. Since the remaining work which contains the work-intensive tasks like the kernel code is executed separately from the virtual prototype, the impact is kept low. Hence, the longer a kernel runs the less overhead is experienced.

4.3   Realtime Processor

Since the AURIX model uses a network connection to connect to the rest of the simulation, the impacts of this code on the system was investigated. To determine the overhead introduced by the proposed approach, synthetic benchmarks were created. They consist of a worker thread that has to be dispatched once each simulated nanosecond meaning a frequency of 1 GHz. It was run first without any networking code to obtain a reference runtime that can be compared. Each measurement was done at least ten times and the average of all runs was taken to minimize the impacts from the host operating system on the results.

At first, only the overhead introduced by the periodic synchronization events was determined. For this, different times between sending the synchronization messages were considered. A period interval of one nanosecond means that the worker thread and the synchronization thread are run alternately. A period interval of two nanoseconds means that for two runs of the worker thread body, one run of the synchronization thread occurs. Figure 4 shows the relative runtime the synchronization messages introduce on the worker thread. A value of zero represents no overhead while a value of one implies a runtime that takes twice as long as the local reference. The measurements were done with two different computers connected via an Ethernet switch and locally on one host by using the loopback device. Additionally, the standard deviation for the measurements was calculated.

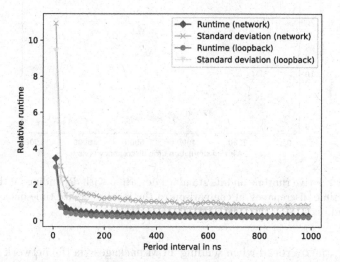

Fig. 4. The relative runtime and its standard deviation with the synchronization messages enabled in comparison to the local reference time once done over network and once using the local loopback device.

As can be seen, a period interval of 1000 ns reduces the overhead to 20–25%. This means that having an interval length that is 1000 times longer than the default clock rate of the system should reduce the impact from more than 300% in case every nanosecond a message is sent to only 20–25%. A similar shape can be seen in Fig. 5 which shows the overhead depending on the allowed simulation time discrepancy between the two SystemC instances. The period was fixed to 1000 ns to reduce the overhead introduced by the periodic sending operation. With an allowed discrepancy of about 8000 ns, the measurable overhead is nearly the same as with only sending the synchronization messages: A little bit above 25%. This should be the time of the best case presented in Fig. 2. It is noticeable that the major impact on the overhead introduced by the synchronization mechanism is depending on the selected period (1000 ns) since the overhead gets reduced at steps of 1000 ns of allowed discrepancy. This is due to the fact that each instance waits for the synchronization message while it is not sent yet. It can be concluded that the allowed discrepancy should be approximately eight times the period time to reduce the overhead.

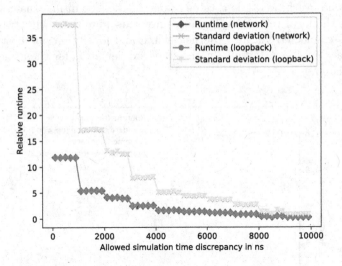

Fig. 5. The relative runtime and its standard deviation with depending on the allowed simulation time discrepancy in comparison to the local reference time once done over network and once using the local loopback device.

Finally, the overhead when sending TLM packages via the network was analysed. The period was fixed to 1000 ns and the discrepancy to 8000 ns. Since the overhead introduced is directly depending on the SystemC design and a generic result cannot be given, the indirect overhead of another TLM data exchange on the synthetic worker was measured. Thus, another thread was introduced that sends as much data as the latency allows. Figure 6 shows that the complete overhead via network is around 50% even for the smallest and greatest evaluated latencies. As a consequence, no real advice can be given regarding the best

suitable latency. The best case would be if the latencies between the remote
and the local simulator instances can be set equal to the latencies of the real
hardware. When using the loopback device, the overall overhead can be reduced
to approximately 30%. However, this cannot be done for the presented virtual
prototype due to the requirement of different host computers.

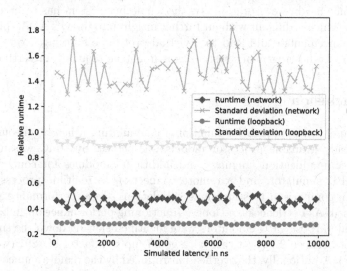

Fig. 6. The overhead and its standard deviation introduced by another thread sending
TLM messages using the presented network approach. This was once done via network
and once via the loopback device.

5   Future Work

From the analysis, the speed can be identified as a major issue in regard to the
usability of the system. While evaluation of small workloads on the heterogeneous system can be feasible, larger sensor processing algorithms (e.g. working
on camera pictures) will take too long for a functional run on the simulated platform. Hence, certain optimization steps from within the involved processor models should be implemented. One simple improvement can be the usage of DMI
as already stated above. Additionally, assertions should be given to allow the
complete exploitation of Just-In-Time techniques. For example, direct changes
of the underlying SystemC memory that may also contain instructions should be
forbidden. Callback functions may then be used to invalidate the memory (like
done for the DMI) if it is changed.

From the findings of this paper, other connection approaches without unconditional compatibility might also achieve higher speeds. Since the isolated way
of execution of the CUDA simulation achieves the best speed, it seems beneficial to also isolate the general purpose CPUs. However, this comes with its own

additional challenges like how to realize direct pointers into the host memory which are required by the GPU emulation.

Further improvements can be expected by using models or enabling features in the selected models that determine the runtime and power behavior of the real hardware when the simulated software is run on it. While this is supported by gem5 and GPGPU-Sim to a certain degree, there are still deviations from the reference hardware. Additionally, the whole bus system has to be modelled accurately which is difficult without further insight into today's ADAS platforms. These enhancements could lead to a virtual prototype allowing a very detailed evaluation of a heterogeneous system as it might be required for certification.

6   Conclusion

In this paper, an approach for functionally simulating a heterogeneous system using already available processor models was shown. SystemC was used as a common communication language and additional modules for connecting the CUDA GPU simulator, and a remote connection to realtime processors were created. In comparison to standalone simulation, severe performance penalties were noticed. As bottlenecks, no longer functioning performance optimizations of the general purpose CPU emulators were identified slowing down the simulation by a factor between 2.7 (best case with gem5) up to a factor of 1291 (worst case with OVP). Additionally, the overhead introduced by the remote connection used to communicate with the realtime processor was analyzed. It could be shown that it stays below 65% for the synthetic benchmarks. For the GPU binding, a very small simulation runtime impact could be observed that stayed below 4% for the observed benchmark applications.

References

1. Aaamodt, T., Boktor, A.: GPGPU-Sim 3.x: a performance simulator for many-core accelerator research. In: International Symposium on Computer Architecture (ISCA) (2012). http://www.gpgpu-sim.org/isca2012-tutorial
2. Anwar Taie, M.: New trends in automotive software design for the challenges of active safety and autonomous vehicles. In: FAST-zero'15: 3rd International Symposium on Future Active Safety Technology Toward Zero Traffic Accidents 2015 (2015)
3. Binkert, N., et al.: The gem5 simulator. SIGARCH Comput. Archit. News **39**(2), 1–7 (2011)
4. Black, F., Scholes, M.: The pricing of options and corporate liabilities. J. Polit. Econ. **81**(3), 637–654 (1973)
5. Delicia, G.S.P., Bruckschloegl, T., Figuli, P., Tradowsky, C., Almeida, G.M., Becker, J.: Bringing accuracy to open virtual platforms (OVP): a safari from high-level tools to low-level microarchitectures. In: IJCA Proceedings on International Conference on Innovations in Intelligent Instrumentation, Optimization and Electrical Sciences ICIIIOES, no. 10, pp. 22–27. Citeseer (2013)

6. Diamos, G.F., Kerr, A.R., Yalamanchili, S., Clark, N.: Ocelot: a dynamic optimization framework for bulk-synchronous applications in heterogeneous systems. In: Proceedings of the 19th International Conference on Parallel Architectures and Compilation Techniques, PACT 2010, pp. 353–364. ACM, New York (2010)

7. Dikmen, M., Burns, C.: Trust in autonomous vehicles: the case of tesla autopilot and summon. In: 2017 IEEE International Conference on Systems, Man, and Cybernetics (SMC), pp. 1093–1098, October 2017

8. Greenblatt, N.A.: Self-driving cars and the law. IEEE Spectr. 53(2), 46–51 (2016)

9. Gutierrez, A., et al.: Lost in abstraction: pitfalls of analyzing GPUs at the intermediate language level. In: 2018 IEEE International Symposium on High Performance Computer Architecture (HPCA), pp. 608–619, February 2018

10. IEEE Computer Society: IEEE Standard for Standard SystemC Language Reference Manual. IEEE Std 1666–2011 (2012)

11. Leupers, R., et al.: Virtual platforms: breaking new grounds. In: 2012 Design, Automation Test in Europe Conference Exhibition (DATE), pp. 685–690, March 2012

12. Menard, C., Jung, M., Castrillon, J., Wehn, N.: System simulation with gem5 and Systemc: the keystone for full interoperability. In: Proceedings of the IEEE International Conference on Embedded Computer Systems Architectures Modeling and Simulation (SAMOS). IEEE, July 2017

13. Power, J., Hestness, J., Orr, M.S., Hill, M.D., Wood, D.A.: gem5-gpu: a heterogeneous CPU-GPU simulator. IEEE Comput. Archit. Lett. 14(1), 34–36 (2015)

14. Reichenbach, M., Liebischer, L., Vaas, S., Fey, D.: Comparison of lane detection algorithms for ADAS using embedded hardware architectures. In: 2018 Conference on Design and Architectures for Signal and Image Processing (DASIP), pp. 48–53, October 2018

15. Schoenwetter, D., Ditter, A., Aizinger, V., Reuter, B., Fey, D.: Cache aware instruction accurate simulation of a 3-D coastal ocean model on low power hardware. In: 2016 6th International Conference on Simulation and Modeling Methodologies, Technologies and Applications (SIMULTECH), pp. 1–9, July 2016

16. Skende, A.: Introducing "parker": next-generation tegra system-on-chip. In: 2016 IEEE Hot Chips 28 Symposium (HCS), August 2016

17. Ubal, R., Jang, B., Mistry, P., Schaa, D., Kaeli, D.: Multi2Sim: a simulation framework for CPU-GPU computing. In: 2012 21st International Conference on Parallel Architectures and Compilation Techniques (PACT), pp. 335–344, September 2012

18. Weinstock, J.H., Leupers, R., Ascheid, G., Petras, D., Hoffmann, A.: Systemc-link: parallel systemc simulation using time-decoupled segments. In: 2016 Design, Automation Test in Europe Conference Exhibition (DATE), pp. 493–498, March 2016

Evaluating Dynamic Task Scheduling in a Task-Based Runtime System for Heterogeneous Architectures

Thomas Becker[1]([✉]), Wolfgang Karl[1], and Tobias Schüle[2]

[1] Karlsruhe Institute of Technology, Kaiserstr. 12, 76131 Karlsruhe, Germany
{thomas.becker,wolfgang.karl}@kit.edu
[2] Siemens AG, Corporate Technology, 81739 Munich, Germany
tobias.schuele@siemens.com

Abstract. Heterogeneous parallel architectures present many challenges to application developers. One of the most important ones is the decision where to execute a specific task. As today's systems are often dynamic in nature, this cannot be solved at design time. A solution is offered by runtime systems that employ dynamic scheduling algorithms. Still, the question which algorithm to use remains.

In this paper, we evaluate several dynamic scheduling algorithms on a real system using different benchmarks. To be able to use the algorithms on a real system, we integrate them into a task-based runtime system. The evaluation covers different heuristic classes: In immediate mode, tasks are scheduled in the order they arrive in the system, whereas in batch mode, all ready-to-execute tasks are considered during the scheduling decision. The results show that the Minimum Completion Time and the Min-Min heuristics achieve the overall best makespans. However, if additionally scheduling fairness has to be considered as optimization goal, the Sufferage algorithm seems to be the algorithm of choice.

Keywords: Dynamic task scheduling · Heterogeneous architectures

1 Motivation

Today's computer systems are highly parallel and possess additional accelerators. Such complex heterogeneous architectures present many challenges to application developers. One of the most important questions developers are faced with is on which processing unit the execution of tasks of an application is most efficient, which may refer to best performance, lowest energy consumption or any other optimization goal. As many systems are dynamic in nature, meaning that they do not always execute the same tasks, and tasks start at unknown points in time, e.g., triggered by signals or user interactions, a static partitioning at design time is not able to optimize the system for all scenarios. To solve this problem, dynamic runtime systems may be employed, which abstract from the underlying system. The application developer simply defines his or her compute

© Springer Nature Switzerland AG 2019
M. Schoeberl et al. (Eds.): ARCS 2019, LNCS 11479, pp. 142–155, 2019.
https://doi.org/10.1007/978-3-030-18656-2_11

kernels representing specific functionality and is then allowed to either provide implementation variants himself or use implementation variants provided by e.g. a library. As dynamic runtime systems also take control of the execution, they can decide at runtime which implementation processing unit pair to use. To make such decisions, dynamic scheduling algorithms are needed. In the literature, a variety of different dynamic algorithms are described. Considering the fact that modern systems are used in a wide range of different scenarios and fields of application, the question remains which algorithm should be used in which scenario and which field of application. Therefore, the goal of this work is to study dynamic scheduling algorithms in several scenarios designed for heterogeneous parallel systems with an additional focus on characteristics of embedded systems, and thereby providing usage guidelines.

Hence, in this work, we evaluate selected dynamic scheduling algorithms in real-world scenarios. We utilize the Embedded Multicore Building Blocks (EMB²), an open source runtime system and library developed by Siemens, which has been specifically designed for embedded applications, to operate the algorithms on a real system. In particular, we make the following contributions:

- We select six dynamic scheduling heuristics that we think are appropriate for the considered field of application.
- We extend the existing scheduling approach in EMB² with more sophisticated ones for heterogeneous systems.
- We evaluate these algorithms on a real system using a GPU as accelerator and investigate their behavior in terms of different metrics.
- We give guidelines which algorithms to choose.

The remainder of this paper is structured as follows: In Sect. 2, we briefly introduce the fundamentals of our work. The scheduling algorithms, EMB² and the extensions to EMB² are presented in Sect. 3. Section 4 describes the experimental setup and presents the results. Finally, we discuss related work (Sect. 5) and conclude with directions for future work (Sect. 6).

2   Fundamentals

2.1   Problem Statement and Task Scheduling

In the basic scheduling problem, a set of n tasks $T := \{t_1, \ldots, t_n\}$ has to be assigned to a set of m resources $P := \{p_1, \ldots, p_m\}$. Next to mapping a task t_i to a resource p_j, scheduling also includes the assignment of an ordering and time slices.

Scheduling problems are generally considered to be NP-hard [10]. As there is no algorithm that can solve all scheduling problems efficiently, there exist many different heuristics. These can be classified into static and dynamic algorithms. The main difference is that static algorithms make all decisions before a single task is executed, whereas dynamic algorithms schedule tasks at runtime. Hence, static algorithms have to know all relevant task information beforehand, while dynamic ones do not need full information and are able to adapt their behavior.

2.2   Optimality Criterion

The standard optimization criterion is the makespan, which is the time an application or a set of tasks spends in a system from start to finish. If several applications are scheduled simultaneously, only considering the makespan can lead to stalling one application in favor of the others. Therefore, it is sensible to also evaluate the algorithms regarding fairness.

A criterion that better reflects scheduling decisions for single tasks is the flow time F_i, which is defined as $F_i = C_i - r_i$, where C_i is the completion time and r_i the release time of a task t_i. Generally speaking, F_i is the time t_i spends within the system. So, the flow time is able to reflect how long a task is in the system before being executed and combines this with its execution time. As the two objectives efficiency and fairness are fundamentally at odds, Bansal et al. [2] suggest minimizing the l_p-norm of the flow time $\|F\|_{l_p}$ for small values of p. $\|F\|_{l_p}$ is defined as follows:

$$\|F\|_{l_p} = \left(\sum_i F_i^p \right)^{\frac{1}{p}}, \tag{1}$$

where p is a value chosen by the user.

3   Dynamic Scheduling Algorithms

This section presents the algorithms and the extensions to EMB^2. We selected these algorithms on the basis of their runtime overhead, scheduling decisions have to be made as fast as possible in dynamic systems, their implementation complexity, and their ability to work with limited knowledge about the set of tasks to be executed. These heuristics can be classified into immediate and batch mode. Immediate mode considers tasks in a fixed order, only moving on to the next task after making a scheduling decision. In contrast, batch mode considers tasks out-of-order and so delays task scheduling decisions as long as possible, thereby increasing the pool of potential tasks to choose from.

3.1   Immediate Mode Heuristics

Opportunistic Load Balancing (OLB). [8] estimates the completion time of the irrevocably scheduled tasks as a measure of load on a processing unit p_j. OLB then assigns a task t_i to the processing unit p_j that has the earliest completion time for its already assigned tasks.

Minimum Execution Time (MET). [7] maps a task t_i to the processing unit p_j that minimizes its execution time. The heuristic considers a task in isolation, not taking the actual load of the processing units in account when making a scheduling decision. Thus, this heuristic can easily lead to load imbalances if for all or most of the tasks a processing unit dominates.

Minimum Completion Time (MCT). [1] combines the execution time of a task t_i with the estimated completion time of the already assigned tasks of a processing unit p_j. In total, MCT predicts the completion time of a task t_i and assigns t_i to the processing unit p_j that minimizes the completion time of t_i.

3.2 Batch Mode Heuristics

Min-Min. [11] extends the idea of MCT by considering the complete set of currently ready-to-execute tasks. The heuristic then assigns the task t_i that has the earliest completion time to the processing unit p_j that minimizes the completion time of t_i. In general, the core idea is to schedule shorter tasks first to encumber the system for as short a time as possible. This can lead to starvation of larger tasks if steadily new shorter tasks arrive in the system.

Max-Min. [14] is a variant of Min-Min that is based on the observation that Min-Min often leads to large tasks getting postponed to the end of an execution cycle, needlessly increasing the total makespan because the remaining tasks are too coarse-granular to partition equally. So, Max-Min schedules the tasks with the latest minimum completion time first, leaving small tasks to pad out any load imbalance in the end. However, this can lead to starvation of small tasks if steadily new longer tasks arrive.

Sufferage. [14] ranks all ready-to-execute tasks according to their urgency based on how much time the task stands to lose if it does not get mapped to its preferred resource. The ranking is given by the difference between the task's minimum completion time and the minimum completion time the task would achieve if the fastest processing unit for this task would not be available. Tasks that do not have a clear preference for a processing unit are prone to starvation.

3.3 Implementation

We integrated the algorithms into EMB², a C/C++ library and runtime system for parallel programming of embedded systems.[1] EMB² builds on MTAPI [9], a task model that allows several implementation variants for a user-defined task. A developer defines a specific functionality, e.g., a matrix multiplication, and is then allowed to provide implementations for this task. MTAPI allows a developer to start tasks and to synchronize on their completion, where the actual execution is controlled by the runtime system. Thereby, the user has to guarantee that only tasks that have their dependencies fulfilled are started. Tasks are executed concurrently to other tasks that have been started and it is allowed to start new tasks within a task. The scheduling implementation of the current EMB² version distributes the task instances between heterogeneous processing units based on the number of already scheduled instances of the same task. For homogeneous

---

[1] https://embb.io/.

multicore CPUs, an additional work stealing scheduler [3,15] is used. As of yet, necessary data transfers for the accelerators are not considered separately. EMB^2 is designed and implemented in a modular fashion that allows developers to add further scheduling policies. However, a few extensions were necessary.

We added a general abstraction for processing units and grouped identical units in classes to allow a uniform treatment. Every unit is implemented using an OS-level worker thread. Workers corresponding to CPU cores are pinned to their respective cores but are assigned a lower priority than device workers.

Scheduling algorithms need task execution times to make sophisticated decisions. These can either be given by the user, an analysis step or predicted at runtime. In this work, we focus on dynamic systems which means static analyses are not possible. Therefore, we extended EMB^2 by a monitoring component that measures task execution times and stores them within a history data base with the problem size as key similar to the mechanism used in [13]. As data transfers are not yet considered explicitly in EMB^2, the execution times on accelerators include necessary data transfers. The stored data is then used to predict execution times of upcoming tasks to improve scheduling decisions. If there is already data stored for a particular task's implementation version and problem size, the data can be used directly. If there is data for a task's implementation version but with different problem sizes, interpolation is used to predict the execution time. If there is no data available at all, the runtime system executes a profiling run of this implementation version.

4   Experiments

To evaluate the scheduling heuristics, we considered a video-processing application using EMB^2's dataflow component, three benchmarks of the Rodinia Benchmark Suite [5], RabbitCT [19], and a benchmark with independent heterogeneous jobs. We chose them as they provide different characteristics, have sufficient problem sizes and thereby running time and possess an easily to parallelize kernel. We included benchmarks where the CPU outperforms the GPU, a benchmark, where the GPU strongly outperforms the CPU, and a benchmark where the difference between the GPU and CPU implementation is not as big. The independent heterogeneous jobs benchmark resembles dynamic systems as the task instances are started sporadically thereby adding a random component to the starting point of a task instance.

All experiments were executed ten times. For the single application benchmarks, we focus on the makespan because a user expects this to be optimized for a single application. We additionally evaluate the average flow time and the l_p-norm (Sect. 2.2) for $p = 3$ for the independent heterogeneous job benchmark. The following figures contain the average, the minimum and the maximum makespan of 10 evaluation runs as errorbars. We omitted the errorbars in the figure for the independent heterogeneous job benchmark to make it more readable.

4.1   Experimental Setup

The experiments were performed on a server with two Intel Xeon E5-2650 v4 CPUs a 12 cores each, an NVIDIA Tesla K80, and 128 GB a 2400 MHz DDR4 SDRAM DIMM (PC4-19200). The software environment includes Ubuntu 16.04.5, the Linux 4.4.0-138-generic kernel, glibc 2.23, and the nvidia-387 driver. EMB[2] was compiled with the GCC 5.4.0 compiler at optimization level-O3. The scheduling algorithms presented in Sect. 3 operate in the so-called pull mode in our experiments. In pull mode, the scheduler gets triggered iff at least one processing unit is idle. We chose this mode because it allows the scheduler to collect a set of tasks, which is needed to benefit from the batch mode heuristics.

4.2   Heterogeneous Video-Processing Application

The dataflow component of EMB[2] takes an arbitrary task graph describing the computation of a single data item, and parallelizes the computations over contiguous chunks of a data stream. They get submitted by a window sliding scheduler to the actual scheduler through reduction to fork-join parallelism while maintaining sequential execution of tasks. So, only tasks that are ready to execute are submitted to the actual scheduler. The application consists of a video-processing pipeline, performing the following steps:

1. Read and decode the next frame from an H.264-encoded video file. The corresponding process in the dataflow network is serial.
2. Convert the frame from the codec-native color space to RGB. This process is again serial because the conversion accesses a shared libswscale context. libswscale is a library that performs highly optimized image scaling and colorspace and pixel format conversion operations.
3. Apply the image transformation in two steps:
   (a) Perform a 3×3 box blur.
   (b) Cartoonify by performing a Sobel operator with a threshold selecting black pixels for edge regions and discretized RGB values for the interior. The Sobel operator consists of two convolutions with different 3×3 kernels followed by the computation of an Euclidean norm.
4. Convert the frame back from RGB to the codec-native color space.

The two image transformation operations have a CPU and GPU implementation. The cartoonify kernel has an average execution time of 165.97 ms on the CPU and 3.1 ms on the GPU for the *kodim23.png* test image by the Eastman Kodak Company. The box blur operation runs on average for 72.8 ms on the CPU and for 3.4 ms on the GPU. As input, we used a 30 s long test video encoded in 854:480 resolution with 30 fps at a bitrate of 2108 kb/s. The results are shown in Fig. 1. The best results are achieved by MCT, Min-Min, Max-Min, and Sufferage with MCT having the best results with an average of 10.3 s. OLB obtains a significantly worse result than the other algorithms with an average of 29.63 s because OLB does not consider task execution times, but rather just takes the next free processing unit, which in our implementation always starts with the CPU cores, and thereby only uses the, in this case slower, CPU.

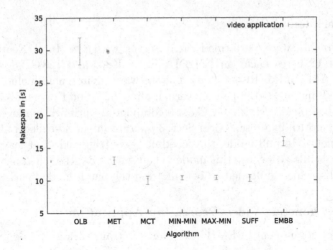

Fig. 1. Makespans for 10 runs of the video application benchmark

4.3   Rodinia Benchmark Suite

Hotspot3D iteratively computes the heat distribution of a 3d chip represented by a grid. In every iteration, a new temperature value depending on the last value, the surrounding values, and a power value is computed for each element. We chose this computation as kernel function for a parallelization with EMB^2 and parallelized it over the z-axis. The CPU implementation then further splits its task into smaller CPU specific subtasks. This is done manually and statically by the programmer to use the underlying parallelism of the multicore CPU and still have a single original CPU task that handles the same workload as the GPU task. For the evaluation, we used a $512 \times 512 \times 8$ grid with the start values for temperature and power included in the benchmark, and 1000 iterations. The average runtime on the CPU is 5.03 ms and 7.36 ms on the GPU.

Figure 2 shows the results of the Hotspot3D benchmark. Min-Min, OLB, MCT, Max-Min, and Sufferage all have an average of around 17 s with Min-Min having the lowest average of 16.94 ms by a very small margin compared to the group's highest average of 17.53 s by Max-Min. In this case, OLB benefits from the fact that it first distributes the load to the CPU. MET obtained the worst result because it does not consider the load of the processing units and just schedules all tasks to the fastest processing unit and so to the same CPU core.

Particlefilter is the implementation of a particle filter, a statistical estimator of the locations of target objects given noisy measurements, included in Rodinia. Profiling showed that *findIndex()* is the best candidate for a parallelization. *findIndex()* computes the first index in the cumulative distribution function array with a value greater than or equal to a given value. As *findIndex()* is called for every particle, we parallelized the computation by dividing the particles into work groups. The CPU implementation again further divides those groups into subtasks. We used the standard parameters 128 for both matrix dimensions, 100 for the number of frames, and 50000 for the number of particles for the evaluation. The average task runtime on the CPU is 17.8 ms and 6.5 ms on the GPU. The results of the Particlefilter benchmark can be seen in Fig. 2. Here, the EMB^2 upstream algorithm got the best result with an average of 15.93 s where all other algorithms except OLB have an average of around 18 s. These results indicate that a distribution of tasks between the CPU and the GPU leads to the best result.

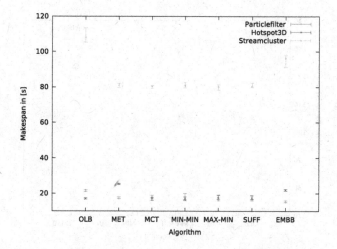

Fig. 2. Makespans for 10 runs of the Rodinia benchmarks

Streamcluster is taken from the PARSEC benchmark suite and solves the online clustering problem. For a stream of input data points, the algorithm finds a user given number of clusters. The main kernel of the algorithm *pgain()* computes if opening a new cluster reduces the total cost. In every iteration *pgain()* is called for each data point, so we parallelized the function by dividing the points into work groups. Again, the CPU implementation then further divides the work group into smaller chunks. We do not provide execution times as Streamcluster iteratively reduces the number of points considered, thereby varying in execution time. The results for the Streamcluster benchmark, see Fig. 2, show that all algorithms except OLB and the EMB^2 upstream version achieved an average makespan of around 80 s with Max-Min getting the best average by a small margin with 80.28 s compared to the second best average of 80.39 s by MCT and the group's worst average of 81.07 s by MET.

4.4   RabbitCT

RabbitCT is a 3D cone beam reconstruction benchmark framework that focuses on the backprojection step. It was created to fairly compare different backprojection algorithms. In backprojection, each voxel is projected onto the projection data, then the data is interpolated and finally, the voxel value is updated. As this means that in every iteration the algorithm iterates over a 3D array, we parallelized the algorithm with EMB^2 by partitioning the volume by the z-axis. The CPU implementation then further partitions these chunks. We measured an average task runtime of 45.9 ms for the CPU and 97.7 ms for the GPU. RabbitCT provides an input data set which we used with a problem size of 512.

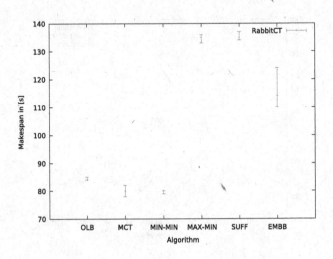

Fig. 3. Makespans for 10 runs of the RabbitCT benchmark

Figure 3 contains the results for the RabbitCT benchmark. We excluded MET as it was significantly worse then the other algorithms with an average of 400.17 s, thereby hiding details in the figure. MCT and Min-Min achieved the best results with MCT achieving an average makespan of 80.56 s and Min-Min achieving a slightly better average makespan of 80 s.

4.5 Independent Heterogeneous Jobs

Additionally, we evaluated the algorithms in a scenario with independent heterogeneous jobs. We chose three video-processing tasks that have both an OpenCL and a CPU implementation:

- J_1 (**Mean**): A 3×3 box blur.
- J_2 (**Cartoonify**): The cartoonify operation introduced in Sect. 4.2.
- J_3 (**Black-and-White**): A simple filter which replaces (R,G,B) values with their greyscale version ($\frac{R+G+B}{3}$, $\frac{R+G+B}{3}$, $\frac{R+G+B}{3}$).

All operations were applied to the *kodim23.png* test image. The three operations execute for 72.8 ms, 165.97 ms, and 11.4 ms on the CPU and 3.4 ms, 3.1 ms, and 3.1 ms on the GPU. We used a sporadic profile to create task instances of these three jobs. New task instances were released with a minimum interarrival time of $\frac{1}{k}$ *secs*, where k is the parameter to control the load, plus a random delay drawn from an exponential distribution with parameter $\lambda = k$. By varying k, we can generate a range of different loads. The evaluation workload consists of 3000 tasks corresponding in equal proportions to instances of all three jobs. We conducted the experiment from $k = 500$ to 2000 with increments of 500. For this experiment, we measured the average makespan, the average flowtime and the l_3-norm. The EMB^2 upstream algorithm was excluded from the flowtime and l_3-norm measurements. In contrast to the other algorithms, which only schedule a new task iff at least one processing unit is idle, the EMB^2 upstream version always schedules a task as soon as it arrives in the system. Thereby, the time a task spends in the system is not really comparable to the other algorithms. The makespan results are shown in Fig. 4.

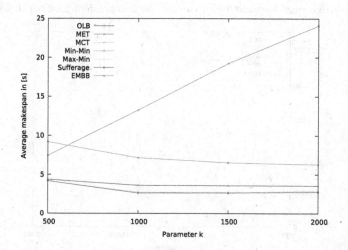

Fig. 4. Average makespan for 10 runs of the independent jobs benchmark

Here, Max-Min, Min-Min, MCT, and Sufferage nearly got the same results with Max-Min achieving the best results. Clearly, the worst results were obtained by MET. The figure of the average flowtimes (see Fig. 5) also show the best results for Max-Min, Min-Min, MCT, and Sufferage. However, for greater values of k there is a distinction between Max-Min and Sufferage, and Min-Min and MCT with the later two obtaining a worse average flowtime. Figure 6 shows the results for the l_3-norm. We excluded MET from the figure as its results were by far worse and so important details would get lost. Again, Sufferage and Max-Min got the best results. but this time for larger values of k Sufferage achieved better results.

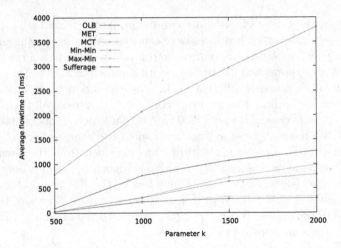

Fig. 5. Average flowtime for 10 runs of the independent jobs benchmark

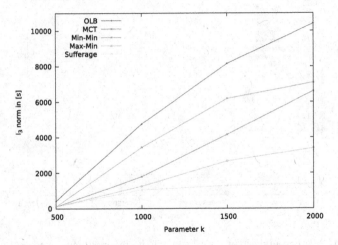

Fig. 6. Average l_3-norm for 10 runs of the independent jobs benchmark

5   Related Work

Task scheduling is a well-known research field which has lead to many heuristics for dynamic task scheduling. These can generally be classified into list scheduling heuristics [14,20], clustering heuristics [16], immediate mode heuristics [1,8,15], duplication scheduling heuristics [12] and guided-random-search-based algorithms including genetic algorithms [17,18], and swarm intelligence algorithms [6]. List scheduling heuristics sort all ready-to-execute tasks according to a priority criterion and then map the tasks to processing units in that order. In contrast, immediate mode heuristics assign a task to a processing unit as soon as it arrives. Clustering heuristics assume that communication costs are a main factor of the total makespan. They try to minimize communication by clustering tasks and executing a cluster on a single processing unit. The goal of duplication scheduling is to reduce communication costs by executing key tasks on more than one processor, thereby avoiding data transfers. Contrary to the heuristic-based algorithms, guided-random-search-based algorithms try to efficiently traverse the search space by sampling a large number of candidates while also allowing temporary degradation of the solution quality. These algorithms are often only evaluated in simulations making it hard to judge their real world applicability. There also exist extensive studies that evaluate and compare different scheduling algorithms. Kim et al. [14] evaluate dynamic scheduling heuristics with independent tasks and task priorities. Braun et al. [4] compare eleven static scheduling heuristics that could also be used as batch-mode heuristics in a dynamic system. However, the heuristics are again evaluated in simulations only.

6 Conclusion and Future Work

In this work, we evaluated six heuristics. We integrated immediate and batch mode heuristics to see if it is possible to leverage sophisticated scheduling decisions in real-world scenarios. To evaluate the algorithms on a real system, we integrated them into EMB^2. The added heuristics and the EMB^2 upstream version were evaluated with six different benchmarks. In particular, we used a video-processing application, Particlefilter, Streamcluster and Hotspot3D of Rodinia, RabbitCT, and a benchmark consisting of three image filter jobs. As evaluation metric, we used the makespan for the application benchmarks. Additionally, we used the average flowtime and the l_3-norm for the independent jobs to measure fairness.

In five of six makespan-focused benchmarks, MCT and Min-Min achieved the lowest makespan or are within a 5% margin of the best makespan. The exception is Particlefilter where the best result is obtained by the EMB^2 upstream algorithm with a speed up of 11.6% to Sufferage. MCT and Min-Min still lie within a 17.9% and a 13.9% margin or a total difference of around 2.5 s. Max-Min and Sufferage also achieve the best or close to the best results in five out of six benchmarks but have a bigger outlier with the RabbitCT benchmark. Here, Max-Min and Sufferage have an makespan increase of around 70% or around 55 s. MET, OLB and the EMB^2 upstream algorithm constantly have worse results than the aforementioned ones. Considering the flowtime and the l_3-norm, Sufferage achieves the best results for the larger k values and is close to the best result for the smaller values. MCT and Min-Min both have increasingly worse results with larger values of k for both the average flowtime and the l_3-norm. In the worst case, the result increases by over 500%. So, in summary iff the focus only lies on the makespan, MCT or Min-Min seem to be the best choice with MCT being the significantly simpler algorithm. If fairness is an additional consideration, Sufferage seems to be the best choice. As future work, we want to consider task priorities, thus enabling soft real-time. The aforementioned starvation issues can also be improved by adding task priorities.

References

1. Armstrong, R., Hensgen, D., Kidd, T.: The relative performance of various mapping algorithms is independent of sizable variances in run-time predictions. In: Proceedings of 1998 Seventh Heterogeneous Computing Workshop, (HCW 98), pp. 79–87, March 1998. https://doi.org/10.1109/HCW.1998.666547
2. Bansal, N., Pruhs, K.: Server scheduling in the Lp norm: a rising tide lifts all boat. In: Proceedings of the Thirty-fifth Annual ACM Symposium on Theory of Computing, STOC 2003, pp. 242–250. ACM, New York (2003). https://doi.org/10.1145/780542.780580
3. Blumofe, R.D., Leiserson, C.E.: Scheduling multithreaded computations by work stealing. J. ACM 46(5), 720–748 (1999)
4. Braun, T.D., et al.: A comparison of eleven static heuristics for mapping a class of independent tasks onto heterogeneous distributed computing systems. J. Parallel Distrib. Comput. 61(6), 810–837 (2001). https://doi.org/10.1006/jpdc.2000.1714
5. Che, S., et al.: Rodinia: a benchmark suite for heterogeneous computing. In: Proceedings of the 2009 IEEE International Symposium on Workload Characterization (IISWC), IISWC 2009, pp. 44–54. IEEE Computer Society, Washington DC, (2009). https://doi.org/10.1109/IISWC.2009.5306797
6. Elhady, G.F., Tawfeek, M.A.: A comparative study into swarm intelligence algorithms for dynamic tasks scheduling in cloud computing. In: 2015 IEEE Seventh International Conference on Intelligent Computing and Information Systems (ICICIS), pp. 362–369, December 2015. https://doi.org/10.1109/IntelCIS.2015.7397246
7. Freund, R.F., et al.: Scheduling resources in multi-user, heterogeneous, computing environments with SmartNet. In: Proceedings of 1998 Seventh Heterogeneous Computing Workshop, HCW 1998, pp. 184–199, March 1998. https://doi.org/10.1109/HCW.1998.666558
8. Freund, R.F., Siegel, H.J.: Guest editor's introduction: heterogeneous processing. Computer 26(6), 13–17 (1993). http://dl.acm.org/citation.cfm?id=618981.619916
9. Gleim, U., Levy, M.: MTAPI: parallel programming for embedded multicore systems (2013). http://multicore-association.org/pdf/MTAPI_Overview_2013.pdf
10. Graham, R., Lawler, E., Lenstra, J., Kan, A.: Optimization and approximation in deterministic sequencing and scheduling: a survey. In: Hammer, P., Johnson, E., Korte, B. (eds.) Discrete Optimization II, Annals of Discrete Mathematics, vol. 5, pp. 287–326. Elsevier, Amsterdam (1979)
11. Ibarra, O.H., Kim, C.E.: Heuristic algorithms for scheduling independent tasks on nonidentical processors. J. ACM 24(2), 280–289 (1977). https://doi.org/10.1145/322003.322011
12. Josphin, A.M., Amalarathinam, D.I.G.: DyDupSA - dynamic task duplication based scheduling algorithm for multiprocessor system. In: 2017 World Congress on Computing and Communication Technologies (WCCCT), pp. 271–276, February 2017. https://doi.org/10.1109/WCCCT.2016.72
13. Kicherer, M., Buchty, R., Karl, W.: Cost-aware function migration in heterogeneous systems. In: Proceedings of the 6th International Conference on High Performance and Embedded Architectures and Compilers, HiPEAC 2011, pp. 137–145. ACM, New York (2011). https://doi.org/10.1145/1944862.1944883

14. Kim, J.K., Shivle, S., Siegel, H.J., Maciejewski, A.A., Braun, T.D., Schneider, M., Tideman, S., Chitta, R., Dilmaghani, R.B., Joshi, R., Kaul, A., Sharma, A., Sripada, S., Vangari, P., Yellampalli, S.S.: Dynamically mapping tasks with priorities and multiple deadlines in a heterogeneous environment. J. Parallel Distrib. Comput. **67**(2), 154–169 (2007). https://doi.org/10.1016/j.jpdc.2006.06.005. http://www.sciencedirect.com/science/article/pii/S0743731506001444

15. Mattheis, S., Schuele, T., Raabe, A., Henties, T., Gleim, U.: Work stealing strategies for parallel stream processing in soft real-time systems. In: Herkersdorf, A., Römer, K., Brinkschulte, U. (eds.) ARCS 2012. LNCS, vol. 7179, pp. 172–183. Springer, Heidelberg (2012). https://doi.org/10.1007/978-3-642-28293-5_15

16. Mishra, P.K., Mishra, A., Mishra, K.S., Tripathi, A.K.: Benchmarking the clustering algorithms for multiprocessor environments using dynamic priority of modules. Appl. Math. Model. **36**(12), 6243–6263 (2012). https://doi.org/10.1016/j.apm.2012.02.011.   http://www.sciencedirect.com/science/article/pii/S0307904X12000935

17. Nayak, S.K., Padhy, S.K., Panigrahi, S.P.: A novel algorithm for dynamic task scheduling. Future Gener. Comput. Syst. **28**(5), 709–717 (2012). https://doi.org/10.1016/j.future.2011.12.001

18. Page, A.J., Naughton, T.J.: Dynamic task scheduling using genetic algorithms for heterogeneous distributed computing. In: 19th IEEE International Parallel and Distributed Processing Symposium, pp. 189a–189a, April 2005. https://doi.org/10.1109/IPDPS.2005.184

19. Rohkohl, C., Keck, B., Hofmann, H., Hornegger, J.: RabbitCT— an open platform for benchmarking 3D cone-beam reconstruction algorithms. Med. Phys. **36**(9), 3940–3944 (2009). https://doi.org/10.1118/1.3180956. http://www5.informatik.uni-erlangen.de/Forschung/Publikationen/2009/Rohkohl09-TNR.pdf

20. Topcuouglu, H., Hariri, S., Wu, M.Y.: Performance-effective and low-complexity task scheduling for heterogeneous computing. IEEE Trans. Parallel Distrib. Syst. **13**(3), 260–274 (2002). https://doi.org/10.1109/71.993206

Dynamic Scheduling of Pipelined Functional Units in Coarse-Grained Reconfigurable Array Elements

Philipp S. Käsgen[1(✉)], Markus Weinhardt[1], and Christian Hochberger[2]

[1] Osnabrück University of Applied Sciences, Osnabrück, Germany
{p.kaesgen,m.weinhardt}@hs-osnabrueck.de
[2] Technische Universität Darmstadt, Darmstadt, Germany
hochberger@rs.tu-darmstadt.de

Abstract. *Coarse-Grained Reconfigurable Arrays (CGRAs)* promise higher computing power and better energy efficiency than *field programmable gate arrays (FPGAs)*. Thus, they are attractive not only for embedded applications, but also for *high-performance computing (HPC)*. Yet, in such applications floating point (FP) operations are the main workload. Most of the previous research on CGRAs considered only operations on integral data types, which can be executed in one clock cycle. In contrast, FP operations take multiple clock cycles and different operations have different latencies. In this contribution, we present a new mechanism that resolves data and structural hazards in *processing elements (PEs)* that feature in-order issue, but out-of-order completion of operations. We show that our mechanism is more area efficient than scoreboarding in most of the relevant cases. In addition, our mechanism is universal, i.e. not only restricted to PEs in CGRAs, but also applicable to microprocessors.

Keywords: Coarse-Grained Reconfigurable Array ·
Floating point unit · Processor pipeline

1 Introduction

CGRAs consist of arrays of PEs which perform computations in parallel and can transmit their results to neighboring PEs. CGRAs are most commonly used for accelerating multimedia applications. In this application domain, the PEs only have to support integer operations, as demonstrated in [7]. Since the latencies of integer operations are low ($\approx$1 clock cycle), handling data dependencies is achieved with little hardware effort such that an application can immediately make use of the parallelism of the CGRA architecture.

Other application domains such as HPC can also benefit from the parallelism in CGRAs. In contrast to multimedia applications, HPC applications require the support of FP operations. When using results of FP operations in the same PE which usually take mutliple clock cycles, either a hardware mechanism must be

© Springer Nature Switzerland AG 2019
M. Schoeberl et al. (Eds.): ARCS 2019, LNCS 11479, pp. 156–167, 2019.
https://doi.org/10.1007/978-3-030-18656-2_12

implemented in these PEs which will detect and prevent *read-after-write (RAW)*, *write-after-read (WAR)*, *write-after-write (WAW) Hazards*, and structural hazards or the compiler or programmer has to anticipate such conflicts and prevent them to guarantee the correct processing. In this document, we explore the hardware option. We will explain the implications on the hardware in detail in Sect. 4. The area overhead of such a mechanism must be as small as possible, as this overhead is proportional to the number of PEs. In addition, this mechanism should enable the efficient use of pipelined *FP units (FPUs)* via dynamic scheduling since this can further improve the performance. Hence, we propose an area-efficient, yet performance-optimized dynamic scheduling mechanism in each PE for handling long-latency operations as in FPUs.

In the remainder of this paper, we will proceed as follows: In Sect. 2 we analyze related work. Then we briefly explain the crucial points of our PEs in Sect. 3 which are necessary to understand our proposed mechanism in Sect. 4. After that, we evaluate our proposal in Sect. 5 and conclude in Sect. 6.

2   Related Work

In this section, we first review three other dynamic scheduling algorithms which enable the efficient use of FPUs or, more generally, pipelined functional units *(FUs)* with high latencies in CPUs in general. To the authors' knowledge, there are no CGRAs whose PEs use register values after they have performed a FP operation in the *same* PE. Nevertheless, we analyze CGRAs which also support FP operations.

Beside [10], scoreboarding [9] is one of the early techniques for dynamic scheduling in computer architecture and still used where small area is preferred over performance. Scoreboarding will stall the instruction pipeline if a RAW, a WAW, or a structural hazard is detected until the hazard disappears. If a short-latency operation is issued after a long-latency operation, and no hazards are present, the short-latency operation might finish earlier than the long-latency operation. To achieve this functionality, a scoreboard monitors the status of the instructions, of the FUs, and of the registers and detects said hazards based on the information in these status registers. Our approach behaves similar to this approach but occupies less area according to our estimation.

Because of the simplistic pipeline stalling when using scoreboarding, performance is not optimal. Therefore, in [10] a more sophisticated solution is proposed which lays the foundation for out-of-order execution in microprocessors. The key techniques here are *register renaming* and the use of *reservation stations*. Although this algorithm is very efficient, it occupies significantly more chip area than scoreboarding.

The author of [4] proposes an out-of-order execution architecture which requires special compiler support, but is more area efficient than [10]. By delaying the execution of the instructions with the help of compiler annotations, i.e. statically, the instructions are executed in another order than initially specified. In summary, the area savings are traded for a static out-of-order execution instead of a dynamic one. This approach requires additional register bits in the program memory for the timing annotations done by the compiler, and thus, is probably more costly than [9] with a reasonably sized program memory.

In [8], a CGRA called WaveScalar is proposed whose PEs can process FP values but always forward the results to other PEs while our architecture can forward and reuse results from FPUs. Due to the strict dataflow architecture, the PE's instructions can be executed in out-of-order fashion. The CGRA performs approximately as well as superscalar processors, but requires less area.

The concept proposed in [1] also enables FP operations. It is a data-driven, yet instruction-processing architecture similar to our CGRA. A token generator manages multiple FUs and instructs them how to deal with the input values by sending tokens to the FUs. Therefore, detecting and resolving hazards are the responsibility of the central token generator, and are not decentralized as designed in our approach. Hence, it is the obligation of the token generator to schedule operations accordingly.

The architecture proposed in [3] is a CGRA embedded as an execution pipeline in the OpenSPARC architecture. It can process FP values in a few PEs, but the PEs do not reuse their results and, hence, do not have to resolve data or structural hazards.

Most of the other CGRAs, e.g. [6,7], and [2], only feature support of integer operations as they target multimedia applications. Although the PEs of all of them can use previously computed results in each PE, data and structural hazards do not occur because the PEs are not pipelined and their latencies are zero.

3   The Processing Element

The architecture of our proposed PE is depicted in Fig. 1. The bold arrows represent multiple bit wide wires (i.e. data and addresses), and the thin arrows represent one bit wires used for control signal transmission. The block shapes indicate how the according modules behave: Rounded rectangles represent combinatorial modules, normal rectangles represent registers/memories which can combinatorially be read, but written data is only visible after one time step. Normal rectangles with bold lines are standard registers. Rounded rectangles with bold lines are complex modules with inner states. The trapezoidal blocks labeled *MUX* are multiplexers. The *ALU* and the *FP adder* are depicted only for demonstration purposes. In general, there can be various and more FUs in one PE. These FUs might also have different pipeline lengths. The dashed blocks are optional result registers. They are optional, because for operations with latency $= 0$, they are necessary for a reliable timing closure, but for pipelined long-latency operations they might be unnecessary and only increase the processing latency of an algorithm without adding any benefit.

Basically, a PE is a RISC-like processor pipeline which can fetch, decode, and execute contexts (which are similar to instructions), and write-back the results to the internal register file. Besides that, they can exchange data with other PEs and with the memory. The blocks of interest are the *decoder*, the *data hazard detector (DHD)*, and the *structural hazard detector (SHD)*. The former resolves data and structural hazards by stalling the pipeline, while the two latter detect data and structural hazards, respectively. A detailed description of the entire CGRA an remaining PE architecture is beyond the scope of this paper but is explained in [5].

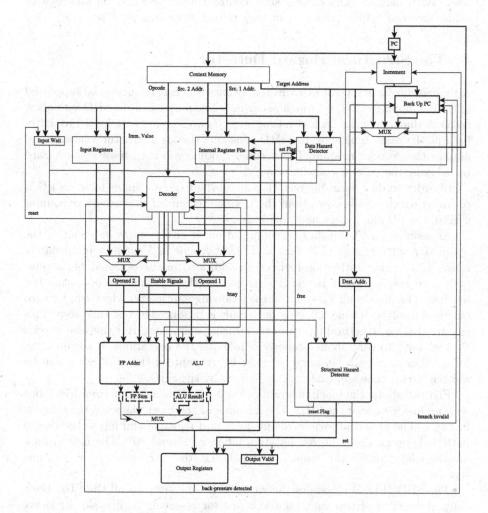

Fig. 1. Overview of a processing element

The DHD consists of a vector of bits, each associated with an internal register file entry. Such a bit or flag will be set if its associated internal register file entry is the destination of computation's result and this computation is in execution. As soon as the result is written back, the according flag is reset. This module is connected to the decoder which can read and set it. The reset signal is sent by the SHD. The SHD is discussed in Sect. 4.

The presence of data hazards is detected by checking the DHD to which the current context refers. If the flag of a source operand is set, a RAW will be detected. If the flag of the destination operand is set, a WAW hazard will be detected. In both cases, the decoder stalls the pipeline until the conflicting flag is reset. WAR hazards cannot occur since contexts are issued in order and register values are read before writing them back in our processing pipeline.

4   The Structural Hazard Detector

A PE can consist of several FUs which may have differing latencies and supported initiation intervals (IIs), i.e. pipelined or not. The purpose of the SHD is to allow no more than one write-back at a time step. If two FUs are anticipated to write-back at the same time step, the SHD considers this as a structural hazard and notifies the decoder module. The decoder module will then resolve the hazard by delaying the current context issue.

In order to deal with different IIs among the FUs, a counter for each FU is provided which counts down from the II value to zero. If the respective counter is zero, the FU can accept new operands.

As soon as an FU finishes its computation, it either stores its result in the optional result register (*FP Sum* and *ALU Result* in Fig. 1) or immediately forwards it to the destination register. In addition, an also optional flag accompanying a result register is set. It signalizes to the PE that the operation has finished. The flags of all FUs control the following multiplexer which can forward only one result at a time, i.e. only one result is produced at one time step. This ensures that no structural hazards occur during write-back. But this also implies that we have to care about properly scheduling the operations in advance, i.e. for an operation with latency l, it must be guaranteed that the result can be written back l time steps later. This is done by the SHD.

Figure 2 shows the block diagram of the SHD. It is a cutout from Fig. 1 but with an inside view of the SHD. The meaning of the block shapes is the same as in Fig. 1. The clouds are wildcards for logic and registers and follow the design pattern between the lightgrey registers labeled "1" and "0". The dotted lines are the wildcards for the respective signals, i.e. they might represent multiple signals.

The SHD (Fig. 2) schedules the write-back time slots for all the FUs. Basically, it consists of two shift registers: one for reserving a time slot or ticket (light grey; the label corresponds to the shift register's index) and another one for the according destination address (dark grey). The length of the SHD's shift registers is equal to the longest latency of the FUs implemented in the respective PE, plus one.

When a context is processed by an FU, the reservation shift register at the index equal to the latency of the FU is set to one, and the destination address is stored in the accompanying address shift register (dark grey in the figure).

In each time step, those shift registers move their information (ticket) towards index zero. When such a pair reaches index zero, the according FU concurrently finishes its computation, and the SHD grants write access for either writing to the *output registers* or to the *internal register file*, depending on the target address.

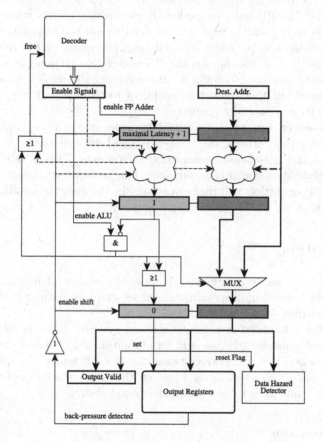

Fig. 2. Structural hazard detector (lightgray: ticket shift register (ticket SR); darkgray: address SR)

Structural hazards during write-back are anticipated and resolved as follows: If an enable signal from the decoder is set, it is checked whether the write-back time slot required in the future is available by looking at the reservation one time step before. If the preceding time slot is already reserved, the operation has to wait until it is available, resulting in a pipeline stall. If it has not been reserved yet, the operation may proceed. For instance, in Fig. 2 the *enable ALU* signal is set. An ALU operation has a latency of 0, meaning that in the next time step the result will be available if the operation is performed. If reservation register 1 already has a reservation, the *free* signal will turn zero; the decoder has to try again in the next time step. If no reservation has been made before, the reservation will succeed and the ALU operation is performed. This simple mechanism can be enhanced such that even more than two FUs can be handled both with equal and different latencies.

Beside the write access, the respective control signals are set (valid for the *output registers*, reset for the DHD). Also, if back-pressure is detected, shifting is disabled, i.e. the PE halts execution. Back-pressure occurs when an output register wants to transmit a value to another PE, but the respective input register still contains a value which has not been processed by the receiving PE. The receiving PE notifies the sending PE about this circumstance (*wait* signal = 1) and the sending PE waits for the receiving PE until it uses the input register value. When this conflict is resolved (*wait* signal = 0), the sending PE can continue to process other contexts.

As a side-effect, due to the different latencies of the FUs, contexts which are issued later than others, might overtake and finish earlier, i.e. it features in-order-issue and out-of-order-completion of contexts. This is valid, since the decoder resolves data hazards in advance. For instance, an integer operation following a FP operation will likely overtake. In the end, the conditions which allow overtaking are similar to scoreboarding.

5   Evaluation

The scope of this section is, firstly, to show the benefit of implementing our approach over a naive implementation, and secondly, to compare our approach with scoreboarding with respect to area.

Our CGRA is modeled and simulated using SystemC to verify its functionality. The model is parametrizable, and for evaluating our proposal, we simulated a CGRA with one PE. The correct behaviour of a PE under back-pressure was verified by testing two neighboring PEs, but this is not the focus of this section since we only want to test the aspects mentioned above.

5.1   Performance

To analyze the performance impact of our approach, two PEs, one without and one with the SHD, are tested with the same contexts. The sole purpose of this subsection is to demonstrate that our approach works similarly to scoreboarding.

For preserving a correct execution of the contexts, the PE without the SHD waits until each operation has finished its execution because it must presume that there is a data hazard. Both PEs provide result registers at the output of the FUs. The measurements on the PE without the SHD will serve as a base-line. In the following, we refer to these PEs as PE_B for the base-line PE and PE_T for our approach. For the evaluation, we run synthetic test cases which target certain corner cases to examplary demonstrate the impact of our mechanism and behaviour when data hazards are present.

For the first test case (A in Table 1), we generate contexts with no data hazards. Therefore, the contexts only rely on PE internal values and only write to the PE's internal register file, so the contexts do not have to wait for values from other PEs or that results are accepted by other PEs. Also no context operand depends on another context's result to exclude RAWs, WARs, and WAWs (WARs are impossible anyway since data is read before writing back in our PE design). The contexts themselves execute (precisely: issue) 100 long-latency operations on pipelined FUs, i.e. $II = 1$ and latency $= 9$.

For the second test case (B in Table 1), we test a context with $II = 1$, and latency $= 3$ followed by a context with $II = 1$, and latency $= 1$, i.e. in total two contexts. We measure the number of clock cycles from issuing the first context through the write-back of the second result. Also, both contexts are data independent. For the other two test cases (C and D in Table 1), we slightly change test case B such that C has a RAW, and D has a WAW while the rest is exactly setup as B.

The test case A shows that PE_T is significantly quicker than PE_B. The required *clock cycles per context (CPC)* are 9.82 for PE_B and 1 for PE_T, disregarding the configuration time. In test case B, out-of-order completion is demonstrated since the second context, although issued in-order, writes back its result before the first context. If the first context executed solely, i.e. without the second, the cycle count would also be 6. The measurements of C and D proof that when a hazard is detected both PEs perform the same.

In summary, the PE_T will reach a CPC of 1 if no RAW or WAW are present. The PE_B's CPC is approximately $1 +$ latency.

Table 1. Execution time evaluation

Test case	PE	Number of clock cycles
A	PE_B	982
	PE_T	100
B	PE_B	8
	PE_T	6
C	PE_B	10
	PE_T	10
D	PE_B	10
	PE_T	10

5.2   Area

In this section, we compare scoreboarding with our approach with respect to area under the aspects

- number of FUs to manage in one PE,
- maximal latency among all FUs in one PE, and
- the maximal II among all FUs in one PE.

As the CGRA is only simulated in SystemC, we have estimated the occupied area of both designs. In order to estimate the area, we determine the number of required registers. A single one bit register occupies significantly more area on a chip than any logic gate and, hence, the overall number of registers gives a profound point of comparison of two designs. Yet, in the following, we use the terms area and number of registers synonymously.

$$
\begin{aligned}
n &:= \text{number of FUs} \\
r &:= \text{number of register file entries} \\
l_{\max} &:= \text{maximal latency of all FUs in a PE} \\
A_S &:= \text{area overhead of scoreboard (in bit)} \\
A_T &:= \text{area overhead of DHD-SHD (in bit)}
\end{aligned}
$$

$$
A_S \approx \underbrace{2 \cdot 4\,\text{bit}}_{\text{instruction status}} + \underbrace{\underbrace{r\,\text{bit}}_{\text{internal register file}} \cdot \lceil \log_2 n \rceil\,\text{bit} + n}_{\text{register status}}
$$

$$
\cdot (\underbrace{1}_{\text{busy}} + \underbrace{3 \cdot \lceil \log_2 r \rceil}_{F_i, F_j, F_k} + \underbrace{2 \cdot \lceil \log_2 n \rceil}_{Q_i, Q_k} + \underbrace{2}_{R_j, R_k})\,\text{bit}
$$

$$
\underbrace{\phantom{\cdot (1 + 3 \cdot \lceil \log_2 r \rceil + 2 \cdot \lceil \log_2 n \rceil + 2)\,\text{bit}}}_{\text{functional status}}
$$

$$
= (r + 2n) \cdot \lceil \log_2 n \rceil\,\text{bit} + (3 \cdot \lceil \log_2 r \rceil + 3)n\,\text{bit} + 8\,\text{bit} \tag{1}
$$

$$
A_T \approx \underbrace{r\,\text{bit}}_{\text{DHD}} + \underbrace{n\,\text{bit}}_{\text{result available flags}} + \underbrace{(l_{\max} + 1)\,\text{bit}}_{\text{ticket SR}}
$$

$$
+ \underbrace{\lceil \log_2 r \rceil \cdot (l_{\max} + 1)\,\text{bit}}_{\text{address SR}} + \underbrace{\sum_{i \in \cup_{k \in n} II(FU_k)} \lceil \log_2 i \rceil\,\text{bit}}_{\text{counters for II}}
$$

$$
= (r + n)\,\text{bit} + (l_{\max} + 1)(1 + \lceil \log_2 r \rceil)\,\text{bit}
$$

$$
+ \sum_{i \in \cup_{k \in n} II(FU_k)} \lceil \log_2 i \rceil\,\text{bit} \tag{2}
$$

$$
A_T \overset{!}{<} A_S \tag{3}
$$

$$
\Leftrightarrow \quad r + n + (l_{\max} + 1)(1 + \lceil \log_2 r \rceil)
$$

$$
+ \sum_{i \in \cup_{k \in n} II(FU_k)} \lceil \log_2 i \rceil < (r + 2n)
$$

$$
\cdot \lceil \log_2 n \rceil + (3 \cdot \lceil \log_2 r \rceil + 3)n + 8 \tag{4}
$$

$$
\forall i \in \cup_{k \in n} II(FU_k) : (i = 1)
$$

$$\Rightarrow l_{max} < \frac{1}{1 + \lceil \log_2 r \rceil} \cdot ((r + 2n) \cdot \lceil \log_2 n \rceil$$
$$+ (3 \cdot \lceil \log_2 r \rceil + 2)n + 7 - r - \lceil \log_2 r \rceil) \tag{5}$$
$$\forall i \in \cup_{k \in n} II(FU_k) : (i = l_{max} + 1)$$
$$\Rightarrow (1 + \lceil \log_2 r \rceil) \cdot l_{max} + n \lceil \log_2(l_{max} + 1) \rceil < (r + 2n)$$
$$\cdot \lceil \log_2 n \rceil + (3 \lceil \log_2 r \rceil + 2)n + 7 - r - \lceil \log_2 r \rceil \tag{6}$$

Formulas (1) and (2) compute the number of register bits of scoreboarding and our DHD-SHD combination, respectively (ticket shift register (ticket SR), and address SR are both components of the SHD module).

The requirement that the area of our mechanism is smaller than the area of the scoreboard implementation is stated in (3). As long as it holds, our area overhead is smaller than that of scoreboarding.

From this inequation we can deduce bounds for the maximal latency of all FUs in a PE which have to hold for the DHD-SHD to be smaller. For instance, if the FUs are pipelined such that every II $= 1$, the sum term in (2) disappears and we get inequation (5) as a lower bound. The upper bound II = maximal latency $+ 1$ is given, since there cannot be a larger II. If we assume that every FU hits this bound, we get (6). This is the worst case regarding the II property.

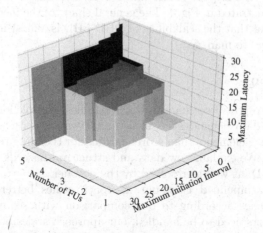

Fig. 3. Area comparison DHD-SHD vs. scoreboard, 32 registers, address width $= 5$ b

In Fig. 3, the design space is depicted. The three axes are number of FUs, maximum II, and maximum latency. The surface shown in the figure is the set of points in which our approach requires as much area as scoreboarding. The set of data covered by this surface from the viewer's perspective comprises the points in the design space for which the DHD-SHD occupies less area than scoreboarding. Scoreboarding is better when choosing any design point in front of the surface from the viewer's perspective. For example, given an ALU (latency $= 0$, II $= 1$), an integer multiplier (latency $= 0$, II $= 1$), a FP adder (latency $= 3$, II $= 1$), and

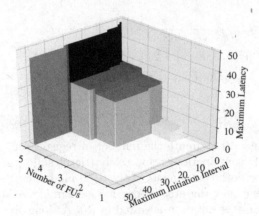

Fig. 4. Area comparison DHD-SHD vs. scoreboard, 128 registers, address width = 7 b

a FP multiplier (latency = 3, II = 1), the point n = 4, $l_{max} = 3$, and II = 1 lies in the space where DHD-SHD is more area-efficient than scoreboarding.

Figure 3 illustrates how well DHD-SHD scales with the number of FUs to manage in contrast to scoreboarding, in particular with three and more FUs. For completeness, the impact of the number of the register file entries on the design space is illustrated in Fig. 4. The general shape of the inequation surfaces in both figures hint that the scalability of DHD-SHD is almost indifferent to the number of registers to manage.

6   Conclusion

In summary, we propose a mechanism which handles multiple long-latency operations even with data dependencies in a similar way as scoreboarding [9], but requires less storage elements than scoreboarding for the more relevant points in the design space. We explain how data and structural hazards are detected by the SHD and DHD, as well as resolved by the decoder.

Obviously, for pipelined FUs, our approach scales better than for non-pipelined approaches according to our comparison with scoreboarding. Even when more registers need to be handled, our approach scales better than scoreboarding. The II's impact on the number of registers is almost negligible. For a few FUs with very high latencies and a few register file entries, scoreboarding uses less registers.

In conclusion, our approach scales better in terms of the number of storage elements than scoreboarding which suggests that this rationale also applies to the area overhead, since registers occupy significantly more area than logic gates on a chip. In the future, we will implement our PE with the DHD and the SHD on a chip and evaluate how much area it will actually occupy.

Acknowledgment. This project is funded by the Deutsche Forschungsgemeinschaft (DFG, German Research Foundation) - 283321772.

References

1. Gatzka, S., Hochberger, C.: The AMIDAR class of reconfigurable processors. J. Supercomput. **32**(2), 163–181 (2005)
2. Goldstein, S., et al.: PipeRench: a coprocessor for streaming multimedia acceleration. In: Proceedings of the 26th Interntional Symposium on Computer Architecture (Cat. No. 99CB36367), pp. 28–39 (1999)
3. Govindaraju, V., et al.: DySER: unifying functionality and parallelism specialization for energy-efficient computing. IEEE Micro **32**(5), 38–51 (2012)
4. Grossman, J.: Cheap out-of-order execution using delayed issue. In: Proceedings 2000 International Conference on Computer Design(ICCD), p. 549, September 2000
5. Käsgen, P.S., Weinhardt, M., Hochberger, C.: A coarse-grained reconfigurable array for high-performance computing applications. In: 2018 International Conference on ReConFigurable Computing and FPGAs (ReConFig), pp. 1–4. IEEE (2018)
6. Lu, G., Singh, H., Lee, M.H., Bagherzadeh, N., Kurdahi, F.J., Filho, E.M.C.: The MorphoSys parallel reconfigurable system. In: European Conference on Parallel Processing, pp. 727–734 (1999). citeseer.ist.psu.edu/461299.html
7. Mei, B., Vernalde, S., Verkest, D., De Man, H., Lauwereins, R.: ADRES: an architecture with tightly coupled VLIW processor and coarse-grained reconfigurable matrix. In: Y. K. Cheung, P., Constantinides, G.A. (eds.) FPL 2003. LNCS, vol. 2778, pp. 61–70. Springer, Heidelberg (2003). https://doi.org/10.1007/978-3-540-45234-8_7
8. Swanson, S., et al.: The wavescalar architecture. ACM Trans. Comput. Syst. **25**(2), 4:1–4:54 (2007)
9. Thornton, J.: Parallel operation in the control data 6600. In: AFIPS 64 (Fall, Part II): Proceedings of the Fall Joint Computer Conference, Part II: Very High Speed Computer Systems, 27–29 October 1964 (1964)
10. Tomasulo, R.M.: An efficient algorithm for exploiting multiple arithmetic units. IBM J. Res. Dev. **11**(1), 25–33 (1967)

Memory Hierarchy

CyPhOS – A Component-Based Cache-Aware Multi-core Operating System

Hendrik Borghorst[1][✉][ID] and Olaf Spinczyk[2]

[1] Department of Computer Science, TU Dortmund, 44227 Dortmund, Germany
hendrik.borghorst@udo.edu
[2] Institute of Computer Science, Osnabrück University, 49090 Osnabrück, Germany
olaf.spinczyk@uos.de

Abstract. Off-the-shelf multi-core processors provide a cost-efficient alternative to expensive special purpose processors at the cost of complex time predictability due to shared resources like buses, caches and the memory itself. This paper presents an operating system concept that takes control over the shared cache to minimize contention, by creating a component-based operating system, that is structured in small data chunks to allow better control over data and code movement in and out of the cache. An evaluation of the operating system shows that the system is able to reduce the difference between the ACET and observed WCET of a synthetic memory load test by 93% for ARM and 98% for Intel systems. Some noteworthy improvements were also achieved for the TACLe benchmarks.

Keywords: Operating system · Multi-core ·
Component-based design · Timing predictability · Real-time

1 Introduction and Related Work

Today's commercially available off-the-shelf multi-core processors offers high performance at a very attractive price point, making them a compelling platform for designers of embedded or cyber-physical systems. The raw computational power would allow for several real-time applications to be run on such a processor. The necessity for timing guarantees, however, presents a challenge as the processors are usually not analyzable with existing tools due to an increase in complexity. It stems from shared resources like memory controllers, caches and interconnects, which enable high computational performance at cheap manufacturing costs. The use of shared resources however introduces variations to the execution times of tasks running in parallel. A simplified multi-core hardware architecture with the main contention points of shared resources highlighted is shown on Fig. 1.

Special hardware units are used to mitigate the effect of shared resources on the execution times. A memory prefetching unit can be used to hide the latency

© Springer Nature Switzerland AG 2019
M. Schoeberl et al. (Eds.): ARCS 2019, LNCS 11479, pp. 171–182, 2019.
https://doi.org/10.1007/978-3-030-18656-2_13

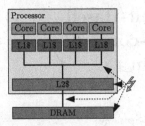

Fig. 1. Simplified exemplary target hardware with contention points highlighted

Table 1. Hardware platforms used for evaluation purposes (CPU speed in GHz, memory speed in MHz).

Platform	Architecture	CPU	Mem.
i.MX6	ARMv7 (Cortex-A9)	1.2	880
Exynos 4412	ARMv7 (Cortex-A9)	1.4	1600
Xeon E5-1620 v4	AMD64 (Broadwell)	3.5	2400

caused by simultaneous accesses to the main memory from different processor cores. These prefetching units can detect common memory access patterns [11] and therefore try to prefetch the data that will be requested in the future by an application. The performance of a prefetching unit depends on the access pattern an application exhibits and on the ability to fetch the data in time before the access occurs. Another way to hide memory access latency is to use caches to keep necessary data local to the processor and thereby reducing the need for bus and memory accesses. A disadvantage however is that the hardware is in control of the caches that commonly is only optimizing the average case of execution times. Furthermore, multiple processor cores are competing over space of a shared cache which results in execution times depending on the load of all other processor cores - an undesirable scenario for real-time applications.

Cache management strategies can be used to reduce the impact of caches on execution times. Instruction cache partitioning during compilation shows that it is possible to reduce the cache miss rate substantially [9]. Similar methods are applicable on data caches as well, which is known to increase the predictability of a system with caches [10]. Both techniques rely on comprehensive knowledge of the hardware the software is executed on after compilation, which makes the approach inflexible, because hardware changes are not possible without recompilation. An alternative to compilation-based cache partitioning is operating system controlled cache partitioning with virtual to physical address translation and memory page colouring [7]. Further work on the integration of cache coloring with cache locking was done for mixed criticality systems [12]. Cache management strategies also have been integrated within an existing operating system [8]. Instead of locking a whole dataset of a task within the cache the approach works by profiling applications on a Linux system and determining which memory pages are important for the applications. These memory pages are preloaded and locked within the cache to prevent eviction. A problem of existing operating systems is that they usually do not control the flow of data within applications which can result in data spread over a large range within the memory, thus making it challenging to keep applications data and code inside the cache and therefore creating accesses to contended resources and causing execution time variations.

We present an operating system, called **CyPhOS** (**Cy**ber **Ph**ysical **O**perating **S**ystem), that is designed to overcome the challenge with a component-based design that features an operating system-based cache management system to partition the cache on a global scale. In Sect. 3 we explain how the system manages the cache to isolate components. While Sect. 4 provides an overview of implementation details, a survey of the performance is given in Sect. 5. The basic idea behind this paper was published before as a research proposal paper [3], but since then it has been implemented completely for ARM and x86 and is evaluated as a whole only now.

Other component-based operating systems have been publicized before. One popular example is the operating system TinyOS [6]. Although some of TinyOS properties are similar to CyPhOS, the main focus is a different one. TinyOS was designed for very small footprint devices that feature only few resources with no multi-processor support. The interaction between components however is similar in that both systems provide an event-based system for interaction and are not permitting blocking operations.

2   System Model

In general embedded software systems are built by creating a single binary file that consists of both the application and the operating system, mostly arbitrarily linked together with respect to the hardware's memory layout (e.g. ROM vs. RAM placement). With this approach the operating system can hardly control how different applications compete within a shared cache because data is widely spread across the memory. A function call from one task to, for example, an operating system function could even evict the task's own data from the cache. The hereby presented concept differs from this approach by creating self-contained software components that are independent of other components. These components contain the program code and all data the components require for their execution. The logical arrangement of program code and data is done statically by the linker for the final binary and thus confining components to a contiguous memory region.

Interaction between components is strictly regulated to allow the operating system to maintain complete control over data and control flow. For this an event-driven approach is chosen. This prevents direct function calls between components. Instead components can export *events* that are broadcast within the operating system. Other components are able to subscribe to these events with so-called *triggers*, that will be executed if a subscribed event is triggered. This concept ensures that the operating system will never loose control over inter-component communication. This concept shares some similarities with the concept of a microkernel [1], as the operating system itself provides only very limited functionality, mainly to moderate communication between components. One of the key differences to most existing microkernel is that CyPhOS only allows asynchronous communication between components whereas microkernel often allow synchronous communication.

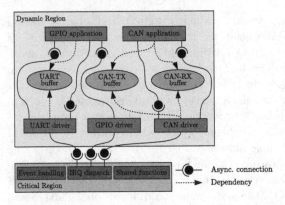

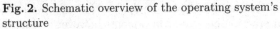

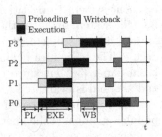

Fig. 2. Schematic overview of the operating system's structure

Fig. 3. Exemplary task execution for a quad-core system (PL - Preloading, EXE - Execution, WB - Writeback)

The concept of events and triggers allows to create a system that is not dependent on the execution of traditional tasks or processes. Instead of starting traditional tasks with a main entry point, an initial trigger of a component can be called to start an application. Alternatively a system can be designed to only react to external events that are converted to internal software events by a minimal interrupt handling system. This enables components to react to outside events in the same manner as to internal events. A device driver component would need to subscribe to the interrupt event of its corresponding device to be able to react to the interrupt requests. The operating system executes only one trigger per component simultaneously, ensuring that no data is modified or read by multiple triggers at once. This synchronization mechanism is comparable to the monitor synchronization. It will automatically serialize all data access to components and renders further synchronization of data unnecessary. Data sharing between multiple components is possible by defining dependencies between components. A trigger can depend on another component which ensures that no other access to the dependent component will occur during the trigger execution.

A schematic overview of the operating system's structure is shown in Fig. 2 with multiple drivers and two example applications accessing a shared component. The block at the bottom represents the critical memory region that contains all operating system functionality that is vital for the execution of components triggers, including at least one stack per processor. It also includes a basic IRQ handler, that forwards all hardware interrupts as software events to the subscribed corresponding driver components, and commonly used functionality like generic lists and the event handling code itself. Above this layer three driver components are located that can communicate to example applications over shared buffers. The access to the shared buffers is possible with normal memory access, for example via pointer passing.

3   Cache Management

In this section we describe how a cache management system can be designed to make use of the aforementioned operating system model and therefore reduce execution time variations caused by the access of contended resources. The idea of the cache management is to give the operating system more knowledge about the memory hierarchy it is running on to be able to reduce the contention of shared resources. With this knowledge the system should be able to execute trigger functions with all necessary data inside the shared cache, so that *not a single* main memory access occurs. To achieve this the execution of a components trigger is split up into a preloading phase, an execution phase and a writeback phase. The preloading phase will load the complete component including all dependencies to a part of the shared cache that is not in use by another core. This can be done using prefetching instructions [2], which have a rather predictable execution time due to their sequential memory access pattern. Following the preloading phase the component can be run without any main memory access because the data is guaranteed to reside in the cache. Any modification of component's data will flag the data as dirty, in need to be written back to the main memory when the component gets deactivated. This can be forced with selective cache cleaning operations, e.g. the CLFLUSH instruction on AMD64 or a *clean by way* operation on ARM. This phase is called the writeback phase.

Several precautionary measures are necessary to be able to control the cache content from the system software, otherwise the components will just evict each other during the preloading phase. One way to prevent cache eviction is partial cache locking [12] that would allow parts of a shared cache to stay locked, so that no eviction in a locked range occurs. A similar technique is cache partitioning [12] which allows to dedicate a part of a shared cache to one processor core, preventing other cores from allocating new data in the same space. Although hardware-based mechanism for cache locking and cache partitioning are preferred, they are not mandatory for the hereby presented concept. If a system does not feature the ability to lock down or partition the cache by processor core granularity, it is important, that only one processor at a time is executing a preloading phase, thus changing the content of the shared cache. Otherwise the cache content would be unpredictable. This increases the complexity of the schedulability analysis of a system and affects overall system performance. The critical memory region, see Fig. 2, is loaded at system boot-up and stays locked permanently within the cache.

When a trigger of a component is activated the system will create a *task* that handles the execution of a component's method to react to an event. These tasks are scheduled by a fixed-priority non-preemptive scheduler. This method is selected to reduce the number of cache preloading and writeback phase executions as each preemption could result in two of each. This might increase the worst-case response time of the operating system. A possible mitigation would be to use short trigger functions and multiple processor cores for interrupt handling. A simplified view of a possible execution of tasks is shown in Fig. 3 with four processors running tasks. Each task's execution is preceded by a preloading phase and superseded by a writeback phase. Only one processor at a time is accessing the main memory (via the preloading or writeback phase). To mitigate the effect of the preloading and writeback phase on the system's response time, the system can be configured, so that components stay inside the cache until the space is needed by other components. The eviction could, for example, be done by selecting the *least recently used* component to be evicted.

4   Implementation

We created a prototype implementation of the presented operating system model to evaluate if it is feasible to use it for real-world applications and how the cache management reduces the execution time variations. The component-based design calls for something that is able to structure program code accordingly. Therefore, C++ was chosen as the programming language. Its object-orientated programming model properly represents the component-based design. In addition, it is possible to make use of namespaces to group several classes of C++ code. This is used to specify to which *operating system component* (OSC) a class belongs.

This information is used during compilation of the operating system to link the operating system components correctly together. This process is done in two steps. At first, each source file is compiled separately. Components are identified by their namespace. This information is picked up by a linker-script generation tool that scans all object files for component names. Afterwards a contiguous data block is created for each found component namespace.

To evaluate the concept, the used hardware has to fulfill two conditions: First, it is necessary for the software to be able to control cache allocation of data. This means that the operating system can control at which part of the shared cache new data is loaded from the main memory. The second requirement that should be fulfilled by the hardware is the ability for software to prevent eviction of cache content from the shared level cache. Both features are available on two platforms for which the prototype implementation, called CyPhOS, is developed. One platform is the ARM Cortex-A9 processor that uses an external cache controller (PL310) with the ability to lock cache allocation by cache way granularity. This mechanism is called *lockdown by way* and can be used to force data to a specific cache way and preventing data eviction by locking all cache ways for new allocations, thus freezing the content of the cache.

The second platform is based on an Intel Xeon processor that provides a similar hardware feature called *Cache Allocation Technology* [5]. This technology provides an interface to the system software to partition the shared level cache between participating processor cores. For each hardware thread (e.g. a physical or logical processor core) a *class of service* (COS) can be assigned. For each COS a bitmask within the processors exists that specifies which part of the cache is assigned to the COS. Although no official mapping between a bit of the bitmask to cache ways exists, our tests have shown that the processor presents a bitmask with a length of the number of cache ways.[1] Two of the available cache

---

[1] Evaluated on an Intel Xeon E5-1620 v4 processor with 20 cache ways.

ways are in shared use with integrated peripherals, e.g. the GPU, and cannot be used exclusively by a processor core, resulting in 18 usable cache ways. With this feature it is also possible to specify to which part of the shared cache new data is allocated, comparable to the *lockdown by way* feature. Prevention of data eviction would, in theory, be possible by setting the bitmask to zero, thus deactivating the allocation of new data altogether. A requirement of the technology, however, is that a bitmask is never allowed to be set to zero, otherwise a *General Protection Fault* is thrown. To work around this limitation each hardware thread needs to be set to a parking cache way configuration during component execution. Two solutions for this problem exist. The first solution is to the set the bitmask to the so called *shared bitmask* which is shared by peripheral hardware components. An evaluation of this solution however revealed that this will result in bad timing behavior as execution times are subject to great variations. An alternative to this would be to dedicate a cache way for each processor core that is used as a standby cache way. This method results in much more stable execution times during component execution and was selected as the preferred method. A disadvantage of this is, that the number of cache ways available for component execution is reduced by the number of processor cores.

Another necessity for the cache management is the ability to force data from the main memory to the managed shared cache. Both the AMD64 and the ARMv7 architecture provide an instruction to preload data in the cache. Although the preload instruction of the ARM-ISA is only a hint to the processor, tests have shown that, at least for the used Cortex-A9 processors, the use of the instruction will result in data being preloaded to the shared level cache.[2]

The ARM Cortex-A9 platform with its cache controller features 1 MiB of second level cache with an associativity of 16. This means that the operating system can simultaneously hold 16 components with a size of 64 KiB in the cache. This data can be used to generate a linker script that aligns every component to a 64 KiB boundary. The alternatively used Intel-based platform features a associativity of 20 (18 available exclusively) with a cache way size of 512 KiB, resulting in a cache size of 10 MiB for the last level cache.

5 Evaluation

In order to evaluate the presented approach several experiments were conducted. The main focus of the evaluation is to demonstrate that hardware-based cache management, controlled by the operating system, can be used to reduce execution time variations substantially. All tests were done on three platforms listed in Table 1. SMT (Hyper-Threading) was disabled for the Intel processor because it will only result in cache and compute resource contention on level 1 and level 2 of the cache hierarchy, thus having a negative impact on the cache management at level 3.

---

[2] Verified on NXP i.MX6 and Samsung Exynos 4412.

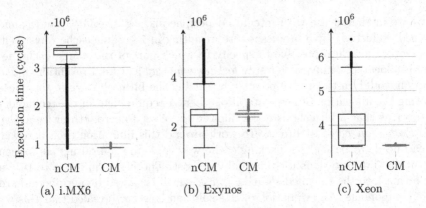

Fig. 4. Comparison of maximum memory load execution times without (nCM) and with cache management (CM) (Access count per component execution: 0.5 * size of cache ways)

All measurements were done using cycle counters provided by the hardware. They are accessible by reading out cycle counter registers of the PMU (performance measurement unit) on ARM and with the help of the RDTSCP instruction for the Intel-based system. It was ensured that no system management interrupts (SMI) occurred during the experiments with the help of a machine-specific register. All tests were compiled with *GCC* at version 8.2 and optimization level O3.

To generate an extreme workload, a test-case was created to stress the whole memory subsystem with a synthetic load, running in parallel on all available processor cores. Dummy OSCs that only stress the memory subsystem with load instructions in a loop are generated to test the approach at maximum memory load possible. Although the load is not completely realistic it provides an overview of the limits of the cache management. For the evaluation 128 dummy components were used. The memory access count per component execution is relative to the cache way size of the architecture, so that the results are comparable for both the ARM and the Intel system architecture. The components were generated with a size depending on the cache way size of the architecture, specifically set to 90% of the cache way size. The resulting components have a size around 58 KiB for the ARM-based system and about 461 KiB for the Intel-based system. After each loop a component finishes its execution and another stress test component is called, thus being preloaded, executed and evicted from the cache. Each experiment is repeated for 80 000 times. The memory access pattern executed by these components is random (within the component's memory range) to prevent hardware prefetching mechanisms from hiding the memory latency. Although a random access pattern is used, each execution of a components trigger is done with the same random seed, thus resulting in the same access pattern for each execution. All execution times are given in processor cycles. Absolute execution times can be calculated with the help of the clock speeds given in Table 1.

Table 2. Relative standard deviations (a) and reduction of difference between observed WCET and ACET (b) of stress test components for different access counts (relative to the cache way size) in %, without (nCM) and with (CM) cache management.

Access size		0.25		0.5		1		2		4	
Platform		(a)	(b)	(a)	(b)	(a)	(b)	(a)	(b)	(a)	(b)
i.MX6	nCM	26.39	75.08	26.12	74.78	26.13	76.18	25.54	75.76	25.61	74.99
	CM	1.14		0.68		0.47		0.43		0.40	
Exynos 4412	nCM	40.41	82.91	37.60	80.37	39.76	85.63	40.13	92.51	21.13	67.00
	CM	1.68		2.01		2.07		1.98		1.85	
Xeon	nCM	20.76	−2.64	18.56	98.02	18.56	97.64	2.41	97.32	1.21	94.82
	CM	0.62		0.27		0.28		0.28		0.27	

The results of one example configuration are shown in Fig. 4. The used configuration for this diagram is an access count of 0.5 times the size of the architectures cache way (in bytes), resulting in 32 768 accesses for the ARM system and 262 144 for the Intel system per component execution. It is apparent that the cache management has a significant impact on the execution times for all three systems. Both the average execution time and the measured worst-case execution time were reduced by a significant amount. For the Xeon system the difference between ACET and observed WCET was reduced by 98.0%. It is noteworthy that though both ARM systems run at nearly the same CPU clock rate, the i.MX6 system is almost twice as fast as the Exynos system. This is probably owed to the fact that the memory of the i.MX6 CPU is clocked at twice the rate, see Table 1. A broader overview of benchmark results is given by Table 2. It shows the relative standard deviations and reduction of difference between the ACET and observed WCET for all three platforms and five configurations that were evaluated. Overall it is noticeable that all configurations reduce the variations of execution times by some degree. For all but one configuration, caused by few outliers, the cache management is able to considerable reduce the difference between ACET and observed WCET. With higher access counts the Intel system is able to compensate the variations via a sophisticated hardware caching strategy, that is effective for repeated memory accesses within the same range. The hardware cache controller of the Cortex-A9 systems evidently is not as capable as the Intel one.

For a more realistic load the TACLe benchmark suite, containing multiple applications with real-world scenario workloads, is used [4]. Each benchmark from the suite is bundled in one component and executed independently of each other repeatedly per OSC execution. To provide a baseline all tests were run without an additional load on the system, providing a best-case measurement, with no contention and no interrupts enabled. Then the tests were repeated with an additional stress load, generated by the aforementioned dummy components, once with the cache management disabled and enabled. Each benchmark component was executed 100 000 times with a repetition of 20 per component

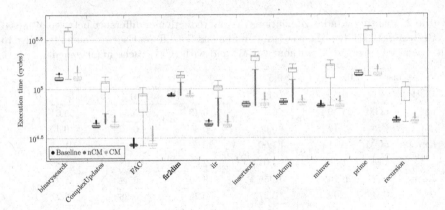

Fig. 5. Selected execution times of TACLe benchmarks (20 repetitions per OSC execution on i.MX6). From left to right: baseline (no additional load), no cache management (additional load), cache management (additional load)

execution to reduce the baseline variation of the benchmarks a bit. A selection of benchmark results is shown on Fig. 5 that shows results for the i.MX6 platform, because it is the main platform for this work and showed the most promising results for the synthetic load as well. It is noticeable that the dummy load has a large impact on the execution time variations for all benchmarks and that the cache management is able to reduce the variations significantly for this platform, bringing it close to the optimal baseline results, but with the dummy load active. Although the cache management was able to reduce the variations for all 21 benchmarks of the TACLe benchmark on the i.MX6 system, the OS was only able to reduce the variations for 16 benchmarks on the Xeon system and 11 on the Exynos system. The results for the Exynos system might be caused by an locked down TrustZone of the system with potential management code polluting the shared cache during the preloading phase. This circumstance calls for further investigation in the future.

Finally the execution times of both the preloading and the writeback phases were evaluated, to verify whether the approach will shift the unpredictable behavior of memory accesses to those phases. The results are listed in Table 3 and show that both preloading and writeback is more stable than the execution phases without cache management. Although the variations for the ARM-based systems appear quite high it should be noted that the minimum and maximum preload time for the Exynos system was 51 792 and 91 911 (69 137/83 807 for writeback) which is comparable low to the variations of the stress test itself, s. Figure 4b, that exhibit a minimum of 1 157 943 and a maximum of 5 535 192 without and respectively 1 840 559 and 3 081 563 with cache management active. This demonstrates that it is possible for applications, under certain circumstances, to run faster with cache management enabled, even if preloading and writeback is considered.

Table 3. Relative standard deviations in % of preloading and writeback phases for all three platforms (without and with stress load)

Platform	PL (no load)	WB (no load)	PL (load)	WB (load)
i.MX6	3.6%	1.2%	1.9%	1.4%
Exynos	9.4%	5.7%	2.3%	0.5%
Xeon	0.9%	0.2%	1.0%	0.2%

6   Future Work and Conclusion

Multi-core (and future many-core) processors provide very cheap computing power at the cost of predictability. Memory hierarchies are becoming more complex and need operating system support to be fully utilized by applications running on these systems. We present an operating system concept that is able to greatly reduce the variations of execution times and, thus, providing a more stable execution base by controlling which data is inside the cache at which point of time. This is achieved by grouping the data, necessary to execute certain applications, within components that can easily be swapped in and out of the cache. The approach enables a maximum reduction of the difference between ACET and the measured WCET of about 92% for an ARM-based system and about 98% for the Intel-based system. The real-world tests conducted with help of the TACLe benchmarks showed some noteworthy improvements as well. To provide a base for further research and verification of the results, the concept operating system is made available as open source software.[3]

Although the OS currently is limited to ARM Cortex-A9 and Intel CAT, AMD also published an documentation for QoS extensions for their future processors, providing a potential new platform for CyPhOS.[4] At the moment this approach is limited to hardware platforms providing some kind of hardware cache management interface, but the concept would also work on other systems, e.g. with scratchpad memories. Future work can be done by leveraging software cache partitioning strategies, for example page coloring [13], thus, getting rid of the hardware requirement. Another interesting research topic could be an automatic optimization to load multiple components at once during preloading. This would decrease the necessary preloading phases for commonly used components. Dynamic memory management is also a topic of research interest for this operating system, especially the question of how to design the memory allocator interface and how to structure dynamic data to fit well in a cache component.

---

[3] The source code of the prototype implementation is available under: https://github.com/ESS-Group/CyPhOS.

[4] https://developer.amd.com/wp-content/resources/56375.pdf.

References

1. Accetta, M., et al.: Mach: a new kernel foundation for UNIX development (1986)
2. Advanced Micro Devices: AMD64 architecture programmer's manual volume 3: General-purpose and system instructions, December 2017. http://support.amd.com/TechDocs/24594.pdf
3. Borghorst, H., Spinczyk, O.: Increasing the predictability of modern COTS hardware through cache-aware OS-design. In: Proceedings of the 11th Workshop on Operating Systems Platforms for Embedded Real-Time Applications (OSPERT 2015), July 2015
4. Falk, H., et al.: TACLeBench: a benchmark collection to support worst-case execution time research. In: Schoeberl, M. (ed.) 16th International Workshop on Worst-Case Execution Time Analysis (WCET 2016). OpenAccess Series in Informatics (OASIcs), vol. 55, pp. 2:1–2:10. Schloss Dagstuhl-Leibniz-Zentrum für Informatik, Dagstuhl (2016)
5. Intel Corporation: Improving real-time performance by utilizing cache allocation technology, April 2015. https://www.intel.com/content/dam/www/public/us/en/documents/white-papers/cache-allocation-technology-white-paper.pdf
6. Levis, P., et al.: TinyOS: an operating system for sensor networks. In: Weber, W., Rabaey, J.M., Aarts, E. (eds.) Ambient Intelligence, pp. 115–148. Springer, Heidelberg (2005). https://doi.org/10.1007/3-540-27139-2_7
7. Liedtke, J., Härtig, H., Hohmuth, M.: OS-controlled cache predictability for real-time systems. In: Proceedings Third IEEE Real-Time Technology and Applications Symposium, pp. 213–224, June 1997. https://doi.org/10.1109/RTTAS.1997.601360
8. Mancuso, R., Dudko, R., Betti, E., Cesati, M., Caccamo, M., Pellizzoni, R.: Real-time cache management framework for multi-core architectures. In: 2013 IEEE 19th Real-Time and Embedded Technology and Applications Symposium (RTAS), pp. 45–54, April 2013. https://doi.org/10.1109/RTAS.2013.6531078
9. Mendlson, A., Pinter, S.S., Shtokhamer, R.: Compile time instruction cache optimizations. In: Fritzson, P.A. (ed.) CC 1994. LNCS, vol. 786, pp. 404–418. Springer, Heidelberg (1994). https://doi.org/10.1007/3-540-57877-3_27
10. Mueller, F.: Compiler support for software-based cache partitioning. In: Proceedings of the ACM SIGPLAN 1995 Workshop on Languages, Compilers & Tools for Real-time Systems, LCTES 1995, pp. 125–133. ACM, New York (1995). https://doi.org/10.1145/216636.216677
11. Tullsen, D.M., Eggers, S.J.: Effective cache prefetching on bus-based multiprocessors. ACM Trans. Comput. Syst. 13(1), 57–88 (1995). https://doi.org/10.1145/200912.201006
12. Ward, B.C., Herman, J.L., Kenna, C.J., Anderson, J.H.: Making shared caches more predictable on multicore platforms. In: 2013 25th Euromicro Conference on Real-Time Systems, pp. 157–167, July 2013. https://doi.org/10.1109/ECRTS.2013.26
13. Zhang, X., Dwarkadas, S., Shen, K.: Towards practical page coloring-based multicore cache management. In: Proceedings of the 4th ACM European Conference on Computer Systems, EuroSys 2009, pp. 89–102. ACM, New York (2009). https://doi.org/10.1145/1519065.1519076

Investigation of L2-Cache Interferences in a NXP QorIQ T4240 Multi-core Processor

Jonathan Fish[✉][ID] and Alfred Bognar

Hensoldt Sensors, Ulm, Germany
{jonathan.fish,alfred.bognar}@hensoldt.net

Abstract. The CPU cache memory was invented to reduce access latency between the processor and the main memory. Instructions and data are fetched from a fast cache instead of a slow memory to save hundreds of cycles. But new kinds of cache interferences were introduced with the arise of multi-core technology.

Safety-critical systems and especially higher functional integrated systems in avionics require an assurance that interferences do not influence functionality to maintain certification capability. Furthermore, interferences caused by cache misses result in a decrease of the processors overall performance.

This paper focuses on the investigation of the L2 cache interferences of a modern commercial-of-the-shelf (COTS) PowerPC based processor as in to how and why they occur. The investigation regards to interferences caused by the multi-core design. In order to realise the problem, a comprehensive understanding of the underlying architecture and the principle function of cache is a necessary prerequisite.

A detailed analysis investigates vulnerabilities in the architecture before these are then exploited by the use of targeted memory arithmetic. A series of measurements performed by a simulation framework, reveals the extent to which these vulnerabilities can affect the runtime of applications.

The results clearly show that the design of a multi-core processor (SMT) not only brings benefits but also risks in terms of performance and runtime. Thus, interferences due to the multi-core design should be avoided if possible, especially given safety-critical guidelines.

1 Introduction

High performance embedded architectures seek to accelerate performance in the most energy-efficient and complexity-effective manner. The current development for computation platforms is shifting from increasing the frequency to increasing the numbers of cores on the same die. Driven by the ongoing challenge of more performance, smaller physical size and reducing costs multi-core processors which have been evolving over the last decades, have become very interesting. But with the advent of the new technology, new problems arise. The limited complexity of

© Springer Nature Switzerland AG 2019
M. Schoeberl et al. (Eds.): ARCS 2019, LNCS 11479, pp. 183–194, 2019.
https://doi.org/10.1007/978-3-030-18656-2_14

single-core based systems compared to multi-core systems allows a partitioned development of individual steps. But this is no longer possible with multi-core systems, since the dependencies caused by the architecture can lead to significant critical interactions between functionally independent components. Among the most important are the conflicts between cores that are resulting from the limited capacity of the memory hierarchy, above all shared caches.

These systems have their own challenges with regards to safety certification such as preserving determinism and assuring certifiability. Ideally, safety critical systems would like to reap the same benefits considering consolidation, performance and migration while keeping certification costs as low as possible. There are well-known challenges including interrupt handling and bus contention, but with multi-core processors new problems have occurred. It has been shown that highly associative shared caches have a number of potential areas of conflict.

As an example for such potential conflicts this paper will be investigating the shared L2 cache of a NXP QorIQ T4240 processor on interferences caused by the multi-core design. The results are intended to shed light on how much the L2 cache can influence the runtime of processes in the worst case scenario. Deriving from this, guidelines for software development can be devised.

2   Related Work

Chip Multiprocessor (CMP) which the QorIQ T4240 belongs to, are currently the prevalent architecture for most modern high-performance processors. The performance advantage of the principle of sharing components is followed by the problem of interferences occurring. Investigations concerning interferences in the memory subsystem were carried out by [3] and [7]. There has also been a considerable amount of research into what types of cache interferences there are and to how to reduce them [1,2,4]. Most solutions are based on the technique of providing a fair distribution of interferences across the participating threads or by using Quality of Service (QoS), for instance by partitioning all shared resources amongst the threads. However, with regard to safety-critical systems, the technique of a fair distribution of interferences is not an option, due to the lack of determinism. Partitioning shared resources is also a very common method, but performance degradation due to segregation is often so severe that single-core processors outperform multi-core ones. Furthermore, most investigations concentrate on the impact of the summary of interferences within the entire memory subsystem, instead of focusing on individual layers.

This work on the other hand focuses on the research of worst case scenarios of L2 cache interferences based on the multi-core architecture. It provides realistic values related to the QorIQ T4240 to indicate the worst case scenarios due to shared cache interferences. These values are intended to help evaluate concurrent running applications within a safety-critical environment.

3   Processor Architecture QorIQ T4240

The T4240 has three L2 caches each serving a cluster of four physical cores. One of the cluster shared L2 caches has a total size of 2 MB. It is divided into 4 banks of 512 KB, which are organised as 16 ways and 512 sets. A bank can only handle one access at a time. It is inclusive for cache lines storing data and generally inclusive for ones storing instructions. The write hit policy is implemented as write-back, as the platform cache would not support write-though due to is smaller size. The write-miss policy is unknown as it is not stated by the manual. Furthermore, to maintain coherency of the cluster cores' L1 caches the MESI protocol is fully implemented [6].

4   Detailed Analysis

4.1   Identifying Architectural Weaknesses

To identify the architectural weaknesses it is necessary to provoke as many cache misses as possible. In other words, the more misses occur, the more the architectural weakness affects cache performance. Cache misses can be classified into four categories: Compulsory miss, capacity miss, conflict miss and coherency miss.

The T4240 consists of a shared set associative L2 cache which is split into banks each of them shared by 4 cores. In view of these facts all four types of misses are able of occurring. But because compulsory misses are inevitable and capacity misses boil down to the cache size, which cannot be changed, they are not covered by this investigation. Conflict and coherency misses on the other hand, are among the types of misses caused by multi-core technology and they can be avoided through targeted implementation.

4.2   Expected Interferences

The T4240 with its twelve e6500 cores is a complex construct, offering multiple kinds of L2 cache interferences. Considering the construction of there are the following possibilities to induct an interference:

Private Memory on Same Cluster. The first and most obvious way to cause an interference is by letting multiple processes which are each individually assigned to a different core, discard each others data in the L2 cache. The single assignment of a process to a core is essential to prevent influences coming from other components. There are basically two ways to cause this condition. Firstly, by filling the entire cache until there is no alternative to having to discard data (capacity miss). Another possibility is to only occupy a single cache set until no cache line of this set is available (conflict miss).

Various Load Distribution on Cache Banks. A cluster shared L2 cache has 4 banks to prevent access congestion. The second way to cause an interference is to let multiple cores utilise only one of four banks. Due to the fact that one bank can only handle one access at a time, the expected performance is approximately the reciprocal value of the number of cores accessing it simultaneously. This test provides information about how large the performance loss is by parallel use of a single cache bank.

Using Shared Memory on Different Clusters. The clusters are connected by a bus system which implements the MESI protocol to prevent cache incoherence. The third way is to use shared memory for threads which are distributed over different clusters. Thereby, the L2 caches have to be kept coherent by the bus system. This test is not a true interference but it is a flaw that can be traced back to the architectural design of the L2 cache. Without the multi-core architecture, the division into clusters would not be required.

5   Evaluation

5.1   Evaluation Setup

The Test Bench. The aim of this investigation is to do a theoretical research on how the L2 cache can be stressed in such a manner, that it causes interferences. To verify and prove the findings of the detailed analysis, a test bench was written in the shape of a software application. The approach to using a software application instead of hardware-based solutions (e.g. performance counters) is to make it independent of the underlying architecture.

- Selection of executable cores (from 0–23 and any combination up to 4 cores)
- Memory type (shared or private)
- Number of cache ways (up to 20)
- Number of cache sets (greater than 1)
- Cache bank occupancy (mixed, thread assigned or single bank)
- Data structure alignment (aligned or unaligned)
- Data arrangement (contiguous or non-contiguous)

The Core Algorithm. The pseudocode of Algorithm 1 is an extracted core function corresponding to the benchmark with n ways. It starts by setting the step size and the offset depending on the bank occupancy. Due to the fact that processors fulfil memory transaction in size of a cache line, it is sufficient to request a single item in a cache line to load the entire line. Therefore the step size over the data is a multiple of a cache line size. The actual operation takes places within the inner loops. The arrays start from the calculated offset and increments with the set step size. The loops work in a cyclic way by assigning the subsequent element to the current one. The decisive factor here is the final assignment just after the loop has ended. This assignment connects the last

Algorithm 1. The core of a 2-way benchmark

```
function N-WAYS(data, num_sets, bank_occupancy)
    δ = SETSTEPSIZE(bank_occupancy)
    γ = SETOFFSET(bank_occupancy)
    i_max = num_sets
    way_0 = data[0]
    way_1 = data[1]
    ...
    way_n = data[n − 1]

    STARTTIMEMEASURING()
    for n = 0 to n_max do
        for i = γ to i_max do
            way_0[i] = way_0[i + δ]
            i = i + δ
        end for
        way_0[i_max] = way_1[γ]
        for i = γ to i_max do
            way_1[i] = way_1[i + δ]
            i = i + δ
        end for
        way_1[i_max] = way_0[γ]
        ...
        for i = γ to i_max do
            way_n[i] = way_n[i + δ]
            i = i + δ
        end for
        way_n[i_max] = way_n[γ]
    end for
    STOPTIMEMEASURING()
end function
```

element of the current loop to the first element of the next loop. Without this connection the compiler would optimise the assembler code to the extent of cutting out the entire loop. It would recognise the redundancy while unrolling the loop and thus perform only a single iteration.

After assigning the number of sets, the data array is split into its ways. This happens due to performance reasons. It is also the reason why there are separate functions for each number of ways. The division from a 2-dimensional into multiple 1-dimensional arrays removes unwanted pointer arithmetic.

The fast and unhindered execution of the operation itself is crucial to the measurement, to minimise the influence of the execution units. According to [5], the assignment operation is performed by the simple unit of which there are four in one e6500 core. Although the redundancy of an execution unit does not guarantee the exclusion of influences from it, but it at least minimises them substantially.

5.2   Evaluation Considerations

Cache Pollution. In order to raise the accuracy of the results, all non-participating cores in the affected cluster should be left untouched by the OS and other applications during the benchmark. The concerning reason is not the utilisation of the core but the pollution of its L1 and L2 caches. For this reason a spinlock is invoked on the concerning cores during the benchmark.

Hugepages. To recap the hardware specifications, the L2 cache has 16 ways of which each have 4×512 sets yielding 128 KB per way. In order to store data in specific sets, specific physical memory addresses are required. For reasons of efficiency, Linux allocates memory in pages of 4 KB, which are not necessarily contiguous.

The problem with pages of 4 KB is that they do not offer the possibility of placing data in certain areas of the L2 cache. However, this is a prerequisite for the benchmark. To make sure that the memory is contiguous *Hugepages* were used by the test bench application for the following measurements.

6   Synthetic Interferences

6.1   Private Memory on Same Cluster

Number of Participating Cores. The lines plotted in Fig. 1 correspond to measurements that were performed with 1, 2, 3 and 4 parallel running cores within a single cluster. Considering two concurrently running cores for instance, the first performance drop is during the transition from 8 to 9 ways. But in contrast to the sharp increase of the blue curve at 17 ways, this increase is significantly smaller.

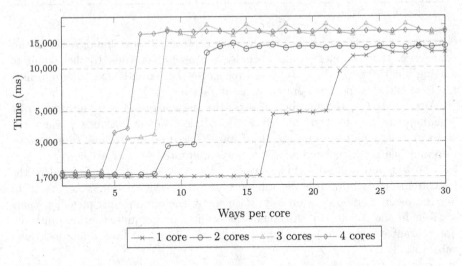

Fig. 1. Runtime of private, contiguous and L2 way aligned memory

In order to get a better insight into why the performance drop is divided into two steps, it is necessary to review the single runtimes. The relative runtime of each core is a good indicator to estimate how the interferences are distributed across the cores with a balanced time showing each core sacrificing the same amount of performance to interferences and an unbalanced time indicating that

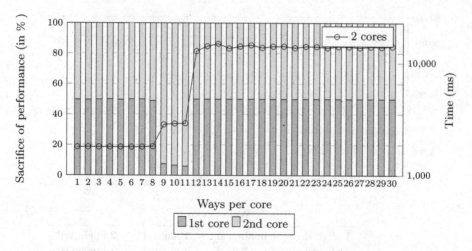

Fig. 2. Sacrifice of performance due to interferences 2 cores

they are unevenly spread. Thus, Fig. 2 illustrates exemplary the sacrifice of performance to interferences of 2 cores. The same applies to measurements with 3 and 4 cores. Figure 2 shows the uneven distribution of L2 cache interferences. The test bench uses s thread barrier (POSIX) to synchronise the threads and although the implementation of a thread barrier is closely tied to the hardware and consists of atomic operations, it does not perfectly synchronise all threads. When the barrier is released, the threads are released almost simultaneously - but only almost.

This situation is aggravated by the cache replacement strategy (SPLRU). Regarding the core algorithm, this means as soon as the leading core reaches the end of the last available L2 cache way, the replacement strategy starts replacing least recently used data. The least recently used data at this point is the first way of the leading core. But because it is reused for the next operation it cannot be replaced. Instead, the first way of another core is replaced, which in turn causes interferences for the core in question. Thus, if only one of the threads receives a very small lead, the impact on the interference distribution is substantial.

Note that this effect is due to the way the core algorithm works and does not represent a general L2 cache issue.

Data Alignment. Most architectures do not support unaligned memory access, but since Freescale does, the possible penalty for reading or writing misaligned memory needs to be investigated.

The solid lines show a significant drop in performance at all levels compared to the dotted ones. The use of unaligned memory is not primarily associated with performance degradation as long as the data is within a cache line. But dealing with unaligned memory overlapping cache lines involves much more effort than it does dealing with aligned memory (Fig. 3).

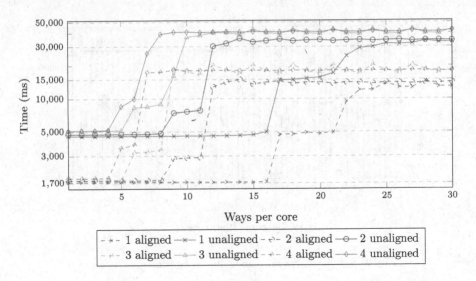

Fig. 3. Runtime of private and contiguous memory

The e6500 core supports the access on unaligned data but at the cost of performance degradation, as it is necessary to perform a realignment process to prepare the data for the upcoming use. For loads that hit in the cache, the load and store units throughput degrades to a third of its normal speed, as it has to handle an interrupt. It takes 3 cycles to translate an unaligned store to make it readable. In addition, after the translation has taken place, the unaligned store is treated as two distinct entries in the load and store queue, each requiring a

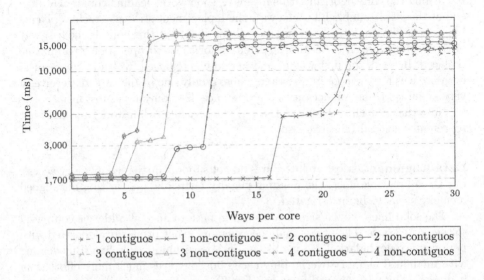

Fig. 4. Runtime of private and L2 way aligned memory

cache access [6]. In other words, the access of unaligned data overlapping cache lines requires an extra translation and an additional cache access compared to aligned data or unaligned data within one cache line.

Data Arrangement. When memory gets allocated by the application, the allocation takes place in the main memory. Figure 4 shows that it makes no difference considering the L2 cache whether the memory was allocated contiguous or non-contiguous.

6.2   Various Load Distributions on Cache Banks

Cores Assigned to Individual Banks. The assignment of cores to individual banks is strictly speaking no measurement of interferences as non occur. Nevertheless, it is interesting to see that assigning cores to banks actually improves performance compared to a default distribution.

From now on, *default memory* is referred to as memory, which is distributed evenly amongst all banks, as it is the default case for standard memory allocations (Fig. 5).

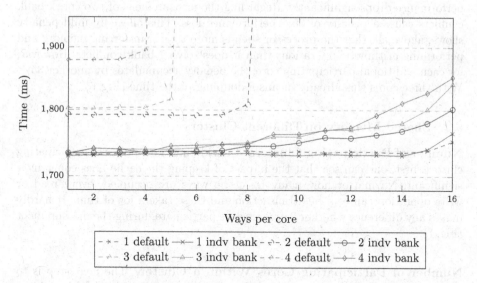

Fig. 5. Runtime of private, contiguous and L2 way aligned memory

Cores Assigned to the Same Bank. The second constellation considering the L2 cache banks is to assign all cores to the same bank. This case is highly unlikely given the use of an operating system, but it still needs be considered.

The deliberate assignment of several cores to a single bank shows very clearly to which extent L2 cache bank conflicts affect performance. Considering the impact of bank conflicts when the data is stored in the L2 cache, one can see that

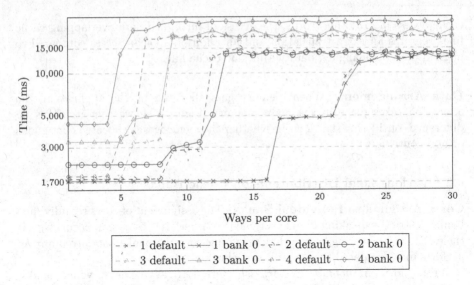

Fig. 6. Runtime of private, contiguous and L2 way aligned memory

performance drops significantly. Regarding the measurement of two cores, bank conflicts cause a penalty of 35% performance loss. This allegedly mild penalty shows, above all, that the processor spends more time transferring memory and performing arithmetic operations than it does solving bank conflicts. However, for each additional participating core, the penalty accumulates by another 35%. With three cores this already means a doubling of the time (Fig. 6).

6.3　Shared Memory on Different Clusters

Number of Participating Clusters. Considering the number of participating clusters first, one can see that the impact of keeping the cache lines coherent is significant. No matter how many L2 cache ways are occupied, every read or write operation causes a bus transaction and these take a lot of time. It hardly makes any difference whether 2 or 3 clusters participate during the measurement (Fig. 7).

Number of Participating Cores Within a Cluster. The next step is to investigate whether interferences by bus contention can be increased by adding a second core per cluster (Fig. 8).

The results show that more cores do not affect the performance any more than 1 core did already. The interferences are caused by the interconnect bus, that has to switch between the cluster on every coherency miss. It does not seem to be the amount of data being transferred from one cluster to the other that causes the loss, but switching between the clusters which requires time. And as the bus needs to switch forth and back between the clusters no matter how many cores participate, all bus transactions are done within the time window two clusters are connected with each other.

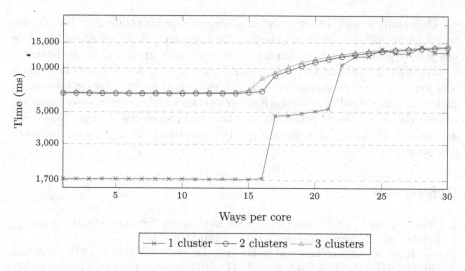

Fig. 7. Runtime of shared, contiguous and L2 way aligned memory regarding to the number of participating clusters (1 core per cluster)

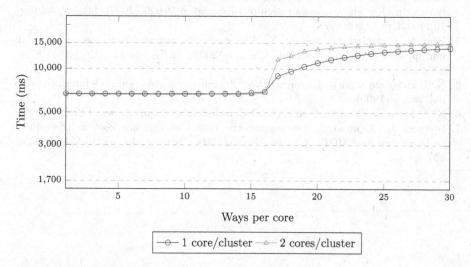

Fig. 8. Runtime of shared, contiguous and L2 way aligned memory regarding to the number of participating core per cluster (2 clusters)

7 Conclusion

The Detailed Analysis pointed out three kinds of interferences that occur based on conflict and coherency misses - private memory on the same cluster, shared memory on different clusters and the load distribution over the L2 cache banks. All three kinds of interferences differ in the performance impact, but what all have in common is that they should be avoided if possible.

The results revealed that cache interferences significantly reduce overall processor performance to such an extent in the worst case that multithreading does not yield a profit, since inter-thread interferences are greater than the benefit.

The NXP T4240 was developed and for general purposes, foremost in network solution. It is a universal-processor, highly optimised for the average usecase. In particular, embedded or real-time applications for which worst case scenarios are critical should pay close attention to a targeted use of the storage subsystem, as this is a key factor in achieving good application performance on multicore processors.

References

1. Chang, J., Sohi, G.S.: Cooperative cache partitioning for chip multiprocessors, pp. 402–412 (2014). https://doi.org/10.1145/2591635.2667188
2. Iyer, R., et al.: QoS policies and architecture for cache/memory in CMP platforms. SIGMETRICS Perform. Eval. Rev. 25–36 (2007). https://doi.org/10.1145/1269899.1254886
3. Jahre, M., Grannaes, M., Natvig, L.: A quantitative study of memory system interference in chip multiprocessor architectures, pp. 622–629 (2009). https://doi.org/10.1109/HPCC.2009.77
4. Kim, S., Chandra, D., Solihin, Y.: Fair cache sharing and partitioning in a chip multiprocessor architecture, pp. 111–122 (2004). https://doi.org/10.1109/PACT.2004.15
5. NXP Freescale Semiconductor: AltiVec^{TM} Technology Programming Interface Manual, rev. 0 (1999)
6. NXP Freescale Semiconductor: e6500 Core Reference Manual, rev. 0 (2014)
7. Stärner, J., Asplund, L.: Measuring the cache interference cost in preemptive real-time systems. SIGPLAN Not. 146–154 (2004). https://doi.org/10.1145/998300.997184

MEMPower: Data-Aware GPU Memory Power Model

Jan Lucas[✉] and Ben Juurlink

Embedded Systems Architecture, TU Berlin, Einsteinufer 17, 10587 Berlin, Germany
{j.lucas,b.juurlink}@tu-berlin.de
http://www.aes.tu-berlin.de/

Abstract. This paper presents the MEMPower power model. MEM-Power is a detailed empirical power model for GPU memory access. It models the data dependent energy consumption as well as individual core specific differences. We explain how the model was calibrated using special micro benchmarks as well as a high-resolution power measurement testbed. A novel technique to identify the number of memory channels and the memory channel of a specific address is presented. Our results show significant differences in the access energy of specific GPU cores, while the access energy of the different memory channels from the same GPU cores is almost identical. MEMPower is able to model these differences and provide good predictions of the access energy for specific memory accesses.

Keywords: GPU · Memory · Power modeling · Data dependent power

1 Introduction

GPUs focus on applications with high computational requirements and substantial parallelism that are insensitive to latency [1]. Large caches are ineffective for GPUs due the execution of thousands of parallel threads [2]. These factors cause GPUs and many GPU applications to require memory interfaces that provide significantly higher DRAM bandwidth than what is required and provided for regular CPUs. GPUs usually achieve the high memory bandwidth by using special graphics DRAM memories with lower capacity but wider and faster interfaces, such as GDDR5. These high throughput memory interfaces consume a significant amount of power. Modeling their power consumption accurately is thus important for architectural GPU power simulators.

In our previous work, we have shown that data values influence the energy consumption of GPU ALU operation significantly [3]. While executing the same sequence of instructions the power consumption changed from 155 W to 257 W, when the processed data values were changed. In this work we demonstrate that energy cost of memory transaction also is influenced significantly by the data values written to the DRAM or read from the DRAM. MEMPower provides

© The Author(s) 2019
M. Schoeberl et al. (Eds.): ARCS 2019, LNCS 11479, pp. 195–207, 2019.
https://doi.org/10.1007/978-3-030-18656-2_15

predictions that consider the data values used in transaction as well as the location of the transaction.

Most current discrete GPUs employ GDDR5 or GDDR5X memories [4,5]. Both employ pseudo open drain signaling (POD) [6]. In POD signaling, current flows when transmitting a zero, while no current flow happens when transmitting a one. To improve energy consumption as well as to limit the number of simultaneously switching outputs, both types of memories use data bus inversion (DBI) [7,8]. DBI encoding transmits data inverted, if that results in a lower energy consumption and uses an extra signal line to allow the receiver to reverse the inversion of the data, if required. POD signaling, together with DBI encoding, is a source of data dependent energy consumption of the memory interface.

CMOS circuits consume dynamic power when their internal circuit nodes are recharged to a different state. How much energy is consumed, depends on the load capacitance of this node and the voltages. Bus wires providing long on-chip distance routing are usually structures with high load capacitance. External off-chip interfaces, also contain large loads in their drivers, receivers, wires as well as parasitic package capacitances. How often each of the wires is recharged, depends on the data and the encoding of the data transmitted over the wire. The recharging of wires and other circuit nodes partly explains, why the energy cost of memory transaction depends on the transmitted data.

Memory transactions are generated within the GPU cores, also called streaming multiprocessors (SM). In the GTX580 GPU, the SMs are organized into graphics processor clusters (GPCs) [9]. Each GPC contains 4 SMs. The GTX580 uses a full GF100 die with all four 4 SMs activated in each of the 4 GPCs.

This paper is structured as follows: We present related work in Sect. 2. Section 3 describes our experimental setup including our microbenchmarks. The following Sect. 4 shows how latency measurements can be used to discover the mapping between memory addresses and memory channels. It also describes the properties of the mapping and insights gained from latency measurements. Section 5 introduces the design of the data dependent power model and evaluates the accuracy of the model. Section 6 concludes the paper.

2   Related Work

GPUWattch [10] and GPUSimPow [11] do not take data values and locations into account when predicting the energy cost of each memory transaction. MEM-Power takes data values into account and thus bridges the gap between architectural simulators and slow but precise RTL power simulators.

Wattch [12] collects some activity factors related to data for some memories and busses but does not model high performance GPUs and graphics DRAM.

Wong et al. used microbenchmarking to reveal various latency and cache characteristics of the GT200 [13], but do not consider energy and memory channel mapping. Mei and Chu used microbenchmarks to analyze the structure of the caches, shared memory as well as latency and throughput of the DRAM in more recent NVidia GPUs [14].

Table 1. GPU configuration in experimental evaluation.

Parameter	Value	Parameter	Value
GPU cores (SMs)	16	Integer units/core	16
GPCs	4	Float units/core	32
Core clock	1.5 Ghz	Memory clock	2 Ghz
CUDA	6.5	Driver	343.36

3   Experimental Setup

For our experiments, we used an NVidia GTX580 GPU with a full GF100 chip using the Fermi architecture [9]. A short overview of its parameters is provided in Table 1. This GPU was selected for two main reasons: 1. GPGPU-Sim currently does not support more recent GPU architectures. Energy was measured using a GPU power measurement testbed that has been described in a previous work [11]. 2. Our previous work resulted in a data-dependent power model for the ALUs of this GPU [3]. This work adds the missing memory power model to enable the creation of architectural power model of the GTX580 GPU, that includes both ALU and memory data dependent power.

In order to measure the power consumption of memory transactions we developed custom microbenchmarks. These microbenchmarks execute the tested memory transaction millions of times. This allows us to measure the small energy used per transaction. In order to measure only the data dependent energy of each transaction we measure every transaction twice: Once with the test vector and once with a baseline vector of all ones. Then the energy consumed by the baseline vector is subtracted to calculate the energy difference caused by the specific test vector. Both measurements are performed at nearly the same time to ensure that the GPU temperature stays approximately constant in both measurements to avoid errors. Without this step GPU temperature variations could result in different amounts of static (leakage) power.

The microbenchmarks use inline PTX assembler to generate special load and store instructions that mostly bypass the L2 cache (`ld.global.cv.u32` and `st.wt.u32`). Even with these instructions, using the nvprof profiler, we detected that multiple accesses to the same address, issued at nearly the same time, are still combined at the DRAM. Our microbenchmark was then redesigned to avoid this issue by making sure that the different SMs are not generating accesses to the same location at nearly the same time. The profiler was used to verify that our microbenchmark generates the expected number of memory transactions. Each measurement was performed 128 times and averaged. The order of the measurements was randomized.

4   Memory Layout

According to NVIDIA the GTX580 features 6 different memory channels [9]. CUDA allows us to allocate space in the GDDR5 but does not provide any control over which memory channels are used for the allocation. We suspected that the different memory channels might have different properties in terms of energy consumption due to different PCB layout of the memory channels as well as internal layout GF100 differences. To use all available memory bandwidth, allocations are typically spread over all memory channels, so that all the capacity can be used and all memory bandwidth can be utilized. However, when we want to measure a specific memory channel we need to identify where a specific memory location is actually allocated. As no public API is available to query that information, we hypothesized that the differences in physical distance between the GPU cores and the memory channels would also result in slightly different latencies when accessing the memory. CUDA offers a special %smid register that can be used to identify the SM executing the code and a %clock register that allows very fine-grained time measurements. We used these two features to measure the memory latency of reading from each location from each SM. We measure the latency of each location 32 times and averaged our measurements to reduce measurement noise. For each location, this results in a 16 element latency vector, where each element of the vector shows the average memory read latency from that SM to the memory location. We detected that the latency to the same memory location is indeed different from different SMs and different memory locations show different latency patterns. We noticed that the latency pattern stays constant for 256 consecutive naturally aligned bytes. This means the granularity of the mapping from addresses to memory channels is 256 bytes, and we only need to perform our latency measurements once for each 256 byte block to identify the location of the whole block.

As the memory latency is not completely deterministic but changes slightly, e.g. due to background framebuffer accesses running in parallel to the measurement, all the latency vectors are slightly different. We solved this issue using k-means clustering [15]. We initially tried to map our latency vectors into six clusters corresponding to the six memory controllers listed in NVIDIA's descriptions of the GF100 [9]. This, however, failed to provide a plausible mapping of the memory locations, but mapping the latency vectors into twelve clusters was successful.

When we assume twelve clusters, all latency vectors are located close to one of the twelve centroids and the second closest centroid is much farther away. The number of points that gets assigned to each cluster is also approximately equal. When we access only locations mapped to one centroid, we achieve approximately 1/12 of the bandwidth achieved, when all locations from all channels are used. This pattern also continues if we selected larger subsets of the centroids, e.g. selecting locations from two clusters results in 1/6 of the bandwidth. The nvprof profiler also provides additional hints that the identified mapping is correct: Many DRAM counters are provided twice, one counter for something called subpartition 0 and another counter for subpartition 1. If we access only locations from a single cluster, we notice that only one of these two performance counters is incremented significantly, while the other counter stays very close to zero. This indicates all locations in each of the clusters are part of the same subpartition.

Lopes et al. list six L2 Cache banks with two slices each for GTX580 [16]. The GTX580 has a 384-bit wide memory interface. Six 64-bit wide channels together with the 8n prefetch of GDDR5 would result in a fetch-granularity of 64 bytes per burst. Memory access patterns that only access 32 consecutive bytes and do not touch the next 32 bytes would always overfetch 32 bytes per transaction and would result in an effective bandwidth of less than half the peak bandwidth. However, our experiments showed better than expected performance for 32 byte fetches. An additional hint at 32 byte transaction is also provided by the NVIDIA profiler, where many DRAM related performance counters are incremented by one per 32 bytes. This indicates that the GTX580 can fetch 32 bytes at a time, which is consistent with twelve 32-bit channels. From these findings, we estimate that the GTX580 uses six memory controllers with two subpartitions in each controller and one 32-bit wide channel per subpartition.

As twelve is not a power of two, the GTX580 cannot simply use a few address bits to select the memory channel. Round-robin mapping of addresses to memory channels is conceptually simple but would require a division of the addresses by twelve.

Figure 1 provides a graphical representation of the recovered memory mapping of 1 MB block of memory. Each pixel represents a 256 byte block, each of the 64 lines represents $64 \times 256\,\text{B} = 16\,\text{kB}$. The memory mapping seems to be

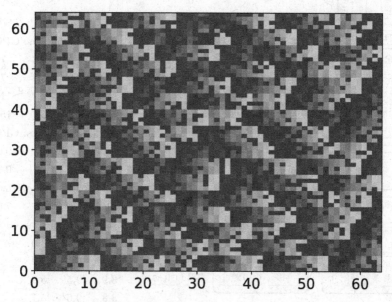

Fig. 1. 1 MB memory block with recovered memory channel mapping, each pixel is equivalent to a 256 byte block

structured, but does not use any simple round robin scheme. With this mapping twelve consecutive 256B blocks, on average, use 10.6 different memory channels. A simple round robin scheme would likely result in some applications having biased memory transaction patterns that favor some memory channels over others, which would result in a performance reduction. The mapping is likely the output of a simple hash function, that makes it unlikely for applications to use a biased memory access patterns by chance. Sell describes a similar scheme used by Xbox One X Scorpio Engine [17].

We also analyzed the latency vectors (Table 2) to reveal more information about the internal structure of the GPU. We first notice that all SMs in the same GPC have nearly the same latency pattern for the memory channels. The first SM in each GPC seems to have the lowest latency. The other SMs are approximately 2, 6 and 8 cycles slower. This additional latency within the GPC does not depend on the memory channels addressed. It is also identical for all four GPCs. This indicates an identical layout of all four GPCs and a shared connection of all SMs of a GPC to the main interconnect. The latency of four memory channels is lowest at GPC1. This is also true for GPC2 and GPC3. There are no memory channels where GPC0 provides the lowest latency. We suspect that is the result of a layout such as shown in Fig. 2. This also matches well with the PCB layout of a GTX580 where DRAM chips are located on 3 of the four sides of the GF100 and the PCIe interface can be found at the bottom.

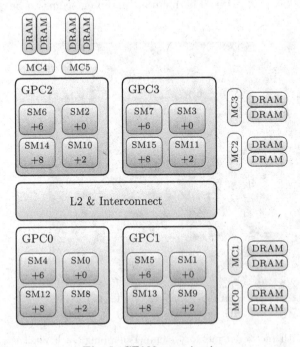

Fig. 2. GF100 organization

Table 2. DRAM latency.

GPC0	GPC1	GPC2	GPC3
Added latency vs. GPC1			
3.6	-	3.6	7.5
3.9	-	3.8	7.5
7.4	-	3.7	11.2
11.3	-	5.7	15.1
Added latency vs. GPC2			
3.6	3.8	-	0.0
3.8	3.8	-	0.1
9.4	3.8	-	5.8
11.2	2.0	-	7.6
Added latency vs. GPC3			
4.0	7.6	4.0	-
3.9	7.7	3.9	-
3.9	9.5	5.9	-
3.8	9.6	5.7	-

5 Data-Dependent Energy Consumption

As already described in the introduction, we expect two main reasons for data dependent energy consumption: 1. Special signaling lines such as the GDDR5 DQ lines with additional energy consumption at a certain signal level. 2. State changes of wires and other circuit nodes. Our model allows a fast and simple evaluation, for this reason, we selected a simple linear model. Every memory transaction is mapped to a small vector that describes the relevant properties of the block. A dot product of this vector with a coefficient vector results in the estimated energy consumption for this transaction. The coefficient vector is calculated in a calibration process.

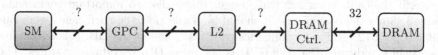

Fig. 3. Memory datapath

The following properties of the block are used to estimate the energy consumption. We model signal level related energy consumption by including the population count of the block. The population count is the number of set bits. We also need to estimate the amount of recharging of internal wires and circuitry caused by the transaction. Memory transactions travel through several units and various connections until they finally reach the DRAM. A simplified diagram is shown in Fig. 3. We know that the transaction travels through a 32-bit wide interface between DRAM and memory controller. Unless a reordering of bits is performed, we know which bits will be transmitted through the same wire and could cause switching activity on these wires, e.g: bits $0, 32, 64, \ldots$ are transmitted on the same DQ line, bits $1, 33, 65, \ldots$ are transmitted on the next DQ line, etc. While we know the width of the DRAM interface itself, the width of the various internal interconnections is unknown. We assume the internal link width are powers of two and are at least byte wide. The coefficients for all potential link sizes are first added to the model. During the calibration of the model, the best subset of coefficients is selected, and we indirectly gain knowledge about the internal interconnections. Because GDDR5 memory can use DBI encoded data, an extra version of each of the previously described coefficients is added to our model. This second version assumes DBI encoded data.

A synthetic set of test vectors was generated to calibrate the model. The calibration test vectors are designed to span a wide range of combinations in terms of toggles at various positions and in terms of population count. We measured the real energy consumption of our test vectors. Initially, the model uses a larger number of coefficients and some of these likely have no corresponding hardware structure in the GPU. This causes a significant risk of overfitting the coefficients to our calibration measurements. We avoid this issue by using LASSO regression as an alternative to regular least square fit [18]. Instead of fitting the calibration data as closely as possible LASSO also tries to reduce the number of used coefficients and reduces their size. The hyperparameter α controls the trade off between number and size of the coefficients and prediction error with the calibration set.

In addition to the set of calibration vectors, we generated another set of test vectors to validate our model. The validation vectors are generated to mimic real application data. The vectors use various integer and floating-point data types, a mixture of random distributions with different parameters was used to generate realistic data. Real application data is often also highly correlated, some test vectors used a Gaussian process to provide correlated data.

Figure 4 shows the prediction error at various values of α. $\alpha = 0.007$ results in the smallest error in the validation set for store transaction. Smaller values of α overfit the calibration set, while larger values discard important coefficients. Table 3 shows the coefficients, it should be noted that the coefficients were calculated per 512 bitflips for numerical reasons. None of the DBI coefficients are used, which indicates that the GPU is not using DBI encoding for stores. The largest coefficient corresponds to a 32 byte wide link. Coefficients for 4 and 8

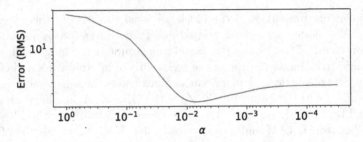

Fig. 4. Store access prediction accuracy vs. α

Table 3. 128B transaction coefficients

Store			Load		
Coefficient	DBI	Value (nJ)	Coefficient	DBI	Value (nJ)
Const	No	7.631	Const	No	9.001
Pop Cnt.	No	-3.060	Pop Cnt.	No	-3.905
Pop Cnt.	Yes	-0.551	Pop Cnt.	Yes	-0.491
Toggle 1	No	0.031	Toggle 1	No	0.009
Toggle 1	Yes	0.036	Toggle 1	Yes	-0.005
Toggle 2	No	0.013	Toggle 2	No	0.011
Toggle 2	Yes	0.025	Toggle 2	Yes	-0.018
Toggle 4	No	0.933	Toggle 4	No	1.676
Toggle 4	Yes	0.084	Toggle 4	Yes	0.000
Toggle 8	No	0.810	Toggle 8	No	0.435
Toggle 8	Yes	-0.035	Toggle 8	Yes	-0.004
Toggle 16	No	2.276	Toggle 16	No	1.021
Toggle 16	Yes	0.042	Toggle 16	Yes	0.000
Toggle 32	No	9.354	Toggle 32	No	7.446
Toggle 32	Yes	0.156	Toggle 32	Yes	0.020
Toggle 64	No	5.169	Toggle 64	No	9.919
Toggle 64	Yes	0.132	Toggle 64	Yes	1.872

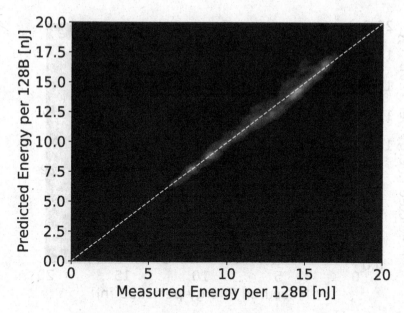

Fig. 5. MEMPower energy prediction for store access

byte wide links are small. Narrow 1 or 2 byte wide links are not employed. The large coefficient for a 64 byte wide link could be linked to SM internal power consumption, as the SMs use 16 wide SIMD units with 32-bits per unit.

The heatmap in Fig. 5 shows the prediction accuracy of our model for 128 byte store transactions. If the model would offer perfect prediction all points would be on the dashed white line. However, all our predictions are very close to the line which indicate a great prediction accuracy. Our RMS error is 0.39 nJ and the relative error is just 3.1%. Smaller transactions use different coefficients, results are not shown here because of the limited space. But one interesting result is that register values from disabled threads influence the energy consumption. Likely these register values are still transmitted through parts of the interconnect but marked as inactive. Taking data values into account instead of assuming a constant average energy per transaction improves the prediction error from an average error of 1.7 nJ to a error of just 0.39 nJ.

Figure 6 shows the prediction accuracy of our load model. In general, the model achieves a good prediction accuracy of 9.1% but tends to underestimate the energy required for cheaper transactions. Our load kernel achieves a significantly lower bandwidth than the store kernel as it will not send the next load transaction before the last transaction returned, while stores will be pipelined. The lower bandwidth results in a reduced signal to noise ratio of the measurements. The load coefficients printed in Table 3 indicate that load transaction are employing DBI encoding. Error improves from 2.3 nJ to 1.43 nJ.

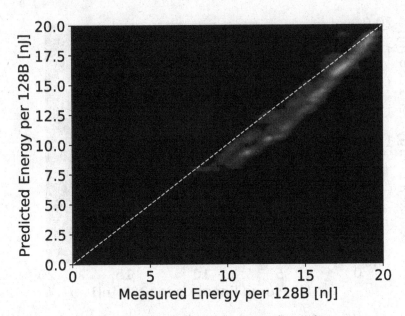

Fig. 6. MEMPower energy prediction for read access

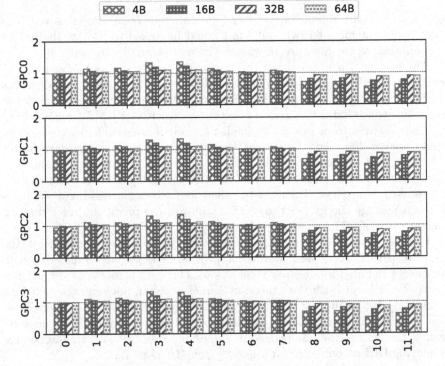

Fig. 7. Normalized memory channel energy consumption

We combined the microbenchmarks with the memory channel identification technique from Sect. 4 to check for energy differences between different memory channels and SMs. We tested the first SM from each GPC and used simplified test vectors to check for changes of our most important coefficients. The normalized results are shown in Fig. 7. We detected only small differences between the different SMs, however, the blue coefficient for switching activity on a 4 byte wide bus shows a large variance between different memory channels. Memory transactions to channels 8 to 11 are significantly cheaper than memory transactions on Channels 0 to 3 and 5 to 7. Memory transactions on Channels 3 and 4 are more expensive. As these results are consistent for all four GPCs, these differences are likely the result of slightly different PCB layout of the different memory channels instead of chip internal routing.

6   Conclusion

In this paper, we have presented the MEMPower power model for GPU memory transactions. Our contributions can be summarized as follows:

- We presented a novel technique to identify in which memory channel a specific memory address is located.
- Our microbenchmarks uncovered previously unknown architectural details of GF100-based GPUs.
- We show that memory channels are not completely identical, but differ in latency and energy consumption.
- The MEMPower model improves the energy predictions accuracy by on average 37.8% for loads compared to non-data dependent models and provides a 77.1% improvement on our validation set for stores.

At peak bandwidth data dependent changes to energy can influence the total power consumption of the GTX580 GPU by more than 25 W or around 10% of the total power. Future Work includes software and hardware techniques to reduce the energy consumption. Common but expensive data patterns could be recoded to patterns with reduced energy consumption. As memory transactions are significantly more expensive than simple ALU operations, even software solutions could be beneficial. Programmer control over data allocation could allow rarely used data to be placed in memory channels with costlier memory access and often used data in memory channels with reduced energy consumption.

Acknowledgements. This work has received funding from the European Union's Horizon 2020 research and innovation programme under grant agreement No. 688759 (Project LPGPU2). A prior version of this work is part of the first author's defended, but currently unpublished, doctoral thesis.

References

1. Owens, J.D., Houston, M., Luebke, D., Green, S., Stone, J.E., Phillips, J.C.: GPU computing. Proc. IEEE **96**(5), 879–899 (2008)
2. Fatahalian, K., Houston, M.: A closer look at GPUs. Commun. ACM **51**(10), 50–57 (2008)
3. Lucas, J., Juurlink, B.: ALUPower: data dependent power consumption in GPUs. In: IEEE Modeling, Analysis and Simulation of Computer and Telecommunication Systems (MASCOTS) (2016)
4. JEDEC Standard: Graphics Double Data Rate (GDDR5) SGRAM Standard. JESD212C, February 2016
5. JEDEC Standard: Graphics Double Data Rate (GDDR5X) SGRAM Standard. JESD232A, August 2016
6. JEDEC Standard: POD15 - 1.5 V Pseudo Open Drain I/O. JESD8-20A (2009)
7. Hollis, T.M.: Data bus inversion in high-speed memory applications. IEEE Trans. Circuits Syst. II: Express Briefs **56**, 300–304 (2009)
8. Kim, J.H., et al.: Performance impact of simultaneous switching output noise on graphic memory systems. In: Electrical Performance of Electronic Packaging. IEEE (2007)
9. Wittenbrink, C.M., Kilgariff, E., Prabhu, A.: Fermi GF100 GPU architecture. IEEE Micro **31**(2), 50–59 (2011)
10. Leng, J., et al.: GPUWattch: enabling energy optimizations in GPGPUs. In: Proceedings of the 40th Annual International Symposium on Computer Architecture (ISCA) (2013)
11. Lucas, J., Lal, S., Andersch, M., Alvarez-Mesa, M., Juurlink, B.: How a single chip causes massive power bills GPUSimPow: a GPGPU power simulator. In: Proceedings of the IEEE International Symposium on Performance Analysis of Systems and Software (ISPASS) (2013)
12. Brooks, D., Tiwari, V., Martonosi, M.: Wattch: a framework for architectural-level power analysis and optimizations. In: Proceedings of the International Symposium on Computer Architecture, ISCA. ACM (2000)
13. Wong, H., Papadopoulou, M.M., Sadooghi-Alvandi, M., Moshovos, A.: Demystifying GPU microarchitecture through microbenchmarking. In: 2010 IEEE International Symposium on Performance Analysis of Systems and Software (ISPASS), pp. 235–246. IEEE (2010)
14. Mei, X., Chu, X.: Dissecting GPU memory hierarchy through microbenchmarking. IEEE Trans. Parallel Distrib. Syst. **28**(1), 72–86 (2017)
15. Hartigan, J.A., Wong, M.A.: Algorithm AS 136: a k-means clustering algorithm. J. R. Stat. Soc. Ser. C (Appl. Stat.) **28**(1), 100–108 (1979)
16. Lopes, A., Pratas, F., Sousa, L., Ilic, A.: Exploring GPU performance, power and energy-efficiency bounds with cache-aware roofline modeling. In: International Symposium on Performance Analysis of Systems and Software (ISPASS) (2017)
17. Sell, J.: The Xbox One X Scorpio engine. IEEE Micro **38**(2), 53–60 (2018)
18. Tibshirani, R.: Regression shrinkage and selection via the lasso. J. R. Stat. Soc. Ser. B (Methodol.) **58**, 267–288 (1996)

Open Access This chapter is licensed under the terms of the Creative Commons Attribution 4.0 International License (http://creativecommons.org/licenses/by/4.0/), which permits use, sharing, adaptation, distribution and reproduction in any medium or format, as long as you give appropriate credit to the original author(s) and the source, provide a link to the Creative Commons license and indicate if changes were made.

The images or other third party material in this chapter are included in the chapter's Creative Commons license, unless indicated otherwise in a credit line to the material. If material is not included in the chapter's Creative Commons license and your intended use is not permitted by statutory regulation or exceeds the permitted use, you will need to obtain permission directly from the copyright holder.

FPGA

Effective FPGA Architecture
for General CRC

Lukáš Kekely[1(✉)], Jakub Cabal[1], and Jan Kořenek[2]

[1] CESNET a. l. e., Zikova 4, 160 00 Prague, Czech Republic
{kekely,cabal}@cesnet.cz
[2] IT4Innovations Centre of Excellence, FIT BUT,
Božetěchova 2, 612 66 Brno, Czech Republic
korenek@fit.vutbr.cz

Abstract. As throughputs of digital networks and memory interfaces are on a constant rise, there is a need for ever-faster implementations of error-detecting codes. Cyclic redundancy checks (CRC) are a common and widely used type of codes to ensure consistency or detect accidental changes of transferred data. We propose a novel FPGA architecture for the computation of the CRC values designed for general high-speed data transfers. Its key feature is allowing a processing of multiple independent data packets (transactions) in each clock cycle, what is a necessity for achieving high overall throughput on very wide data buses. The proposed approach can be effectively used in Ethernet MACs for different speeds, in Hybrid Memory Cube (HMC) controller, and in many other technologies utilizing any kind of CRC. Experimental results confirm that the proposed architecture enables reaching an effective throughput sufficient for utilization in multi-terabit Ethernet networks (over 2 Tbps or over 3000 Mpps) on a single Xilinx UltraScale+ FPGA. Furthermore, a better utilization of FPGA resources is achieved compared to existing CRC implementation for HMC controller (up to 70% savings).

Keywords: FPGA · CRC · High-speed processing · Ethernet · HMC

1 Introduction

The Cyclic Redundancy Check (CRC) codes are widely deployed in digital communications and storage systems to detect accidental error introduced into data. The binary data are divided into transactions (packets) and each transaction is subjected to a CRC which results in a fixed-length binary check sequence. The computed check sequence value is then attached to the original data to determine its correctness. After being transferred/processed, the data are subject to the same CRC computation one more time and the new result is compared with the older attached CRC value. In case of a match, the data transaction is most likely not corrupted. Because of their simple implementation in hardware and good characteristics, the utilization of CRCs is very popular [5,6].

© Springer Nature Switzerland AG 2019
M. Schoeberl et al. (Eds.): ARCS 2019, LNCS 11479, pp. 211–223, 2019.
https://doi.org/10.1007/978-3-030-18656-2_16

The computation of CRC codes is based on the remainder of a polynomial division where coefficients are elements of the finite field $GF(2)$. There are many different CRC codes, each defined by a specific dividing polynomial and output (code) width. The mathematical background of CRC and forms of its hardware representation have been extensively studied in various works like [10,11,13] and is not the primary focus of this paper. All we need to know is that an approach capable of processing multiple input bits in parallel exists and is based on XOR equations set up for each output bit. A specific set of these equations (CRC table) can be easily constructed for any given dividing polynomial and input data word width. Furthermore, multiple results of these CRC tables can be aggregated (accumulated) together to obtain code value of longer data transaction.

Although basic CRC computation can be easily represented, practical processing of high-speed data is much harder. The data packets usually have variable lengths and are not completely aligned with data bus words. Unaligned ends and starts must be handled correctly, which requires additional logic and more complex architecture than a single CRC table. Furthermore, as the data bus width is growing to raise throughput, transfers of multiple packets per clock cycle (data bus word) must be supported. This challenge must be addressed in practical high-speed CRC implementation and that is indeed the main focus of our work.

We propose a novel FPGA architecture for practical computation of CRC codes for general high-speed transfers of data packets with variable lengths. The architecture enables effective computation of multiple values per clock cycle in a single pipeline thus allows handling of multiple packets in each data bus word. Furthermore, it supports configurable pipelining (before synthesis) so optimal tradeoff between frequency (throughput) and utilized resources can be selected. When fully pipelined, the CRC architecture achieves unprecedented throughput of over 2 Tbps or 3000 millions of packets per second (Mpps) in a single FPGA.

2   Related Work

The mathematical background of CRC computation has been extensively studied in many previous works like [7,10,11,13] and it is not the focus of this paper. Rather, we want to use the results and proposed effective hardware representation of basic CRC calculations from these papers as primary constructional blocks of a new architecture. However, the challenge of practical high-speed CRC computation for variable-length data packets is more complicated.

Some attempts to address this additional challenges are made in [4]. Architectures arranging basic CRC calculation into more complex structures are proposed to enable processing of unaligned packets ending. However, the proposed architectures are shown to scale well only up to throughputs around 10 Gbps (256 b wide bus) what is insufficient for current high-speed data handling.

More advanced general CRC implementations are described in many papers like [1,3,15]. All of them use a kind of advanced pipelining and parallelization to achieve higher frequencies (throughputs) than other simpler solutions. The Ethernet CRC-32 implementations by these architectures use input data widths of

64 to 512 bits and can run at hundreds of MHz. This leads to reported through-puts sufficient for wire-speed traffic processing of up to 100 Gbps Ethernet. But scaling for higher speeds is not properly addressed in any of these works and would bring exponential growth in required FPGA area or significant degradation of effective throughput on short packets (i.e. data rate limited by packet rate). Furthermore, the extension of these architectures to allow multiple packets per clock cycle (i.e. sufficiently increasing their packet rate) would be non-trivial.

Interesting CRC architecture [8,9] uses pipelining similar to the above works to achieve high throughput and focuses primarily on reconfigurability of CRC polynomial, but it also partially addresses the challenge of limited packet rate on short packets. The architecture can process parts of two subsequent packets in a single clock cycle (data bus word). A maximal throughput of 40 Gbps reported in the paper can be thus easily scaled up to 100 or even 200 Gbps. But because the parallel processing is structurally limited to only two packet parts, further scaling would again hit the same obstacles as mentioned above.

Fastest commercially available CRC architecture is part of Ethernet MAC IP core [14]. In the product description, its authors claim to be able to achieve up to 400 Gbps line-rate processing of packets using only a small portion of FPGA area. But no throughput measurements nor exact resource requirements are provided to back up those claims. Furthermore, any details about their CRC architecture or its parameters (e.g. frequency, data bus width) are also lacking.

3   Architecture Design

Here we describe the proposed CRC architecture. First, data bus format with multiple packets per clock cycle is defined. This is crucial for efficient scaling above 100 Gbps. After that, basic utilized CRC computing blocks are introduced. Finally, the architecture itself is presented in serial and parallel versions.

3.1   Input Bus Format

To enable multiple packets per clock cycle, we define the input data bus word format as illustrated in Fig. 1. The figure also shows an example of possible packet placement under the proposed format. One should notice that without the support of multiple packets per clock cycle, each of the depicted data frames should occupy separate word on the bus (5 words would be required), but word sharing enables more dense packing (only 3 words are needed in the example). The proposed bus format is shown at the bottom of the figure, each data word is divided into several *regions*. These restrain the maximum number of data packets per word as at most one packet can start and one end (can be a different one) in each region. Each region is further separated into multiple *blocks* of basic data *elements* (items) to constraint possible positioning of packet starts. Notice that each packet must start aligned with the start of a block, but can end on any data element (packets A and B both end in the middle of a block).

To support the described bus format, additional metadata must accompany each data word. For each region the following information must be given:

– a flag for the presence of a packet start (SOP),
– a flag for the presence of a packet end (EOP),
– a position of packet start if present (SOP_POS),
– a position of packet end if present (EOP_POS).

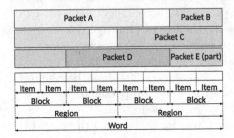

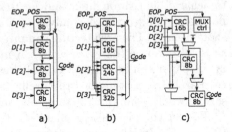

Fig. 1. Data bus format illustration.   **Fig. 2.** CRC end realizations possibilities.

The proposed data word format enables definitions of multiple bus versions with different parameters. We describe them by these four attributes:

– *Number of regions (n)* match the maximal number of packets per word.
– *Region size (r)* defines the number of blocks in a region.
– *Block size (b)* states the number of elements in a block.
– *Element width (e)* defines the size of the smallest piece of data in bits.

Using these attributes, we derive bus word width in bits like $dw = n \times r \times b \times e$.

3.2   CRC Computation Blocks

In both versions of the proposed architecture, we utilize 4 basic computational units: (1) basic CRC table for fixed input width, (2) accumulation logic capable of aggregating multiple intermediate CRCs, (3) correction of input data based on packet start position, and (4) finalization of CRC based on packet end position.

As already mentioned in the Introduction, based on given dividing polynomial and input width a specific implementation of basic **CRC table** can be easily generated [13]. It has a form of parallel XOR equations on input bits, one equation for each output (code) bit. In FPGAs, these XORs are implemented in LUTs. The CRC table basically only converts the input data word into an intermediary CRC code value without regard to packet borders.

Specific **CRC accumulation** can be similarly generated for any polynomial. It has a form of parallel XOR equations and it aggregates two or more intermediary CRC values computed from separate parts of data (e.g. by CRC tables). This enables to divide handling of longer data packets in multiple smaller steps.

Correction of **CRC start** based on packet position can be achieved by masking – the part of the input before packet start is filled with zeros. CRC computations are based on XOR operations and zero is a neutral value for them ($0\ xora = a$ for any a). Therefore, it is possible to show that extension of any data by prepending any number of leading zeros has no effect on computed CRC value, which remains the same as for original data [7]. Note, that also the initial (intermediary) value of CRC register must be shifted and applied accordingly.

Finally, correct handling of **CRC end** is a bit more complicated. Masking similar to start correction cannot be directly applied, as appending trailing zeros to data will change the computed CRC value. A workaround is to use a barrel-shifter to shift the last data part so that the end of the packet is aligned with the end of the region. This way, the masking operation is converted from trailing zeros into leading zeros and can be applied in the same way as in CRC start. Another possible type of approach is to utilize some arrangement of multiple smaller CRC tables [4]. Illustration of these arrangements for 32 bit wide region and $e = 8$ are shown in Fig. 2. On the left, we can see a serial version, where multiple tables are pipelined each processing one input data element and correct output code is selected afterward based on packet end position. In the middle, there is a parallel version, where each possible position of the end has its own accordingly wide table. These basic approaches do not scale well for wider data buses – depth of the pipeline (critical path) in (a) or amount of resources in (b). To issue the scaling challenge a more sophisticated approach illustrated as (c) can be used. Each pipeline step corresponds to one layer of a binary search tree and performs CRC computation with a gradually halving table width which can be applied or bypassed. The binary tree is evaluated for a given packet end position (MUX ctrl) and bypass multiplexors at each pipeline step are controlled accordingly. At the end an implicit CRC finalization table with width e is present. For example, for the computation of 24 bit long packet end only the middle 8 bit table is bypassed, and for 16 bit end the top 16 bit table is bypassed.

Thanks to division and encapsulation of all basic CRC computations into the described blocks, the subsequently designed architecture will be general and easily usable for any given division polynomial. Because, the change of the polynomial only requires re-generation of used CRC tables (XOR equations) in these blocks and will not affect structure of the whole architecture.

3.3 Serial and Parallel Architectures

Both versions of the proposed CRC architecture divide processing of input data word between n submodules – one for each region. Each submodule can process an independent packet in each clock cycle or they can cooperate together and handle longer packets. Serial and parallel version differ primarily in the distribution of intermediate CRC values between these submodules. Figure 3 shows top level structure of the serial implementation. One region of the input bus (width $rw = r \times b \times e$) is connected to each submodule. The submodule calculates final CRC value if an end of the packet is present in his part of input bus. To support cooperation on longer packets, each submodule is passing its intermediate CRC

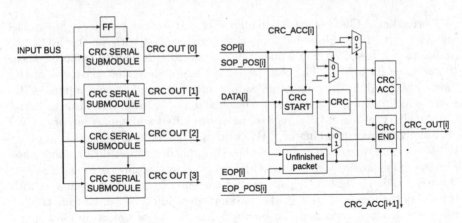

Fig. 3. Serial top level architecture.   **Fig. 4.** Serial submodule internal structure.

result to the next submodule. The last submodule is passing its result to the first over a register, so the calculation can continue in the next data bus word.

In Fig. 4 we can see internal structure of one serial submodule. It is composed of several logic stages and optional registers for better timing. Base CRC table of width rw is used as a core computational block and handling of corrections required for starting, ending or continuing packets is realized by multiple separate blocks around it. They are controlled by metadata about packet positioning in the assigned region of the bus. The CRC start block masks input data before the packet start so that subsequent base CRC calculation is performed correctly for starting packets. If no start of a packet is present, the input data word is not altered. If a packet continuing from the previous words is present in the input data, the output value of CRC table is aggregated with an intermediate CRC value from the previous submodule in accumulation block. Otherwise (starting packet), the input CRC value is masked and no aggregation is performed – only locally computed result is passed. The output of accumulation block is used as intermediate CRC value on the input of the next submodule. Finally, CRC end block performs CRC calculation for packets ending in data region assigned to this submodule. When the whole packet data (start and end) are present in the region of this submodule, the final CRC value is calculated only from masked input data. Otherwise, output CRC value is calculated from the intermediate result from the previous submodule and unaltered input data.

The serial implementation has a weak point – long critical path from the output of the CRC register, through CRC aggregation in all submodules, and back to the register (Fig. 3). This critical path cannot be resolved using pipelining as correct CRC intermediate value must be present in the register when processing of the next word starts. That is why, we propose the parallel version of CRC aggregation. In Fig. 5 we can see that, the output value of CRC submodule is shared with each subsequent submodule not just with the next one. In Fig. 6 we can see internal structure of CRC submodule accommodated for the parallel aggregation. There are several major changes present. The output value of CRC accumulation block now serves only for the final CRC calculation in the CRC end block of the next submodule. So, the intermediate CRC results are not accumulated in steps through the whole pipeline of submodules. Now, each CRC accumulation block must independently aggregate intermediate CRC values from all previous submodules including value stored in the top-level register. The other parts of the parallel implementation remain the same as in the serial one. This version has significantly improved critical path and allows to achieve much higher operating frequencies. On the other hand, it requires considerably more logic resources as more complicated CRC accumulation modules are used.

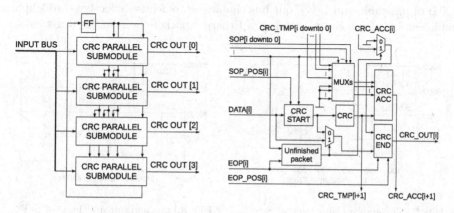

Fig. 5. Parallel top level architecture.   **Fig. 6.** Parallel submodule internal structure.

4   Measured Results

We evaluate the proposed CRC architecture in two high-speed cases: Ethernet networks and HMC controller. CRC ensures consistency of data packets in both cases, but different polynomials are used. A detailed evaluation is performed for the networking case, where effects of various architecture parameters are explored. In HMC case we directly select the best configurations and compare them with existing CRC implementation in the OpenHMC controller.

4.1   Ethernet Based Networks

Ethernet uses CRC with the CRC-32 division polynomial [6] as a frames check sequence. As already discussed in the Related Work, published architectures can be effectively used for Ethernet traffic processing at speeds up to 200 Gbps and commercially available solutions promise throughputs of up to 400 Gbps. Their scaling towards higher speeds is limited by insufficient packet rates on the shortest packets for wider data buses. The proposed architecture addresses exactly this issue and should be able to scale well even at higher throughputs.

When adjusting the proposed architecture for Ethernet, the parameters of the bus format should be configured to appropriate values. Ethernet operates with bytes (octets) as the smallest data elements – therefore $e = 8$. Lower layers of Ethernet (PCS/PMA layers) usually operate with frame starts aligned at $8\,B$ lanes – so $b = 8$ is convenient. Size of a region should correspond with the size of the smallest allowed packets $(64\,B)$ – so $r = 64/b = 8$. Smaller regions would needlessly allow more packets per word than possible and larger regions would reduce bus saturation for the shortest packets. Using these attributes $(r = b = e = 8)$ and considering the shortest packets to be $64\,B$ long, the bus format impose no more than $b - 1 = 7$ bytes of alignment overhead per packet. Furthermore, as lower layers of Ethernet operate with larger overhead per packet $(20\,B$ of preamble and IFG), our bus enables us to achieve effective throughput sufficient for wire-speed processing of Ethernet packets even in the worst case.

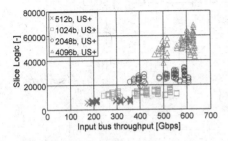

Fig. 7. Throughput and logic of S-S.   **Fig. 8.** Throughput and logic of S-T.

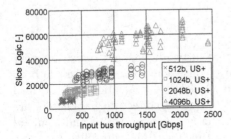
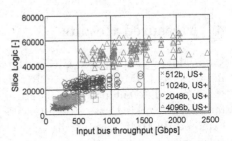

Fig. 9. Throughput and logic of P-S.   **Fig. 10.** Throughput and logic of P-T.

Evaluation for Ethernet compares four versions of the proposed architecture: (1) **S-S** – *serial* architecture with *shifter* CRC end, (2) **S-T** – *serial* architecture with *tree* CRC end, (3) **P-S** – *parallel* architecture with *shifter* CRC end, and (4) **P-T** – *parallel* architecture with *tree* CRC end. For each, we measure results for different data bus widths $(dw = 512, 1024, 2048, 4096)$ and various combinations of pipeline registers. In all cases, we use data bus parameters $r = b = e = 8$ that are sufficient for wire-speed processing of even the shortest frames, only the value of n is changing with the width of the bus. The results of all the combinations form the state space of CRC implementations with different throughput, working frequency, latency and resource usage. All values are obtained for the Xilinx Virtex-7 XCVH870T or UltraScale+ XCVU7P FPGAs using the Vivado 2017.3.

Figures 7, 8, 9, and 10 compare the four versions of Ethernet CRC architecture. They show resource utilization and achieved throughput on the Ultra-Scale+ FPGA. Each point represents one specific implementation with a different combination of parameters (data width and pipeline enabling). The resources utilization linearly increases with the achieved throughput in both parallel versions (Figs. 9 and 10). Unfortunately, in both serial versions (Figs. 7 and 8) the resources increase considerably faster with throughput. In the case of the P-S and the P-T implementations, we are able to reach effective throughputs of well over 2 Tbps (over 3000 Mpps). Achieved throughputs for the S-S and the S-T implementations are notably worse while the used resources remain similarly high. This is because the serial CRC generators reach notably lower frequencies due to an expected longer critical path.

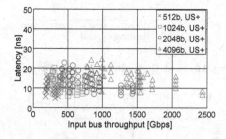 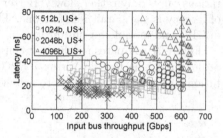

Fig. 11. Throughput and latency of S-S.   **Fig. 12.** Throughput and latency of S-T.

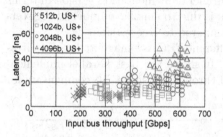 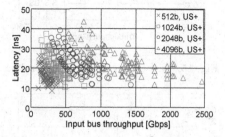

Fig. 13. Throughput and latency of P-S.   **Fig. 14.** Throughput and latency of P-T.

Figures 11, 12, 13, and 14 bring the latency into the picture. Generally, the latency depends on the number of enabled pipeline registers in CRC implementations and achieved working frequency. From the graphs, we can see that the latencies of the serial implementations are increasing notably as the achieved throughput (word width) is rising. On the other hand, the latencies of the parallel implementations remain approximately within the same bounds. This is again due to the higher frequency of parallel implementations even for wider buses.

Figure 15 shows the evaluated four versions of Ethernet CRC implementations together. Only Pareto optimal set of results in resource utilization and achieved throughput space is selected for each implementation version. From the graph, we can more clearly see the difference between the serial (dashed lines) and the parallel (full lines) implementations in achieved throughput. The parallel implementations are able to reach the effective throughput of over 2 Tbps, while the serial implementations cannot reach significantly more than 600 Gbps. Furthermore, parallel-tree has slightly better resource utilization than parallel-shifter.

Figure 16 shows Pareto optimal results of latency to achieved throughput for the four evaluated versions of Ethernet CRC implementations. Again, we can see the notable difference between the serial (dashed lines) and the parallel (full lines) implementations. The latency of the serial implementations steeply increases with the throughput (bus width), but the latency of parallel implementations raises only rather slowly. Better parallel implementation version in terms of latency is the parallel-shifter one. This is due to smaller number of registers in CRC end module for shifter version compared to tree version.

Figure 17 compares results between different FPGAs – magenta for the Ultra-Scale+ and blue for the Virtex-7 FPGA. It shows the best parallel implementations in resource utilization to achieved throughput space. To compensate for

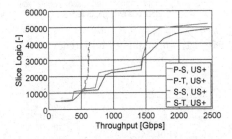

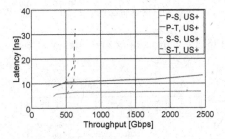

Fig. 15. Best throughput × logic results.   **Fig. 16.** Best throughput × latency results.

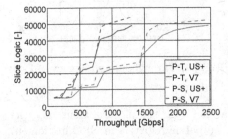

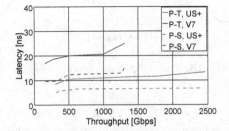

Fig. 17. Throughput × logic, varied chip.   **Fig. 18.** Throughput × latency, varied chip.

the 1.5-2 times lower achieved frequencies on the Virtex-7 chip compared to the UltraScale+, nearly 2 times larger implementations must be used when trying to achieve the same throughputs. The stairs in the graphs are caused by the changing data bus width. Finally, Fig. 18 compares latencies of the best parallel implementations of Ethernet CRC generator between different FPGAs. Again, we can see the positive effect of the higher frequencies and sparser registering on the UltraScale+, where the latency is nearly 2 times better.

4.2 OpenHMC Controller

Hybrid Memory Cube (HMC) is a high-performance RAM interface that uses a 32 bit version of CRC with the CRC-32K (Koopman) division polynomial [2,12]. Again, an appropriate adjustment of the data bus format parameters should be considered first. HMC operates with data divided into 128 bit wide 'flits' as the smallest data elements, therefore $e = 128$. Each data transaction (packet) is a continuous sequence of 1 or more flits, so $r = b = 1$. Finally, the number of regions n depends on the width of the memory interface, commonly used widths are 4, 6 or 8 flits. This kind of bus arrangement leads to a considerably simplified computation in each submodule. As packets start and end only aligned to the region borders, CRC start and CRC end blocks are not needed.

Table 1. Comparison of OpenHMC CRC implementation to the proposed.

Bus width	Implementation	LUTs	FFs	Fmax
512	OpenHMC	4988	2477	700 MHz
	proposed	2262	1858	807 MHz
768	OpenHMC	12071	3778	594 MHz
	proposed	3935	2791	802 MHz
1024	OpenHMC	23599	5125	517 MHz
	proposed	6340	3728	798 MHz

An existing opensource controller implementation of HMC interface is called OpenHMC controller [2]. It utilizes its own specific implementation of CRC architecture capable of handling multiple flits per clock cycle. The CRC implementation is a critical part of the whole controller, as it consumes the majority of all FPGA logic required. We compare this default implementation to our proposed CRC architecture in the parallel version for different data widths. The results for the UltraScale+ FPGA are provided in the Table 1. While our architecture is configured to have the same latency and throughput as the OpenHMC default CRC implementation, a clear difference in resource utilization is visible. Our implementation requires less than half of the logic and around 75% of registers for 512 b (4 flits) wide bus. Resource saving increases even further for wider data buses, up to only a quarter of logic and around 70% of registers. Achieved frequency is also better in our implementations, it especially scales considerably better with rising bus width compared to default OpenHMC implementation.

5   Conclusion

This paper introduces and elaborates a novel FPGA architecture of general CRC computation that enables achieving very high processing throughputs. The proposed architecture is able to process multiple packets per clock cycle and offers good scalability even for very wide data buses. Thanks to a well defined and configurable structure, the architecture can be easily adjusted for CRC computation based on any given polynomial. Furthermore, we can optimize achieved parameters for specific application requirements in terms of processing latency, FPGA resources utilization, and total computational throughput.

Our experimental evaluation shows, that when computing CRC (FCS) for Ethernet frames in high-speed networks the proposed concept enables to achieve unprecedented wire-speed throughput. At a cost of just a few percents of total resources available in a single UltraScale+ FPGA, the achieved throughput can be as high as 2.4 Tbps (over 3500 Mpps). That is, to our knowledge, considerably higher than in any other published work. It is especially thanks to favorable frequency scaling of the designed parallel version of the proposed architecture. The second part of the measurements shows results of our CRC architecture adjusted for high-speed HMC interface. Our approach achieves much better results than default CRC implementation inside OpenHMC controller in terms of both resources as well as frequency (throughput). For the same data width (number of parallel flits), we can save up to 73% logic and 27% registers.

The proposed architecture has been verified in simulations and is also currently tested on a real FPGA as part of our semi-finished implementation of 400 GbE MAC. As part of our future work, we want to propose a feasible approach to high-speed RS-FEC computation in a single FPGA. RS-FEC is based on similar mathematical principles as CRC (finite fields) and is required part of 400G Ethernet implementation.

Acknowledgments. This research has been supported by the MEYS of the Czech Republic project Reg. No. CZ.02.1.01/0.0/0.0/16_013/0001797, the IT4Innovations excellence in science project IT4I XS–LQ1602, and by the Ministry of the Interior of the Czech Republic project VI20172020064.

References

1. Bajarangbali, Anand, P.A.: Design of high speed CRC algorithm for ethernet on FPGA using reduced lookup table algorithm. In: IEEE India Conference (2016)
2. Computer Architecture Group and Micron Foundation: OpenHMC: a configurable open-source hybrid memory cube controller. University of Heidelberg (2014)
3. Hamed, H.F.A., Elmisery, F., Elkader, A.A.H.A.: Implementation of low area and high data throughput CRC design on FPGA. Int. J. Adv. Res. Comput. Sci. Electron. Eng. **1**(9) (2012)

4. Henriksson, T., Liu, D.: Implementation of fast CRC calculation. In: Proceedings of the Asia and South Pacific, Design Automatation Conference, pp. 563–564 (2003)
5. HMC Consortium: hybrid memory cube specification 2.1. Altera Corp. (2015)
6. IEEE Computer Society: Amendment 10: media access control parameters, physical layers and management parameters for 200 Gb/s and 400 Gb/s operation. IEEE Standard 802.3bs-2017, pp. 1–372 (2017)
7. Kennedy, C., Reyhani-Masoleh, A.: High-speed parallel CRC circuits. In: 42nd Asilomar Conference on Signals, Systems and Computers, pp. 1823–1829 (2008)
8. Mitra, J., Nayak, T.K.: Reconfigurable concurrent VLSI (FPGA) design architecture of CRC-32 for high-speed data communication. In: IEEE International Symposium on Nanoelectronic and Information Systems, pp. 112–117 (2015)
9. Mitra, J., Nayak, T.: Reconfigurable very high throughput low latency VLSI (FPGA) design architecture of CRC 32. Integr. VLSI J. **56**, 1–14 (2017)
10. Pei, T.B., Zukowski, C.: High-speed parallel CRC circuits in VLSI. IEEE Trans. Commun. **40**(4), 653–657 (1992)
11. Perez, A.: Byte-wise CRC calculations. IEEE Micro **3**(3), 40–50 (1983)
12. Schmidt, J., Bruning, U.: OpenHMC: a configurable open-source hybrid memory cube controller. In: ReConFigurable Computing and FPGAs. IEEE (2015)
13. Shieh, M.D., Sheu, M.H., Chen, C.H., Lo, H.F.: A systematic approach for parallel CRC computations. J. Inf. Sci. Eng. **17**(3), 445–461 (2001)
14. Tamba Networks: Datacenter Ethernet. Tamba Networks, LLC (2018). http://www.tambanetworks.com/products/datacenter-ethernet/
15. Walma, M.: Pipelined cyclic redundancy check (CRC) calculation. In: International Conference on Computer Communications and Networks, pp. 365–370 (2007)

Receive-Side Notification for Enhanced RDMA in FPGA Based Networks

Joshua Lant[✉], Andrew Attwood, Javier Navaridas, Mikel Lujan, and John Goodacre

University of Manchester, Manchester M13 9PL, UK
{joshua.lant,andrew.attwood,javier.navaridas,
mikel.lujan,john.goodacre}@manchester.ac.uk
http://apt.cs.manchester.ac.uk/

Abstract. FPGAs are rapidly gaining traction in the domain of HPC thanks to the advent of FPGA-friendly data-flow workloads, as well as their flexibility and energy efficiency. However, these devices pose a new challenge in terms of how to better support their communications, since standard protocols are known to hinder their performance greatly either by requiring CPU intervention or consuming excessive FPGA logic. Hence, the community is moving towards custom-made solutions. This paper analyses an optimization to our custom, reliable, interconnect with connectionless transport—a mechanism to register and track inbound RDMA communication at the receive-side. This way, it provides completion notifications directly to the remote node which saves a round-trip latency. The entire mechanism is designed to sit within the fabric of the FPGA, requiring no software intervention. Our solution is able to reduce the latency of a receive operation by around 20% for small message sizes (4 KB) over a single hop (longer distances would experience even higher improvement). Results from synthesis over a wide parameter range confirm this optimization is scalable both in terms of the number of concurrent outstanding RDMA operations, and the maximum message size.

Keywords: FPGA · Transport layer · Micro-architecture · Reliability

1 Introduction

The use of FPGAs as the main compute element within HPC systems is becoming very attractive, as we are seeing burgeoning demands from potentially communication bound workloads such as Deep Learning. These workloads are well suited to FPGA based architectures as they can use data-flow style processing [11], and are capable of leveraging custom data types (lower precision than floating-point). One of the key issues towards the uptake of FPGAs for HPC is

This work was funded by the European Union's Horizon 2020 research and innovation programme under grant agreements No 671553 and 754337.

© Springer Nature Switzerland AG 2019
M. Schoeberl et al. (Eds.): ARCS 2019, LNCS 11479, pp. 224–235, 2019.
https://doi.org/10.1007/978-3-030-18656-2_17

the need to truly decouple the FPGA resources from the host CPU [1,16]. This way, the FPGA will be able to communicate with other FPGA resources directly, rather than having to initiate transactions via the CPU, which will dramatically reduce the latency of communications and better facilitate data-flow style processing among FPGAs. In theory this is relatively simple, and IP cores are available and can be readily used to provide Ethernet based communications within the fabric of the FPGA. Unfortunately these existing solutions are unsuited for HPC, due to the requirements for high reliability in the network. Packet dropping is simply not an option within HPC environments, as guarantee of delivery is required. Leveraging these IPs with a TCP stack is not really feasible since it would require either either a software implementation (running in the CPU) or a full hardware-offloaded solution. The former is antithetical to our requirement that the FPGA acts as an independent peer on the network. The latter is also inappropriate due to high resource consumption and limited scalability due to its connection-based nature. In prior work [2,9] we discussed in greater detail why traditional network protocols are unsuited for FPGA-based HPC systems, and presented a Network Interface (NI) to enable FPGA based communication using RDMA (Remote Direct Memory Access) and NUMA (Non-Uniform Memory Access) type communications over a custom HPC network protocol. Our NI is leveraged along with our custom FPGA-based switch design [2], which lowers area and power overheads by means of a geographic addressing scheme.

The main contribution in this work is the presentation of a microarchitectural design which provides a significant enhancement in the architecture over the preliminary RDMA infrastructure presented in [9]. RDMA is a technique for transferring data to remote nodes which frees the CPU to perform useful work while network transactions are in progress, and is supported in the majority of high performance interconnection networks today. We enhance the performance of receive operations in our system by tracking incoming RDMA transfers in order to provide a receive side notification upon completion. Thus avoiding the round trip latency for the ACK, required for sender-side notifications. We show results of a send and receive operation using varying message sizes and show that the latency of small messages can be improved significantly. Our results show that we are able to scale the mechanism out to a large number of outstanding DMA operations, and achieve a latency reduction of up to 20% on small RDMA operations over a single hop distance.

Our mechanism is able to handle out-of-order packet delivery, maintaining a fully connectionless (datagram based) approach to the transport layer, and enabling the use of fully adaptive routing at packet level granularity within the network. A connectionless approach is essential to provide full decoupling of CPU and FPGA resources. Managing connection state information and the associated retransmission buffers is complex [10]. This is prohibitively expensive to implement within the FPGA fabric, given that the amount of Block RAM is limited (around 35 Mb on the Zynq Ultrascale+ [17]). This is particularly true in a HPC context where the number of outstanding connections may be very large. This is the main reason why reliability is typically offered as a software solution; because the complexity of offloading is too great when rapid connection setup/teardown is required, especially for large number of concurrent connections. We argue for a connectionless approach for just this reason, to reduce the area overhead of the transport layer, and increase the scalability by reducing the information required in the NIC. For example, we need no retransmission buffering for RDMA, and push the responsibility for flow control into the network. As well as this, having the ability to route packets adaptively (as our switch design does [2]) presents the opportunity for much better load balancing within the network and enhanced fault tolerance due to the ability to properly utilize path-diversity [3].

2   Related Work

Our earlier work [9] has shown that traditional protocols such as Ethernet and Infiniband are unsuitable for use in FPGA based HPC systems, due to performance and area concerns respectively. We therefore propose the use of a custom protocol in order to avoid some of the issues with traditional networking stacks. Likewise, the majority of solutions for offering reliable communications in FPGAs are also unsuitable for our needs. This is because they typically rely on software mechanisms to enable retransmission, or hold connection states. We argue that a connectionless approach is necessary in order to enable accelerators to communicate directly with one another without CPU involvement (a key requirement for harnessing the potential of FPGAs within a HPC context [16]), and that hardware offloading of the whole transport mechanism is the only way to achieve this.

There are several FPGA based TCP-offload engines available commercially such as [12] and [13]. TCP offloading aims to either offload fully or partially the functionality of the TCP protocol into hardware. They are often touted as a good solution to the performance issues associated with the TCP/IP software stack. (These problems being latency issues due to excessive memory copying and context switching etc.) However, the TCP stack is very complex, and as such fully offloading the transport layer to hardware is very difficult, particularly for FPGA implementations. The majority of solutions therefore only offload portions of the stack to hardware such as checksumming or segmentation. To our knowledge, the only fully hardware offloaded solutions for FPGA are used for financial trading. These systems are latency-critical so the solution is fully offloaded at the expense of dramatically reduced scalability [12,13]. Obviously this is inappropriate in the context of HPC. In [15] a solution is proposed to overcome this scalability issue, allowing for over 10,000 simultaneous connections. However, this connection based approach still suffers massive memory utilization. They require external session buffers in DRAM, amounting to 1.3 GB for 10,000 sessions. Without a huge dedicated RAM for the offload engine this is extremely wasteful in terms of both memory usage and memory bandwidth.

The Infiniband specification defines a reliable, connectionless transport [8], but there is no actual hardware implementation. Grant et al. [5] propose a scheme for performing RDMA transfers using "Unreliable Datagrams" in Ethernet or

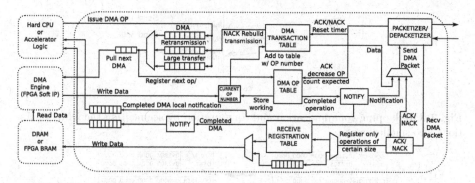

Fig. 1. Architecture of the transport layer for RDMA communications within our custom NI.

Infiniband networks. They propose a method of using existing structures present in the iWARP protocol [14], writing the incoming RDMA to memory as normal at the receiver, but recording the incoming datagrams and posting to a *completion queue*, which indicates that segments of a full RDMA operation have completed successfully. Their solution eliminates much of the network stack processing but is implemented in SW and does not consider reliability.

A similar approach to ours is presented by Xirouchakis et al. [18]. It describes the design of a system composed of a virtualized RDMA engine and mailboxes [6]. This features several key differences in design from our own. They do not describe a method to store and retransmit shared memory operations as we do in [9]. They rely on software-based retransmissions, meaning that accelerator logic within the FPGA fabric is incapable of talking directly to the NI without CPU involvement. While the authors target user-level initiation of transfers to avoid the TCP/IP stack overheads, they still use a connection based approach, and only allow for multiple paths to be taken at the granularity of blocks forming these connections, not fully adaptive multipath routing and support for out-of-order delivery at the packet level as we do [9].

3 Implementation

Figure 1 shows the architecture of our hardware-offloaded transport mechanism for RDMA transfers. It can be seen here that both FPGA based accelerator logic and the hard CPU are able to utilize the NIC, issuing commands and pushing data to the network in exactly the same manner. The NIC provides reliable transmissions and allows for out-of-order packet reception using a connectionless approach. This is split into two major separate control and data-paths, one for the sending side and one for the receiving side. On the send side the CPU/accelerator issues DMA operations which are then pulled by the DMA engine from the command queues. The DMA engine is currently the Xilinx CDMA IP, running in Scatter-Gather mode. Every new operation which is pulled by the DMA engine is logged in the DMA OP Table in the NI. This table issues an OP number for

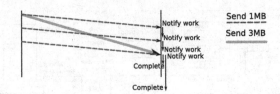

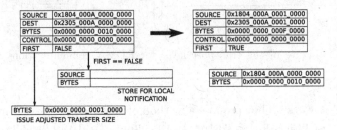

Fig. 2. Overlapping communication and computation by segmenting the DMA operations into smaller ones.

Fig. 3. Shows the update of the "Large Command" queue head for an operation of 1 Mb, to be split into 64K transfers.

every packet within the operation which is sent to the network and returned in the acknowledgement, keeping a count of the number of successful transfers in a given operation. Individual packets are tracked in the DMA Transaction Table. This keeps a timeout for individual packets, and builds retransmission operation entries in the event of lost/timed out or negatively acknowledged packets. Notification of completion is given locally, to let the processor know that a DMA operation has finished sending data, and remotely, to tell the remote processor that it has new data at a given location.

3.1 Segmentation

Due to our connnectionless approach and out-of-order delivery of packets, the receiver needs to know when a whole operation is finished before it can begin work on the data, as it cannot guarantee which data has arrived at which point. Due to the importance of overlapping computation and communication for many data-intensive workloads [4] we attempt to ameliorate the additional latency that this imposes on the system by allowing for segmentation of large RDMA transfers into multiple smaller ones (as in Fig. 2). Doing this is simple as the RDMA commands issued by the CPU/accelerator pass through the NI, and information can be captured and altered at this point. Figure 3 shows how the segmentation mechanism works. If a given command is seen to be over a certain threshold size it can be sent to a special "Large Transfer" queue. In this instance when the command is processed it can be assigned a status flag in the DMA Operation table. When an operation completes with this special status flag then no local notification is posted; only the notification to the receiver.

If the command is of size M, and the segment size is N, then the head of the "Large Transfer" queue remains in place for M/N operations. The offset for the base address and the number of bytes to be transferred are simply updated at the head of the queue following a new segmented command being pulled by the DMA engine (Fig. 3). Upon the issue of the last command, the special status flag remains deasserted, so local completion notification for the original full transfer can be formed. The threshold for the optimal maximum size of a segmented operation is highly dependent on the structure of the application and so should be defined by the programmer during configuration of the NI.

There is little overhead in actually performing these modifications to the DMA commands. The DMA engine is set up in a cyclic buffer mode so it simply posts read requests to the NIC to pull new operations into the engine. The only difference in this instance is that the DMA engine will see a modified work item from that which the CPU/accelerator posted to the NI. Since the DMA engine can queue the next command to be performed internally, the new modified command can be formed while the current operation is in flight, so no additional latency is caused by this mechanism.

3.2 Receiver Registration

To reduce latency we track the receive side RDMA operations to provide local completion notification, and to handle out-of-order packets. Upon receiving an RDMA transaction, the operation can be logged in the Receive Registration Table (see Fig. 1). It may or may not require registration depending on the transfer size (this will be discussed further in Sect. 4). Operations are registered by using a special entry in the "Type" field in the packet header, which is given to the first transfer of an operation. When the receiver sees this transaction they register the range of addresses which are expected from the whole operation.

Out-of-order packet delivery is handled here by creating an escape channel for any packets which currently have not had a table entry created. Until the first packet has arrived any out-of-order packets which arrived first will be put in the escape channel in order not to stall the pipeline. We are able to do this because the data that enters the NI is written to memory in a store-and-forward fashion. The data cannot be allowed to enter into memory until a CRC has confirmed the validity of the packet, so there is an (X cycles) latency corresponding to the number of flits within the packet. In this time we are able to drain the previous packet into the escape channel.

Once the first packet associated with the DMA is seen, registration of the operation is completed and a mask is used to determine when all corresponding packets have been received for the operation, and to drop duplicates. An initial mask is required to account for the fact that an operation may be smaller than the maximum possible registered operation ($Maskbitwidth \times Packetsize$). This mask is created by a barrel shifter which uses a field in the header of the first packet of the operation, which denotes the number of expected packets. We shift in zeroes to form the appropriate initial operation state. A single 1 is added to the end of this process (as the first packet must have arrived to begin this

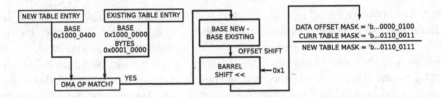

Fig. 4. Creating the bitmask for the new dma data, to check for duplicates and completion status.

registration process). For example, if we assume a 4 KB operation, a 16 KB mask size and a packet size of 512 B, the initial mask after registration would be 'b1111_1111_1111_1111_1111_1111_0000_0001 (8 packets are needed and the first one is received).

3.3   Receiver Notification and Duplicate Data

Every time a new packet arrives the table is checked in order to determine whether any existing entry matches with the new packet. This is done by calculating whether the incoming destination is within the range of the entry currently being checked. If there is no corresponding entry in the table then the data is sent to the escape channel, and an associated timer is started. If this times out then the packet and its associated data is dropped. This timeout can happen for two reasons: (*i*) The packet is a duplicate and the corresponding operation has already completed. The packet is rightfully dropped as the operation has completed and been removed from the table of active operations. In this case dropping the packet is safe because the previous packet must have sent a correct acknowledgement back to the sender. (*ii*) The first packet in the operation is severely delayed or lost in the network, so registration never happens. In this case dropping the packet is safe because the sender will have received no acknowledgement or negative acknowledgement, and will itself time out and retransmit the packet. In the event that data is found to correspond to an entry in the table, but is a duplicate, the data can be safely dropped straight away and there is no need for the timer.

Figure 4 shows how the mask is updated upon receiving a new packet. If the table entry being checked is found to match the incoming data, then it proceeds to create a new mask. The base address of the entry and the number of bytes of the operation are used to calculate whether the operation being checked in the table relates to the new packet arriving. An offset is then created for a barrel shifter, which generates a mask to cause a bit flip. If the mask is found to be all 1's then the operation must be completed. If $Newmask == Originalmask$ then the packet must be a duplicate and can be dropped.

Once a full operation has been completed the receiver is notified locally of the RDMA operation, which saves a full round-trip packet latency compared to waiting for the sender to provide a completion notification upon receiving the last acknowledgment (see Fig. 5). The notification is currently sent to a queue which

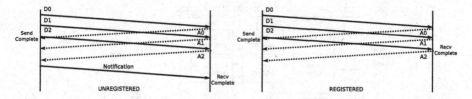

Fig. 5. Time for send and receive operations to complete for registered and unregistered transfers.

can be polled by the receiver. Doing this allows for a non-blocking or a blocking receive to be performed in the application. Polling the notification queue when empty returns a special default value. This can be used to effectively create a spin-lock in the software, only returning from the blocking receive function when the notification has indeed been posted, and the return value is not equal to the default value.

3.4 Non-Registered Operations

There may be points where either registering an operation is unnecessary, or is not sensible given the number of communications (for example in a many-to-one collective involving many nodes). In this case the operation remains unregistered and we must suffer the additional round trip latency for acknowledgement. However, in this case there is no need to track and handle duplicate packets, or out-of-order delivery. The addresses of the packets which form the DMA operations are simply memory locations within a global virtual address space (described in [7]), it does not matter if this memory location is overwritten, because the acknowledgement for the operation happens only once all the corresponding packets have been acknowledged to the sender. We provide strong ECC protection for ACK packets so that they will only be lost or corrupted in the most exceptional circumstances. If packets arrive out-of-order then they are simply written to the correct place in memory regardless, as the packet has a base address associated with it, which is formed in the DMA engine at the sender.

4   Evaluation

The Network Interface, and thus all the components shown and discussed in Sect. 3 are implemented completely within the fabric of the FPGA. For all evaluation within this Section we use the Xilinx Zynq Ultrascale+ ZCU102 development board (part number EK-U1-ZCU102-G). The test setup is shown in Fig. 6. There are two entirely segregated datapaths within the FPGA, emulating completely the action of a distributed setup except we implement the send node's IP and the receiving node's IP within a single FPGA. We have shown in previous work communication over a complete networked solution including the router/switch [2,9], but in order to more accurately measure time, we

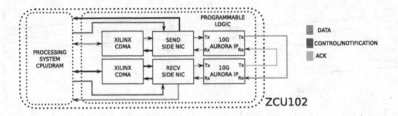

Fig. 6. Experimental setup on the Zynq Ultrascale+ FPGA.

use a loopback setup. Using the NIC in conjunction with the switch allows for a much higher number of connections to/from a single node. The processing system contains four hard-core ARM-A53 processors, as well as cache-coherent interconnect, IOMMU, DRAM controller etc, while the programmable logic is just that; the FPGA fabric of the device. It can be seen that the current DMA engine is the Xilinx CDMA IP, and we use Aurora PHY IP to enable 10G line-rate across the links. This IP is used simply to perform serialization and 64/66b line encoding/decoding, and does not wrap the packet using any other protocol. The frequency of all components implemented within the FPGA fabric is 156.25 MHz. The processing system runs at 1GHz.

4.1 Latency of Send and Receive Operations

In order to balance the requirements for low latency transfers with reduced area overheads, only a limited range of message size for registration is required. Figure 7 shows the results of an experiment to show the performance benefits of registered receive side transactions. This shows the latency for the transfer of data and notification of completion in a user-space application for a single hop transfer. The latency of the send operation is the time taken to configure the DMA engine from user-space, and for notification to be received at the sender that the DMA engine has pushed all the data into the network. The measurement we take is thus for a non-blocking send, for the data to simply enter the network. A blocking send operation would have higher latency than the registered receive operation since it must wait for the last ACK to arrive. The latency of receive operations are measured from the time the sender begins to initialize the transfer, until the receiver gets notification that the DMA data is placed in memory, either by local notification from the NI (Registered), or as a notification packet from the sender.

As shown in Fig. 7, the latency of a receive operation for a 1 KB transfer is around 5.23 μs, and for a registered receive is only 4.21 μs, cutting ≈20% from the latency of the receive side being notified of the transaction. We also see that the performance gains from this registration technique diminish with transfer size and become insignificant at around 32 KB. At much larger transfers the measured latency for send/recv/registered recv are very similar, as is seen in the convergence of the results in Fig. 7. This is because the extra round trip latency

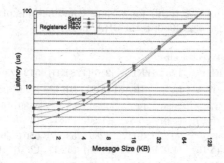

Fig. 7. Latency of a send/recv operation over a single hop distance.

is dwarfed by the overall transfer time for the data. What this means in practice is that registered transactions will only show significant benefits within a certain range of smaller message sizes. Although this is dependent on the distance from the destination and the network load (affecting latency). As the distance between source and destination increase, or the load of the network goes up, we would see larger and larger message sizes be able to benefit from receive side registration. The distance between sender and receiver can be worked out easily owing to the geographical routing scheme which we employ [2], so adjusting the threshold for registration based upon this would be trivial. However, dynamically adjusting these thresholds based upon the network load may be very difficult and be potentially very wasteful of resources.

4.2   Area of Receiver Registration Module

Clearly there will be high variability in the performance gains of registering the receive side operations, depending on the distance of communications. It therefore seems appropriate to perform a parameter sweep for various configurations of number of simultaneous outstanding operations the node can handle, and the largest possible size of operation for receiver registration. Table 1 shows the area utilization of the *Receive Registration* module (shown in Fig. 1), under differing configurations. We consider bitmasks for between 32 KB and 512 KB, using a packet size of 512B–a small packet size is used to ease congestion and help with load balancing. We vary the number of outstanding operations (table entries) between 64 and 1024.

The results show that varying the maximum DMA operation size for registration has little effect on the number of LUTs. This is because the logic to decode/encode the mask is not significant, compared with other components in the module. The number of BRAMs jumps considerably at certain boundaries, which is due to the odd bit width of the table entries. Effectively this creates a scenario where we can gain "free" entries to the table because of the fixed size BRAMs being utilized more efficiently. It is also worth noting that the number of BRAMs for the smallest 64×64 configuration does not correspond to the utilization of the table. This is because the storage for the data in the escape

Table 1. Area utilization (% total) for various combinations of max packet size and table depth. Total LUTs = 274080, total BRAMs = 912.

		Bitmask vector size								
		64 (32 KB)		128 (64 KB)		256 (128 KB)		512 (256 KB)		1024 (512 KB)	
		LUT	BRAM	LUT	BRAM	LUT	BRAM	LUT	BRAM	LUT	BRAM
Table size	64	2230 (0.81)	47 (5.15)	2936 (1.07)	49 (5.37)	4286 (1.56)	53 (5.81)	6589 (2.40)	60 (6.58)	11072 (4.04)	74 (8.11)
	128	2282 (0.83)	47 (5.15)	2942 (1.07)	49 (5.37)	4289 (1.56)	53 (5.81)	6501 (2.37)	60 (6.58)	11092 (4.04)	74 (8.11)
	256	2266 (0.82)	47 (5.15)	2973 (1.08)	49 (5.37)	4366 (1.59)	53 (5.81)	6842 (2.49)	60 (6.58)	11124 (4.05)	74 (8.11)
	512	2298 (0.84)	47 (5.15)	2974 (1.08)	49 (5.37)	4367 (1.59)	53 (5.81)	6843 (2.49)	60 (6.58)	10965 (4.00)	74 (8.11)
	1024	2273 (0.83)	47 (5.15)	2976 (1.09)	52 (5.70)	4363 (1.59)	57.5 (6.30)	6575 (2.39)	68 (7.45)	11088 (4.04)	89.5 (9.81)

channel is set to enable 64 full packets to be held in the NI. This uses 43 BRAMs, which is why we still see a baseline for the BRAM utilization at this small configuration. Although this value is highly acceptable, and not prohibitive for the implementation of accelerators in combination with our NI, with the largest possible configuration only requiring 10% of the total BRAMs, and uses no DSP slices, which are key for performing efficient floating point arithmetic.

5   Conclusions

In this paper we have presented an optimization for the hardware-offloaded transport layer of an FPGA based Network Interface. A micro-architecture is presented which allows for the receiver of an RDMA operation to register the operation, thereby enabling receive side notification upon completion of the operation. We show that for small RDMA operations the latency of the receive operation can be reduced by ≈20%. This can be leveraged with a method of segmenting large DMA operations into a number of smaller ones, thereby enabling us to maintain a connectionless (datagram based) approach to our transport layer, while allowing communication and computation to overlap. The connectionless approach maintains scalability of the system, and allows for fully adaptive routing at packet level granularity, giving better load-balancing properties to the network.

We provide an analysis of the area utilization of various configurations of the receive-side registration module, and show that, due to the fixed sized BRAMs and the odd bit-width of table entries, certain configurations make better use of the BRAMs. In the most aggressive implementation, the total BRAM use of the receive registration module is below 10% of the available, whereas the number of LUTs is around 4%. More reasonable configurations lower these to around 6% and 1.5%, respectively. Hence, the overall area utilization is very acceptable, leaving plenty for use by accelerator blocks etc. Particularly when noting that our implementation does not utilize any DSP blocks on the FPGA.

References

1. Caulfield, A.M., et al.: A cloud-scale acceleration architecture. In: The 49th Annual IEEE/ACM International Symposium on Microarchitecture, p. 7. IEEE Press (2016)
2. Concatto, C., et al.: A CAM-free exascalable HPC router for low-energy communications. In: Berekovic, M., Buchty, R., Hamann, H., Koch, D., Pionteck, T. (eds.) ARCS 2018. LNCS, vol. 10793, pp. 99–111. Springer, Cham (2018). https://doi.org/10.1007/978-3-319-77610-1_8
3. Dally, W.J., Aoki, H.: Deadlock-free adaptive routing in multicomputer networks using virtual channels. IEEE Trans. Parallel Distrib. Syst. **4**(4), 466–475 (1993)
4. El-Ghazawi, T., El-Araby, E., Huang, M., Gaj, K., Kindratenko, V., Buell, D.: The promise of high-performance reconfigurable computing. Computer **41**(2), 69–76 (2008)
5. Grant, R.E., Rashti, M.J., Balaji, P., Afsahi, A.: Scalable connectionless RDMA over unreliable datagrams. Parallel Comput. **48**, 15–39 (2015)
6. Katevenis, M., et al.: Next generation of exascale-class systems: exanest project and the status of its interconnect and storage development. Microprocess. Microsyst. **61**, 58–71 (2018)
7. Katevenis, M., et al.: The exanest project: interconnects, storage, and packaging for exascale systems. In: 2016 Euromicro Conference on Digital System Design (DSD), pp. 60–67. IEEE (2016)
8. Koop, M.J., Sur, S., Gao, Q., Panda, D.K.: High performance MPI design using unreliable datagram for ultra-scale infiniband clusters. In: Proceedings of the 21st Annual International Conference on Supercomputing, pp. 180–189. ACM (2007)
9. Lant, J., et al.: Enabling shared memory communication in networks of mpsocs. Concurr. Comput. Pract. Exp. (CCPE), e4774 (2018)
10. Mogul, J.C.: TCP offload is a dumb idea whose time has come. In: HotOS, pp. 25–30 (2003)
11. Ovtcharov, K., Ruwase, O., Kim, J.Y., Fowers, J., Strauss, K., Chung, E.S.: Accelerating deep convolutional neural networks using specialized hardware. Microsoft Res. Whitepaper **2**(11), 1–4 (2015)
12. PLDA: An implementation of the TCP/IP protocol suite for the Linux operating system (2018). https://github.com/torvalds/linux/blob/master/net/ipv4/tcp.c
13. Intilop Corporation: 10 g bit TCP offload engine + PCIe/DMA soc IP (2012)
14. Ohio Supercomputing Centre: Software implementation and testing of iWarp protocol (2018). https://www.osc.edu/research/network_file/projects/iwarp
15. Sidler, D., Alonso, G., Blott, M., Karras, K., Vissers, K., Carley, R.: Scalable 10Gbps TCP/IP stack architecture for reconfigurable hardware. In: 2015 IEEE 23rd Annual International Symposium on Field-Programmable Custom Computing Machines (FCCM), pp. 36–43. IEEE (2015)
16. Underwood, K.D., Hemmert, K.S., Ulmer, C.D.: From silicon to science: the long road to production reconfigurable supercomputing. ACM Trans. Reconfigurable Technol. Syst. (TRETS) **2**(4), 26 (2009)
17. Xilinx Inc.: Zynq UltraScale + MPSoC Data Sheet: Overview (2018). v1.7
18. Xirouchakis, P., et al.: The network interface of the exanest hpc prototype. Technical report, ICS-FORTH / TR 471, Heraklion, Crete, Greece (2018)

An Efficient FPGA Accelerator Design for Optimized CNNs Using OpenCL

Manoj Rohit Vemparala[1](✉), Alexander Frickenstein[1], and Walter Stechele[2]

[1] BMW Group, Munich, Germany
Manoj-Rohit.Vemparala@bmw.de
[2] Technical University of Munich, Munich, Germany

Abstract. Convolutional Neural Networks (CNNs) require highly parallel Hardware (HW) accelerators in the form of Graphical Processing Units (GPUs), Application Specific Integrated Circuits (ASICs) or Field Programmable Gate Arrays (FPGAs) to build low latency solutions necessary for implementing image processing applications. FPGAs have the ability to provide a right balance between flexibility, performance and energy efficiency. The design of FPGA based accelerator design traditionally required a tedious Register Transfer Level (RTL) design flow process. To improve design productivity, the proposed work uses High-Level Synthesis (HLS), described in OpenCL, to generate the FPGA bitstream for the CNN model. The 2D Winograd transformation is integrated in the pipeline to reduce the overall number of Multiply and Accumulate (MAC) operations in the CNN. Instead of increasing the batch size to improve the throughput, this work discusses a mixed precision approach which can counter the limited memory bandwidth issue within the CNN. The obtained results are competitive against other FPGA based implementations proposed in literature. The proposed accelerator can achieve more than 1.9× higher energy efficiency compared to an embedded Nvidia Jetson TX1 implementation of VGG-16.

Keywords: FPGA · CNN · Winograd transform · HLS · Quantization

1 Introduction

In the last few years, Deep Learning has emerged as the most promising approach for solving problems in various fields like image classification [1], video classification [2], object detection [3], speech recognition [4] and natural language processing [5]. CNNs are biologically inspired algorithms which are able to detect prominent features and provide an output as image classification or object detection. Previously in the field of computer vision, hard-coded algorithms were required for image processing. Over the years, popular CNN architectures like AlexNet [1], VGG-16 [6], ResNet-152 [7] have increased the classification accuracy and further serve as feature extractors for well known object detectors such as SSD [8] or FCN [9]. This makes the CNN a promising candidate for computer

© Springer Nature Switzerland AG 2019
M. Schoeberl et al. (Eds.): ARCS 2019, LNCS 11479, pp. 236–249, 2019.
https://doi.org/10.1007/978-3-030-18656-2_18

vision applications. However, the improved prediction accuracy of CNNs comes at the expense of higher computational and memory demand. The state-of-the-art CNN architectures require millions of training parameters and billions of operations to process one single image. For instance, AlexNet [1] requires more than 1.4 billion Floating-Point Operations (FLOPs) to process a single image and produces a Top-1 accuracy of 57.6% on ImageNet 12 validation dataset. Whereas, ResNet-152 [7] takes more than 22.6 GFLOP and produces a Top-1 accuracy of 77%. Caziani et al. [10] show that the inference time and model accuracy follows a hyperbolic relationship as small increment in accuracy results in lot of computation time. The computational demand for image segmentation and scene labelling tasks is even higher. Therefore, deployment of CNN inference task on the right HW platform and applying HW friendly optimization techniques are really important.

The hardware accelerators such as GPUs, FPGAs and ASICs are commonly used to accelerate CNNs. The GPU is the most common choice among these accelerators because of its high compute capability and memory bandwidth. However, the model deployment using GPUs is costly and energy inefficient, which is a major concern in low power embedded and real-time applications. On the other extreme end, ASIC design can achieve high throughput with lower power consumption. However, it requires long development time and offers less flexibility compared to other solutions. The re-configurable hardware in the form of an FPGA is another potential alternative which can accelerate the existing CNNs and provide a balance between performance, energy efficiency and flexibility. The conventional FPGA design flow requires a hardware design methodology, which involves programming in VHSIC Hardware Description Language (VHDL) or Verilog making it difficult to design and debug. Complicated accelerator designs such as CNNs would result in higher time to market. The introduction of HLS tools enables the developers to program the FPGA in high-level languages such as C++ or OpenCL to accelerate the development process.

This work places importance to both FPGA accelerator design and network level optimization methods for obtaining higher performance and energy efficiency compared to the state-of-the-art approaches. For this purpose, *WinoCNN*, a CNN based FPGA accelerator design is proposed, which can reduce the high compute and memory demand by leveraging the Winograd convolution and mixed precision approach. The main contribution of this work is the design of flexible FPGA accelerator which can support different kinds of optimization methods for different CNN layers to reduce internal pipeline stalls and improve the overall performance. Section 2 discusses about related work concerning various quantization techniques and FPGA based accelerator designs. Section 3 describes about the Winograd fast convolution algorithm, mixed precision approach and the proposed accelerator design. Section 4 evaluates the performance of the accelerator on various CNN models like VGG-16 and FCN-8s.

2   Related Work

The existing CNN models are computationally expensive and memory intensive, preventing their deployment in devices with low memory resources or in applications with strict latency requirements. On one side, there are improvements on applying optimization techniques to CNN models and on the other side there are on-going efforts to develop specialized hardware architectures to suite compute requirements of CNNs.

The most common method to deploy CNN models on embedded or low power hardware platforms is to approximate them using low precision data types with minimum accuracy loss, without needing to re-train the model. Using quantization methods, weights, activations, biases are represented with smaller bit width and the complexity of MAC operation is reduced. Popular CNN approximation framework named *Ristretto* by Gysel et al. [11], converts the weights and activations in Caffe-based neural networks to fixed-point format. It has the ability to automatically determine the number of integer, fractional bits and scale factors for weights and activations of each layer, which is necessary to avoid serious degradation of the resulting classification accuracy. The authors are able to quantize AlexNet to 8-bit weights and activations with an accuracy drop well below 1%. *Binarized Neural Networks* proposed by Courbariaux et al. [12] converts both weights and activations to binary format. This effectively replaces the power hungry MAC operation to an XNOR and popcount operation. The work by Rastegari et al. [13], investigate larger CNN models like AlexNet using *XNOR Networks*. However, the accuracy degradation is still visible. In this work, a mixed precision approach adopting 16-bit weights and activations in convolutional layers, binary weights for Fully Connected (FC) layers is adopted in order to tackle the accuracy degradation and decrease the demand for external memory bandwidth and local memory requirement for FC layers.

Many FPGA based accelerator designs have been proposed in the literature to accelerate CNN models. In order to accelerate both convolutional and FC layers, high performance computing libraries such as NVIDIA's cuBLAS in GPU and Intel's MKL in CPU are used during inference and leverage the conventional Matrix Multiplication (MM) representation resulting in transformation of filters and input feature maps. The work proposed by Suda et al. [14], adopts similar MM approach to FPGA based CNN implementation. They flatten the filters, rearrange the input feature maps and output maps are thereby calculated using matrix multiplication. The matrix multiply approach comes at an expense of data duplication of input feature maps and filters. Thus, MM approach finally ends up being memory bounded and throughput limited especially in FPGA platforms. Zhang et al. [15] show that the data duplication can result upto 25× more DRAM memory access for AlexNet. Thus, they propose an FPGA based CNN accelerator *Caffeine* adapting a convolutional MM representation. Caffeine converts the FC layers to convolutional MM representation, which is compatible with both convolutional and FC layers. Additionally, they have integrated the accelerator with a Deep Learning framework *Caffe* on Xilinx KU060 FPGA.

Wang et al. proposed PipeCNN in [16], which is an OpenCL based CNN accelerator using similar approach as [15]. They employ a sliding window based data buffering scheme to maximize the data reuse and reduce the number of external memory accesses. They further reduce the demand for external memory bandwidth by fusing CNN operations like convolution, max pooling without the need to store inter layer results back. This framework can be further deployed in wide number of FPGA devices just by changing few compile hardware parameters.

Winograd minimal filter algorithm and Fast Fourier Transformation (FFT) are well known algorithms to accelerate the convolution operation resulting in Element Wise Matrix Multiplication (EWMM) in their respective domains. Compared to traditional convolutions and Winograd, FFT is more efficient with kernel size greater than 5. The complexity of the FFT depends on the size of the output feature map and becomes ineffective for smaller filter sizes [17]. The work by Zhang et al. [18] propose an FFT based CNN accelerator design using overlap and add method to further reduce the arithmetic complexity and perform well on small filter sizes. Aydonat et al. [19] accelerate AlexNet using OpenCL based Deep Learning Accelerator (DLA) using 1-D Winograd transform to reduce the arithmetic complexity in convolutional layers and thus achieves higher performance. DLA performs multiplications using half precision 16-bit floating point weights, activations and stores the intermediate input feature maps in local memory to improve the performance.

As the current trend of deep CNN topologies such as FCN-8s use small filters and more convolutional layers, the proposed accelerator in this work uses 2D Winograd algorithm to reduce the number of multiplications by $2.25\times$ in the convolutional layers. As the computational demand in the convolutional layers is high, the amount of logic and buffer sizes required for the intermediate Winograd transformation is decided using design space exploration to avoid intermediate stalls in the pipeline. The previous CNN based FPGA accelerators in the literature simultaneously classify multiple images grouped as a batch to reuse the filters of each layer. As a result, the global memory accesses significantly reduces and further increases the throughput per image. In low latency applications like in the field of autonomous driving, there is significantly less advantage by implementing batch parallelism. Thus, accelerator design in this work is strictly limited to batch size of 1 and leverages the mixed precision approach.

3 Methodology

3.1 Winograd Convolution

The traditional convolution usually works by sliding the filters across an input activation. As an alternative, convolution can be implemented more efficiently using Winograd algorithm by reducing the number of MAC operations which was generalized for CNNs by Lavin et al. [20]. The traditional convolution computes every output feature map separately, whereas 2D Winograd convolution generates output maps in tiles. It reduces the number of multiplication by reusing the intermediate outputs and is suitable for small kernel size and stride values.

The work in [20] demonstrates that the Winograd algorithm using $F(2 \times 2, 3 \times 3)$ has the ability to produce theoretical speed up of $2.25\times$ and $F(4 \times 4, 3 \times 3)$ can produce a speed up of $4\times$. Nevertheless, it introduces intermediate transformation which can be computed using addition, subtraction and bit shift operations. Winograd convolution follows a four stage approach (a) Input transform (b) Kernel transform (c) Element wise multiplication in Winograd domain (d) Inverse Winograd transform of the output feature maps.

The proposed accelerator uses 2D Winograd Convolution $F(2 \times 2, 3 \times 3)$, where the generated output tile size is 2×2 and the filter size is 3×3. The required input tile size is 4×4 ($4 = 3 + 2 - 1$). The output of the Winograd convolution can be expressed as shown in Eq. 1. Here g and b are input activation and filter before Winograd transform respectively.

$$Y = A^T \left[G^T g G \odot B^T b B \right] A \tag{1}$$

For $F(2 \times 2, 3 \times 3)$, the constant matrices required for transformations G, B, and A are expressed in Eq. 2. The element wise multiplications are performed using the DSP blocks in FPGA and the input transformations are computed on FPGA logic.

$$G = \begin{bmatrix} 1 & 0 & 0 \\ \frac{1}{2} & \frac{1}{2} & \frac{1}{2} \\ \frac{1}{2} & -\frac{1}{2} & \frac{1}{2} \\ 0 & 0 & 1 \end{bmatrix} \quad B = \begin{bmatrix} 1 & 0 & -1 & 0 \\ 0 & 1 & 1 & 0 \\ 0 & -1 & 1 & 0 \\ 0 & 1 & 0 & -1 \end{bmatrix} \quad A = \begin{bmatrix} 1 & 0 \\ 1 & 1 \\ 1 & -1 \\ 0 & -1 \end{bmatrix} \tag{2}$$

This work performs the weight transformations during the compile time and stores the transformed weights in the external DRAM to save additional logic utilization. However, it comes with an expense of extra local memory utilization. It is also challenging to implement Winograd convolutions using low precision integers. Each transformed input feature map is obtained after 4 addition/-subtraction operations. Thus, the intermediate transformations could result in overflows to the transformed matrices and can affect the overall model accuracy. As an example, performing Winograd convolution with 8-bit activations and weights, is effectively equivalent to performing a traditional convolution with 6-bit activations and 8-bit weights. In this case, the Winograd layers must be retrained to avoid accuracy degradation. However, proposed accelerator in this work considers only 16-bit weights and activations to perform Winograd convolutions.

3.2   Mixed Precision Approach

Unlike the convolutional layers, the FC layers do not share the weights and typically require higher off-chip memory bandwidth. Thus, the mixed precision approach is leveraged to reduce the pipeline stalls. The mixed precision approach leverages the 16-bit weights in the convolutional layers and binary weights in the FC layer. The training procedure for mixed precision approach is similar to the proposed *Binary Weight Network* proposed in [13]. The training procedure for VGG-16 is demonstrated in the Algorithm 1. In each iteration of training, there are three steps; 1. forward propagation, 2. backward propagation and 3. parameter update. In the forward propagation, the weights of only FC layers are binarized as shown in lines 1–7. In case of VGG-16, the layer 14 to 16 are FC layers as shown in line 2. In the backward propagation, the gradients of the binarized weights are calculated in line 8. In the parameter update phase, the calculated gradients are updated to full precision weights of the FC layers as line 9.

The mixed precision approach decreases the demand of external memory bandwidth as the weights are reduced from 16-bit to 1-bit. The FC layers with 16-bit weights demand higher local memory which remains unused for the convolutional layers. Thus, the mixed precision approach can also be adopted to avoid the higher local memory demand. As the binary weights are leveraged, the output of the FC layers can be performed using additions/subtraction operations. The compute units of mixed precision approach can be mapped to FPGA logic.

Algorithm 1. Training the FC layers of CNN model with binary weights

---

Input: Minibatch of training dataset with Images, labels, predictions $(I, Y, \overline{Y})$, cost function $C(Y, \overline{Y})$, time step t, current full precision weights W^t and learning rate η^t
Output: updated full precision weights W^{t+1}, FC layers with binary weights W_{fc}^b and learning rate η^{t+1}

1: Binarizing the FC layers:
2: **for** i = 14 to 16 **do**
3:     $Weight_{mean} \leftarrow Mean(W_i^t)$
4:     **for** kth weight ith layer **do**
5:         $W_{ik}^b \leftarrow sign(W_{ik}^t)$
6:         $W_{ik}^b \leftarrow W_{ik}^b \times Weight_{mean}$
7: $\overline{Y} \leftarrow Forward(I, W^t, W_{fc}^b)$
8: $\frac{\partial C}{\partial W_t}, \frac{\partial C}{\partial W_{fc}^b} \leftarrow Backward(I, W^t, W_{fc}^b)$
9: $W^{t+1} \leftarrow UpdateParameter(W^t, \frac{\partial C}{\partial W_t}, \frac{\partial C}{\partial W_f c^b}, \eta^t)$
10: $\eta^{t+1} \leftarrow UpdateLearningRate(\eta^t, t)$

3.3   WinoCNN Accelerator Design

The high level architecture description of the proposed WinoCNN accelerator is presented in Fig. 1, which can accelerate large variety of layers in CNN models. WinoCNN consists of a set of OpenCL kernels which can be interconnected using Intel's OpenCL extension channels. Four of the subsystems are directly connected to the external DDR which can fetch the input feature maps, weights and write back the layer outputs using high throughput data streams of different bandwidth. WinoCNN accelerator involves design parameters like convolution group n, parallelization factors M_{vec} and D_{vec}, quantzation Q which effect the utilization of local memory, compute units and logic.

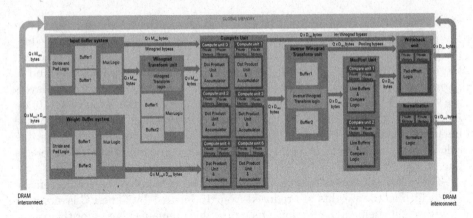

Fig. 1. High level architecture design of WinoCNN described in OpenCL.

The Local Response Normalization (LRN) subsystem directly fetches the features from the DDR, normalizes them and sends it back again to the DDR. It is isolated from the pipeline as the LRN operation can be started only after computing all the output feature maps of a particular layer. Each layer of the CNN fetches the input feature maps and stores it in the input buffer. Since the neighbouring output of the convolution operations share input features, one can leverage the data reuse opportunity. The convolution can be performed in groups and the input features required for one group can be buffered. The corresponding features are sent either to the Winograd transform units or directly to the compute units of the convolution system when input maps do not need Winograd transformation. This is particularly useful when kernel size of the convolutional layer is not 3×3. The Winograd transformation units in the WinoCNN accelerator are limited to 3×3 kernel size. Winograd transformation stages are bypassed for layers with non 3×3 kernel sizes such as 1×1, 4×4, 5×5, 7×7 and regular convolution bypassing Winograd transformations is performed. The input buffer system is also capable to rearrange the input and pad additional zeros in between and across the borders when the layer is required to perform the transpose convolution.

The weight buffer system fetches the required weights from the external DDR and provides it to the compute units of the convolution system. The size of the interconnect between the DDR and weight buffer is naturally higher than the size of the input buffer interconnect, as more number of weights are required to calculate an output tile than input feature maps. Due to the limited external memory bandwidth of FPGAs, the input and weights are first cached to the local memory before being fed to the compute units of the convolution system. Thus, the double buffers are helpful which are operated in a pipelined manner to make sure data transfer and computation does not overlap. The Winograd transformation for the weights are performed at compile time after the training phase to prevent additional logic utilization on FPGA. However, it has a limitation of additional local memory requirement as the kernel size is increased from 3×3 to 4×4.

WinoCNN also provides an option of computing the convolution with binary weights. As an example, in VGG-16, the weights due to FC layer contribute 90% of the overall CNN's weights of the CNN. Further, the amount of local memory allocated to the weight buffer depends on the amount of weights in FC6. Thus, most of the local memory remains unused for other CNN layers. This problem can be prevented by leveraging binary weights for the FC layers resulting in minimal accuracy loss. On the hardware side, separate weight buffer could be used to perform binary convolutions.

When the Winograd convolution mode is desired, the input feature maps must undergo Winograd transformation before feeding it to the compute units. For this sake, the Winograd transform kernel buffers array of 4×4 tiles of input feature maps. Since the input Winograd transformation consists of only addition and subtraction operations, additional DSP blocks are not required and the complete transformation can be implemented in logic. Using additional local memory replication of buffered input feature maps, the Winograd transformation of all the 16 elements can be performed in parallel. This would obviously result in higher Block RAM (BRAM) utilization due to the limited number of read and write ports of M20K block[1]. The transformed input features are stored in a buffer before passing it to the compute units to implement the data flow in a pipelined manner.

The most compute intensive unit is the Compute Unit kernel which can perform convolution or element wise multiplications. It contains several processing elements which get mapped to the underlying DSP blocks of the FPGA, performing fixed-point multiplications. Each DSP block can perform two 8-bit or 16-bit multiplications on Arria-10 FPGA platform. If desired, these processing elements can be leveraged for computation of FC layers. As mixed precision approach performs binary convolutions in the fully connected layers, dedicated compute units which can perform multiplication operation with 16-bit and 1-bit operands are synthesized on logic.

Apart from these kernels, other OpenCL kernels responsible for pooling, LRN and an output kernel for writing back the layer outputs to the DDR are included. Pooling kernel is flexible to perform down sampling for both Winograd and tile based convolution outputs. CNN topologies like AlexNet can leverage the LRN kernel. Output kernel is responsible to transfer the outputs of convolution/Pooling kernel to DDR. It can also perform the functionality of fuse layer, whereby output of the previously generated layer must be added to the output generated by the current layer. This feature is required for fuse layers of FCN-8s.

---

[1] Each M20K block of Arria 10 consists of 3 read ports and 1 write port. Double pumping is possible with $2 \times$ clock frequency.

4   Experimental Results

4.1   Case Study: VGG-16

The mixed precision model is retrained on ImageNet dataset by initializing the convolutional layers with pretrained full precision weights and FC layers are initialized using Gaussian distribution with zero mean and 0.005 standard deviation. ImageNet is a large-scale dataset from ILSVRC challenge [21]. The training dataset contains 1000 classes and 1.2 million images. The validation dataset contains 50,000 images, 50 images per class. The classification performance is reported using Top-1 and Top-5 accuracy. Top-1 accuracy measures the proportion of correctly-labeled images. If one of the five labels with the largest probability is a correct label, then this image is considered to have a correct label for Top-5 accuracy. The validation accuracy of the mixed precision approach is compared with different fixed-point implementations in the convolution layers and also the full precision implementation of VGG-16 in Table 1. There is no accuracy degradation with more than 18× reduction in weights compared to the full precision model after retraining. The mixed precision approach cannot be used in the case of FCN-8s as it does not use FC layers.

Table 1. Accuracy comparison of mixed precision VGG-16.

Precision Conv layer weights	Precision FC layer weights	Top-1 accuracy	Top-5 accuracy	Parameters
32-bit float	32-bit float	68.08%	88.00%	560 MB
32-bit float	Binary	69.85%	89.65%	72 MB
16-bit fixed	**Binary**	**69.56%**	**89.40%**	**44 MB**
8-bit fixed	Binary	69.24%	89.12%	30 MB

VGG-16 consists of 13 convolutional layers with 3×3 kernels. Since WinoCNN is based on F(2 × 2, 3 × 3) Winograd algorithm, there is scope for increase in throughput for 13 convolutional layers because they can leverage the Winograd convolutions. The remaining three layers can use binary weights to avoid the higher local memory demand. The effect of M_{vec} and D_{vec} (parallelization factors) is investigated in terms of resource utilization and performance for VGG-16 with mixed precision quantization. The Table 2 discusses the HW resource utilization and throughput for mixed precision VGG-16 using WinoCNN. To summarize, using Winograd convolutions and mixed precision approach, an overall throughput of 24 img/sec with a batch size of 1 is achieved for VGG-16.

4.2   Case Study: FCN-8s

The semantic segmentation on Cityscapes dataset [22] is evaluated using FCN-8s architecture. VGG-16 is used as the feature detector and additional layers

Table 2. Resource consumption of mixed precision VGG-16 implementation.

Parallelization $M_{vec} \times D_{vec}$	Throughput measurement (ms)	BRAM usage	DSP usage	Logic (ALM)
16×16	121.83	1.561 MB/6.6 MB	12%	28%
16×32	71.15	2.42 MB/6.6 MB	20%	45%
16×64	41.766	5.44 MB/6.6 MB	37%	61%

are added for up-sampling the image. The convolutional layers are initialized with the weights obtained for ImageNet classification and the upsampling layers are trained in an iterative manner as [9]. The Intersection over Union (IOU) is an essential metric which calculates the number of pixels overlapped between ground truth labels and the obtained predictions. The IOU score is evaluated for each class in the dataset separately and finally mean Intersection over Union (mIOU) is obtained by taking average over all the IOU values. The mIOU are compared for different quantizations in Table 3.

Table 3. Comparing mIOU for FCN-8s with different quantizations.

Precision	mIOU	Parameters
32-bit float	61.0%	537 MB
16-bit fixed	59.8%	269 MB
8-bit fixed	58.4%	134 MB

The proposed FCN-8s in [9] consists of more than 102M training parameters and demands more than 52.6 billion MAC operations to execute the FC6 layer. As the kernel size is not 3×3, WinoCNN accelerator cannot leverage Winograd algorithm. Further, this layer demands 6.4 MB of local memory only for weight buffer with $M_{vec} = 16$, $D_{vec} = 64$ and $Q = 16$. The local memory in the form of BRAMs are also leveraged for input buffer and Winograd transformations. Thus, the kernel size is changed from 7×7 to 3×3 in FC6 layer and modified version of FCN-8s is retrained. The 7×7 kernel is observed to be too large and results in redundancy for Cityscapes dataset as a similar accuracy is achieved with 3×3 kernel. The computations of the last upscore layer have been reduced by upsampling with a factor of 2 instead of 8. This change would result in a smaller segmentation output with dimension 128×256. The input of modified FCN-8s is 512×1024 image and output is 128×256. The overall computational complexity of modified FCN-8s is 358 GOP. For $M_{vec} = 16$, $D_{vec} = 64$, $Q = 16$, we obtain a throughput of *494 ms* on Arria10 GX FPGA to perform inference using the modified version of FCN-8s. The theoretical and practical inference times in ms is presented for FCN-8s with various degrees of parallelization factors (M_{vec} and D_{vec}) in Fig. 2. The theoretical values are obtained after realizing a similar kind of roof-line model in [15] for WinoCNN.

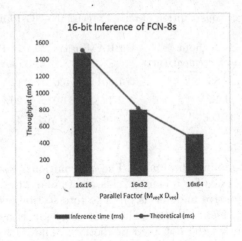

Fig. 2. Throughput comparison of 16-bit FCN-8s for different parallelization schemes.

4.3   Comparision with Related Work

The best performance results obtained from WinoCNN for VGG-16 is compared with the state-of-the-art FPGA accelerators in Table 4. The overall performance is calculated in Giga Operations Per Second (GOPS) by dividing the computational complexity of CNN architecture in GOP and inference time. The proposed accelerator design extracts the best performance per DSP block and also offers best performance for VGG-16 while there is further scope for increase in performance with the future release of Altera Offline Compiler (AOC) compiler. Currently, the DSP utilization is less than 40% and still delivers best performance for VGG-16. We also present the performance results without Winograd convolution and Mixed Precision quantization for VGG-16 indicating as "Non Optimal". The work in [19] applies 1-D Winograd on AlexNet using Arria-10 FPGA with float-16 as their quantization scheme. They achieve 6.89× better performance than WinoCNN as they use Winograd algorithm for all the convolutional layers with maximum DSP utilization. Further, they were using a batch size of 96 for FC layers. The obtained result is reported for FCN-8s also in Table 4. GPU delivers better throughput for VGG-16 (5.2×) compared to the proposed accelerator design. However, the power consumption is an important parameter for real-time and embedded applications. WinoCNN dominates by a factor of 1.8× in VGG-16 compared to the full precision GPU implementation in terms of energy efficiency measured in (GOPS/Watt). WinoCNN also achieves 1.9× better energy efficiency than full precision embedded GPU Jetson TX1 implementation for VGG-16. The energy efficiency comparison against Jetson TX1 is based on the results produced by Caziani et al. [10]. The power consumption on Arria 10 GX development kit is measured using the MAX V device on board which communicates with host using JTAG bus. There is also standalone application for power monitoring GUI which measures power across various power rails.

Table 4. Performance comparison with state-of-the-art FPGA accelerators for different VGG-16.

Work	FPGA platform	CNN model	Batch size	Quantization scheme	Overall performance GOPS	Performance per DSP GOPS/DSP[a]
Ours	Arria-10 GX 1150	FCN-8s	1	16-bit fixed	724.692	1.36
Ours	Arria-10 GX 1150	VGG-16	1	Mixed precision	742.478	1.47
Non optimal	Arria-10 GX 1150	VGG-16	1	16-bit fixed	286.416	0.56
[14]	Stratix-V GSD8	VGG-16	1	16-bit fixed	117.9	0.11
[18]	QuickAssist QPI	VGG-16 conv	1	32-bit Float	123.48	0.55
[15]	Ultrascale KU060	VGG-16	32	16-bit fixed	266	0.66
[15]	Virtex 690t	VGG-16	32	16-bit fixed	354	0.16
[23]	Arria-10 GX 1150	VGG-16	1	16-bit fixed	645.25	0.424
GPU	Nvidia-TitanX	VGG-16	1	32-bit float	3722	-
Embedded GPU	Nvidia-Jetson TX1	VGG-16	1	32-bit float	172	-

[a] Arria-10 consists of 1536 DSP elements. Only 37% of the DSP blocks are leveraged with the current release of AOC compiler.

5 Conclusion

This work uses OpenCL to describe the CNN based FPGA accelerator and reduces overall design time. The Winograd based fast convolutional algorithm is leveraged for kernel size of 3×3 to decrease the number of MAC operations by $2.25\times$ and thereby achieving close to theoretical speed up values on FPGA. The reuse of filter weights, feature maps is maximized to perform the convolution for a given channel and decrease the amount of DRAM access. The buffered feature maps are also parallely used for computing outputs from various channels. The Intel OpenCL channels have been efficiently used to fuse various operations of a layer such as Winograd transformations, convolution and pooling.

The performance bottlenecks caused by the fully connected layers have been identified in VGG-16 due to higher external memory bandwidth demand. As the fully connected layers consist of 90% of the weights in VGG-16, they demand for higher on chip memory which remains unused for other convolutional layers and thus limits the amount of parallelism in accelerator design. Thus, the pipeline stalls have been reduced by introducing a mixed precision approach with no accuracy loss in VGG-16. This approach uses binary weights and higher precision activations leveraging the dedicated on chip memory and compute logic on FPGA. With these HW and SW optimizations, WinoCNN achieves $1.8\times$ better energy efficiency than full precision implementation of Nvidia-Titan X. Finally, a practical application like semantic segmentation is implemented using FCN-8s CNN model with the same accelerator design achieving an overall throughput of 725 GOPS.

References

1. Krizhevsky, A., Sutskever, I., Hinton, G.E.: Imagenet classification with deep convolutional neural networks. In: Pereira, F., Burges, C.J.C., Bottou, L., Weinberger, K.Q. (eds.) Advances in Neural Information Processing Systems, vol. 25, pp. 1097–1105. Curran Associates Inc. (2012)
2. Karpathy, A., Toderici, G., Shetty, S., Leung, T., Sukthankar, R., Fei-Fei, L.: Large-scale video classification with convolutional neural networks. In: Proceedings of the 2014 IEEE Conference on Computer Vision and Pattern Recognition, pp. 1725–1732. IEEE Computer Society, Washington (2014)
3. Girshick, R.: Fast R-CNN. In: Proceedings of the 2015 IEEE International Conference on Computer Vision, pp. 1440–1448, Washington, DC, USA (2015)
4. Abdel-Hamid, O., Mohamed, A.-R., Jiang, H., Deng, L., Penn, G., Yu, D.: Convolutional neural networks for speech recognition. IEEE/ACM Trans. Audio Speech Lang. Proc. **22**(10), 1533–1545 (2014)
5. Socher, R., Perelygin, A., Wu, J., Chuang, J., Manning, C.D., Ng, A., Potts, C.: Recursive deep models for semantic compositionality over a sentiment treebank. In: Proceedings of the 2013 Conference on Empirical Methods in Natural Language Processing, pp. 1631–1642. Association for Computational Linguistics (2013)
6. Simonyan, K., Zisserman, A.: Very deep convolutional networks for large-scale image recognition. CoRR, abs/1409.1556 (2014)
7. He, K., Zhang, X., Ren, S., Sun, J.: Deep residual learning for image recognition. In: 2016 IEEE Conference on Computer Vision and Pattern Recognition, pp. 770–778, June 2016
8. Liu, W., Anguelov, D., Erhan, D., Szegedy, C., Reed, S., Fu, C.-Y., Berg, A.C.: SSD: single shot MultiBox detector. In: Leibe, B., Matas, J., Sebe, N., Welling, M. (eds.) ECCV 2016. LNCS, vol. 9905, pp. 21–37. Springer, Cham (2016). https://doi.org/10.1007/978-3-319-46448-0_2
9. Shelhamer, E., Long, J., Darrell, T.: Fully convolutional networks for semantic segmentation. IEEE Trans. Pattern Anal. Mach. Intell. **39**(4), 640–651 (2017)
10. Canziani, A., Paszke, A., Culurciello, E.: An analysis of deep neural network models for practical applications. CoRR, abs/1605.07678 (2016)
11. Gysel, P.: Ristretto: hardware-oriented approximation of convolutional neural networks. CoRR, abs/1605.06402 (2016)
12. Courbariaux, M., Bengio, Y.: Binarynet: training deep neural networks with weights and activations constrained to +1 or -1. CoRR, abs/1602.02830 (2016)
13. Rastegari, M., Ordonez, V., Redmon, J., Farhadi, A.: XNOR-Net: ImageNet classification using binary convolutional neural networks. In: Leibe, B., Matas, J., Sebe, N., Welling, M. (eds.) ECCV 2016. LNCS, vol. 9908, pp. 525–542. Springer, Cham (2016). https://doi.org/10.1007/978-3-319-46493-0_32
14. Suda, N., et al.: Throughput-optimized OpenCL-based FPGA accelerator for large-scale convolutional neural networks. In: Proceedings of the 2016 ACM/SIGDA International Symposium on Field-Programmable Gate Arrays, pp. 16–25. ACM, New York (2016)

15. Zhang, C., Fang, Z., Zhou, P., Pan, P., Cong, J.: Caffeine: towards uniformed representation and acceleration for deep convolutional neural networks. In: Proceedings of the 35th International Conference on Computer-Aided Design, pp. 12:1–12:8. ACM, New York (2016)
16. Wang, D., An, J., Xu, K.: PipeCNN: an OpenCL-based FPGA accelerator for large-scale convolution neuron networks. CoRR, abs/1611.02450 (2016)
17. Sze, V., Chen, Y., Yang, T., Emer, J.S.: Efficient processing of deep neural networks: a tutorial and survey. Proc. IEEE **105**(12), 2295–2329 (2017)
18. Zhang, C., Prasanna, V.: Frequency domain acceleration of convolutional neural networks on CPU-FPGA shared memory system. In: Proceedings of the 2017 ACM/SIGDA International Symposium on Field-Programmable Gate Arrays, pp. 35–44. ACM, New York (2017)
19. Aydonat, U., O'Connell, S., Capalija, D., Ling, A.C., Chiu, G.R.: An OpenCL™ Deep learning accelerator on Arria 10. In: Proceedings of the 2017 ACM/SIGDA International Symposium on Field-Programmable Gate Arrays, pp. 55–64. ACM, New York (2017)
20. Lavin, A.: Fast algorithms for convolutional neural networks. CoRR, abs/1509.09308 (2015)
21. Deng, J., Dong, W., Socher, R., Li, L.-J., Li, K., Fei-Fei, L.: ImageNet: a large-scale hierarchical image database. In: IEEE Conference on Computer Vision and Pattern Recognition (2009)
22. Cordts, M., et al.: The cityscapes dataset for semantic urban scene understanding. CoRR, abs/1604.01685 (2016)
23. Ma, Y., Cao, Y., Vrudhula, S., Seo, J.-s.: Optimizing loop operation and dataflow in FPGA acceleration of deep convolutional neural networks. In: Proceedings of the 2017 ACM/SIGDA International Symposium on Field-Programmable Gate Arrays, pp. 45–54. ACM, New York (2017)

Energy Awareness

The Return of Power Gating: Smart Leakage Energy Reductions in Modern Out-of-Order Processor Architectures

Elbruz Ozen[✉] and Alex Orailoglu

University of California, San Diego, La Jolla, CA 92093, USA
elozen@eng.ucsd.edu, alex@cs.ucsd.edu

Abstract. Leakage power has been a significant concern in power constrained processor design as manufacturing technology has scaled down
dramatically in the last decades. While power gating has been known
to deliver leakage power reductions, its success has heavily relied on
judicious power gating decisions. Yet delivering such prudent decisions
has been particularly challenging for out-of-order processors due to the
unpredictability of execution order. This paper introduces an intelligent
power gating method for out-of-order embedded and mobile processor
execution units by monitoring and utilizing readily available hints on
the pipeline. First, we track the counts of different instruction types in
the instruction queue to identify the execution units slated to remain idle
in the near future. As the presence of an instruction is not a definite indicator of its execution start due to stalls, our second guidance improves
the accuracy of the first approach by tracking the stalling instructions
in the instruction queue due to memory dependencies. While tracking
IQ content delivers dramatically better results than the state-of-the-art
timeout-based methods in the literature with 48.8% energy reductions,
the memory-aware guidance boosts energy savings up to 72.8% on average for memory intensive applications.

Keywords: Power gating · Embedded and mobile processors ·
Out-of-order execution

1 Introduction

Distributed computing at the edge with embedded and mobile devices creates
numerous opportunities for a variety of applications. While empowering The
Internet of Things (IoT), mobile devices and distributed intelligent systems,
embedded and mobile processors need high-performance hardware and accelerators to meet real-time processing requirements. For instance, today's high-end
mobile processors have deeper pipelines than before, they contain specialized
hardware to accelerate common tasks and they exploit the performance benefits of out-of-order execution [1]. At the same time, most embedded or mobile

© Springer Nature Switzerland AG 2019
M. Schoeberl et al. (Eds.): ARCS 2019, LNCS 11479, pp. 253–266, 2019.
https://doi.org/10.1007/978-3-030-18656-2_19

devices have to operate on a strict energy budget unlike desktop and server systems, and the workload characteristics can vary dramatically during the device operation which necessitates aggressive power saving methods while keeping the specialized execution units available when they are needed.

Micro-architectural techniques for execution unit power gating are widely explored in the literature for in-order embedded processors for almost a decade now. The embedded and mobile processors have dramatically evolved since then by employing out-of-order and super-scalar execution and equipping various accelerators. The clock speeds have also scaled by an order of magnitude from a few hundred MHz to the GHz range as reported by Halpern et al. [2] whereas memory latency has failed to keep up with the down-scaling of processor cycle times. Therefore, despite a slew of emerging memory technologies, the memory bottleneck remains a limiting factor for these high-performance computing devices which require an extensive amount of data to fully utilize their computational power. In addition, the memory requirements of applications continue to expand, consequently forcing a larger amount of RAM to be integrated into these systems to meet computation requirements. While the memory access times increase proportionally with the memory size, the impact has become even more striking today when it is measured in the scaled processor cycle times. As a result, the previous methods fall short of providing effective power gating guidance due to being oblivious to the unpredictability of the out-of-order execution and large memory stall times in the decision process.

Leakage power is a critical problem for low-power embedded devices, constituting a significant portion of the total energy consumption as CMOS technology is being scaled down in the last few decades. As a solution, it is possible to cut off the leakage power by turning off the circuit components when they are not needed. The previous works in the literature focused on power gating cache lines [3], re-sizing the branch predictor [4] or turning off the individual cores on a multicore system [5]. Modern embedded and mobile processors contain a variety of execution units including multiple integer ALUs (arithmetic logical units), FPUs (floating point units), vector units, and specialized accelerators embedded into the pipeline. The diversity of the execution units in embedded processors notwithstanding, most applications utilize a subset of them during a particular time window, with many units not being used at all in numerous intervals during the application execution. If these units are not put into sleep mode, they dissipate power as static leakage. While the benefits can be appreciable, power gating the execution units is a challenging problem in the face of execution uncertainty, as outlined by Kaxiras and Martonosi [6], because their idle periods tend to be much shorter and less predictable than other processor elements.

The primary challenge in execution unit power gating is to find "long enough" intervals so that the leakage energy saved by turning off the processor exceeds the energy dissipated by switching between on and off states. This period is denoted as $T_{break-even}$ (break-even point) in prior literature. Also, an execution unit that is off, but needed, requires a certain amount of time ($T_{wake-up}$) to become ready for execution. As a result, the idle interval should be greater than the sum of these two values as shown in Eq. 1 to deliver overall savings at no performance penalty; otherwise, power gating the units unnecessarily may not only cause energy loss, but it might also affect the performance of the processor.

$$T_{idle} > T_{break-even} + T_{wake-up} \tag{1}$$

The solution to this problem in in-order processors is evident because of the predictable nature of the execution pipeline. It can be solved by using a compiler analysis to determine the distance between two consecutive same type instructions and if warranted issuing turn-off signals through the instruction set. These methods are not readily applicable to out-of-order cores because the processor can dynamically reorder the instruction execution. The existing power gating methods in out-of-order execution do not aim to strictly satisfy the requirement given in Eq. 1 as pessimism in the face of uncertainty will result in forgoing many profitable power gating opportunities; instead, a predictive approach optimizes the decisions so that Eq. 1 will be with rare exceptions satisfied, resulting in overall energy savings. Previous works [7,8] in out-of-order processors rely on predictive methods such as timeouts to turn-off the execution units after observing prolonged idle periods. Although predictive methods can perform well in numerous cases, their accuracy inherently depends on how past instructions correlate with future execution. When the correlation fails to be satisfied for a particular application, prediction based methods not only fail to deliver any benefit but can induce a severe energy and performance penalty.

Although out-of-order cores have a significant amount of unpredictability in the execution, the pipeline contains numerous information sources which can be tracked easily and used as a hint for smart power gating decisions. This paper aims to discover the useful and readily trackable information sources and utilize them for smart power gating decisions. The guidance obtained from the pipeline consequently reduces the reliance on prediction and dramatically improves decision accuracy. We introduce two primary sources of guidance and the required hardware to track this information. We follow this up by measuring their impact on energy reduction and outline the results in the following sections. We emphasize the following points in this work as our contribution to the literature:

1. Use of IQ (instruction queue) content as a lookup for future instructions to be executed leading to making power gating decisions accordingly.
2. Introduction of a comprehensive methodology for "snooze bits" based tracking of missed load dependencies and consequent selective turn off of the execution units.
3. Utilization of the out-of-order execution flexibility to extend the sleep time and eliminate expensive early wake-ups without degrading performance.

2   Related Work

In [7], Hu et al. present a time-based and branch misprediction guided power gating policy for execution units in out-of-order processors. They turn off the execution units after observing prolonged periods of idleness or upon undergoing a branch misprediction. Since the success rate of the timeout-based power gating is strictly related to the determined timeout value, Bournoutian et al. [8] examine instruction type ratios in one application to determine timeout values of execution units in a timeout-based policy. Their method targets out-of-order mobile processor execution units with reservation stations. MAPG [9] turns off the in-order cores in a multiprocessor system when a load instruction misses on the cache. It is reasonable in this context to turn off the entire in-order core as it would stall until the processor retrieves the data from memory. Similarly, TAP [10] provides lower bound estimates for memory access time using tokens with out-of-order cores turning off themselves when they access the main memory, resulting in an aggressive overcompensation for an out-of-order processor which may continue executing instructions which do not depend on the load result on the same core while waiting for the memory.

A number of previous works as in [11–14] use a combination of compiler-based analysis and architectural support to determine the minimum cycle distance between two consecutive same type instructions, and signal turn-off commands to hardware when the former instruction is issued if there is sufficient distance between them. Wake-up is achieved by using explicit instructions or when the second instruction is decoded in the pipeline. These works present in the context of in-order execution, with their approaches being challenging to adapt to out-of-order processors as instructions may end up being executed differently than the program order. As an alternative method, pipeline balancing [15] dynamically changes the issue width and turns off pipeline resources when the applications fail to exhibit sufficient parallelism to utilize them. The approach saves power by monitoring the processor performance and setting the execution resources accordingly.

3   Power Gating Method

3.1   Instruction Queue Based Power Gating Guidance

Out-of-order processors look ahead in the instruction window to find sufficient parallelism in the code and utilize the pipeline resources more efficiently. Performance efficiency is typically attained by dispatching many instructions into the IQ and issuing instructions out-of-order when their operands are ready. Since the IQ holds the instructions to be executed in the near future, the information content of IQ can be exploited to make more accurate decisions and diminish the need for prediction in this process. The monitoring in IQ is performed by dynamically tracking the count of each instruction group that is executed on the same type of execution unit. We update the counts of each group by setting two checkpoints in the pipeline. We check the instruction opcode and increment the corresponding counter when an instruction is dispatched into IQ. When an instruction completes execution, we decrease its group's counter. The hardware issues a turn-off signal to the execution units whose group counter becomes zero. If a counter makes a transition from zero to a non-zero value, it issues a turn-on signal to the related execution unit so that it can wake itself up and become ready within the next few cycles. The main advantage of this aspect of our proposed approach is its simplicity and the improvement it provides over the timeout-based methods. It requires no more hardware or energy than any timeout-based method (in fact, the same timeout counters can be utilized for tracking instruction counts) but it yields dramatically higher average sleep ratios at the cost of the same performance penalty.

3.2   Memory-Aware Power Gating Guidance

The IQ content provides information regarding the instructions which will be executed in the future. In this aspect, the information is useful but incomplete, as many instructions continue to reside in the IQ despite their inactivity and cause the system to pessimistically turn on the units even though they are neither being executed nor slated for execution in the near future. If perfect information of the stall times were available, it would be possible to make highly accurate power gating decisions. It is possible to design a system which can track all dependency chains to provide an accurate estimation of the execution times. Yet such tracking requires a significant amount of information with the tracking hardware easily overpowering the improvement that is hoped for. As the majority of the stalls are in the order of few cycles, tracking them provides no benefit over counting instructions in the IQ. However, one primary source of long stalls is the lower-level cache and memory access latency. When a load instruction misses on the first-level cache, it causes all directly and indirectly dependent dispatched instructions to stall in the IQ for tens of cycles until it retrieves its result. Tracking such information can boost the accuracy of decisions made with IQ guidance by particularly favoring the applications with high cache miss rates.

We introduce a memory-aware power gating guidance with a hardware mechanism to keep track of instructions which directly or indirectly depend on the missed load instructions on the L1 cache. We mark these instructions temporarily by using *snooze bits* and exclude them from consideration while making power gating decisions. Snooze bits display similarities to *poison bits* [16] which implement a speculation inheritance mechanism to enable squashing of misprediction-reliant instructions. In our context, we store snooze bits per each instruction instead to track missed load dependencies. The decision algorithm is similar to the method which is presented with instruction queue-based guidance, but it excludes the instructions from the count when they are snoozed.

The determination of the number of unmarked instructions necessitates additional effort over merely counting the instructions in the IQ. To achieve this, we keep the snooze bits explicitly in the IQ for each instruction. It is to be noted that an instruction can be snoozed by multiple loads in the pipeline. In addition to these multiple snooze bits, we add one more bit and denote therein the logical OR of all the snooze bits of an instruction as the *overall snooze bit*.

An instruction's snooze bits can be marked as a result of two events: while an instruction is being dispatched, it can inherit snooze bits from its parents, namely the instructions which provide its source operands. Besides, when a load instruction misses on L1, it can snooze its descendants, namely all the instructions which are directly or indirectly in the dependency chain of the missed load.

The snoozing event marks an instruction's snooze bit indicated with the missed load's ID. If the instruction had no marked snooze bits previously, the overall snooze bit is also marked. Similarly, when a previously missed load instruction retrieves its result, it clears its descendants' snooze bits affiliated with its load ID, and the instructions' overall snooze bits are also cleared if this is the only missed load instruction which they depend on. As a result of these events, we distinguish three distinct scenarios to update the unmarked instruction counts:

1. An instruction increments the unmarked instruction count of its group when it is dispatched unless it inherits snooze bits from its parents.
2. An instruction decrements the unmarked instruction count of its group when its execution is completed.
3. In addition, when a load instruction misses on L1 or returns data after the miss, we track how many of its descendants have changed their overall snooze bit, and adjust the counters accordingly.

Even though the memory-aware guidance requires quite a bit of information to track, we show that the necessary hardware can be implemented by utilizing the existing issue logic to update the snooze bits. As a result, the update process is dramatically simplified, and it can be performed no differently than the update of other information in the IQ. The described implementation method in Sect. 4.2 conveniently achieves these tasks with only four basic operations and without needing any associative look-ups in the IQ. As a result, these operations do not impact timing, and the energy impact is minimized.

In addition, we deliberately avoid an early wake-up mechanism to cut down on the hardware cost, but this design decision necessitates examination of the concomitant performance issues. To illustrate, an instruction may become ready for the execution in the cycle subsequent to receiving the awaited result from the memory, but it might end up waiting for the execution unit wake-up. Although this is a critical problem for an in-order processor, the incurred wake-up time overhead barely leads to any performance loss because of the flexibility of out-of-order execution. Unless the wake-up stalling instructions clog the IQ and impede further instruction dispatch, no consequent material performance issue ensues. The experimental results confirm that the extra performance loss is negligible as we expected.

4   Hardware Design

4.1   Base Hardware to Track IQ Content

The IQ tracking hardware and power gating control logic can be implemented as in Fig. 1. We employ an execution unit detector to detect the type of dispatched instructions. The detector consists of a combinational logic which maps the instruction opcodes into execution groups. We keep the count of the instructions in the IQ for each execution unit by using shift registers. The length of each shift register equals the IQ size. We use a shift register as a counter because it

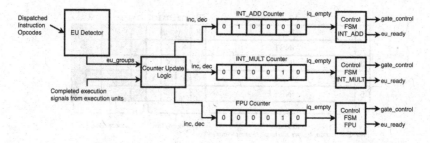

Fig. 1. Overview of the IQ tracking hardware

reduces dynamic power consumption due to the reduced number of bit flips and it simplifies the update logic. We initialize each counter to "0...01" indicating the zero value where the position of bit "1" shows the instruction count. The counter is shifted left to increment and right to decrement. In this hardware scheme, we can directly use the least significant bit as an empty signal without checking the entire register. Finally, each execution unit has a simple FSM (finite state machine) with three states as its transition diagram shows in Fig. 2 which indicates the conditions for the transitions to happen (bold) as well as the asserted signals (italics) in each state. The FSM controls the gating transistor and the ready signal to inform the pipeline control logic when the execution unit is ready.

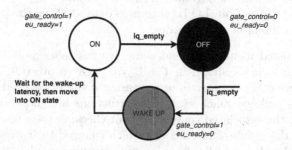

Fig. 2. FSM transition diagram

4.2 Extension Hardware to Track Memory Dependencies

This section introduces our novel IQ extension hardware to track cache-missed load dependencies. Its design helps us to fully utilize the existing issue logic in the pipeline, and perform the tracking by making use of simple operations at each stage. To keep the load dependencies and the snooze bits, we introduce $2N + 1$ extra bits to each IQ entry where N is the LQ (Load Queue) size. N bits are used to indicate dependencies with an additional N bits to indicate snooze bits and 1 bit for the OR'ed summary of the snooze bits as shown in Fig. 3. A bit in the ith dependency column indicates that the instruction is dependent on

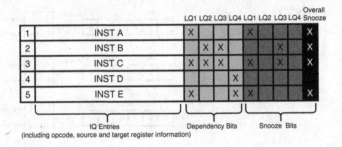

Fig. 3. Extension hardware to track missed memory dependencies

the load instruction in LQ's ith entry. Similarly, a mark in the snooze column i indicates that the instruction is snoozed by the missed load instruction at LQ's ith entry. The overall snooze summary bit becomes "1" if at least one snooze bit is "1". The dependency and the snooze bits are updated as follows:

- When an instruction is dispatched, its dependency bits are set to the OR of the dependency bits of the instructions which provide its operands. Similarly, its snooze bits are set to the OR'ed version of its parents' snooze bits.
- When a load instruction (LQ ID i) is dispatched, it marks its ith dependency bit in addition to the dependencies inherited by its parents.
- When a load instruction (LQ ID i) misses on L1, it copies the ith dependency column of all IQ entries into the ith snooze column.
- When a load instruction (LQ ID i) returns data, it clears the ith dependency and snooze column of all IQ entries.

Tracking missed memory dependencies requires some modifications to the counter update logic as shown in Fig. 1. We need to override the increment signal and prevent the counter from increasing if the dispatched instruction is snoozed by its parents. Since executed instructions are snooze mark free, we can decrement the associated counter without checking their mark. Finally, we need to check the group of instructions which changed their overall snooze bit due to load related events (cache miss and returning result). Both load miss and load result return after miss can trigger counter updates if they cause an instruction's overall snooze bit to flip. In this case, the hardware detects how many instructions changed their overall snooze bit and updates the counters accordingly.

5   Experimental Results

We implemented the proposed design by modifying the out-of-order CPU model in the gem5 simulator [17]. The pipeline resources of the processor are shown in Table 1. We tested the proposed system with various SPEC2006 integer and floating point benchmarks by assuming $T_{break-even}$ as 10 cycles. We used various typical $T_{wake-up}$ latency values to observe the performance impact.

The $T_{break-even}$ and $T_{wake-up}$ values are selected to be within a similar range as in the previous out-of-order processor focused work [7,8] and in the most recent publications on power gating [18]. We have taken measurements for Integer ALU, Integer Multiply/Divide Unit and Floating Point Unit. The reported average values refer to arithmetic means unless stated otherwise for a particular value. Some geometric mean values are used for comparison with previous work [7].

Table 1. Implemented out-of-order CPU parameters

Clock frequency	1 GHz
Dispatch & Issue width	4-Wide
L1I cache, L1D cache	32 kB, 2-Way, 2 Cyc. Lat.
L2 cache	128 kB, 4-Way, 20 Cyc. Lat.
Memory latency	120 ns
IQ size, LQ size, ROB size	16, 16, 32 entries
Int-ALU, FP-ALU, Int-Mult Count	4, 2, 1

Figure 4 illustrates the sleep time of the execution units as a percentage of the total execution time for a variety of benchmarks. IQG represents the model only with instruction queue guidance. IQG+MAG monitors the IQ content and makes use of the cache miss information to snooze instructions. We have also included the total idle cycles and for comparison the power gating potential, the sum of all idle periods which are larger than $T_{break-even} + T_{wake-up}$, as defined in [7]. The power gating potential incorporates all idle periods in which power gating delivers a net energy profit, without affecting performance; yet the reader will note that this idealistic assessment is not achievable without a perfect oracle of future execution. IQG provides 66.2% and 53.4% average sleep ratio for integer and floating point units, respectively. The memory-aware guidance boosts these rates up to 73.6% and 75.1%, thus considerably extending the sleep rate for the floating point units. A remarkable observation may be the occurrence of cases when IQG+MAG exceeds the power gating potential that we can see in some benchmarks in Fig. 4. While this augurs well, no energy benefit should be expected as this excess stems from the inability to predict the appropriate reactivation times of components in an out-of-order environment. Actually a concern in this context may be that conversely the aggressive policy of turning off units when they are not needed at a particular time point may be impacted by the arrival of an instruction soon after the turn-off. Figure 5 shows that this concern is unwarranted as the energy savings of IQG+MAG track the potential savings closely.

Figure 5 shows the summary of total energy savings for each benchmark. We have used the simulation statistics together with the static and dynamic power values in [13,19] to calculate the energy savings in the execution pipeline which

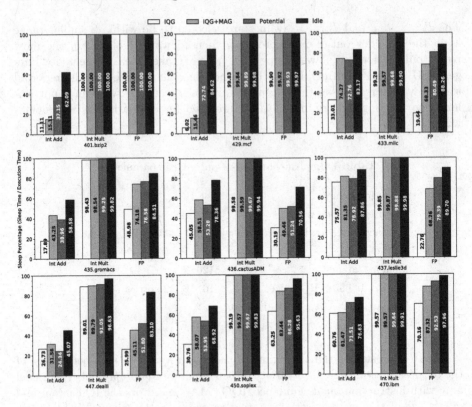

Fig. 4. Execution unit sleep time percentage

combines execution units, IQ and scheduling logic. The calculations include static and dynamic power consumption of each unit, the switching cost of power gating decisions, the static and dynamic energy cost of the additional hardware, and the energy cost of the extended execution time due to the performance impact of these methods. We use a realistic non-zero leakage model as in [13] to account for when the execution unit is turned off. The energy impact of the additional hardware is incorporated in the reported energy values by first calculating the extra bit requirements for each guidance type, followed up by a scaling of the area, leakage and dynamic power of the IQ to accurately model the energy overhead introduced by the tracking hardware. In a quite pessimistic scenario, IQG and MAG can approximately lead to 10% and 120% inflation in the IQ area and consequently to a similar increase in static and dynamic energy consumption. Despite the dramatic energy cost of the tracking hardware, we still attain 48.8% net energy savings in average by merely monitoring the IQ content. Memory-aware guidance helps to increase the average energy savings up to 72.8%. Interestingly, IQG+MAG results in slightly smaller energy savings than IQG for *bzip2* despite a higher sleep rate because the energy overhead of tracking stalling instructions counteracts its benefit if the gain is short of substantial for

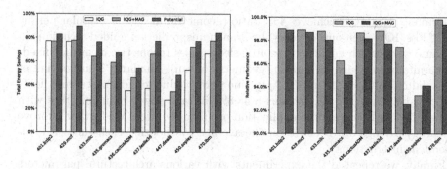

Fig. 5. Total energy savings   **Fig. 6.** Performance impact

a particular benchmark. Memory-aware guidance improves the energy savings as the cache miss rate increases. The performance impact of the suggested models is also demonstrated in Fig. 6. We obtain the relative performance values under the assumption of 4 cycles $T_{wake-up}$. The average performance reduction with IQG and IQG+MAP is around 2.1% and 3.1% respectively.

The main advantage of only monitoring IQ is its simplicity, yet it achieves remarkable power savings when compared to the timeout-based power gating methods in out-of-order processors. Hu et al. [7] can put the floating point units to sleep at 28% (geometric mean) of the execution cycles with around 2%

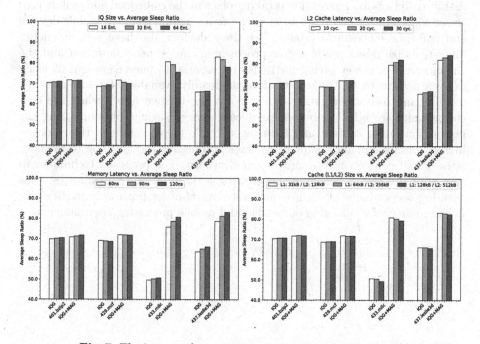

Fig. 7. The impact of processor parameters on the sleep ratio

performance loss. IQG achieves 45% ratio (geometric mean) at a similar performance loss. IQG even outperforms the branch misprediction guided technique in the same work which enables up to 40% sleep cycles (geometric mean) for fixed-point units by reaching 51% ratio (geometric mean). Similarly, Bournoutian et al. [8] claims around 27% and 19% pipeline power reduction for integer and floating point benchmarks. IQG attains a 48.8% average power reduction rate with comparable hardware, and no application profiling required. We further improve the energy savings up to 72.8% on the average by snoozing cache-missed load-dependent instructions.

Finally, we repeated the experiments with various architectural parameters to measure the effect of IQ size, L2 latency, memory latency and the cache sizes on the result. The results shown in Fig. 7 indicate that the average number of sleep cycles never fluctuate more than 6–8% for either of the policies despite the remarkable variance in processor parameters. While IQG results almost stay constant as the parameter changes, the sleep rate of IQG+MAG positively correlates with the cache and memory latencies as we expected. Larger cache sizes have a minor negative impact on IQG+MAG due to the reduced number of cache miss rates. Larger IQ sizes also reduce the benefit of IQG+MAG, but the benefits still stay prominent over IQG for practical IQ sizes.

6   Conclusion

A shift to out-of-order execution is taking place in the embedded and mobile processor space influenced by the strict performance requirements in mobile devices and real-time embedded systems. Yet these devices also have a tight energy budget, unlike desktop and server processors. The proper adaptation and the enhancement of power saving methods are essential to pursue energy efficiency in these architectures. We keep track of the readily available information on the pipeline and use power gating to cut down the leakage power when the execution units are idle. We obtain significant energy savings by monitoring the instruction queue content and reducing the role of prediction in this process. Memory-aware guidance helps us to track stalling instructions due to memory latency and consequently improves our decisions. The proposed techniques in this work promise to alleviate the growing leakage energy expenditures, thus ensuring the viability of high-performance out-of-order processors particularly in the context of challenging embedded and mobile processing environments.

References

1. Rupley, J.: Samsung M3 processor. In: 2018 IEEE Hot Chips 30 Symposium (HCS), Cupertino, CA, USA (2018)
2. Halpern, M., Zhu, Y., Reddi, V.J.: Mobile CPU's rise to power: quantifying the impact of generational mobile CPU design trends on performance, energy, and user satisfaction. In: 2016 IEEE International Symposium on High Performance Computer Architecture (HPCA), pp. 64–76 (2016). https://doi.org/10.1109/HPCA.2016.7446054
3. Kaxiras, S., Hu, Z., Martonosi, M.: Cache decay: exploiting generational behavior to reduce cache leakage power. In: Proceedings 28th Annual International Symposium on Computer Architecture, pp. 240–251 (2001). https://doi.org/10.1109/ISCA.2001.937453
4. Chaver, D., Piñuel, L., Prieto, M., Tirado, F., Huang, M.C.: Branch prediction on demand: an energy-efficient solution. In: Proceedings of the 2003 International Symposium on Low Power Electronics and Design, pp. 390–395 (2003). https://doi.org/10.1145/871506.871603
5. Leverich, J., Monchiero, M., Talwar, V., Ranganathan, P., Kozyrakis, C.: Power management of datacenter workloads using per-core power gating. IEEE Comput. Archit. Lett. **8**, 48–51 (2009). https://doi.org/10.1109/L-CA.2009.46
6. Kaxiras, S., Martonosi, M.: Computer architecture techniques for power-efficiency. In: Synthesis Lectures on Computer Architecture (2008). https://doi.org/10.2200/S00119ED1V01Y200805CAC004
7. Hu, Z., Buyuktosunoglu, A., Srinivasan, V., Zyuban, V., Jacobson, H., Bose, P.: Microarchitectural techniques for power gating of execution units. In: International Symposium on Low Power Electronics and Design, pp. 32–37 (2004). https://doi.org/10.1145/1013235.1013249
8. Bournoutian, G., Orailoglu, A.: Mobile ecosystem driven dynamic pipeline adaptation for low power. In: Pinho, L.M.P., Karl, W., Cohen, A., Brinkschulte, U. (eds.) ARCS 2015. LNCS, vol. 9017, pp. 83–95. Springer, Cham (2015). https://doi.org/10.1007/978-3-319-16086-3_7
9. Jeong, K., Kahng, A.B., Kang, S., Rosing, T.S., Strong, R.: MAPG: memory access power gating. In: Design, Automation & Test in Europe Conference (DATE), pp. 1054–1059 (2012)
10. Kahng, A.B., Kang, S., Rosing, T., Strong, R.: TAP: token-based adaptive power gating. In: International Symposium on Low Power Electronics and Design, pp. 203–208 (2012). https://doi.org/10.1145/2333660.2333711
11. Rele, S., Pande, S., Onder, S., Gupta, R.: Optimizing static power dissipation by functional units in superscalar processors. In: Horspool, R.N. (ed.) CC 2002. LNCS, vol. 2304, pp. 261–275. Springer, Heidelberg (2002). https://doi.org/10.1007/3-540-45937-5_19
12. You, Y.-P., Lee, C., Lee, J.K.: Compilers for leakage power reduction. ACM Trans. Des. Autom. Electron. Syst. **11**, 147–164 (2006). https://doi.org/10.1145/1124713.1124723
13. Roy, S., Ranganathan, N., Katkoori, S.: A framework for power-gating functional units in embedded microprocessors. IEEE Tran. Very Large Scale Integr. (VLSI) Syst. **17**, 1640–1649 (2009). https://doi.org/10.1109/TVLSI.2008.2005774
14. Kondo, M., et al.: Design and evaluation of fine-grained power-gating for embedded microprocessors. In: Design, Automation & Test in Europe Conference (DATE), pp. 145:1–145:6 (2014). https://doi.org/10.7873/DATE.2014.158

15. Bahar, R.I., Manne, S.: Power and energy reduction via pipeline balancing. In: 28th Annual International Symposium on Computer Architecture, pp. 218–229 (2001). https://doi.org/10.1109/ISCA.2001.937451

16. Hennessy, J.L., Patterson, D.A.: Computer Architecture: A Quantitative Approach, 5th edn, Appendix H. Elsevier (2011)

17. Binkert, N., et al.: The gem5 simulator. SIGARCH Comput. Archit. News. **39**, 1–7 (2011). https://doi.org/10.1145/2024716.2024718

18. Chiu, K.W., Chen, Y.G., Lin, I.C.: An efficient NBTI-aware wake-up strategy for power-gated designs. In: Design, Automation & Test in Europe Conference (DATE), pp. 901–904 (2018). https://doi.org/10.23919/DATE.2018.8342136

19. Li, S., Ahn, J.H., Strong, R.D., Brockman, J.B., Tullsen, D.M., Jouppi, N.P.: McPAT: an integrated power, area, and timing modeling framework for multi-core and manycore architectures. In: Proceedings of the 42nd Annual IEEE/ACM International Symposium on Microarchitecture, pp. 469–480 (2009). https://doi.org/10.1145/1669112.1669172

A Heterogeneous and Reconfigurable Embedded Architecture for Energy-Efficient Execution of Convolutional Neural Networks

Konstantin Lübeck[(⊠)] and Oliver Bringmann

Department of Computer Science, University of Tübingen, Tübingen, Germany
{konstantin.luebeck,oliver.bringmann}@uni-tuebingen.de

Abstract. Machine learning based convolutional neural networks (CNN) are becoming increasingly popular for identification tasks like image classification or speech recognition. However, CNNs have high memory and computational demands which makes it challenging to implement them on cost-efficient and energy-autonomous hardware. To cope with this challenge we present a heterogeneous and reconfigurable embedded architecture implemented on an inexpensive and widely available entry-level system on chip (SoC). Our architecture combines an ARM CPU and a coarse-grained reconfigurable architecture (CGRA) which execute a CNN in parallel to reach a higher energy-efficiency. Our results show up to 130% higher performance and 78% better energy-efficiency compared with an embedded Nvidia GPU.

1 Introduction

Embedded computer vision systems are becoming an important part of our everyday life. For instance, smartphones are used for object classification and face recognition. Also safety critical systems like highly automated driving cars employ computer vision systems for trajectory planning and obstacle avoidance, which often rely on convolutional neural networks (CNNs) to extract information from images due to their high precision [1,2]. However, CNNs have large memory and computational demands which leads to outsourcing CNN executions from mobile devices to data centers equipped with high performance general purpose graphics processor units (GPGPUs). Outsourcing solves the problem of computational and memory demands, but introduces latency and privacy issues. Moreover, the high energy demand and cost of GPGPUs need to be taken into account. To cope with those issues energy-autonomous and inexpensive embedded hardware for the execution of CNNs is necessary.

In this paper we present a heterogeneous and reconfigurable embedded architecture for energy-efficient offline execution of CNNs. To address cost-efficiency our architecture is implemented on an entry-level Xilinx Zynq SoC making it low-cost and easily adoptable for mid and large-scale deployment. We use the

© Springer Nature Switzerland AG 2019
M. Schoeberl et al. (Eds.): ARCS 2019, LNCS 11479, pp. 267–280, 2019.
https://doi.org/10.1007/978-3-030-18656-2_20

ARM Cortex-A53 quad-core CPU and the FPGA of the Xilinx Zynq Ultra-Scale+ MPSoC in parallel to accelerate CNN layers. On the FPGA a coarse-grained reconfigurable architecture (CGRA) is implemented which enables us to almost arbitrarily connect the digital signal processors units (DSPs) for the execution of different CNN layers without the need of a time consuming FPGA synthesis and implementation. On the ARM Cortex-A53 CPU the packed SIMD NEON registers and the available CPU cores are used to execute CNN layers. Those two pieces of hardware are connected through the 128-bit wide accelerator coherency port (ACP), which provides a low-latency and high-bandwidth com-munication via the level-2 (L2) cache of the ARM CPU. With this architecture we are able to achieve a 78% higher energy-efficiency and up to 130% better per-formance compared with a Nvidia Tegra K1 GPU when executing a LeNet-5 [1] inspired CNN.

2   Convolutional Neural Networks

Convolutional neural networks are a variant of artificial neural networks which have been used very successfully for the detection, classification and segmenta-tion of objects in images [4]. In addition, new precision records are being set continuously [1,3,5,6].

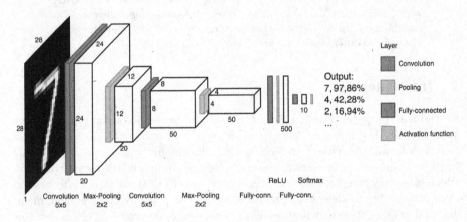

Fig. 1. Typical structure of a CNN [7]. (Color figure online)

CNNs are composed of several layers which successively filter abstract fea-tures from the input data and pass them on to the next layer. The most common layers are convolution, pooling, and fully-connected. In Fig. 1 a typical CNN structure with the mentioned layers is depicted. This CNN is based on LeNet-5 [1] a CNN which is used to classify grayscale images of hand-written digits from 0 to 9 of the MNIST data set [7]. The convolution layer (marked red) applies a convolution operation with previously trained filter kernels to its input data channels and emphasizes local features in those channels. Usually, several different filter kernels are applied to the same input data channel which leads to many more output data channels than input data channels. This can be seen in Fig. 1 where the first convolution layer takes the original image with only one grayscale channel as input and applies 20 different filter kernels to it, which produces 20 output data channels. Convolution layers are often followed by a pooling layer (marked green) which reduces the output data of the previous layer by only selecting the maximum (max pooling). This brings formerly emphasized local features closer together and makes it possible to combine them into a more global feature. Pooling also drastically shrinks the data size which helps to reduce memory consumption and the execution time of following layers. The last CNN layers are generally an array of fully-connected layers. A fully-connected layer takes all input elements from all channels and combines them into one vector of global features. This global feature vector is then further reduced by successive fully-connected layers until the vector size is equal to the number of classes. In Fig. 1 the fully-connected layers (marked blue) reduce their input data consisting of 800 elements down to 10, which represent the classes 0 to 9. In the very last step of the CNN in Fig. 1 a softmax function is applied to the feature vector, which converts the elements to pseudo-probabilities that represent to which class the original input image belongs.

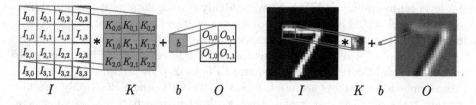

Fig. 2. Convolution operation.

The most computationally demanding layer is the convolution layer. The input data of this layer forms a tensor I with a width w_I, height h_I, and depth (channels) d_I. The filter kernels K of a convolution layer are usually quadratic with a width and height of n. The stride s describes how many pixels the filter kernel will be moved after it was applied to the input data I. In each single application of a filter kernel all filter elements are multiplied with the corresponding elements of the input data channel. All products of those multiplications are summed up and a bias b is added to the sum, which forms one output data element $O_{*,*}$. Figure 2 shows the application of a filter kernel K and bias b to input data I and the resulting output data O.

3 Related Work

Due to the broad range of applications where CNNs can be used [4] and due to the high computational and memory demands a lot of research efforts have been undertaken to accelerate the execution of CNNs on different hardware architectures. The most popular platform for the acceleration of CNNs are GPGPUs [2,8,9] because of the existence of software libraries [8,10,11] which offer great flexibility to train and execute CNNs. However, GPGPUs have an extremely high energy demand up to 650 W [12], which is not suitable for energy-autonomous applications. Also the use of application specific integrated circuits (ASICs) to energy-efficiently accelerate CNNs has been studied extensively [13–21]. ASICs offer a much better energy-efficiency than GPGPUs since all circuits can be tailored to the given problem set. On the other hand, designing, layouting, and actually manufacturing an ASIC is very costly and time consuming. Moreover, an ASIC can mostly only be used to execute the specific task it was designed for while meeting the given performance and energy constraints. A good trade-off between the flexible programmability of GPGPUs and the energy-efficiency of ASICs are FPGAs. FPGAs offer programmable logic blocks which are connected together over a configurable network. This enables programmers to tailor the FPGA resources to efficiently execute a given algorithm. Due to the flexibility, energy-efficiency and relatively low costs of FPGAs they have become a popular platform for the energy-efficient acceleration of CNNs [22–25]. Since the configuration of FPGAs through a synthesis and implementation process is time and memory consuming CGRAs are often used for CNN accelerator architectures [14,16,18,19,22]. In contrast to FPGAs, which offer complex fine-grained bit level configurability, CGRAs provide highly regular data path configurability on word level [26]. This makes it possible to change the data path in a CGRA on-the-fly without the need for a time consuming synthesis and implementation.

Contemporary embedded systems consist of different pieces of hardware such as multiple multi-core CPUs, GPUs, and FPGAs [27]. In [24] and [25] heterogeneous embedded systems are used, however, the CPU and FPGA only execute certain tasks on their own rather than working in real parallel fashion where both pieces of hardware are combined to execute a task.

4   Hardware

Our heterogeneous architecture is implemented on a Xilinx Zynq UltraScale+ MPSoC (ZU3EG) using the ARM Cortex-A53 quad-core CPU (APU) and the programmable logic (PL/FPGA). Both hardware components are used to execute a CNN in parallel. Figure 3 shows an overview of our architecture with computing elements, storages blocks, and their connections over data busses.

4.1   Configurable Reconfigurable Core (CRC)

On the PL/FPGA side the Configurable Reconfigurable Core (CRC) [28,29] is implemented. The CRC is a two-dimensional systolic array composed of 28 identical processing elements (PEs) connected over a nearest-neighbor network, which can be reconfigured at run time, block RAMs (BRAMs) to store

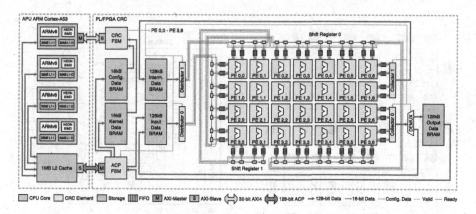

Fig. 3. Hardware architecture overview.

computation and configuration data, and two finite-state machines (FSMs) which take care of communication with the APU and configuration of the PE network (see Fig. 3).

The PEs are connected through a nearest-neighbor network with a data width of 2×16-bit. Via the North and South, PEs are able to send and receive data over two channels. From the West, PEs can only receive data and, vice versa, can only send data to the East. All PE-to-PE connections are implemented as FIFO buffers. To enqueue and dequeue data into and from a FIFO each 16-bit data channel is accompanied by a valid and a ready wire. The valid wire signals the FIFO whether data coming from a PE is valid and can be enqueued. The valid wire also signals the receiving PE that the FIFO holds data. The ready wire signals the FIFO if the receiving PE is ready to process the data at its input. Those PE-to-PE connections can be seen on the left hand side of Fig. 4. Additionally, each PE is connected to a 32-bit wide configuration data wire to load a configuration or a numeric constant. Inside of each PE resides a 16-bit constant register to store a numeric value, a 32-bit configuration register which is connected to multiplexers and demultiplexers (MUX/DEMUX) to configure a PE's internal data path, and a functional unit (FU) which acts as an arithmetic logic unit. Each PE output has a 16-bit register that stores the data which is going to be enqueued into the connected FIFO during the next clock cycle. Those PE internals are depicted on the right hand side of Fig. 4.

The FU has three 16-bit fixed point data inputs and is capable of the following operations: addition, subtraction, multiplication, multiply-accumulate, and maximum of two or three numbers, which are implemented using the digital signal processor resources (DSPs) of the PL/FPGA. Through the PE's MUXes all input data channels from the North, West, South, and the constant register can be configured as input for each of the three FU data inputs (see Fig. 4). In each clock cycle the FU checks whether all data values for the configured operation are present at its data inputs by checking the corresponding valid wires. If all input data values are present and all configured valid wire are set, the FU

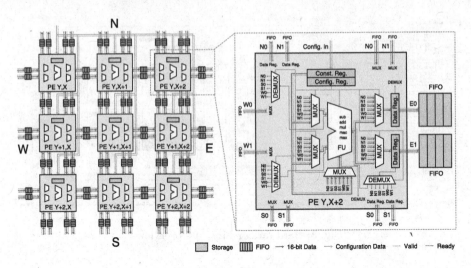

Fig. 4. CRC nearest-neighbor network and PE internals.

executes the operation and sets the valid wire at its output to store the result in the configured output registers. However, if not all data values are available, the FU unsets the ready wires for the inputs on which the data is available. This stalls the data paths leading to those data inputs, which is propagated through the whole PE network, until all required data values are valid.

This stalling mechanism allows for two-dimensional data pipelining. One-dimensional instruction pipelining is a well known technique employed in all modern processors. It speeds up the overall run time of programs by overlapping the execution of consecutive instructions. This is accomplished by splitting instructions into different steps whereas each step is then processed by the corresponding pipeline stage while all stages work in parallel [30]. Complex arithmetic expressions, like a convolution, can also be split into steps whereas each step represents a single operation. Those single operations are mapped onto PEs. Via the nearest-neighbor network those single operations on PEs are connected to form the desired arithmetic expression. On the left hand side of Fig. 5 such a mapping is shown using a 3×3 convolution. The elements of the kernel K and the bias b are stored in the constant register of the PEs.

The border PEs (PE$*, 0$ and PE$\{0; 3\}, *$ in Figs. 4 and 5) are connected to a shift register which supplies those PEs with the input data I. Because for the calculation of adjacent output data elements $O_{*,l}$ and $O_{*,l+1}$ of a $n \times n$ convolution the input data columns $I_{*,l+s}, \ldots, I_{*,l+n-s}$ are needed the shift register only has to be shifted $n \cdot s$ times to apply the kernel K to the next part of the input data I. This shifting mechanism exploits data locality of the row-wise application of a kernel for $s < n$.

On the right hand side of Fig. 5 the data flow graph of the three PEs in the northmost row and the connected shift register cells for a 3×3 convolution is extracted and displayed at four consecutive points in time $(t_0, \ldots, t_3)$.

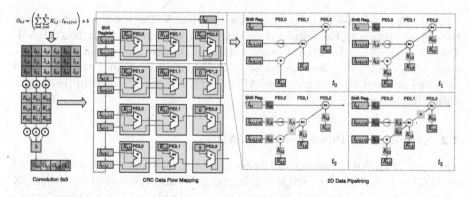

Fig. 5. Mapping and data flow of a 3×3 convolution onto the CRC. (Color figure online)

The rectangular vertices on the left hand side represent the shift register cells and the rectangular vertices at the bottom represent the constant registers. The circular vertices depict the configured PE function whereas each column of vertices in the data flow graph represents one PE. At t_0 all vertices are ready to process data (marked green) and no data path leading to any vertex is stalled. In the next step t_1 all shift register cells and constant registers have valid data. Since the multiply-accumulate operation in PE0,2 is missing the operand coming from PE0,1 the data path coming from the shift register is stalled (marked red). At t_2 the multiply and forward operation in PE0,0 have been processed and the data values for the next kernel application are present in the shift register. In the last step t_4 all operands for the multiply-accumulate operation in PE0,2 are available such that the stalled data path coming from the shift register can be unlocked.

By employing two-dimensional data pipelining it is possible to have input and intermediate data values of multiple consecutive kernel applications of a convolution simultaneously and in a chronological order on the CRC. If the pipeline is completely filled one output value is calculated in each clock cycle. By mapping multiple consecutive kernel applications onto the CRC this can be increased further by employing intra and inter output feature map parallelism (intra/inter-OFMP) [17].

The configuration, kernel, and input data for the CRC is read from a configuration file stored on flash memory and placed into the L2 cache by the APU. The APU sends a command over the 32-bit wide AXI4 bus to the CRC FSM containing the address and number of the configurations, kernels, and input data in the L2 cache. The ACP FSM then loads this data over the 128-bit wide ACP bus from the L2 cache of the APU into the corresponding BRAMs. Afterwards the APU sends a start command to the CRC FSM which triggers the configuration of the distributors, PEs, and collectors. This takes one clock cycle for each component. The distributors are responsible for reading input data from the BRAMs and inserting it into the shift registers. The distributors are programmed to generate complex address patterns to read data from the sequential

BRAMs like column-wise input data as seen in Fig. 5. The collectors either store the output data into the output data BRAM or the intermediate data BRAM. The intermediate data BRAM is used if an arithmetic expression is too large to fit onto the 28 PEs and has to be split. When all configurations have been executed on the CRC it signals the APU that the result is stored in the output data BRAM (see Fig. 3).

4.2   Application Processor Unit (APU)

The APU is an ARM Cortex-A53 64-bit quad-core processor with a clock speed of 1.1 GHz. It supports the ARMv8 instruction set and the packed SIMD NEON extension with 128-bit wide registers, which can hold up to four 32-bit floating point values at once. Each APU core has an in-order two-way superscalar 8-stage pipeline, two separate 32 kB level-1 caches for instructions (L1-I) and data (L1-D). All four cores share a coherent 1 MB level-2 cache (L2) for instructions and data. Each core has master access to the 32-bit wide AXI4 bus which is connected as slave to the PL/FPGA. The 128-bit wide Accelerator Coherency Port (ACP) is connected as master to the PL/FPGA and as slave to the APU's L2 cache (see Fig. 3). The ACP allows the implemented hardware on the PL/FPGA, in our case the CRC, to coherently share data with the APU over a low latency interconnect. Each transaction over the ACP consists of 64 Byte of data, which is equal to the length of one L2 cache line. The APU is also connected to 2 GB DDR4 RAM which serves as main memory [27].

5   Software (Pico-CNN)

Pico-CNN [32] is responsible for the execution of CNNs on the APU and the communication with the CRC. It runs under Ubuntu Linux 16.04 LTS on the APU. Pico-CNN is completely written in C and implements convolution, max-pooling, fully-connected, and softmax optimized for the ARM Cortex-A53 processor cores and the packed SIMD NEON extension. Except for the softmax layer all layers are implemented in a parallel fashion using OpenMP [31] to utilize all available four APU cores.

Figure 6 shows how a single kernel application of a 5×5 convolution is mapped onto the packed SIMD NEON registers Q. Each Q register is 128-bit wide, which makes it possible to execute four 32-bit floating point operations in parallel. After loading all elements of the input data I and the kernel K into registers Q0–Q5 and Q6–Q11 (left hand side of Fig. 6) all products $P_{i,j}$ are calculated by multiplying each input data element $I_{i,j}$ with the corresponding kernel element $K_{i,j}$ (middle part of Fig. 6). Subsequently, all products $P_{i,j}$ will be accumulated into a single 128-bit register. In the end, the partial sums $S_0, \ldots, S_3$ will be summed up and the bias b is added to form one output element $O_{k,l}$ (right hand side of Fig. 6).

Due to the fact, that each kernel of a convolution will be applied to the whole input data set it is easy to distribute the computation of each convolution layer

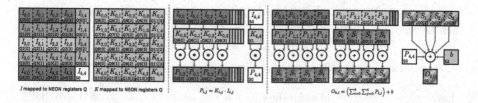

Fig. 6. Mapping of a 5×5 convolution onto packed SIMD NEON registers.

to multiple hardware components. In case of our architecture the input data of a convolution layer is split into four parts. Three of those parts are of equal size and intended for the APU. The fourth part is intended for the CRC. The APU-CRC split ratio is determined by executing each layer separately and then picking the CRC ratio which leads to the highest energy-efficiency for this layer. This step is repeated for each CNN layer. Since the input data size and the structure of a CNN is fixed the execution time is the same for different inputs such that the CRC ratios only have to be determined once.

On the APU all CNN layers are processed using 32-bit floating point data values. The CRC, however, uses 16-bit fixed point values for its calculations. This means all kernel elements are available as 32-bit floating point and 16-bit fixed point values. This conversion of kernel elements is only done once. The CRC input and output data has to be converted for each layer and each execution of a CNN. This conversion is carried out by one APU core and consists of one multiplication and one type cast using the packed SIMD NEON extension, which allows us to calculate four conversions at once. After the conversion of CRC input data is done it is placed into the L2 cache and read by the CRC. When the CRC has finished its calculations it moves its output data to the L2 cache where it will be converted to 32-bit floating point values. The 16-bit fixed point values are not overwritten since those can be reused for the next layer to save computational resources. This conversion affected the classification accuracy by less than 2%. The read and write operations on the L2 cache and the communication via the AXI4 and ACP busses are implemented as Linux kernel modules.

The configuration of the CRC is done manually using a graphical editing program, which allows us to set the PEs' internal data paths, FU operations, and PE-to-PE connections [33]. The configuration can be assessed using a cycle-accurate simulator. The final CRC configuration is imported into Pico-CNN, which takes care of actually configuring the CRC during the execution of a CNN.

6   Results

To evaluate our heterogeneous architecture we executed a LeNet-5 [1] inspired CNN depicted in Fig. 1. This CNN consists of eight layers and was trained, using the Caffe LeNet tutorial [34], to classify grayscale images of hand-written digits from 0 to 9 taken from the MNIST data set [7]. For the classification of one image 4.6 GOP have to be executed. Table 1 provides detailed information for each layer.

Table 1. Detailed layer overview of the LeNet-5 inspired CNN.

Layer		Data values [$w \times h \times d$]			#Opera. [OP]
No.	Name	Input	Output	Kernels	
1	Convolution 5 ×5	$28 \times 28 \times 1$	$24 \times 24 \times 20$	$5 \times 5 \times 20$	576,000
2	Max-Pooling 2×2	$24 \times 24 \times 20$	$12 \times 12 \times 20$	0	11,520
3	Convolution 5×5	$12 \times 12 \times 20$	$8 \times 8 \times 50$	$5 \times 5 \times 1000$	3,200,000
4	Max-Pooling 2×2	$8 \times 8 \times 50$	$4 \times 4 \times 50$	0	3,200
5	Fully-Connected	800	500	$500 \times 800 \times 1$	800,000
6	ReLU	500	500	0	500
7	Fully-Connected	500	10	$10 \times 500 \times 1$	10,000
8	Softmax	10	10	0	30

To determine the best CRC ratio we executed each convolution layer and max-pooling layer separately for four different architecture configurations and measured the number of input data frames it is able to process per second (FPS). During the execution we measured the power by requesting it through PMBus commands [35] send to the voltage regulators of the UltraZed-EG IO Carrier Card which contains the Xilinx UltraScale+ MPSoC (ZU3EG) with our implemented architecture. We either set a 100 MHz or 250 MHz CRC clock speed and used either one or three APU cores. Figure 7 shows the measured performance in FPS (1st row), mean power in W (2nd row), and the resulting energy-efficiency in $GOP\,s^{-1}\,W^{-1}$ (3rd row) for the convolution and max-pooling layers with different CRC ratios. One can clearly see that the best performance and energy-efficiency for the convolution layers can be reached with a CRC at a 250 MHz clock speed and one APU core. This is due to the fact, that the performance increase of a 2.5 times higher CRC clock speed only increases mean power by an average of 10%. The fact that the use of one APU core clearly dominates the use of three APU cores can be explained by the small input data size such that the accelerated execution can not compensate the communication overhead of OpenMP. The same can be seen for the max-pooling layers where a parallel execution on the APU and the CRC leads to a performance and energy-efficiency drop. The best energy-efficiency for the first convolution layer is reached with a CRC ratio of 0.75 at $0.32\,GOP\,s^{-1}\,W^{-1}$ and a 0.2 CRC ratio at $0.14\,GOP\,s^{-1}\,W^{-1}$ for the second convolution layer.

We compared our heterogeneous architecture with the Nvidia Tegra K1 ASIC [36]. We executed the LeNet-5 inspired CNN with Pico-CNN on two architecture configurations with the previously determined optimal CRC ratios. On the Tegra K1 GPU we executed the same CNN using Caffe with CUDA acceleration [8] and measured the FPS and the mean power to determine the energy-efficiency.

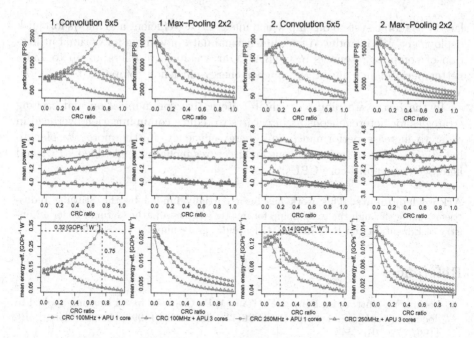

Fig. 7. Evaluation of different architecture configurations and CRC ratios.

The results of those measurements are depicted in Fig. 8. Both of our architecture configurations show an up to 2.3 times better performance than the Tegra K1 GPU. However, the Tegra K1 shows a lower mean power than our architecture configurations which have a 1.78 times higher energy-efficiency of $0.132\,\mathrm{GOP\,s^{-1}\,W^{-1}}$ when executing the LeNet-5 inspired CNN.

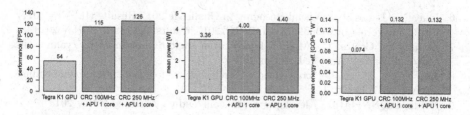

Fig. 8. Comparison of the Tegra K1 GPU with our heterogeneous architecture.

7 Conclusion

In this paper we presented a novel heterogeneous and reconfigurable embedded architecture for energy-efficient execution of convolutional neural networks. Our architecture successfully combines a general purpose CPU with a coarse-grained reconfigurable architecture. It is implemented on an inexpensive and largely available system on chip which makes it cost-efficient and allows for quick deployment. We introduced two-dimensional data pipelining for optimal utilization of compute resources in CGRAs. Our architecture offers an up to 130% better performance and a 78% higher energy-efficiency compared to a Nvidia Tegra K1 GPU.

In the future we plan to evaluate alternative communication and caching strategies for heterogeneous architectures to reduce communication overhead in order to increase performance and energy-efficiency. Furthermore, we plan to investigate different heterogeneous architectures including embedded GPUs and heterogeneous multi-core CPUs.

Acknowledgments. This work has been partially funded by the Stiftung Industrieforschung through the scholarship for master's theses and the German Federal Ministry of Education and Research (BMBF) under grant number 16ES0876 (GENIAL!).

References

1. LeCun, Y., Buttou, L., Bengio, Y., Haffner, P.: Gradient-based learning applied to document recognition. Proc. IEEE **86**(11), 2278–2324 (1998). https://doi.org/10.1109/5.726791
2. Krizhevsky, A., Sutskever, I., Hinton, G. E.: ImageNet classification with deep convolutional neural networks. In: Proceedings of the 25th International Conference on Neural Information Processing Systems (NIPS 2012), Lake Tahoe, NV, pp. 1097–1105 (2012)
3. Simonyan, K., Zisserman, A.: Very deep convolutional networks for large-scale image recognition. arXiv:1409.1556 (2014)
4. LeCun, Y., Bengio, Y., Hinton, G.: Deep learning. Nature **521**, 436–444 (2015). https://doi.org/10.1038/nature14539
5. Hu, J., Shen, L., Sun, G.: Squeeze-and-excitation networks. arXiv:1709.01507 (2017)
6. ImageNet Large Scale Visual Recognition Challenge 2017 Results (ILSVRC2017). http://image-net.org/challenges/LSVRC/2017/results. Accessed 19 Nov 2018
7. LeCun, Y., Cortes, C.: MNIST handwritten digit database. http://yann.lecun.com/exdb/mnist. Accessed 29 Oct 2018
8. Jia, Y., et al.: Caffe: convolutional architecture for fast feature embedding. arXiv:1408.5093 (2014)
9. Nvidia cuDNN. https://developer.nvidia.com/cudnn. Accessed 2 Nov 2018
10. Abadi, M., et al.: TensorFlow: large-scale machine learning on heterogeneous systems. http://tensorflow.org. Accessed 14 Nov 2018
11. Paszke, A., et al.: Automatic differentiation in PyTorch. In: Proceedings of the NIPS 2017 Workshop Autodiff, Long Beach, CA (2017)
12. Nvidia Titan RTX. https://www.nvidia.com/en-us/titan/titan-rtx. Accessed 20 Feb 2019
13. Chen, T., et al.: DianNao: a small-footprint high-throughput accelerator for ubiquitous machine-learning. In: Proceedings of the 19th International Conference on Architectural Support for Programming Languages and Operating Systems (ASPLOS 2014), Salt Lake City, UT, pp. 269–284 (2014). https://doi.org/10.1145/2541940.2541967

14. Tanomoto, M., Takamaeda-Yamazaki, S., Yao, J., Nakashima, Y.: A CGRA-based approach for accelerating convolutional neural networks. In: Proceedings of the 2015 IEEE 9th International Symposium on Embedded Multicore/Many-core Systems-on-Chip (MCSOC 2015), Turin, pp. 73–80 (2015). https://doi.org/10.1109/MCSoC.2015.41

15. Shi, R., et al.: A locality aware convolutional neural networks accelerator. In: Proceedings of the 2015 Euromicro Conference on Digital System Design, Funchal, pp. 591–598 (2015). https://doi.org/10.1109/DSD.2015.70

16. Fan, X., Li, H., Cao, W., Wang, L.: DT-CGRA: dual-track coarse-grained reconfigurable architecture for stream applications. In: Proceedings of the 2016 26th International Conference on Field Programmable Logic and Applications (FPL), Lausanne, pp. 1–9 (2016). https://doi.org/10.1109/FPL.2016.7577309

17. Jafri, S.M.A.H., Hemani, A., Kolin, P., Abbas, N.: MOCHA: morphable locality and compression aware architecture for convolutional neural networks. In: Proceedings of the 2017 IEEE International Parallel and Distributed Processing Symposium (IPDPS), Orlando, FL, pp. 276–286 (2007). https://doi.org/10.1109/IPDPS.2017.59

18. Chen, Y.H., Krishna, T., Emer, J.S., Sze, V.: Eyeriss: an energy-efficient reconfigurable accelerator for deep convolutional neural networks. IEEE J. Solid-State Circuits 52(1), 137–138 (2017). https://doi.org/10.1109/JSSC.2016.2616357

19. Zhao, B., Wang, M., Liu, M.: An energy-efficient coarse grained spatial architecture for convolutional neural networks AlexNet. IEICE Electron. Express 14(15), 20170595 (2017). https://doi.org/10.1587/elex.14.20170595

20. Shin, D., Lee, J., Lee, J., Yoo, H. J.: DNPU: an 8.1TOPS/W reconfigurable CNN-RNN processor for general-purpose deep neural networks. In: Proceedings of the in 2017 IEEE International Solid-State Circuits Conference (ISSCC), pp. 240–241, San Francisco, CA (2017). https://doi.org/10.1109/ISSCC.2017.7870350

21. Du, L., et al.: A reconfigurable streaming deep convolutional neural network accelerator for Internet of Things. IEEE Trans. Circuits Syst. I Regular Papers 65(1), 198–208 (2018). https://doi.org/10.1109/TCSI.2017.2735490

22. Chakradhar, S., Sankaradas, M., Jakkula, V., Cadambi, S.: A dynamically configurable coprocessor for convolutional neural networks. In: Proceedings of the 37th Annual International Symposium on Computer Architecture (ISCA 2010), Saint-Malo, pp. 247–257 (2010). https://doi.org/10.1145/1815961.1815993

23. Zhang, C., Li, P., Sun, G., Xiao, B., Cong, J.: Optimizing FPGA-based accelerator design for deep convolutional neural networks. In: Proceedings of the 2015 ACM/SIGDA International Symposium on Field-Programmable Gate Arrays (FPGA 2015), Monterey, CA, pp. 161–170 (2015). https://doi.org/10.1145/2684746.2689060

24. Qiu, J., et al.: Going deeper with embedded FPGA platform for convolutional neural network. In: Proceedings of the 2016 ACM/SIGDA International Symposium on Field-Programmable Gate Arrays (FPGA 2016), Monterey, CA, pp. 26–35 (2016). https://doi.org/10.1145/2847263.2847265

25. Gokhale, V., Zaidy, A., Chang, A.X.M., Culurciello, E.: Snowflake: an efficient hardware accelerator for convolutional neural networks. In: Proceedings of the 2017 IEEE International Symposium on Circuits and Systems (ISCAS), Baltimore, MD, pp. 1–4 (2017). https://doi.org/10.1109/ISCAS.2017.8050809

26. Hartenstein, R.: A decade of reconfigurable computing: a visionary retrospective. In: Proceedings of the Design, Automation and Test in Europe Conference and Exhibition 2001 (DATE 2001), Munich, pp. 642–649 (2001). https://doi.org/10.1109/DATE.2001.915091

27. Xilinx: Zynq UltraScale+ Device Technical Reference Manual, UG1085 v1.7 (2017)
28. Oppold, T., Schweizer, T., Oliveira, J.F., Eisenhardt, S., Kuhn, T., Rosenstiel, W.: CRC - concepts and evaluation of processor-like reconfigurable architectures. Inf. Technol. IT **49**(3), 157–164 (2007). https://doi.org/10.1524/itit.2007.49.3.157
29. Lübeck, K., Morgenstern, D., Schweizer, T., Peterson D., Rosenstiel W., Bringmann O.: Neues Konzept zur Steigerung der Zuverlässigkeit einer ARM-basierten Prozessorarchitektur unter Verwendung eines CGRAs. In: 19. Workshop Methoden und Beschreibungssprachen zur Modellierung und Verifikation von Schaltungen und Systemen (MBMV), Freiburg, pp. 46–58 (2016). https://doi.org/10.6094/UNIFR/10617
30. Hennessy, J.L., Patterson, D.A.: Computer Architecture, 5th edn. Morgan Kaufmann Publisher Inc., San Francisco (2011)
31. Dagum, L., Menon, R.: OpenMP: an industry-standard API for shared-memory programming. IEEE Comput. Sci. Eng. **5**(1), 45–55 (1998). https://doi.org/10.1109/99.660313
32. Pico-CNN. https://github.com/ekut-es/pico-cnn. Accessed 27 Feb 2019
33. CRC Configurator. https://github.com/ekut-es/crc_configurator. Accessed 27 Feb 2019
34. Jia, Y.: Training LeNet on MNIST with Caffe. http://caffe.berkeleyvision.org/gathered/examples/mnist.html. Accessed 20 Feb 2019
35. System Management Interface Forum, PMBus Power System Management Protocol Specification Part II - Command Language, Revision 1.2 (2010)
36. Nvidia, Whitepaper NVIDIA Tegra K1 A New Era in Mobile Computing, V1.0 (2013)

An Energy Efficient Embedded Processor for Hard Real-Time Java Applications

Manish Tewary[(⊠)], Avinash Malik, Zoran Salcic,
and Morteza Biglari-Abhari

Department of Electrical and Computer Engineering, University of Auckland,
Auckland 1010, New Zealand
mtew005@aucklanduni.ac.nz,
{avinash.malik,z.salcic,m.abhari}@auckland.ac.nz

Abstract. Energy management is very important and sometimes critical for certain classes of hard real-time systems. In this paper, we present effective energy reduction techniques for hard real-time systems developed in Java, which execute on bare metal and run on a time-predictable specialized Java processor. We modified traditional clock gating and dynamic frequency scaling methods to include the hardware-based run-time slack calculation in periodic tasks, thus reducing energy consumption in hard real-time systems. Two methods for energy reduction are employed leading to Energy Aware Java Optimized Processor (EAJOP). The first method includes task execution time monitoring and comparison with the estimated worst-case execution time to calculate the slack and bringing the processor to sleep for the slack duration upon task completion. The second method introduces real-time residual slack calculation at so-called checkpoints inside the periodic task, which are then used to lower the system frequency of the rest of the task dynamically, resulting in lower energy consumption. We compare EAJOP with baseline JOP when implemented on FPGA and demonstrate gains in energy consumption.

Keywords: Real-time and embedded systems · Processor · Compiler · Energy management

1 Introduction

Java is a platform-independent object-oriented programming language used in the embedded and real-time world, especially after the introduction of Real Time Specification for Java (RTSJ) and Safety-Critical Java (SCJ). Using Java in embedded systems suffered from a few inherent issues like the use of an extra software layer in the form of the Java Virtual Machine (JVM) and unpredictability in execution time due to automatic garbage collection. Few attempts have been made to solve the extra software layer issue by architecting JVM directly in hardware. A prominent case is Java Optimized Processor (JOP) [1] which also offers timing predictability of execution of Java bytecodes and is open for research and modifications.

Energy consumption is an important concern in real-time embedded applications, especially for battery powered devices. The energy consumption reduction of any

© Springer Nature Switzerland AG 2019
M. Schoeberl et al. (Eds.): ARCS 2019, LNCS 11479, pp. 281–292, 2019.
https://doi.org/10.1007/978-3-030-18656-2_21

processor is achieved by using different techniques, which are based on processor architecture, static analysis of programs and run-time control, which, however consume additional time and energy. We introduce an approach to energy management and reduction targeting hard real-time systems executing on bare metal processor, which relies on compiler additions, analysis of Worst-Case Execution Time (WCET) of a task and new hardware dedicated for run-time slack calculation, supported with small modifications (additions) of original time-predictable JOP processor in the form of energy management modes. The new processor called Energy Aware JOP (EAJOP) provides a hardware-based mechanism for slack measurement at different points (called checkpoints) in the program and it also implements energy reduction algorithms which use hardware-based run-time slack calculation (RTSC). EAJOP together with the Energy Aware Compiler Tool (EACT) constitutes the main contribution of this paper. Close affinity with JOP enables the use of all JOP compilation tools, while the modified toolchain enables evaluation of the results of energy saving algorithms implemented in EAJOP by comparing it with baseline programs which do not utilize energy management.

The rest of the paper is organized as follows: Sect. 2 introduces our motivations, task model and methods of energy consumption reduction. Section 3 explains the modifications that led to EAJOP. Section 4 explains EACT used to support energy consumption reduction. Section 5 presents analysis and validation of the approach containing experimental setup and results. Section 6 presents related works. Section 7 concludes the work and indicates some future research directions.

2   Preliminaries

2.1   Task Model and Energy Optimizations

A Java application may consist of one or more tasks which must execute with predefined dependencies, where a task is a unit of work which can be scheduled and executed on the processor. In this presentation, we focus on a single periodically executed task, represented by a Java program and its control flow graph (CFG). The time interval between two successive execution of the task is called the period of the task. A task has many paths from the beginning to the end of its execution. A task T will take time ET to execute with ET $\in$ [LB, UB], where LB and UB are lower and upper bound on the execution time, respectively. In hard real-time systems, ET must not exceed the UB, which is considered as the Worst-Case Execution Time (WCET). This WCET can be found by using static timing analysis of programs assuming time-analyzable execution architecture [2].

The time difference between the measured total execution time for the task in clock cycles and WCET time in clock cycles is called slack. This slack can be utilized for energy reduction: (1) by bringing the processor to sleep for the duration of slack, where Sleep mode may be implemented using power gating or clock gating inside the processor or (2) by stretching the non-WCET path to WCET by continuously adjusting system frequency, thereby increasing processor utilization to close to 100% on every path in the task. Huang et al. [3] proposed a method for calculating intra-task DVFS schedules called Checkpoint Insertion Method. Checkpoints are the points which serve as hints to the run-time system for taking power/energy management actions. Checkpoints are added to the program by the compiler after the static analysis of the program. In our approach, each checkpoint is also annotated with Worst-Case Remaining Cycles (WCRC) which is a static parameter computed by the compiler considering worst-case execution cycles required from the checkpoint to the end of the task. During run-time, processor calculates a dynamic parameter called Remaining Cycles (RC), by subtracting current execution time (CET) at the checkpoint from the WCET. New system frequency can be calculated at each checkpoint dynamically using the following equation:

$$F_{next} = (WCRC^*F_{min})/RC \qquad (1)$$

where F_{next} is new frequency and F_{min} is the minimum frequency at which worst-case execution times are satisfied. Since processor supports a finite set of frequencies, F_{next} is approximated to next higher frequency in the set of supported frequencies, which is closest to calculated frequency.

Checkpointing method can be implemented in software, which calculates frequency at the checkpoints and as explained in Sect. 5.1, it results in a big overhead, motivating us to use a hardware solution. Processor changes frequency when it encounters checkpoints by using frequency change instructions. Since the time taken by checkpointing and frequency change instructions is fixed and pre-defined, the time-predictability of the original processor is preserved.

2.2 Hardware Based Run-Time Slack Calculation and Energy Management

In this section, we introduce two energy saving methods for a real-time embedded processor, which use hardware-based run-time slack calculation (RTSC) either at the end of the task or at different checkpoints in the code during program execution. Figure 1 shows CFG of a small program with four paths from start to finish of the program. Execution times (ET_i) of these paths in increasing order can be shown by the following relation

$$ET_1 < ET_4 < ET_2 < ET_3$$

where Path3 (ET_3) is the WCET path and Path1 (ET_1) is the best-case execution time path. We will use CFG in Fig. 1 for explaining the energy saving methods. Also, we assume that Path1 to Path4, if taken, are executed in a sequence respectively and then repeated ad-infinitum.

RTSC with Sleep Mode. Compiler's static analysis tool calculates the WCET in clock cycles for a task. This WCET is inserted in the program code at the start of the task by the compiler. Also, the start and end of each task are marked in the program code. The final slack (in clock cycles) is calculated by hardware at the end of the task execution and the processor goes to Sleep mode for the duration of slack. Figure 2 illustrates the RTSC-Sleep method for the CFG shown in Fig. 1. When the processor completes Path1, Path2 or Path4, it has slack which can be used to put the processor to sleep, whereas when the processor is executing WCET path (Path3) it has no slack, so the processor remains in Normal mode.

RTSC with DFS. In this method, the clock frequency for paths with slack is reduced so that they finish at WCET time. Since the frequency of operation is chosen from a finite set of frequencies, the program execution finishes at the nearest time to WCET that is feasible with the available system frequencies. The task program code is marked with checkpoints by compiler's static analysis tool based on the algorithm given in [3]. Checkpoints are inserted on two types of edges in the CFG:

1. Forward branches
2. Outgoing edges from loop body

An example of checkpoint insertion is shown in the CFG of Fig. 1. Compiler calculates WCRC for every checkpoint. Each checkpoint in the program code is annotated by the compiler using a special instruction with the value of WCRC as an operand to the instruction. Compiler re-calculates WCET after insertion of checkpoints and it also inserts WCET at the start of the program code using a special instruction. During task execution, when the processor encounters any checkpoint, it calculates RC using WCET and CET and then calculates the new frequency of operation using Eq. 1. Figure 3 shows that after the application of this method, the execution time for all paths is extended to a time closer to WCET.

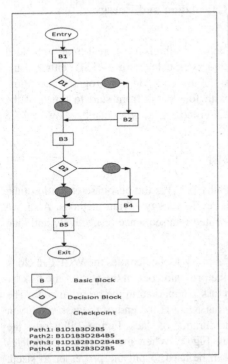

Fig. 1. CFG of a small program

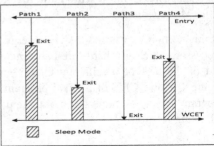

Fig. 2. RTSC with sleep

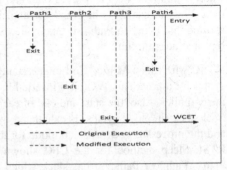

Fig. 3. RTSC with DFS

3 Energy Aware Java Optimized Processor (EAJOP)

EAJOP is a new energy-aware processor based on the JOP architecture, which introduces three modes of processor operation and five new bytecodes for energy management. Figure 4 shows the hardware layout of the EAJOP processor, with the
following additions to the original JOP:

1. New bytecodes and microcodes to the core for energy management.
2. A Power Control Circuit (PCC) which implements processor modes (Normal,
   Sleep, DFS) for energy saving methods.
3. New logic in IO interface for holding (registering) the incoming external events
   when the core is in Sleep mode.
4. Additional logic and memory in IO interface to store experimental data used in
   energy measurements.

EAJOP saves energy by either adjusting the frequency or gating clocks of the
following processor blocks: EAJOP core, memory interface, and other system components except for PCC and IO interface, which are always active.

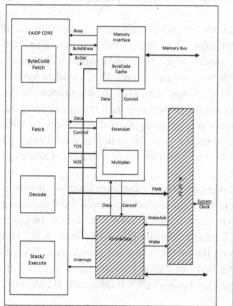

Fig. 4. EAJOP architecture

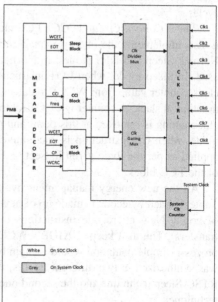

Fig. 5. PCC architecture

EAJOP Core. Changes in JOP core were made to introduce energy management in
the architecture without losing its time analyzability. EAJOP core includes five new
bytecodes which can be used by the programmer and compiler for energy management
actions on PCC. They are supported by five new microcodes. Each energy management

bytecode is implemented using a sequence of microcodes. A new bus called power management bus (PMB) connecting the core to the power control circuit (PCC) was added, as shown in Fig. 4. New bytecodes are explained below.

Mode Bytecode (Mode). The processor has three modes of operation, Sleep, DFS and Normal mode. Each mode can be chosen by executing Mode bytecode with a specific operand.

Clock Change Bytecode (CCI). CCI bytecode changes the frequency of the EAJOP processor where the frequency is given as an operand to the bytecode.

Worst Case Execution Time Bytecode (WCET). WCET bytecode is dual purpose, it marks the start of a task and it is also used to transmit WCET value (which it takes as an operand) to the PCC.

End of Task Bytecode (EOT). End of each task can be marked by EOT bytecode.

Check Point Bytecode (CP). CP bytecode is used to mark each checkpoint in the program code and it takes WCRC as an operand.

Checkpoint Minimum Distance Filter (CMDF). CP bytecode adds a time and energy overhead which can be bigger than the effects of lowering frequency, if the execution time between two checkpoints is too short. To circumvent this issue, we have included a CMDF in the Bytecode Fetch block to do a forced hardware abort of CP bytecode, if the last occurrence of CP bytecode was within a pre-defined number of cycles.

Power Control Circuit (PCC). PCC changes the processor's mode of operation and it also implements the energy management logic. The three modes of operation are Normal, Sleep and DFS modes. In Normal mode, no energy optimization technique is used. In Sleep mode, when EOT instruction is encountered then PCC deducts system clock counter value from WCET to calculate slack and then goes to sleep mode for the duration of slack. A counter in PCC decrements the slack value until it reaches zero, the clock gating is removed at this point and processor resumes normal operation. In DFS mode, when CP instruction is encountered then the new frequency is calculated and applied as per the logic given in Sect. 2.2. Figure 5 shows the functional organization of the PCC block.

All the new energy management bytecodes add fixed execution time as shown in Table 1. Each bytecode is made up of new microcode instructions and a fixed sequence of nop's. New microcode instructions take fixed defined hardware actions (register transfers). This fact keeps EAJOP's WCET analyzable just like JOP. Though the real processor implementation would contain both the methods, but for comparison EAJOP was synthesized in two different flavors, the first one called EAJOP-Sleep implements RTSC-Sleep technique and the second one called EAJOP-DFS implements RTSC-DFS technique.

4   EACT – Energy Aware Compiler Tool for EAJOP

EACT is an EAJOP energy aware compiler tool written in Java, which takes standard Java compiled class file as input and generates an energy-aware memory and executable files for EAJOP as output. The baseline of EACT tool is the original JOP WCET tool (WCA) [2]. WCA uses freely available LpSolve Mixed Integer Linear

Programming (MILP) solver (available as a Java library) to get the worst-case execution time estimates. EACT extends WCA functionality by adding the capability to get WCET estimates for checkpoints (called WCRC). A CMDF was implemented in the EACT to reduce the number of checkpoints in the application. Figure 6 shows the compilation steps involved in the generation of Jop executable files for three different execution platforms.

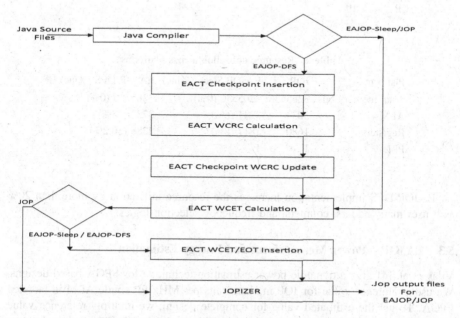

Fig. 6. Compilation steps for three processor platforms

5 Analysis and Validation

5.1 Comparison with Software-Based Implementation of Bytecodes

Hardware actions implemented for the bytecodes and algorithms explained in Sect. 3 may be implemented in software (Java), which can calculate frequency at the checkpoints and switch to new frequency using clock change instruction with current execution time calculated by a software routine. A comparison between software implementation and EAJOP-DFS bytecode implementation is shown in Table 1, it shows that hardware implementation for checkpointing is around a thousand times less expensive than the software implementation.

5.2 EAJOP – Two Execution Platforms

As mentioned before, we synthesized EAJOP in two flavors, thus developing two different energy aware platforms. The results of synthesis for a Cyclone-V Altera (Intel) chip are shown in Table 2.

Table 1. Comparison between EAJOP and software-based implementation

Bytecode	EAJOP hardware clock cycles	Software based implementation
Mode	7	2
CCI	16	28
WCET	7	17
EOT	16	17350
CP	19	22784

Table 2. Resource utilization across platforms

Platform	JOP	EAJOP-Sleep (%inc)	EAJOP-DFS (%inc)
Total memory bits	3265536	3265536 (0%)	3265536 (0%)
ALMs	3034	3241 (6%)	3732 (23%)
Registers	1680	1817 (8%)	2288 (36.2%)
PLLs	1	1	3

EAJOP-DFS implementation increases the resource utilization by more than 20% as it uses many adders, counters, and frequency selection logics.

5.3   EAJOP – Power Measurement and Energy Estimation

Vijay et al. [4] give a dynamic power estimation technique for FPGA based designs. We use a reference value for JOP in Nanowatts per MHz for single ALM in targeted FPGA. To get the estimated value for complete design, we multiply reference value with the number of ALM used by the design. This total value can be multiplied by the frequency in MHz to get the power consumption estimates at different frequencies of operation. We use the same technique to estimate value for EAJOP-Sleep and EAJOP-DFS platforms. Maximum frequency was constrained to 50 MHz in our current implementation. Table 3 gives the estimated average dynamic power consumption for three platforms, where P is average dynamic power consumption for one ALM.

Different power and energy estimation techniques have been explained in [5]. We chose the instruction level power/energy estimation technique for our research. To calculate the energy consumed by the program of a task, program was converted to a sequence of Java bytecodes and then each bytecode was converted to a sequence of microcodes. Since each microcode takes a fixed number of clock cycles to execute, we could calculate the total time taken for execution at different frequencies and the dynamic component of energy consumed then is simply found by multiplication of average dynamic power consumed per unit of time with the total time taken by application to execute.

Let ET be execution time, ST be slack time, P_f be power at frequency f, P_{cg} the power consumed at clock gated state, f_{max} be the maximum frequency supported by processor and P_{fmax} be average power consumed at f_{max}. Let f_s be the set of feasible frequencies

$$f_s = \{f_1, f_2, f_3, \ldots \ldots, f_{max}\}$$

Then consumed energy can be defined by following equations:

$$Energy\_EAJOP\_Sleep = (ET * P_{fmax}) + (ST * P_{cg})$$
$$Energy\_EAJOP\_DFS = \sum_{f \in f_s} ET_f * P_f$$

Table 3. Average dynamic power consumption across platforms

Platform	Operational freq (MHz)	Average power consumption (NanoWatts)
JOP	50	$(3034 \times 50) \times P$
EAJOP-Sleep (Pf_{max})	50	$(3241 \times 50) \times P$
EAJOP-Sleep (P_{cg})	Clock gated	$(184 \times 50) \times P$
EAJOP-DFS (P_f)	f	$(3732 \times f) \times P$

5.4 Experimental Setup and Case Study

We used four applications (Bubble-Sort, Matrix-Multiplication, Sieve, and Lift-Control) from Jembench suite from Java embedded benchmarks [6] for proof of concept. Sixty input patterns were used for each application, each pattern chosen randomly by the test program which calls the applications. WCET was calculated by the EACT tool. Java compiled program was processed by EACT and JOP tools to produce energy aware JOP executable files for experiments on all three platforms as shown in Fig. 6. EAJOP stores the execution time (in clock cycles) of each code section with its operation frequency inside a RAM. Java programs were written as wrappers around applications to read data from EAJOP data RAM and calculate energy consumed for every data point which can then be either stored in a text file or displayed on standard output.

5.5 Experimental Results

Baseline energy consumption, calculated for the specific WCET of the program, remains constant for every input pattern as the program is made to run for WCET cycles irrespective of its ET. Each program has a different WCET, resulting in different baseline energy consumption. Output file size across different platforms is shown in Table 4. WCET comparisons for the four experimental applications normalized to JOP are shown in Table 5. Normalized energy consumption for the four experimental applications is shown in Table 6. RTSC Sleep method tends to save more energy than

Table 4. Output file size across platforms normalized with JOP output file size

Platform	Lift	Bubble	Sieve	Matrix
EAJOP-Sleep	1.001	1.006	1.005	1.005
EAJOP-DFS	1.010	1.076	1.041	1.037

Table 5. WCET across platforms normalized with JOP WCET

Platform	Lift	Bubble	Sieve	Matrix
EAJOP-Sleep	1.0023	1.0023	1.0023	1.0023
EAJOP-DFS	1.32	1.31	1.41	1.19

Table 6. Energy Consumption across platforms normalized with JOP Energy

Platform	Lift	Bubble	Sieve	Matrix
Min energy (EAJOP-Sleep)	0.59	0.12	0.04	0.06
MAX energy (EAJOP-Sleep)	0.66	0.52	0.21	1.018
Avg energy (EAJOP-Sleep)	0.64	0.40	0.14	0.36
Min energy (EAJOP-DFS)	0.782	0.09	0.024	0.009
Max energy (EAJOP-DFS)	0.785	0.58	0.228	1.184
Avg energy (EAJOP-DFS)	0.783	0.43	0.123	0.378

RTSC DFS on an average execution path but on some paths with extremely high slacks, RTSC DFS saves more energy.

Saving in the RTSC Sleep is nearly directly proportional to the ratio of slack to WCET, this is due to near negligible time overhead in the RTSC Sleep which is fixed at 25 clocks irrespective of complexity and length of the program code. We observed that average time overhead added by the RTSC DFS was 1100, 1800, 1500, 5000 cycles in Bubble, Lift, Sieve, Matrix respectively, which on an average is about 1.5% to 13% of WCET. Savings in the RTSC DFS was found to be proportional to left-over slack in the execution path as some slack is consumed by time overheads. For paths with negligible slack, EAJOP consumes more energy than JOP, this is due to higher average power in EAJOP as compared to JOP.

6   Related Works

A survey of system level power-aware design techniques was done in [7]; this work is directed towards real-time systems and provides foundations for our research. The work in [8] was one of the seminal works utilizing compiler and OS assisted power management in the program code to hint the processor on choosing the correct frequency for a real-time system. Their work utilizes slack in the intra-task optimizations, but their treatment uses OS to control and apply frequency changes. The work in [3] defined the checkpoint insertion method for generating a Dynamic Voltage and Frequency Scaling (DVFS) schedule. This method improves average energy savings by

3% to 15% depending upon the process technology. The research in [9] covers both inter-task and intra-task power optimizations using both static and run-time optimizations applied to real-time systems. The work in [10] presents the improvements upon the checkpoint insertion method by implementing a technique to find the correct place to insert checkpoints in the code. They proposed a method for estimating remaining worst-case execution cycles at checkpoints by using execution trace mining for applications. The work in [11] proposes a new online voltage scaling (VS) technique for battery-powered embedded systems with real-time constraints and a novel rescheduling/remapping technique for DVFS schedules. All the above-mentioned research works used OS or supervisory-task controlled energy management whereas our current research focuses on energy management in real-time systems running on bare metal without any controlling software task or OS.

7 Conclusions

In this paper, we presented a brief overview of real-time power aware Java processor called EAJOP and discussed techniques of energy management for a hard-real-time system based on EAJOP architecture. We compared the energy savings of RTSC Sleep and RTSC DFS with baseline JOP platform and found that higher the slack in the programs, more energy is saved by energy management methods implemented in EAJOP. For current implementation and experiments, RTSC Sleep gives better savings than RTSC DFS on low slack paths but on the path with very high slacks RTSC DFS performs better. For any real-time application, selection of the correct platform could be made based on desired WCET, FPGA size, and energy constraints. Our future efforts are directed towards using EAJOP architecture and EACT tool for developing new algorithms for energy optimizations, some of these are:

1. Extending the current work (on single task applications) to systems with multiple periodic tasks.
2. Using the design space exploration technique to find the optimum hardware and compiler solution considering energy, cost and performance for an application.
3. Using the methods in multicore NoC-based architecture context.

References

1. Schoeberl, M.: A Java processor architecture for embedded real-time systems. J. Syst. Archit. **54**(1–2), 265–286 (2008)
2. Schoeberl, M., Pedersen, R.: WCET analysis for a Java processor. In: Proceedings of JTRES 4th International Workshop on Java Technologies for Real Time and Embedded Systems, Paris (2006)
3. Huang, P.K., Ghiasi, S.: Efficient and scalable compiler directed energy optimizations for real time applications. ACM Trans. Des. Autom. Electron. Syst. **12**(3), 27 (2007)
4. Vijay, D., Tim, T.: Methodology for high level estimation of FPGA power consumption. In: Proceedings of the 2005 Asia and South Pacific Design Automation Conference, Shanghai (2005)

5. Sultan, H., Ananthanarayanan, G., Sarangi, S.R.: Processor power estimation techniques: a survey. Int. J. High Perform. Syst. Archit. **5**(2), 93–114 (2014)
6. Schoeberl, M., Preusser, T.B., Uhrig, S.: The embedded Java benchmark suite JemBench. In: JTRES'10 Proceedings of the 8th International Workshop on Java Technologies for Real-Time and Embedded Systems, Prague (2010)
7. Unsal, O.S., Koren, I.: System-level power-aware design techniques in real-time systems. In: Proceedings of the IEEE (2003)
8. Aboughazaleh, N., Mosse, D., Childers, B.R., Melhem, R.: Collaborative operating system and compiler power management for real-time applications. ACM Trans. Embed. Comput. Syst. **5**(1), 82–115 (2006)
9. Takase, H., Zeng, G., Gautheir, L., Kawashima, H.: An integrated optimization framework for reducing the energy consumption of embedded real-time applications. In: Proceedings of the 17th IEEE/ACM International Symposium on Low-Power Electronics and Design (2011)
10. Tatematsu, T., Takase, H., Gang, J., Tomiyama, H.: Checkpoint extraction using execution traces for intra-task DVFS in embedded systems. In: Sixth IEEE International Symposium on Electronic Design, Test and Application (2011)
11. Yuan, C., Schmitz, M.T., Al-hashimi, B.M., Reddy, S.M.: Workload-ahead-driven online energy minimization techniques for battery-powered embedded systems with time-constraints. ACM Trans. Des. Autom. Electron. Syst. (TODAES) **12**(1), 19–24 (2007)

NoC/SoC

A Minimal Network Interface
for a Simple Network-on-Chip

Martin Schoeberl[✉], Luca Pezzarossa, and Jens Sparsø

Department of Applied Mathematics and Computer Science,
Technical University of Denmark, Kongens Lyngby, Denmark
{masca,lpez,jspa}@dtu.dk

Abstract. Network-on-chip implementations are typically complex in
the design of the routers and the network interfaces. The resource consumption of such routers and network interfaces approaches the size of an
in-order processor pipeline. For the job of just moving data between processors, this may be considered too much overhead. This paper presents
a lightweight network-on-chip solution. We build on the S4NOC for the
router design and add a minimal network interface. The presented architecture supports the transfer of single words between all processor cores.
Furthermore, as we use time-division multiplexing of the router and link
resources, the latency of such transfers is upper bounded. Therefore, this
network-on-chip can be used for real-time systems. The router and network interface together consume around 6% of the resources of a RISC
processor pipeline.

Keywords: Network-on-chip · Network interface · Real-time systems ·
Multicore processor · Communication

1 Introduction

With the move to multicore processors to increase performance (both average
case and worst case), the emerging question is how those multiple cores communicate to execute a distributed workload. One of the main aims is to keep the
communication on-chip to avoid the time and energy cost of moving bits off-chip
to and from shared main memory. For this, on-chip communication networks-
on-chip (NoC) architectures have emerged.

The research field of NoC architecture and implementation is large and
diverse. While some general understanding of router designs have evolved (possibly because routers implement well defined and limited functionality), the architecture and implementation of network interfaces (NIs) is more diverse, complex,
and difficult to compare.

NIs can be optimized for quite different uses. We identify five different uses of
NoCs: (1) supporting cache coherence protocols, (2) single word memory accesses
to a different core or input/output device, (3) access to a shared external memory,

© Springer Nature Switzerland AG 2019
M. Schoeberl et al. (Eds.): ARCS 2019, LNCS 11479, pp. 295–307, 2019.
https://doi.org/10.1007/978-3-030-18656-2_22

(4) supporting message passing between cores, and (5) supporting streaming data. Depending on the types of traffic supported, the NoCs and in particular the NIs providing the interface to the NoC may be rather diverse. We see a tendency to implement more support functionality in hardware, e.g., end-to-end flow control and buffer handling with DMA support. In combination with different packet and bus interfaces this results in a large variety of NI designs that are often quite advanced and expensive.

This paper presents a minimal NI that directly supports the synchronous data flow model of computation [7]. It supports sending of single word packets from a sender to a receiver. The resulting NI is lightweight and consumes a fraction of resource compared to other NIs. The resource consumption of the NI and the router is around 6% of the resources of the Patmos processor, which we use in the evaluation. Support for message passing or streaming data can be added in software on top of the service that the NI provides. If needed, flow control can also be handled in software.

As a starting point, we use a simple NoC, the S4NOC [13], that is available in open source.[1] S4NOC uses time-division multiplexing (TDM) of the link and router resources. The tool to generate TDM schedules [3] is also available in open source. We extend the S4NOC with a simple NI with first-in-first-out (FIFO) buffers and connect it to the T-CREST multicore platform [12], similar to the one-way memory [11] project.

The proposed NoC and NI are optimized for the real-time domain. To enable static worst-case execution time analysis of tasks, the computing platform and the communication needs to be time-predictable. The S4NOC was designed to be time-predictable. Therefore, our NI extension aims to be time predictable as well.

The contributions of this paper are: (1) a reestablishing of a minimalistic NoC using static TDM arbitration and simple routers and (2) a minimal NI that supports message passing between processing cores on top of the low-cost NoC. Furthermore, we present a benchmarking framework for NoCs that support data flow applications.

This paper is organized in 6 sections: Sect. 2 presents related work. Section 3 provides background on the S4NOC architecture that we use to build upon. Section 4 presents the minimal NI as a fit for the low-cost S4NOC architecture. Section 5 evaluates the NI design for the S4NOC. Section 6 concludes.

2   Related Work

For time-predictable on-chip communication, a NoC with TDM arbitration allows for bounding the communication delay. Æthereal [5] is one such NoC that uses TDM where slots are reserved to allow a block of data to pass through

---

[1] The original design is available in VHDL at https://github.com/t-crest/s4noc, while a rewrite in Chisel [2] has been made available at https://github.com/schoeberl/one-way-shared-memory.

the NoC router without waiting or blocking traffic. We conform to the TDM approach of Æthereal, but present a simpler NI in this paper. In comparison with the aelite, which is one variant of the Æthereal family of NoCs, the S4NOC, including our proposed NI, is considerably smaller. For a 2×2 NoC, the S4NOC uses 1183 4-input LUTs and 1110 flip-flops. In contrast, aelite uses 7665 6-input LUTs and 15444 flip-flops [16].

The PaterNoster NoC [10] avoids flow control and complexity in the routers by restricting a packet to single standalone flits. The NI of PaterNoster is a simple design to support single word packets. The NI is connected to the memory stage of a RISC-V processor [9]. The RISC-V instruction set has been extended with a transmit instruction that blocks until a free slot is available in the NoC and a receive instruction that explores all input buffers in parallel to find a packet for a source address. If no packet is available, the pipeline blocks. Our NoC uses a similar architecture, but we use TDM based scheduling. Our NI is mapped into an address and can be accessed by normal load and store instructions. Furthermore, by avoiding a full lookup in the receive buffer, our NI is more than a factor of 10 smaller than the PaterNoster NI.

The OpenSoC Fabric [4] is an open-source NoC generator written in Chisel. It is intended to provide a system-on-chip for large-scale design exploration. The NoC itself is a state-of-the-art design with wormhole routing, credits for flow control, and virtual channels. Currently, the interface to the NoC is a ready/valid interface receiving either packets or flits. An extension with a NI is planned. A single OpenSoC router (in the default configuration) is as large as our complete 3×3 NoC including the NIs and open core protocol (OCP) interfaces.

Similar to Æthereal, the Argo NoC [6] uses a TDM based NoC, but also uses the same TDM schedule in the NI [15]. The Argo NI and NoC offer time-predictable transfer of data from a core local memory across the NoC and into a local memory of another core. This TDM-based DMA mechanism is part of the NI, and as a result, data is transferred without any buffering or (credit based) flow control. In comparison with the NI presented in this paper, the Argo NI is substantially larger, as the use of DMA-driven data transfer results in a correspondingly higher throughput across the NoC when larger blocks of data are transferred.

The one-way shared memory [11] project uses the S4NOC to implement a special form of distributed shared memory. Each core contains a local on-chip memory where blocks within those local memories are constantly copied to other cores. The one-way shared memory is also a design with low resource consumption, but the programming interface is very different from our NI.

3   The S4NOC Design

Our work builds on top of the S4NOC NoC design [13] by adding a minimal NI. Therefore, we provide here background information on the S4NOC design. The S4NOC implementation in Chisel does not contain a NI but is just used for a one-way shared memory [11]. Therefore, we add a NI to the S4NOC with the same design philosophy of building a lightweight NoC.

The S4NOC is a statically scheduled, time-division multiplexed (TDM) NoC intended for real-time systems. As all traffic is statically scheduled, there are no conflicts on any shared resource, such as links or multiplexers. Without conflicts, there is no need to provide buffering in the routers, flow control between routers, or credit-based flow control between the NIs.

A static schedule for the TDM NoC is precomputed and results in a TDM round with individual TDM slots. For single word packets, the TDM slot is a single clock cycle. Each core can send one word to every other core in one TDM round. The slot number identifies the virtual circuit to the receiving core. The TDM round repeats for further packets.

The original design supports single word packets and single cycle hops between routers. The routers contain one output register per port and a multiplexer in front of that register. The schedule is stored in the router and drives the multiplexers for the five output ports.

The default configuration of the S4NOC is a bidirectional torus, resulting in five output ports (north, east, south, west and local) and four inputs to the multiplexers, which form the crossbar. The default schedule is a one-to-all schedule where each core has a dedicated virtual circuit to each other core. With such a regular structure of a bidirectional torus and an all-to-all schedule, it is possible to find one schedule that is executed in all routers [3]. That means it is the same for all routers, e.g., if at one clock cycle a word is routed from west to north, it is done in all routers.

The resulting hardware is lean. One register per port, one 4:1 multiplexer per port, a counter for the TDM schedule, and a table for the schedule. With Chisel, the table for the schedule is computed at the hardware generation time.

4   The Minimal Network Interface

Figure 1 shows an overview of a 9-core processor organized in a 3×3 grid. All cores are connected via a NI to the network of routers. The NoC topology is a bidirectional torus. The bidirectional torus minimizes the number of hops for a packet to travel. The corresponding all-to-all core communication graph for N cores has $N \times (N - 1)$ virtual circuits. For a 3×3 multicore, this results in 72 virtual circuits, which can be served by a 10 slot TDM schedule [3] for the NoC. This is only 2 slots more than what is needed by the 8 outgoing and 8 incoming virtual circuits. This short TDM schedule is possible due to the high bandwidth provided by the 36 links connecting the 3×3 multicore.

A straightforward implementation of a NI could use separate FIFOs for each virtual circuit endpoint; in the 9 core example, this would be 8 FIFOs for transmitting data and 8 FIFOs for receiving data. The result would be a relatively large design and a design that scales poorly with a growing number of cores.

In our design, the same functionality is implemented by a combination of hardware and software. By exploiting the TDM scheduling used in the routers and by sacrificing a small amount of bandwidth, we have been able to design a NI that has only a single FIFO for transmission of data and a single FIFO for reception of data. The result is a small NI design, as shown in Fig. 2.

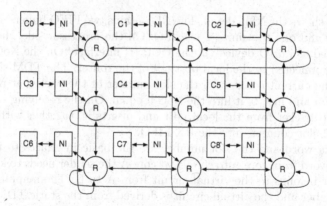

Fig. 1. A 3×3 multicore connected by a bi-torus NoC.

A virtual circuit can be identified at the senders end by the slot number in which its data is transmitted and at the receivers end by the slot number when its data is received. The slot number is stored in the transmit FIFO along with the data to be transmitted. The slot number of the element at the head of the transmit FIFO is compared against the TDM slot counter and the data is sent at the scheduled point of time.

From the view of the processor, the NI is a peripheral device mapped into the address space of the processor. It consists of a transmit and receive buffer and two flags for the status of those buffers. The transmit buffer contains a flag showing if the buffer is empty, the receive buffer contains a flag if there is some data available. The sender and receiver have to poll these flags.

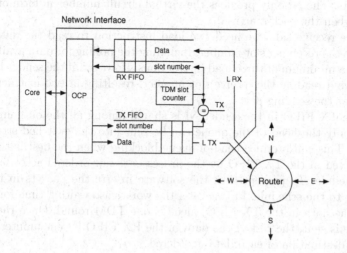

Fig. 2. One processing node consisting of a core, our NI, and a router.

Figure 2 shows the NI in detail. The NI contains two FIFO buffers: one receive (RX) FIFO and one transmit (TX) FIFO. On the processor side, those buffers are connected as an IO device via the OCP [1] interface. On the NoC side, the buffers are connected to the local port (L) of the router. The TDM slot counter compares the current count with the slot number of the packet at the head of the TX FIFO and inserts it into the NoC if equal. On the receiving side, the NI takes a valid packet from the local port and inserts it, together with the value of the TDM slot counter, into the RX FIFO.

The data word and the slot number are the basic interfaces to the NI. To transmit a word from core A to core B, at core A the sender needs to know which slot number belongs to the virtual circuit from A to B. The mapping between the slot number and the virtual circuit is derived from the static TDM schedule. At the receiving end, core B reads the data and the receiving slot number when the packet has arrived. The slot number when a word is received indentifies the source node. Therefore, there is no further information needed in the packet or in the NI to determine the source or destination of a packet.

At the sending side, we optimize the write into the NI by using the lower bits of the address to determine the send slot number. E.g., when the processor writes the data word to BASE_ADDRESS + 3, it requests a send in time slot 3. With the polling of the TX FIFO empty flag, sending a single word needs at least one load and one store instruction.

When a packet is received from the network the payload data is written into the RX FIFO along with the slot number when it was received, which identifies the sender. Before reading the RX FIFO, the core must first read the data available flag to ensure there is data to read. And based on this, the software can identify the virtual circuit and, thus, the sender. The software is in charge to dispatch packets received from different cores to different tasks waiting for the packets. The NI only provides the virtual circuit number in form of the slot number when the packet arrived.

On the receive side, we need two load instruction to read the data and to determine the receiving slot number. Including the polling for data available this results in a minimum of three load instructions. However, if the sender is known, we can avoid reading the receive slot number, resulting in two instructions per word, as at the sending part.

As the TX FIFO in the sender NI is shared among all the outgoing virtual circuits, only the head of the queue can be sent into the switched structure of the NoC. This can produce head-of-queue blocking when the destination of the data injected in the TX FIFO by the processor is not ordered according to the TDM schedule. To prevent this, the software inserts the packets in the order according to the schedule. In this case, the worst-case waiting time for starting to send the data in the TX FIFO queue is one TDM round. Once the head of the queue is sent, the rest of the data in the RX FIFO is sent uninterruptedly, since the destination of each data is ordered.

Having a dedicated TX FIFO per outgoing virtual circuit would remove the head-of-queue blocking and the initial waiting for the TDM slot for the data at the head of the queue. In our approach, we trade a minor reduction in performance (waiting for the head-of-queue TDM slot and ordering in software) for a minimal and simple architecture.

The NI design (and TDM arbitration) might waste bandwidth. However, the key parameter is what bandwidth can be achieved at what hardware cost. If our design is small, we can waste bandwidth at a very low cost.

5   Evaluation

In this section, we evaluate and discuss the presented NI/NoC architecture in terms of performance and hardware cost. As part of the evaluation, we present the custom micro-benchmark framework based on the data flow model of computation that we developed and used to characterize the NI/NoC performance.

The results are produced using Intel/Altera Quartus Prime (v16.1) targeting the Intel/Altera Cyclone IV FPGA (model EP4CE115) which is used on the DE2-115 board. Specifically, performance results are obtained by running the benchmarks on a 3-by-3 multicore platform implemented on the same FPGA using the Patmos [14] processors as cores.

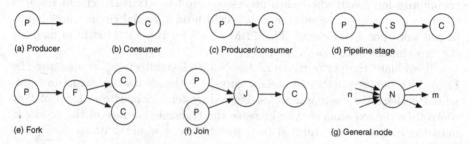

Fig. 3. Elementary structures that can be used to model data flow applications. Structure (c) to (f) are used as benchmarks.

5.1   Benchmarking Method

Our NI is intended to support message passing between processor cores. Therefore, we introduce a benchmarking framework inspired by the synchronous data flow model of computation [7]. In this model of computation, data are processed by a statically ordered sequence of actors. When an actor receives enough input tokens (data units), it starts the computation to produce output tokens to be sent to the next actors.

The benchmarks consist of a selection of elementary structures that can be used to model data flow applications. The actors are running on different nodes of the platform and the NoC supports the communication channels between them. In other words, the elementary structures can be considered as the building blocks of any data flow applications.

Figure 3 shows the elementary structures, where the ones of Figs. 3(c–f) are directly used as benchmarks. The elementary structures are as follows: (a) A producer, with a single output channel, that can produce at a pre-determined rate. (b) An eager consumer, with a single input channel, that can receive as fast as possible. (c) A producer directly connected to a consumer. This benchmark is used to measure the pure NoC throughput between two actors placed in different nodes. (d) A pipeline stage, with one input and one output channels. This benchmark is used to characterize the overhead of the pipeline stage node. (e) A fork stage, with one input and two or more output channels. This benchmark is used to characterize the overhead of the fork node. (f) A join stage, with two or more input and one output channels. This benchmark is used to characterize the overhead of the join node. (g) The general case node, where an actor has n input channels and m output channels. The above classifications are specializations of this general node.

5.2 Performance

The maximum bandwidth offered by the NoC depends on the TDM schedule. The following analysis assumes a schedule that implements a fully connected core communication graph where each processor core has a (virtual) circuit towards all other processors. The maximum bandwidth on a virtual circuit corresponds to one word per TDM round. The TDM round for the 3×3 platform used for the experiments is 10 clock cycles.

To evaluate the performance of the NoC/NI architecture, we measure the bandwidth between actors (processor cores) for the elementary structures presented earlier. We assume a time-triggered system without any form of flow control. In the experiments, we increase the transmission rate of the producer until the consumer is saturated (i.e., just before it would start to miss packets/tokens).

Table 1. Maximum measured throughput, in clock cycles per word, for the four micro benchmarks used in the evaluation.

Benchmark	Throughput (clock cycles per word)
Producer/consumer	10.1
Pipelined stage	10.1
Fork	23.1
Join	25.1

Table 1 presents the measured maximum throughput, expressed in clock cycles per word per channel, for the four elementary structures used in the evaluation. For the first two benchmarks, the measured throughput coincides with the maximum theoretical one of one word per TDM round since all the actors involved are faster than the TDM round. For the fork and join test cases, the throughput is lower. This can be explained by observing that the fork and the join actors have to perform more operations before being able to send a token to the next actors.

If flow-control is introduced in form of credits sent back from the receiver to the sender, the maximum measurable throughput is reduced. Due to more software overhead, the latency of individual words is increased. Hardware support for flow-control would result in a shorter latency. We implemented a version of the producer/consumer example with flow control using a single credit, and in this case the throughput is 23.0 clock cycles per word (as opposed to 10.1 for the time triggered organization).

All the results presented and discussed above are obtained using a FIFO queue of 4 words. Further buffering is managed in software. The sending and the receiving operations consist of two nested for-loops. The outer loop iterates every time an entire buffer is sent or received by the inner loop, which iterates for every word of a buffer. Figure 4 shows the maximum measured throughput for the four benchmarks for buffer sizes from 1 to 64 words.

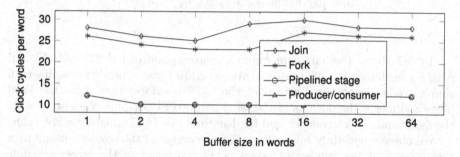

Fig. 4. Maximum measured throughput, in clock cycles per transferred word, for the four micro-benchmark for different buffer sizes. The graphs for the pipelined stage and the producer/consumer benchmarks fall on top of each other.

For all the graphs we observe a similar course or pattern: a decrease to a minimum followed by an increase to a maximum and finally stabilization to a value between the minimum and the maximum. This can be explained by the effect of the loop unrolling executed by the compiler on the inner loop. The minimum occurs when the compiler completely unrolls the loop, while the maximum occurs when the number of loop iterations is too large for the loop to be unrolled.

5.3   Hardware Cost

The resource consumption is given in 4-input look-up tables (LUT), flip-flops (DFF), and memory consumption in bytes. The memory consumption only refers to the memory used in the NoC (e.g., for schedule tables, etc.). The size for the local memory in the Argo NIs is configurable and therefore not shown in the table. Maximum clock frequency is reported for the slow timing model at 1.2 V and 85 C.

Table 2. Resource consumption, maximum frequency, and length of the TDM schedule of different configurations of the S4NOC.

Configuration	LUT	DFF	fmax (MHz)	Sched. length
$2 \times 2 = 4$	1784	1596	235.8	5
$3 \times 3 = 9$	5351	4221	236.1	10
$4 \times 4 = 16$	10761	7568	221.0	19
$5 \times 5 = 25$	17732	11825	216.6	27
$6 \times 6 = 36$	29136	17172	188.6	42
$7 \times 7 = 49$	36783	23373	195.5	58
$8 \times 8 = 64$	55423	30784	183.2	87
$9 \times 9 = 81$	68079	38961	172.8	113
$10 \times 10 = 100$	94540	48500	150.8	157

Table 2 shows the hardware resource consumption of the S4NOC (NI and routers) in different configurations. We generate those synthesize results with simple traffic generators (instead of the OCP interface) that drive the local ports and merge the outputs of the local ports to FPGA pins. We also provide the maximum clock frequency and the length of the TDM schedule in the table.

We observe a slightly higher than linear increase of the resource usage with the increase in the number of nodes. This is a result of the larger schedule tables in the routers for larger NoCs. Furthermore, we observe a decrease in the maximum clocking frequency as the number of nodes increases. However, the maximum frequency is still higher than the maximum frequency of the Patmos core, which is below 80 MHz in the used FPGA.

Table 3 shows the hardware resource consumption of the S4NOC using the presented NI with the OCP interface and other NoCs. The first group of entries in Table 3 shows the resource consumption of a single S4NOC node including the router and the NI for a configuration with 4 buffers in the FIFOs. The resource consumption is further split into the router and NI components. The resource numbers have been collected from a 3×3 configuration, where we took the median value of the resource consumption of the 9 nodes. The maximum clock frequency of the 3×3 configuration is 72 MHz. This critical path is in the processor pipeline and not in any part of the S4NOC router or NI.

The next group of entries in Table 3 report the results for a single node of the Argo NoC [6]. The Argo NoC is available in open source. Therefore, we can obtain the results by synthesizing two configurations of the Argo NoC for the same FPGA.

The next group set of result in Table 3 is for the PaterNoster node for a 2×2 configuration. Similarly to S4NOC and Argo, the PaterNoster NoC is available in open-source, which allows us to synthesize it for the same FPGA. From the results, we can observe that the S4NOC node is more than 10 times smaller than the PaterNoster node. The PaterNoster NI is relatively large, as it contains a fully associative receive buffer to be able to read from any channel independently of the receiving order.

Table 3. Resource consumption of different components of the S4NOC compared with other designs.

Component	LUT	DFF	Memory
S4NOC node	602	453	0
Router	266	165	0
Network interface	336	288	0
Argo node	1750	926	1.3 KB
Router	932	565	0
Network interface	849	361	1.3 KB
PaterNoster node	8030	3546	0
Router	1899	1297	0
Network interface	6131	2249	0
OpenSoC router	3752	1551	0.8 KB
3×3 S4NOC	5423	4382	0
3×3 Argo NoC	15177	8342	12.1 KB

The table also presents the results for a single router of the OpenSoC NoC [4]. For this result, we generated the Verilog code for the default configuration, which is a 2×2 mesh with routing based on virtual channels and one local port. From the results, we can observe that the size of a single OpenSoC router is as large as the entire 3×3 S4NOC with a single buffer.

The next group shows resource consumptions of complete 3×3 NoCs. The S4NOC is around 3 times smaller than the Argo NoC. At this cost, the Argo NoC provides hardware support for message passing and DMA handling.

When comparing an S4NOC node with the size of a Patmos core, which consumes 9437 LUTs and 4384 registers, we can see that we achieved our goal of a small NoC. The resource consumption of one NI and router is around 6% of the Patmos core. When comparing our NoC with a leaner RISC core, such as the RISC-V implementation that is part of the Real-Time Capable Many-Core Model [8] and consumes 5375 LUTs and 1557 registers, our NoC is still in the range of 11% of that RISC pipeline.

5.4 Source Access

The source of the S4NOC and the NI is available as part of the Patmos project at https://github.com/t-crest/patmos. Detailed instructions how to run the experiments from this sections can be found at https://github.com/t-crest/patmos/tree/master/c/apps/s4noc.

6 Conclusion

State-of-the-art network-on-chip implementations tend to provide a lot of functionality in hardware. This results in complex design of the routers and the network interfaces. The resource consumption of such routers and network interfaces approache the size of a simple processor pipeline.

The paper presents a design at the other end of the spectrum: a lightweight network-on-chip solution with a minimal network interface that supports the transmission of single word packets between processor cores. The resulting design consumes about 6% of the resources of a RISC processor pipeline per node. Furthermore, as we use time-division multiplexing of the router and link resources, the latency of the communication is upper bounded and we can use this network-on-chip for real-time systems.

Acknowledgment. We would like to thank Constantina Ioannou for bringing up the idea of simply using a FIFO as a network interface.

The work presented in this paper was partially funded by the Danish Council for Independent Research | Technology and Production Sciences under the project PREDICT (http://predict.compute.dtu.dk/), contract no. 4184-00127A.

References

1. Accellera Systems Initiative: Open Core Protocol specification, release 3.0 (2013). http://accellera.org/downloads/standards/ocp/
2. Bachrach, J., et al.: Chisel: constructing hardware in a scala embedded language. In: The 49th Annual Design Automation Conference (DAC 2012), pp. 1216–1225. ACM, San Francisco, June 2012
3. Brandner, F., Schoeberl, M.: Static routing in symmetric real-time network-on-chips. In: Proceedings of the 20th International Conference on Real-Time and Network Systems (RTNS 2012), pp. 61–70. Pont a Mousson, France, November 2012. https://doi.org/10.1145/2392987.2392995
4. Fatollahi-Fard, F., Donofrio, D., Michelogiannakis, G., Shalf, J.: Opensoc fabric: on-chip network generator. In: 2016 IEEE International Symposium on Performance Analysis of Systems and Software (ISPASS), pp. 194–203, April 2016. https://doi.org/10.1109/ISPASS.2016.7482094
5. Goossens, K., Hansson, A.: The aethereal network on chip after ten years: goals, evolution, lessons, and future. In: Proceedings of the 47th ACM/IEEE Design Automation Conference (DAC 2010), pp. 306–311 (2010)

6. Kasapaki, E., Schoeberl, M., Sørensen, R.B., Müller, C.T., Goossens, K., Sparsø, J.: Argo: a real-time network-on-chip architecture with an efficient GALS implementation. IEEE Trans. Very Large Scale Integr. (VLSI) Syst. **24**, 479–492 (2016). https://doi.org/10.1109/TVLSI.2015.2405614

7. Lee, E.A., Messerschmitt, D.G.: Synchronous data flow. Proc. IEEE **75**(9), 1235–1245 (1987). https://doi.org/10.1109/PROC.1987.13876

8. Metzlaff, S., Mische, J., Ungerer, T.: A real-time capable many-core model. In: Proceedings of 32nd IEEE Real-Time Systems Symposium: Work-in-Progress Session (2011)

9. Mische, J., Frieb, M., Stegmeier, A., Ungerer, T.: Reduced complexity many-core: timing predictability due to message-passing. In: Knoop, J., Karl, W., Schulz, M., Inoue, K., Pionteck, T. (eds.) ARCS 2017. LNCS, vol. 10172, pp. 139–151. Springer, Cham (2017). https://doi.org/10.1007/978-3-319-54999-6_11

10. Mische, J., Ungerer, T.: Low power flitwise routing in an unidirectional torus with minimal buffering. In: Proceedings of the Fifth International Workshop on Network on Chip Architectures, NoCArc 2012. pp. 63–68. , ACM, New York (2012). https://doi.org/10.1145/2401716.2401730

11. Schoeberl, M.: One-way shared memory. In: 2018 Design, Automation and Test in Europe Conference Exhibition (DATE), pp. 269–272, March 2018. https://doi.org/10.23919/DATE.2018.8342017

12. Schoeberl, M., et al.: T-CREST: time-predictable multi-core architecture for embedded systems. J. Syst. Archit. **61**(9), 449–471 (2015). https://doi.org/10.1016/j.sysarc.2015.04.002

13. Schoeberl, M., Brandner, F., Sparsø J., Kasapaki, E.: A statically scheduled time-division-multiplexed network-on-chip for real-time systems. In: Proceedings of the 6th International Symposium on Networks-on-Chip (NOCS), pp. 152–160. IEEE, Lyngby, May 2012. https://doi.org/10.1109/NOCS.2012.25

14. Schoeberl, M., Puffitsch, W., Hepp, S., Huber, B., Prokesch, D.: Patmos: a time-predictable microprocessor. Real-Time Syst. **54**(2), 389–423 (2018). https://doi.org/10.1007/s11241-018-9300-4

15. Sparsø J., Kasapaki, E., Schoeberl, M.: An area-efficient network interface for a TDM-based network-on-chip. In: Proceedings of the Conference on Design, Automation and Test in Europe, DATE 2013, pp. 1044–1047. EDA Consortium, San Jose (2013)

16. Stefan, R.A., Molnos, A., Goossens, K.: dAElite: a TDM NoC supporting QoS, multicast, and fast connection set-up. IEEE Trans. Comput. **63**(3), 583–594 (2014). https://doi.org/10.1109/TC.2012.117

Network Coding in Networks-on-Chip with Lossy Links

Michael Vonbun$^{(\boxtimes)}$ (iD), Nguyen Anh Vu Doan(iD), Thomas Wild,
and Andreas Herkersdorf

Chair of Integrated Systems, Technical University of Munich, Munich, Germany
{fmichael.vonbun,anhvu.doan,thomas.wild,herkersdorf}@tum.de

Abstract. Providing a reliable and efficient communication infrastructure becomes more important and more demanding for current and future Many-core System-on-Chips. The increased amount of communication partners demands for efficient resource usage. At the same time, an ongoing feature size reduction and supply-voltage level reduction renders the SoC vulnerable to bit errors. Our work aims at providing a generalized analysis of network-coded Networks-on-Chip with multicast support and unreliable links. We compare network-coded with dimension-routed NoCs in terms of their hop counts and achievable long-term rates. The results show that for an 8×8 2D-mesh setup, network-coding yields a $1.7\times$ to $8.3\times$ better hop count and can achieve a $1.2\times$ to $3.7\times$ higher rate as dimension-routed 8×8 NoCs for bit error probabilities of 10^{-12} to 10^{-3} and 10% multicast traffic.

1 Introduction

Networks-on-Chip (NoCs) have been developed to provide an efficient and scalable interconnect solution to cope with the high number of processor cores enabled by an increase in silicon real estate. For the sake of more processing resources, the design goals of many NoCs have been low complexity and small area footprint. Nevertheless, if routers are not limited to minimum area designs, one could invest in a higher router complexity.

About two decades ago, that same trend took place in computer networks and culminated with Network Coding (NC), proposed by Ahlswede in 2000 [1] who postulated a paradigm shift towards routing of information, rather than of packets. The key idea was that network routers are not limited to only forwarding incoming data but can perform almost arbitrary operations on the packet level, such as combining the payload of multiple packets, promising an increase in network utilization efficiency.

As NC finds its roots in information theory, it was quickly adopted by the network community, delivering important contributions both towards understanding the theoretical foundations of NC and finding feasible NC schemes. Therefore, with this idea of *information routing*, some of the early works tackled the usage of NC for wireless communication having highly unreliable channels, showing a considerable improvement in network performance [9].

© Springer Nature Switzerland AG 2019
M. Schoeberl et al. (Eds.): ARCS 2019, LNCS 11479, pp. 308–321, 2019.
https://doi.org/10.1007/978-3-030-18656-2_23

With the on-going feature-size reduction, high switching frequencies, and reduced supply voltages, unreliability is becoming now a challenge for SoC designers [8] and NC is a promising candidate to mitigate those effects for the communication infrastructure. Its benefits have, for instance, been shown by Microsoft in a multicast setting [4].

In this paper, we provide an analysis of the benefit of NC over dimension-routing for NoCs for session-operated applications and packet multicast in a scenario with lossy links. We chose an analytic approach for our study, mainly because it allows to assess NoCs with bit error rates as low 10^{-12}, in contrast to event-driven network simulations which, for small bit error rates, show slow convergence and lack statistical confidence.

The benefits of NC in an NoC setting are demonstrated by studying the efficiency gap of dimension-routed and network-coded NoCs (NC NoCs). We assume, that the NoC is operated in sessions, where each session has a set of active sources and associated sinks and thus impose a certain communication demand on the communication infrastructure. We use two different metrics to compare the efficiency of network-coded and dimension-routed networks: (1) their resource utilization in terms of links or router-hops, and (2) their achievable theoretic rate or long-term throughput. In the model we propose for the comparisons, we do not account for both the code overhead in NC NoCs and retransmission request-mechanisms in dimension-routed NoCs.

The paper is organized as follows. In Sect. 2, we review related work. In Sect. 3, we first introduce the concept of NC and the unicast NC model which is the basis of our evaluation. We extend that base model to model network multicasts and provide network-coded metrics used for the comparison with dimension-routed NoCs. Equivalent dimension-routed metrics are introduced in Sect. 4. Section 5 shows the benefits of network-coded over dimension-routed NoCs for 2D-mesh networks with lossy links. Section 6 concludes the paper.

2   Related Work

After NC has been proposed in [1], many information theory centric research groups have focused on this topic. Theoretical foundations of the formulation and the efficiency of network coding have been published [11,15,19]. Code construction, a subproblem of coded networks, was addressed in [5,13] where linear network codes have been proposed.

More practical results using NC have been provided in [4,12] in a peer-to-peer context for content distribution and in [10,14] for wireless networks with relay nodes. While both use-cases showed the benefit of using coded networks, the results can not directly be transferred to NoCs. The key features leveraging coded networks are long packets and user cooperation in the content distribution scenario, and the broadcast advantage as well as a shared wireless medium bottleneck in the wireless networks scenario, which are features not found in NoCs.

Therefore, multiple publications tailored NC for NoCs. [7] presented a basic feasibility analysis of network coded NoCs based on mapping butterfly communication patterns (cf. Fig. 1) onto a 2D-mesh NoC. Extending the work in [7], [17,18] proposed algorithms to calculate the mid-point node to establish butterfly coded NoCs and compared the impact on the network performance of different mid-point selection strategies. [2] showed a router design that stalls packets in order to increase the event that packets that share the same destinations can exploit the butterfly structure. A different NoC architecture was investigated in [6], where unidirectional buses connecting multiple routers instead of bidirectional point-to-point links where used to connect the routers in an NoC. Although all those four works have already shown the potential of NC, their results reflect butterfly communication patterns only.

Considering arbitrary multicast configurations, we have shown, in a prior publication, the benefits of network-coded over dimension-routed NoCs in [20]. In contrast to the present work, we did not consider lossy network operation in our comparison.

To achieve error resilience and an increase in efficiency for unicast connections in NoCs, random linear NC was proposed and evaluated in an analytic model with flit error rates between 5% to 20% in [16]. While lossy networks are addressed in this work as well, we consider using NC in a multicast setting that leverages the potential of NC with bit error rates as low as 10^{-12}.

A NC enabled network architecture that is based on clustering multiple nodes into cooperation regions that combine 4 packets into one network-coded was proposed in [22]. These cooperation regions are interconnected by dedicated links that carry the network-coded packets. To recover the packets at the destination region, the plain packets are sent in addition over a regular 2D-mesh NoC. In contrast, we want to focus on both a comparison of network-coded and dimension-routed NoCs without increasing the network's capacity by adding additional links and the impact of lossy links in our work.

3   Network-Coded NoCs

In general, a network code is the design and mapping of a set of operations performed on packets to distinct nodes in a network. As this definition is a rather abstract one, we provide a short introduction to NC.

3.1   An Introduction to Network Coding

As stated in Sect. 1, by the observation of the increased processing and storage capabilities of state-of-the-art network resources, such as routers and switches, NC was introduced.

Two examples for small network codes are given in Fig. 1. In Fig. 1(a), introduced in [1] and referred to as the Butterfly example, two sources A and B want to transmit data concurrently to two joint sinks E and F. Limited by the common edge connecting nodes C and D, serving both sinks at the same time

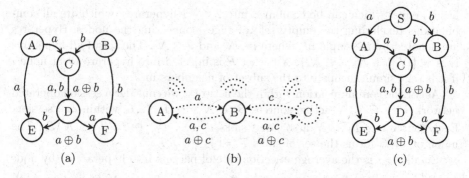

Fig. 1. NC examples: (a) Butterfly, (b) Relay, and (c) Butterfly with super source. The coded operation is indicated in blue. (Color figure online)

reduces the long-term throughput of the two cross connections A–F and B–E to only half the throughput. Instead, with NC, node C performs an XOR ($a \oplus b$) on data streams, which is then forwarded to nodes E and F simultaneously by node D. These changes eliminate the bottleneck and result in a decreased number of edges and timeslots used as well. At the receivers, an additional XOR is required to recover the original information.

In Fig. 1(b), introduced in [10] and referred to as the Relay example, we have a 3 node wireless communication scenario: nodes A and C need to exchange information but, due to distance, have no direct link established. Rather, node B acts as a relay between A and C. Again, broadcasting $a \oplus c$ is more efficient in terms of channel and transmit energy than a consecutive transmission of a and c, as B saves half its transmissions using NC.

These two examples show clearly that a network code requires both a set of operations (forwarding and XOR in both examples) and an operation mapping (choosing which node performs the coding operation on incoming packets) as well as a transmission strategy (broadcasting the coded data to both sinks in the Butterfly example or waiting for the reception of both a and c prior to coding and broadcast in the Relay example).

3.2   Definitions and Notation

Let $\mathcal{G} = (\mathcal{N}, \mathcal{E})$ be a network graph characterizing an arbitrary network with N nodes, where $\mathcal{N} = \{1, \ldots, N\}$ is the set of nodes and $\mathcal{E} = \{(ij) \mid i, j \in \mathcal{N}\}$ is the set of edges. The neighbors of node $i \in \mathcal{N}$, N_i, are collected in the set $\mathcal{N}_i = \{j \mid j \in \mathcal{N}, (ij) \in \mathcal{E}\}$. As the interconnects of routers in 2D-mesh NoCs are bidirectional, we model each link between two nodes by two unidirectional edges. The capacity of an edge is p, which is 1 flit-per-edge-use for lossless and $0 \leq p < 1$ flit-per-edge-use for lossy networks.

When using NC, we focus on information routing rather than packet routing. Therefore, we encapsulate multiple edges of a router into hyperarcs, which are virtual connections carrying the same information. A node with N_i neighbors has N_i edges which can be combined into $2^{N_i} - 1$ hyperarcs, which are all combinations (excluding the empty set) of edges connecting the nodes. Hyperarcs are denoted by the tuple iJ, where $i \in \mathcal{N}$ and $J \subset \mathcal{N}_i$. The set of all hyperarcs is $\mathcal{A} = \{iJ \mid i \in \mathcal{N}, J \subset \mathcal{N}_i\}$. A packet P is injected into hyperarc iJ at node i if it is sent simultaneously to the subset of neighbors in J.

As for the communication within the network, we consider a session operated network with $C \leq N$ active sources $\mathcal{S}_c \in \mathcal{N}, c = 1, \dots, C$ within one session. Each source has $T_c < N$ associated sinks $t_1^{(c)}, \dots, t_{T_c}^{(c)} \in \mathcal{T}_c, \mathcal{T}_c \subset \mathcal{N} \backslash \mathcal{S}_c$. The union of all $\mathcal{T}_c$ forms the set of sinks $\mathcal{T} = \bigcup_{c=1,\dots,C} \mathcal{T}_c$.

Finally, z_{iJ} is the average injection rate of packets into hyperarc iJ by node $i \in \mathcal{N}$, and $x_{ij}^{(t_k^{(c)})}$ is the information flow from node $i \in \mathcal{N}$ to node $j \in \mathcal{N}_i$ contributing to the communication from source $\mathcal{S}_c$ to sink $t_k^{(c)}$, i.e. the amount of information that goes from i to j associated with the source-sink pair $\mathcal{S}_c$, $t_k^{(c)}$.

3.3   Minimum-Cost Network Operation

In [15], the requirements for efficient network operation using NC has been formalized. The determination of the set of operations is referred to as the code construction problem, whereas the right transmission strategy is referred to as the subgraph selection problem, i.e. selecting paths for information flows from the sources to the destinations. In other words, a network can be operated with minimum-cost if (a) there exists a capacity achieving network code and (b) the network supports certain injection rates and information flows. As an independent solution to both problems does not sacrifice optimality, we focus on the subgraph selection problem in our comparison. The code construction problem can be solved using linear network codes (cf. [5,13]).

The Subgraph Selection Problem. According to [15], the rate of packets $r_{t_k^{(c)}}$ arriving at sink $t_k^{(c)}$ per unit time interval can be supported by the network using NC for every source-sink pair $(\mathcal{S}_c, t_k^{(c)})$, $\forall c = 1, \dots, C, t_k^{(c)} \in \mathcal{T}_c$, provided that there exist (a) packet injection rates $z_{iJ} \geq 0, \forall (iJ) \in \mathcal{A}$ and (b) information flows for all source-sink combinations $x_{ij}^{(t_k^{(c)})} \geq 0, \forall i \in \mathcal{N}, j \in \mathcal{N}_i, t_k^{(c)} \in \mathcal{T}_c, c = 1, \dots, C$, such that the flows do not exceed the cut capacities of the network (cf. paragraph 1 on p. 6), which relate to the max-flow/min-cut theorem. In addition, within the network, information is neither generated nor consumed except by sources and sinks (cf. paragraph 2 on p. 6). As we will see in the following paragraphs, the constraints on the packet rate $r_{t_k^{(c)}}$ are linear in nature, which means that the subgraph selection problem is a linear program and can be solved using any common LP-solver.

Although the problem formulation of [15] suffices to solve the problem, we use a modified version introduced in [19], as it reduces the problem formulation in terms of flow variables and is more concise. Using the results of [15,19] a network can be operated with rates $r_{t_k^{(c)}}, \forall t_k^{(c)} \in \mathcal{T}$, if the aforementioned constraints can be fulfilled.

Associated Injection Limits. In a generalized multicast setting, each injection z_{iJ} encapsulates injections associated with a certain multicast group c, i.e. the sum of partial injection rates $y_{iJ}^{(c)}$ is upper bounded by the injection rate z_{iJ}:

$$\sum_{c=1}^{C} y_{iJ}^{(c)} \leq z_{iJ}. \tag{1}$$

Cut Capacity Constraint. The flow of information $x_{ij}^{(t_k^{(c)})}$ of connection c flowing through the cut $K \subset \mathcal{N}_i$ from node i to a subset of its neighbors K is bounded by the capacity of the cut between i and K. This capacity depends on the associated injection rates $y_{iJ}^{(c)}$, as higher injection rates lead to a higher flow of information. If the network is lossy, the probabilities of transmission success influence the information flow as well.

If p_{iJL} is the probability that exactly the nodes in L receive the information injected into hyperarc iJ, then

$$b_{iJK} = \sum_{\{L \subset J | L \cap K \neq \emptyset\}} p_{iJL}, \tag{2}$$

is the capacity associated with this hyperarc and the information flow is bounded:

$$\sum_{j \in K} x_{ij}^{(t_k^{(c)})} \leq \sum_{\{J \subset \mathcal{N}_i | J \cap K \neq \emptyset\}} b_{iJK} \cdot y_{iJ}^{(c)}, \forall i \in \mathcal{N}, K \subset \mathcal{N}_i, t_k^{(c)} \in \mathcal{T}_c, c = 1, \ldots, C. \tag{3}$$

Flow Conservation Law. As information is preserved within a node, the in- and outgoing information flows have to be equal, except for sources and sinks.

$$\sum_{j \in \mathcal{N}_i} x_{ij}^{(t_k^{(c)})} - \sum_{j: i \in \mathcal{N}_j} x_{ji}^{(t_k^{(c)})} = \begin{cases} r_{t_k^{(c)}}, & \text{if } i = \mathcal{S}_c, \\ -r_{t_k^{(c)}}, & \text{if } i = t_k^{(c)}, \\ 0, & \text{otherwise}, \end{cases} \tag{4}$$

$$\forall i \in \mathcal{N}, t_k^{(c)} \in \mathcal{T}, c = 1, \ldots, C.$$

Medium Access Constraint. As we will consider both the link-usage as well as the achievable throughput in our efficiency comparison between NC and dimension-routed NoCs, we need an additional constraint modeling the medium access (MAC) for the rate computation. From Eq. 1 we see that associated injections are upper bounded by the overall injections. To constrain the injections themselves, and therefore the injections associated with multicast group c, we have to upper bound the sum of all injections originating at node i and ending at j by the activity of the edge between i and j, e_{ij}:

$$\sum_{J: J \in \mathcal{A}, j \in J} z_{iJ} \leq e_{ij}, \forall i \in \mathcal{N}, j \in \mathcal{N}_i. \tag{5}$$

Super Source Extension for Network-Coded NoCs. In contrast to the simple examples in Figs. 1(a) and (b), the sources of an NC NoC have to be synchronized somehow due to the network structure. If sources are not synchronized, there is no need for a router to broadcast the message to multiple ports, thus enabling path diversity. Rather, it would fall back to a basic one-to-one connection scheme used by dimension-routed networks.

In our network model, source synchronization is introduced by adding a super-source to the network that is connected to the real sources. The concept and application of a super-source to a network that supports NC can be seen in Fig. 1(c): without NC, the super-source can support both sinks only with a rate of 1.5, needing 10 link uses to deliver both a and b to the sinks E and F instead of rate of 2 with 9 link uses when using NC.

From this example, we can derive additional constraints and properties of an NC NoC in the case of adding a super-source which (a) is connected to all sources, (b) has unit capacity directed edges, and (c) must inject disjoints messages to every source. This implies that, in addition to extending the network itself and modifying the base constraints of Sect. 3.3 by the additional node, we also added a medium access constraint on the links originating at the super-source to ensure disjoint message injection.

3.4   Efficiency of Network-Coded NoCs

Without further constraints, following the ideas of [15], we can find injection rates z_{iJ} large enough such that any rate $r_{t_k^{(c)}}, \forall t_k^{(c)} \in \mathcal{T}$ can be supported.

Given that the routing resources, i.e. edges and routers, are limited in a network and that a network should achieve a high throughput with the available resources, we use two efficiency metrics to characterize the operation of a network which are (a) the hop count or number of edges and (b) the rate at which sinks can be served within a session for a certain communication request.

Hop Count. By dictating unit packet rate and finding the minimum injection rates z_{iJ} that support the packet rate, we get the utilization of hyperarcs. As hyperarcs are virtual connections modeling injections into multiple edges at once, we must also account for the size of an hyperarc to get to the edge utilization of the NC approach. Minimizing the sum of weighted injection rates

$$\gamma_{\mathrm{nc}} = \sum_{i \in \mathcal{N}} \sum_{J \subset \mathcal{N}_i} |J| \cdot z_{iJ}, \tag{6}$$

for some fixed rate $r_{t_k^{(c)}} = r, \forall t_k^{(c)} \in \mathcal{T}$, yields the hop count when multiplied with the number of flits per packet F:

$$\Gamma_{\mathrm{nc}} = \min_{z_{iJ} \geq 0:\, (iJ) \in \mathcal{A}} F \cdot \gamma_{\mathrm{nc}}, \tag{7}$$

$$\text{s.\,t. Eq. (1), (3), (4), (5), and } r_{t_k^{(c)}} = r = 1, \forall t_k^{(c)} \in \mathcal{T}.$$

The hyperarc capacity, in flit per channel use in the case of NoCs just as for regular point-to-point edges, is modeled by b_{iJK} (cf. Eq. (2)). The probabilities in Eq. (2) can be calculated in the case of lossy NoCs by using $p_{ijj} = (1 - p_{\text{out}})^B$ as the edge capacity and using the fact that the edges contributing to hyperarc iJ are disjoint. Therefore, this efficiency metric holds for both lossless and lossy NC NoCs.

Rate. If we want to maximize the rates, we have to constrain the injections of the network, otherwise the linear program becomes unbounded. Therefore, we limit the activity of the edges to unit activity using the medium access constraint (cf. Sect. 3.3), which upper-bounds the injection rates by the edge activity.

$$\max_{r_{t_k^{(c)}}} \sum_{t_k^{(c)} \in T} r_{t_k^{(c)}},$$

$$\text{s. t. Eq. (1), (3), (4), (5), and } e_{ij} = 1, \forall (ij) \in \mathcal{E}. \tag{8}$$

4   Dimension-Routed NoCs

For our comparison, we use XY-dimension routing, although advanced routing algorithms have been proposed for NoCs, mainly because it (a) is well established and therefore makes results more comparable, (b) is deadlock free, (c) comes with low routing overhead, and (d) uses unique predetermined minimum distance routes. Just as with NC NoCs, we base our efficiency characterization both on the edge utilization of network nodes and the rates achievable.

Hop Count. Following a packet from source $\mathcal{S}_c \in \mathcal{N}$ to one of its sinks $t_k^{(c)} \in \mathcal{T}_c$, the packet traverses the nodes along its route $\mathcal{R}_{xy}(\mathcal{S}_c, t_k^{(c)})$, using the edges between each two nodes for one cycle per flit, which sums up to $|\mathcal{R}_{xy}(\mathcal{S}_c, t_k^{(c)})|$ edge usages per flit. For a multicast setting, a routing mechanism that spans a tree and exploits overlapping routes originating from the same source has an edge use per flit per connection

$$\gamma_{xy,c} = \left| \bigcup_{k=1}^{T_c} \mathcal{R}_{xy}(\mathcal{S}_c, t_k^{(c)}) \right|. \tag{9}$$

For lossy NoCs, we have to account for retransmissions caused by invalid packet data as well. We assume that retransmissions will be limited to the sinks that received corrupt packets. Therefore, we have to calculate the probability that the packet was received by the nodes in subset $K \subset \mathcal{T}_c$ but was not received by the nodes in subset $\mathcal{T}_c \backslash K$, which we denote as $Q_{\mathcal{S}_c K}$. The lossless edge use per flit per connection $\gamma_{xy,c}$ of Eq. (9) is then extended to

$$\gamma_{xy,c} = \left| \bigcup_{t \in \mathcal{T}_c} \mathcal{R}_{xy}(\mathcal{S}_c, t) \right| + \sum_{K \subset \mathcal{T}_c : K \neq \emptyset} \frac{\left| \bigcup_{t \in K} \mathcal{R}_{xy}(\mathcal{S}_c, t) \right|}{Q_{\mathcal{S}_c K}}, \tag{10}$$

In our prior work [21], we provided an analytic estimation of end-to-end bit error rates for NoC multicasts, modeling the network as a cascade of binary symmetric channels. Inferring from that results, a recursive equation for $Q_{\mathcal{S}_c K}$ and packets with B bits is

$$Q_{\mathcal{S}_c K} = p_s(K)^B - \sum_{L \subset \{\mathcal{T}_c \setminus K\}:\, L \neq \mathcal{T}_c \setminus K} Q_{\mathcal{S}_c \{\mathcal{T}_c \setminus L\}}, \forall K \subset \mathcal{T}_c, \tag{11}$$

initialized with $Q_{\mathcal{S}_c \mathcal{T}_c} = p_s(\mathcal{T}_c)^B$, which is the probability that all sinks received correct packets and not a single bit flipped at the sinks of multicast group c. Here, $p_s(K)$ is the subset success probability for a single bit of the receivers in subset $K \subset \mathcal{T}_c$, i.e. the probability that the nodes in K received correct bits, irrespective of the nodes in $\mathcal{T}_c \setminus K$. Due to space limitations, the proof for both Eqs. (10) and (11) are omitted in this paper but can be developed based on the results in [21].

The hop count we use for comparison is calculated as the sum of edge usages per connection weighted with the packet length

$$\gamma_{xy} = F \cdot \sum_{c=1}^{C} \gamma_{xy,c}. \tag{12}$$

Rate. Having overlapping routes of traffic originating from different sources means that at least one edge must be shared by all these sources. Every sink ends up with a different rate, depending on the communication demand. The T rates quantify the capabilities of the network. The rate of the connections is obtained by counting the number of all multicast routes that have a common edge and keeping the maximum values. For example, if two multicast connections have a common edge, the long-term rate of both connections reduces to 0.5, whereas disjoint connections have unit rate.

In the case of unreliable NoCs, we need to account for the information loss. If packets are received incorrectly with a probability of p_{out}, we get only every $1 - p_{out}$th packet. Thus, we can sustain only a rate of $1 - p_{out} = p_s(t_k^{(c)})^B$ of the lossless long-term rate $r_{t_k^{(c)}}$ for packets with B bits.

5   Efficiency Assessment of Network-Coded NoCs

In this section we compare NC and dimension routed NoCs with respect to their hop counts and rates as derived in Sects. 3 and 4.

5.1   Experimental Setup

Since the network is operated in sessions, we fix the number of sources and sinks, randomly draw the respective number of communication partners in that session, and calculate both hop counts and rates. An equivalent injection rate per session is calculated from the number of sources active within one session. In our analysis runs, we used random traffic and bit error probabilities

$(p_e = \{10^{-12}, 10^{-9}, 10^{-6}, 10^{-3}\})$. The first analysis run is an exhaustive sweep for a 3×3 2D-mesh for a first interpretation of the basic behavior of NC and routed NoCs. Then we used 4 different parameter sets (constrained random traffic, multicast ratio, injection rate, and packet length) with different mesh sizes (3×3 to 8×8). The comparison results are the mean of 1000 random session realizations, where we sum up the obtained hop counts and average the calculated rates per network realization. If not stated otherwise, we use packets with 256 bit/packet divided into 8 flits/packet and 32 bit/flits.

5.2   Results

3-by-3 NoC. In a first step of our evaluation, we analyze the behavior of a 3×3 NoC. In this network, we can choose from 1 to 9 sources and 1 to 8 sinks per source. To isolate the influence of the communication demand size, i.e. the number of sources and sinks active within one session, we fix the number of sources, and sinks per source to one distinct value.

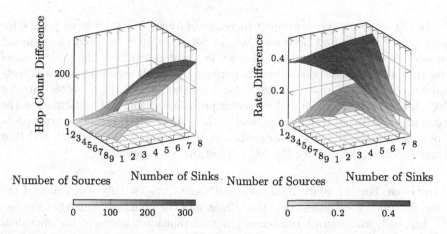

Fig. 2. Averaged differences in hop count (left) and rates (right) of network-coded and dimension-routed 3×3 2D-mesh NoC with lossy links over all source-sink combinations.

The results of Fig. 2 show almost equal results for $p_e \in [10^{-12}, 10^{-6}]$ (bottom surface); only at 10^{-3} can we see a considerable increase in the benefit of NC (top surface). In terms of hop count reduction, we observe that NC is most advantageous when all the nodes in the network are active but serve only about half of the available nodes. In contrast to the almost lossless cases, the hop count advantage increases at $p_e = 10^{-3}$ with a higher number of active sources and the size of the multicast group. This is due to the coded-network being able to recover the information with less redundancy as it distributes the information over the network, therefore making better use of the link capacity. For the rates, however, it is better to keep the number of active sources and sinks low, allowing to exploit path diversity, which is limited in high-traffic scenarios.

Constrained Random Traffic. Next, we investigate networks of different sizes with a randomized communication demand with sources and sinks drawn, without loss of generality, from the discrete uniform distribution $\mathcal{U}[1,8]$ chosen to have a higher variation for the analysis.

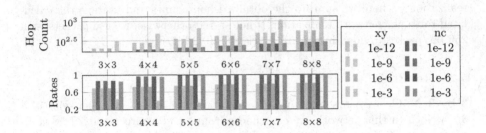

Fig. 3. Averaged hop counts (top) and rates (bottom) of different network sizes and bit error rates NoC for random numbers of sources and numbers of sinks.

In Fig. 3, we observe hop count increases of routed NoCs between 1.2–2× for $p_e \in [10^{-12}, 10^{-6}]$, and between 1.9–4.5× for $p_e = 10^{-3}$ between the different network sizes. Since the main difference in these networks is the packet travel distance, we see that coded-networks perform especially well with increased network sizes. For the rates, we see a local maximum of a 1.3× better rate for NC NoCs in a 5×5 mesh and low error probability, which is attributed to the comparatively dense traffic as opposed to the 8×8 mesh. However, as error probabilities increase, the rate is affected more by the long routes as well, and thus there is a 3.9× increase for the NC NoC in the 8×8 mesh.

Multicast Ratio. Since multicast traffic accounts for only a fraction of the overall traffic [3], we investigate the influence of the multicast traffic percentage. To this end, we generate combined uni- and multicast traffic at an equivalent injection rate of 0.1 flit/cycle/node and use multicast groups of 8 sinks per multicast connection [3].

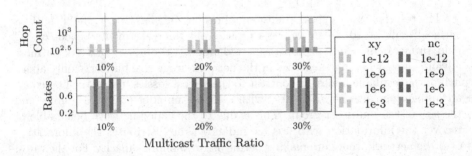

Fig. 4. Averaged hop counts (top) and rates (bottom) at different multicast ratios.

The multicast traffic ratio has an interesting influence, as can be seen from Fig. 4. For the hop count, we see an improvement of 1.7× to 2.0× for $p_e \in [10^{-12}, 10^{-6}]$, which means that the coded network can better cope with multicast groups. However, for $p_e = 10^{-3}$, the opposite is observed: we have a 8.4× to 6.8× increased hop count of the routed network. This means that the NC NoC suffers from the increased traffic as well. For the rates, we see a steady improvement from 1.2× to 1.3× from 10% to 30% multicast traffic in the low error rate case to 4.0× in the high error rate case, meaning that NC exploits path diversity more efficiently even in the case of high error probabilities.

Injection Rate. The influence on the network's load is assessed in this section for different network sizes at an error probability of 10^{-3}. We generated traffic to reach equivalent rates between 0.04 and 0.25 flit/cycle/node with 10% multicast traffic and an 8-ary multicast.

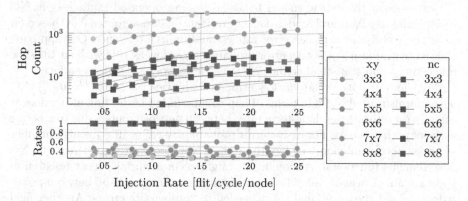

Fig. 5. Averaged hop counts (top) and rates (bottom) at equivalent injection rates.

From Fig. 5, we can see that the NC NoCs curves show a lower hop count than those of the routed NoCs and have the same shape, meaning that NC does not overly benefit from a higher network load. The rates, however, show that NC can sustain almost unit rates, since an 8×8 has a high amount of network resources and does not suffer from corrupted packets as much as the routed NoC.

Packet Length. To conclude our analysis, we investigate the influence of the packet length in Fig. 6. The equivalent injection rate is about 0.1 flit/cycle/node at 10% multicast traffic and multicast groups of size 8 in an 8×8 NoC.

The hop count results show that the packet length has a huge impact on the efficiency of the network. Indeed, while we have only a small increase in hop count of less than 1.1× when using NC for $p_e = 10^{-12}$ and $p_e = 10^{-3}$, the NoC can not be operated anymore using routing with retransmissions, as the packet loss rate becomes too high. For the rates, the same effect can be observed. The routed network is too busy retransmitting at $p_e = 10^{-3}$ while the NC NoC sustains a high rate. For $p_e \in [10^{-12}, 10^{-6}]$, the 1.2× increased rates originate from a better usage of path diversity.

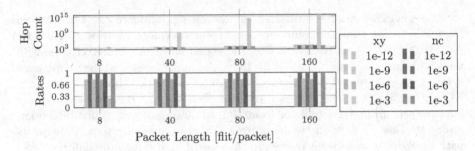

Fig. 6. Averaged hop counts (top) and rates (bottom) of different packet sizes and bit error rates for 8-by-8 2D-mesh NoC.

6 Conclusion

We extended a theoretical model to assess session operated multicasts in NC NoCs with lossy links and modeled an equivalent dimension routed NoC based on an analytic end-to-end packet error rate estimation as a reference. Our approach allowed to evaluate NoCs with error probabilities as low as 10^{12} without the slow convergence and statistical confidence issues a network simulator can face.

We showed that, already at low error probabilities ($p_e \in [10^{-12}, 10^{-6}]$), NC outperforms routed NoCs in terms of hop counts due to better link utilization. It can also establish higher long-term rates between network routers due to a better usage of path diversity. For higher error probabilities ($p_e = 10^{-3}$), a high number of packet retransmissions renders the routed NoC inoperative, whereas the NC NoC remains functional. Although this might seem artificial, recent research in approximate or near-threshold computing have shown a trade-off between power reduction and the additional effort needed to compensate errors. Another field of application are space-grade MPSoCs where, due to an increased exposure to radiation, common SoCs have to be hardened against a high number of bit errors.

In our comparison, we focused on an analytic model of synchronized NoCs operated in sessions. To overcome the inherent limitation of sessions, time-division-multiplexed NoCs, that offers synchronization and control by design, are suitable candidates and will be subject to further research. Additionally, we plan to cover hardware aspects in the analysis of NC NoCs by considering code overhead, power consumption of coding operations as well as latency.

References

1. Ahlswede, R., Cai, N., Li, S.Y.R., Yeung, R.W.: Network information flow. IEEE Trans. Inf. Theory **46**(4), 1204–1216 (2000)
2. Duong-Ba, T., Nguyen, T., Chiang, P.: Network coding in multicore processors. In: IEEE International Performance Computing and Communications Conference, pp. 1–7 (2011)
3. Feng, C., Liao, Z., Zhao, Z., He, X.: A low-overhead multicast bufferless router with reconfigurable banyan network. In: IEEE/ACM International Symposium on Networks-on-Chip, pp. 1–8 (2018)

 4. Gkantsidis, C., Goldberg, M.: Avalanche: File Swarming with Network Coding. Microsoft Research (2005)
 5. Ho, T., et al.: A random linear network coding approach to multicast. IEEE Trans. Inf. Theory **52**(10), 4413–4430 (2006)
 6. Hu, J.H., Zhang, S.W.: NoC architecture with local bus design for network coding. In: International ICST Conference on Communications and Networking in China, pp. 1151–1154 (2011)
 7. Indrusiak, L.S.: Evaluating the feasibility of network coding for NoCs. In: ReCoSoC, pp. 1–5 (2011)
 8. Karnik, T., Hazucha, P.: Characterization of soft errors caused by single event upsets in cmos processes. IEEE Trans. Dependable Secure Comput. **1**(2), 128–143 (2004)
 9. Katti, S., Katabi, D., Hu, W., Rahul, H., Medard, M.: The importance of being opportunistic: Practical network coding for wireless environments (2005)
10. Katti, S., Rahul, H., Hu, W., Katabi, D., Médard, M., Crowcroft, J.: XORs in the air: practical wireless network coding. In: ACM SIGCOMM Computer Communication Review, vol. 36, pp. 243–254 (2006)
11. Koetter, R., Médard, M.: An algebraic approach to network coding. IEEE/ACM Trans. Netw. **11**(5), 782–795 (2003)
12. Li, B., Niu, D.: Random network coding in peer-to-peer networks: from theory to practice. Proc. IEEE **99**(3), 513–523 (2011)
13. Li, S.Y.R., Cai, N., Yeung, R.W.: On theory of linear network coding. In: International Symposium on Information Theory, pp. 273–277 (2005)
14. Louie, R.H.Y., Li, Y., Vucetic, B.: Practical physical layer network coding for two-way relay channels: performance analysis and comparison. IEEE Trans. Wirel. Commun. **9**(2), 764–777 (2010)
15. Lun, D.S., et al.: Minimum-cost multicast over coded packet networks. IEEE Trans. Inf. Theory **52**(6), 2608–2623 (2006)
16. Moriam, S., Yan, Y., Fischer, E., Franz, E., Fettweis, G.P.: Resilient and efficient communication in many-core systems using network coding. In: IEEE International Performance Computing and Communications Conference, pp. 1–8 (2015)
17. Shalaby, A., Goulart, V., Ragab, M.S.: Study of application of network coding on NoCs for multicast communications. In: IEEE International Symposium on Embedded Multicore SoCs, pp. 37–42 (2013)
18. Shalaby, A., Ragab, M., Goulart, V.: Intermediate nodes selection schemes for network coding in network-on-chips. In: NORCHIP, pp. 1–5 (2012)
19. Traskov, D., Heindlmaier, M., Médard, M., Koetter, R., Lun, D.S.: Scheduling for network coded multicast: a conflict graph formulation. In: IEEE GLOBECOM Workshops, pp. 1–5 (2008)
20. Vonbun, M., Wallentowitz, S., Feilen, M., Stechele, W., Herkersdorf, A.: Evaluation of hop count advantages of network-coded 2D-mesh NoCs. In: International Workshop on Power and Timing Modeling, Optimization and Simulation, pp. 134–141 (2013)
21. Vonbun, M., Wild, T., Herkersdorf, A.: Estimation of end-to-end packet error rates for NoC multicasts. In: Hannig, F., Cardoso, J.M.P., Pionteck, T., Fey, D., Schröder-Preikschat, W., Teich, J. (eds.) ARCS 2016. LNCS, vol. 9637, pp. 363–374. Springer, Cham (2016). https://doi.org/10.1007/978-3-319-30695-7_27
22. Xue, Y., Bogdan, P.: User cooperation network coding approach for NoC performance improvement. In: International Symposium on Networks-on-Chip, pp. 1–8 (2015)

Application Specific Reconfigurable SoC Interconnection Network Architecture

Gul N. Khan[✉] and Masoud O. Gharan

Electrical, Computer and Biomedical Engineering, Ryerson University,
Toronto, ON M5B2K3, Canada
gnkhan@ee.ryerson.ca

Abstract. Multi and many-core SoCs (System-on-Chip) are the key solutions to cater for extraordinary demands of high-performance embedded and other applications. It has become more critical with the limits on sub-nanometer technologies for chips that cannot be shrunk further. Network on Chip (NoC) is a scalable interconnection structure that can provide efficient solutions for on-chip interconnection problems of many-core SoCs such as re-configurability for application specific applications. Most of the existing reconfigurable NoCs improve performance of SoC in exchange of larger chip area and higher power. We present a new reconfigurable NoC having improved performance and power for variety of SoC applications. The synthesis and simulation results for our approach show higher performance by comparing our NoC architecture with the past on-chip interconnection structures.

Keywords: Reconfigurable on-chip SoCs · System-on-Chip ·
NoC with router and switch layers · Application specific NoC

1 Introduction

Multi-core systems are continuously improving due to the shrinking of fabrication technology. This trend has changed to integration of simpler processing cores on a single chip [1]. Therefore, multi and many-core System-on-Chip (SoC) architectures have become the new generation of high-performance embedded computer platforms. In parallel with the above progress, the performance of interconnection system is also growing, and Network-on-Chip (NoCs) have emerged to become the communication backbone for systems depending on the application s requiring high performance.

Conventional NoCs (CNoC) is a generic NoC architecture consists of homogenous nodes that are connected by links according to the NoC topology. A conventional 4×4 mesh-topology NoC, as part of the SoC is shown in Fig. 1. CNoCs are scalable and suitable for many-core SoCs as well as generic multi-core CPU architectures [2]. CNoC nodes consist of routers with 5-input and 5-output ports, and communication links for interconnection. Generally, a message is passed as a collection of packets, where a packet is made of multiple flits. A flit is the smallest data unit that travels through the NoC nodes in a pipelined fashion at the NoC clock rate. A wormhole switching is generally employed, where a header flit passes through the network to establish and reserve a route for all the packet flits [2].

© Springer Nature Switzerland AG 2019
M. Schoeberl et al. (Eds.): ARCS 2019, LNCS 11479, pp. 322–333, 2019.
https://doi.org/10.1007/978-3-030-18656-2_24

The main problem with the CNoC is its lack of flexibility, where the communication between two neighboring nodes is always faster than the communication between far nodes (specifically for low/normal traffic). This is due to the pipelined nature of communication where far nodes use more routers and pipeline stages than the neighboring nodes. Application-oriented systems are designed to meet the needs of one or a small set of applications. SoC cores placement for the NoC are fixed, however their communicating targets may differ according to the application being executed on the chip. Consider the NoC system given in Fig. 1, if the CPU core is required to directly communicate with the Memory core (neighboring core) in one application and then it may also have to communicate with the RF core (far core) for the 2nd application. For high-performance SoC design, the NoC should provide adequate flexibility for the far cores to communicate in the same fashion as the neighboring cores.

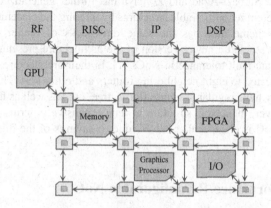

Fig. 1. SoC having a conventional 4 × 4 Mesh NoC.

To alleviate delays of wormhole switching, Virtual Channels (VCs) have been introduced. We argue that by removing or scaling down the VCs in exchange of additional switches to NoC nodes, the NoC becomes more efficient and reconfigurable for an application-oriented high-performance SoCs. Various reconfigurable NoCs have been proposed as suitable interconnection system for high performance SoCs [3–6]. Most of them have added extra hardware to a generic NoC for creating a reconfigurable architecture. Our NoC design approach does add some extra hardware components to the CNoC, however these components also help to remove some of the routers to reduce the hardware cost of NoC. Our reconfigurable NoC provides the flexibility along with the balancing of hardware cost and communication speed.

2   Past Reconfigurable NoCs

A key past work on reconfigurable NoCs has been proposed by Stensgaard and Sparsø [3]. They presented a reconfigurable NoC (ReNoC) that can be organized in the form of a homogeneous topology, where the NoC node consists of a buffered router that is wrapped by an asymmetric Reconfigurable Switch (RS). The main drawback of ReNoC is the utilization of a switch along with the router for each ReNoC node and it consumes more hardware and power. ReNoC was further developed by Chen et al. and they proposed 'SMART' NoC that reconfigures a mesh topology at runtime [4]. They employed additional circuitry in the router that allows a packet to bypass all the way from source to destination core in a single clock cycle.

Modarressi et al. have also built on ReNoC and presented a reconfigurable architecture for NoC to configure arbitrary application specific topologies [5]. The NoC nodes are composed of routers and reconfigurable switches are used to interconnect NoC nodes. They also propose another reconfigurable structure that provides more flexibility by increasing the number of RSs between adjacent routers. The main drawbacks of their approach are higher hardware cost and large delay (in-between two adjacent cores) that is equivalent to two routers and one RS as compared to two router delay in a CNoC. Sarbazi-Azad and Zomaya has further generalized the architecture and explored different reconfigurable structures by altering the placement of routers and RSs [6]. Their scheme also has the same drawbacks of higher cost and delays. Suvorova et al. presented a newer version of the architecture presented by Modarressi et al. [5] to mitigate fault tolerance in NoCs [7]. In their architecture, every router and RS are also connected to eight neighboring routers and other RSs. The interconnection configuration may have regular structure (torus, tree, etc.) as well as irregular or hybrid structures. However, their NoC structure is very expensive in terms of hardware. Our reconfigurable NoC is cheaper than CNoC due to savings of the high cost traditional NoC routers.

3   High Performance Reconfigurable NoC

The main objective of our reconfigurable NoC presented in this paper is to design the NoC with high flexibility in terms of topology and speed with acceptable increase of hardware and power consumption. The proposed NoC architecture can be easily scaled (in two dimensions) for any SoC application to satisfy the constraints of hardware overhead and communication speed. An abstract level of our High Performance Reconfigurable NoC (HPRNoC) architecture is illustrated in Fig. 2. A two-layer HPRNoC architecture consists of separate networks of Reconfigurable Switches (RS) and routers. The RS-network receives messages from the IP cores and passes them through switches and the Router-network to implement the application. Figure 2 illustrates a 4 × 4 mesh example of our HPRNoC1 architecture that consists of two communication layers i.e. RS-network and a router-network. These layers are interconnected together that the IP cores are connected to the router-layer through RS layer. The RS-layer consists of reconfigurable switches that can also have other than mesh topology. The router layer is a conventional router based NoC interconnection that can be of any topology. The routers are active component having buffers, arbiter and crossbar switch to communicate in a pipelined manner in-between the source and sink cores (IPs) [2]. On the other hand, RSs are passive components that only connect their input ports to their output ports. They do not have any buffers, and arbitration logic.

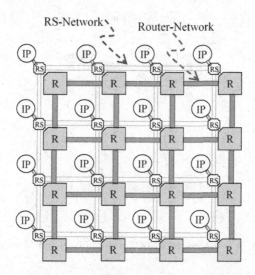

Fig. 2. 4×4 Mesh HPRNoC1: IP, RS & R represent cores, recon-switches & routers respectively.

One of the main features in our NoC design is that each IP core has an exclusive access to a router port through one or more switches. It makes our HPRNoC a subset of router based NoCs and when there is no route for a source core in the RS layer, there is a route in the router layer. When a packet reaches to the router layer, it can benefit of all the protocols and facilities associated with a conventional NoC. The cores that need a high-speed communication route can communicate through RS layer.

A specific HPRNoC2 version of our HPRNoC structure is illustrated in Fig. 3. The RS-layer has the same nodes as the IP layer, but the router layer is scaled down to the extent that it provides a dedicated port for each IP core. The internal structure of a RS node consists of a set of simple switches along with control logic to establish connections between the incoming and outgoing links. The motivation for inserting the RS layer over the router based layer is that the RS components are much more efficient in terms of chip area, power and speed as compared to intelligent complex packet-switching routers. Therefore, we intend to utilize fewer number of routers in the packet communication process as we have employed 4 routers instead of 16 in a the HPRNoC structure shown in Fig. 3. Six-port wormhole routers are used having input and output ports, arbiter and a crossbar switch [2]. In the router micro-architecture, the input-ports utilize buffers for VC organization, and the output ports are data buses. Virtual Channels (VCs) alleviate the congestion and deadlock related routing problems in addition to improving the performance of router layer communication.

Multi-core SoCs designed for multiple applications to be executed will require configurable interconnections for fast execution. An efficient way of message passing in our proposed re-configurable SoC is to put look-up tables in RS and router modules enabling them to inter-connect various communication links according to the applications being executed. Routing mechanism in our proposed HPRNoC is similar to the

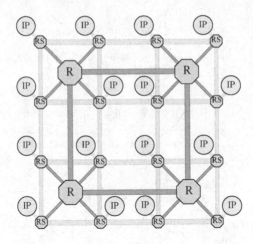

Fig. 3. 4 × 4 Mesh HPRNoC2 with 4 routers and 16 switches.

CNoC, where the IP cores send data in the form of packets whose header (first) flit contains the route information and the tail (last) flit closes the packet communication. When a source core sends the header flit of a packet to an RS module, the RS module connects the input-port from the IP core to a relevant output-port according to the destination address of the header flit. Assume a packet moves only in the RS layer to reach its destination that can be a router or an IP core. When the header flit enters a RS on its route, it is switched toward the destination. The communication among RS layer takes only one clock cycle for the header flit to reach its destination. The communication in the RS layer is fast as no pipelined stages and buffering are involved.

However, a packet may also have to pass through the router layer. When a header flit reaches the input-port of a router, it is stored in the input-port buffer. Then, the input-port issues a request signal to the arbiter. The arbiter performs arbitration among the potential input-ports' flits that are making requests to access the crossbar switch and other shared resources [2]. When the flit wins arbitration and is granted to exit the router, it passes through the crossbar switch. This form of communication in a router needs at least four pipelined stages [2]. For routers utilizing VCs, the structure of router input-port becomes more complex. The crossbar switch can be configured to connect any input buffer of the router to any output port (channel), with the constraints that only one input-port is connected to only one output-port. Arbiter also has a simple hardware however, it will become complex for a VC based router.

We have mentioned a few advantages of our proposed HPRNoC architecture. Firstly, the RS module structure is much smaller as compared to a router. Therefore, by following our approach, the NoC designer can create an optimal NoC by using more RS modules and fewer routers. For instance, in the 4 × 4 2D-mesh HPRNoC2 shown in Fig. 3, only four routers are used. The input-ports of these routers are just enough for accommodating sixteen IP cores in case they need to communicate through the router layer. Moreover, faster communication in the RS layer as compared to the router layer makes our HPRNoC an ideal communication subsystem for high-speed SoCs. We can also increase the number of RS layers (such as 2 RS layers and one reduced router layer) to provide faster interconnection routes for IP cores. More IP cores can communicate through the multiple RS layers and more cores can access through faster RS layers. To summarize our HPRNoC has some advantages that are given below:

- The main advantage of our HPRNoC architecture is its homogeneity and scalability. This feature makes it useful for widespread applications.
- Another feature is the high-speed interconnection required by high performance SoCs. SoC cores can be connected via high speed RS-network layers.
- The third advantage is the flexibility of our HPRNoC architecture to trade between performance and the hardware overhead. The hardware required by the RS layer is a small fraction of the routers. Therefore, by decreasing the router layer size in exchange of increasing the number of RS layers or RSs will lead to a flexible structure with high performance and economical hardware.
- The architecture is scalable and separable in terms of hardware cost and speed. The RS layer impacts the communication speed and the router layer has an impact on the hardware cost.
- The negative point of our HPRNoC is its higher level of interconnection wiring due to large number of RSs and one or more RS layers. It may turn the chip layout of SoCs a bit difficult.

4   Experimental Results

In this section, HPRNoC architecture is compared with the conventional NoC (CNoC) and reconfigurable NoC developed in the past. For the experimental results, we have used 2D-mesh based NoC architectures, where each node consists of a router for a 4×4 mesh topology. The routers of a CNoC architecture are identical in terms of their VCs, arbiter and crossbar switch.

4.1   Synthesis of HPRNoC and CNoCs

To investigate the hardware characteristics of our HPRNoC architecture, we have investigated the NoCs given in Figs. 1, 2 and 3. The NoCs are synthesized in terms of power consumption, chip area, and critical path delay. NoCs are implemented in System-Verilog and chip area, power and critical path delay related parameters are obtained by employing Synopsys Design Compiler with 15 nm NanGate ASIC libraries [8]. A global operating voltage of 0.8 V and time-period of 1 *nsec* (1 GHz) is applied for NoC synthesis. The communication links among the NoC nodes are ignored. The input-ports of routers are setup to utilize zero, 2, 3 or 4 VCs and 8 buffer slots. A buffer slot accommodates 16-bit flits. RS consumes much less hardware than a no-VC router as it only needs a few multiplexer switches and a simple control logic along with registers to keep the look-up table for a packet being transferred. The RS switches the inputs to the outputs according to the routing address carried by the header flit of a packet. Our Verilog-designs indicate that for NoC routers, the chip area of a crossbar switch for a 6-port router is also much smaller than the overall chip area of the router.

We present the hardware characteristics of various size HPRNoCs, CNoCs and past reconfigurable NoC in Table 1. The CNoCs have a mesh topology (5-ports) and listed as CNoC1, CNoC2 and CNoC3 based on the number of VCs utilized in the input-ports. The nodes of CNoC1 is made of simple routers without any VC, and the router of CNoC3 has 3-VCs per input-port. HPRNoC architectures, HPRNoC1 (with no-VC routers) and HPRNoC2 illustrated in Figs. 2 and 3 are evaluated. Table 1 also has two columns presenting the power and area ratios of these NoCs with the 4 × 4 RS network layer shown in Fig. 2. Both HPRNoC versions perform much better than CNoCs due to fast inter-node communication through the RS layer. For our HPRNoCs the delay is just two times of the RS delay. The minimum delay in CNoC router is 18 times of the RS delay. In addition to faster communication potential of HPRNoCs, they consume less hardware. For example, HPRNoC2 uses much lower hardware because only four routers are used as compared to 16 routers in other NoCs.

Table 1. NoCs hardware characteristics

NoC	ASIC design 15 nm NanGate Library			
	Area (μm^2)	[a]Power (mW)	Characteristics ratio with a '4 × 4 RS Network'	
			Area	Power
4 × 4 RS Network	8336	2.5	1.0	1.0
2 × 2 no-VC 6-port Router Network	18640	7.5	2.2	2.9
CNoC1 (Fig. 1) 4 × 4, no-VC 5-port Router Network	39972	14.4	4.8	5.6
CNoC2 (Fig. 1) 4 × 4, 2-VC 5-port Router Network	43180	16.3	5.2	6.3
CNoC3 (Fig. 1) 4 × 4, 3-VC 5-port Router Network	48668	19.0	5.8	7.4
HPRNoC1 (Fig. 2)	48308	17.0	5.8	6.6
HPRNoC2 (Fig. 3)	26976	10.1	3.2	3.9

[a]Total dynamic and static power

4.2   Performance Evaluation

NoC Performance metrics such as latency is also determined for the evaluation and comparisons of HPRNoC by using ModelSim. We have explored four NoCs such as CNoC1, CNoC2, CNoC3 and HPRNoC1 (given in Figs. 1 and 2) for commonly used applications of Audio/Video Benchmark (AV) [9] and DVOPD. Double Video Object Plane Decoder (DVOPD) with the capability to decode two streams in parallel [10]. DVOPD and AV Benchmark applications are mapped to 4 × 7 and 4 × 4 mesh topologies as shown in Figs. 4 and 5 respectively. The mappings to various NoCs such as CNoC1, CNoC2 and CNoC3 follow XY algorithm i.e. a mapping is done in X direction to reach to the Y dimension of its destination, then it maps to Y direction to reach their destination. Figure 5 illustrates this mapping for AV benchmark application for the CNoC2. The arrow lines indicate the direction of packet from sources to sinks. These arrows also specify the number of VCs needed for each channel. For example, three packets require 3 VCs to service the 3 packets without any blockage. AV benchmark performance cannot be improved further with 3 or more VCs (see Fig. 5).

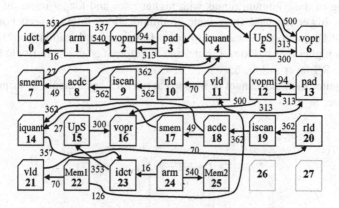

Fig. 4. DVOPD mapped to 4 × 7 mesh CNoC.

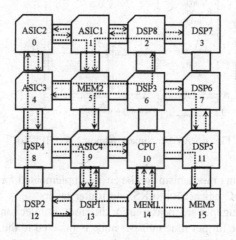

Fig. 5. AV benchmark mapping to a CNoC2.

For a fair comparison, the mapping in HPRNoCs follows the mapping methodology given below and the mapping is shown in Fig. 6 for the AV Benchmark application.

- The mapping follows XY routing in the router layers, and any route mapping in the RS layer. Routers have arbiters and buffers to implement message passing, where RSs are setup in advance for any routing methodology.

- In the RS node, an output-port can receive packet from one input-port as RS does not have buffer and arbiter to support the sharing of an output-port by multiple input-ports. For example, consider the communications from source cores 0 and 5 to a destination core 4 (Fig. 6). The RS 4 cannot deliver two packets to its output port connected to sink 4. Therefore, such communication can only be mapped over the router layer of Fig. 6.
- Mapping of the communications with higher rates and longer routes have priority over the lower rate and short route communications in RS layers. For example, among different communications to core 10, the communication from source core 15 has a higher rate and longer route, and therefore it is given priority to be mapped over the RS layer in Fig. 6.
- A communication that cannot be mapped to only RS layer should be mapped via RS and router layers.

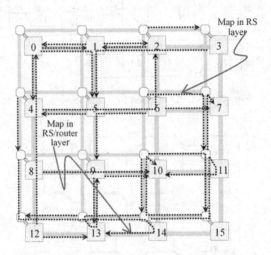

Fig. 6. AV benchmark mapping for HPRNoC1

The above mapping mechanism can be easily implemented for all the HPRNoCs as each node of the NoC has access to RS and router layers.

Latency and throughput are measured for different flit injection rates. The inject rate of '1' means that one flit per time unit per node is injected to the NoC. We have set a time unit to be equal to 9 clock cycles. Injection rate cannot be set beyond 9 in our simulation meaning that 9 flits per time unit per node are injected to the NoC where a source core cannot inject more than one flit per clock cycle.

To measure the latency and throughput, a specific number of packets are injected. In the case of DVOPD and AV Benchmark 221888 and 1520512 packets are sent to each NoC respectively. NoC communication is based on wormhole switching where the channel width is equal to the flit size of 16-bits. A packet is made of 16 flits, and each input-port has an 8-slot central buffer to implement VCs. As mentioned before, the routers in CNoC1 and HPRNoC1 do not support VCs and the routers for CNoC2 and

CNoC3 has 2- and 3-VCs respectively in their input-ports. The flit arrival/departure for all the routers takes 2 cycles. The NoCs throughput and latency results are presented for DVOPD and AV benchmark in Figs. 7 and 8 respectively. Please note that AV benchmark application only require two VCs due to which CNoC2 and CNoC3 based results are identical. It can be observed from the results that the average latency in HPRNoC1 is less than those of CNoC3, CNoC2, and CNoC3 for all the flit injection rates. The average latencies of DVOPD and AV benchmark in HPRNoC1 are 37% and 58% less than those of CNoC3 respectively. The average throughput for HPRNoC1 is higher than those of CNoC1, CNoC2, and CNoC3. For both applications, the average throughputs for HPRNoC1 are 5% higher than CNoCs.

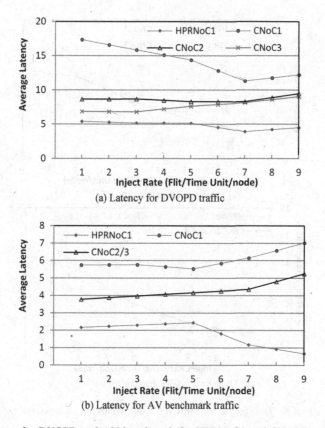

(a) Latency for DVOPD traffic

(b) Latency for AV benchmark traffic

Fig. 7. Latency for DVOPD and AV benchmark for HPRNoC1 and CNoC mesh topologies.

The advantage of HPRNoC1 becomes more interesting when we consider the hardware characteristics. As we have observed form the synthesis data of Table 1, a 4 × 4 HPRNoC1 consumes 0.7% and 11% less area and power as compared to a 4 × 4 CNoC3 respectively. The critical path delay of HPRNoC1 is determined by its slowest component that is a 5-port no-VC router, and in the case of CNoC3 5-port

3-VC router is the slowest one. Therefore, the HPRNoC1 operating frequency can be set almost three times faster than the CNoC3 clock.

The results presented in Fig. 7 depict non-linear latency graphs. This is due to irregular communications among the nodes. Another consideration is that the contentions in CNoC depend on the number of utilized VCs. Higher VC utilization decreases the contention and improves performance. HPRNoC1 provides higher performance at higher flit injection rates. For lower to moderate traffic, there are time intervals without a flit injection, which leads to lower contention in CNoCs. However, at a high injection rate of 7–9, HPRNoC1 delivers flits via RS along with the router layers resulting in lower contention.

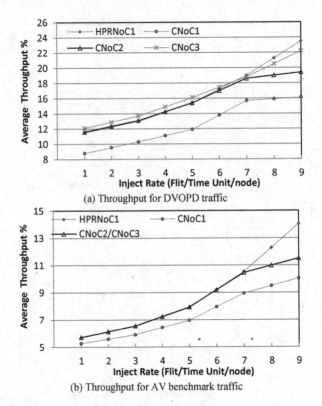

(a) Throughput for DVOPD traffic

(b) Throughput for AV benchmark traffic

Fig. 8. Throughput for HPRNoC1 and CNoC mesh topologies.

5   Conclusions

We have presented a High-performance Reconfigurable NoC (HPRNoC) architecture that consists of a network of reconfigurable switches and a trimmed network of routers. Our novel architecture has allowed us to reduce the number of routers to balance the hardware cost due to additional RSs. HPRNoC design shows a minimal delay between

SoC cores with fewer RSs as compared to the past reconfigurable NoC architectures [5]. The main features associated with our HPRNoC architectures are scalability, high speed communication and lower hardware. The experimental results do not cover all the benefits of our proposed HPRNoC architectures, however, the results can illustrate the efficiency of our approach. For example, the average latencies of some well-known application-specific SoCs such as DVOPD and AV benchmark are 37% and 58% less than conventional NoCs. The average throughput in HPRNoC1 is also higher than those of other conventional NoCs. The advantage of HPRNoC becomes more interesting when we also consider the lower hardware overhead. A 4×4 HPRNoC1 consumes 11% less power and can run three times faster when compared to a conventional 4×4 NoC.

Acknowledgment. The authors acknowledge the financial support from Ryerson University and Computing System support from CMC microsystems.

References

1. Zhang, Z., Refauvelet, D., Greiner, A., Benabdenbi, M., Pecheux, F.: On-the-field test and configuration infrastructure for 2D-Mesh NoCs in shared-memory many-core architectures. IEEE Trans. VLSI Syst. **22**(6), 1364–1376 (2014)
2. Khan, G.N.: Efficient and low power NoC router architecture. In: Choi, J., Iniewski, K. (eds.) High-Speed and Low Power Technologies: Electronics and Photonics, pp. 211–251. CRC Press, Taylor & Francis (2018)
3. Stensgaard, M., Sparsø, J.: ReNoC: a network-on-chip architecture with reconfigurable topology. In: Proceedings 2nd ACM/IEEE International Symposium Networks-on-Chip (NOCS), Newcastle Upon Tyne, UK, pp. 55–64, April 2008
4. Chen, C.H.O., Park, S., Krishna, T., Subramanian, S., Chandrakasan, A.P., Peh, L.S.: SMART: a single-cycle reconfigurable NoC for SoC applications. In: Proceedings Design Automation and Test in Europe (DATE) Conference, Grenoble, pp. 338–343, March 2013
5. Modarressi, M., Tavakkol, A., Sarbazi-Azad, H.: Application-aware topology reconfiguration for on-chip networks. IEEE Trans. on VLSI Systems **19**(11), 2010–2022 (2011)
6. Sarbazi-Azad, H., Zomaya, A.Y.: A reconfigurable on-chip interconnection network for large multicore systems. In: Sarbazi-Azad, H., Zomaya, A.Y. (eds.) Large Scale Network-Centric Distributed Systems, pp. 3–29. Wiley-IEEE Press (2014)
7. Suvorova, E., Sheynin, Y., Matveeva, N.: Reconfigurable NoC development with fault mitigation. In: Proceedings of the 18th Conference on Open Innovations Association and Seminar on Information Security and Protection of Information Technology, pp. 335–344 (2016)
8. Matos, J.M., et al.: Open cell library in 15 nm FreePDK technology. In: Proceedings of the International Symposium on Physical Design, pp. 171–178, March 2015
9. Dumitriu, V., Khan, G.N.: Throughput-oriented NoC topology generation and analysis for high performance SoCs. IEEE Trans. VLSI Syst. **17**(10), 1433–1446 (2009)
10. Concer, N., Bononi, L., Soulié, M., Locatelli, R., Carloni, L.P.: The connection-then-credit flow control protocol for heterogeneous multicore systems-on-chip. IEEE Trans. Comput. Aided Des. Integr. Circ. Syst. **29**(6), 869–882 (2010)

Author Index

Printed in the United States
by Bookmasters

Printed in the United States
By Bookmasters